Public Lands Politics
*Interest Group Influence on the Forest Service
and the Bureau of Land Management*

PAUL J. CULHANE

Published for RESOURCES FOR THE FUTURE, INC.
By The Johns Hopkins University Press
Baltimore and London

HD
216
.C84

Copyright © 1981 by Resources for the Future, Inc.

All rights reserved
Manufactured in the United States of America

Published for Resources for the Future
By The Johns Hopkins University Press, Baltimore, Maryland 21218

Dabney Lancaster Library
Longwood College
Farmville, Virginia

Library of Congress Cataloging in Publication Data

Culhane, Paul J.
  Public lands politics.
  Includes bibliographical references and index.
  1. United States—Public lands. 2. Forests
and forestry—Government ownership—United States.
3. Forests and forestry—United States—Multiple
use. 4. United States. Forest Service.
5. United States. Bureau of Land Management.
I. Resources for the Future. II. Title.
HD216.C84   333.1'0973   80-8776
ISBN 0-8018-2598-9   AACR2
ISBN 0-8018-2599-7 (pbk.)

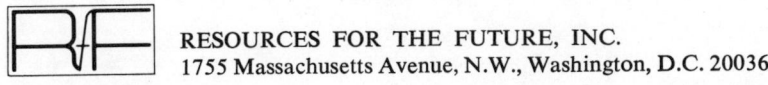 RESOURCES FOR THE FUTURE, INC.
1755 Massachusetts Avenue, N.W., Washington, D.C. 20036

Board of Directors: M. Gordon Wolman, *Chairman,* Charles E. Bishop, Roberto de O. Campos, Anne P. Carter, Emery N. Castle, William T. Creson, Jerry D. Geist, David S. R. Leighton, Franklin A. Lindsay, George C. McGhee, Vincent E. McKelvey, Richard W. Manderbach, Laurence I. Moss, Mrs. Oscar M. Ruebhausen, Janez Stanovnik, Charles B. Stauffacher, Carl H. Stoltenberg, Russell E. Train, Robert M. White, Franklin H. Williams

Honorary Directors: Horace M. Albright, Erwin D. Canham, Edward J. Cleary, Hugh L. Keenleyside, Edward S. Mason, William S. Paley, John W Vanderwilt

President: Emery N. Castle

Secretary-Treasurer: Edward F. Hand

Resources for the Future is a nonprofit organization for research and education in the development, conservation, and use of natural resources and the improvement of the quality of the environment. It was established in 1952 with the cooperation of the Ford Foundation. Grants for research are accepted from government and private sources only if they meet the conditions of a policy established by the Board of Directors of Resources for the Future. The policy states that RFF shall be solely responsible for the conduct of the research and free to make the research results available to the public. Part of the work of Resources for the Future is carried out by its resident staff; part is supported by grants to universities and other nonprofit organizations. Unless otherwise stated, interpretations and conclusions in RFF publications are those of the authors; the organization takes responsibility for the selection of significant subjects for study, the competence of the researchers, and their freedom of inquiry.

This book is a product of RFF's Renewable Resources Division, Kenneth D. Frederick, director. Paul J. Culhane is assistant professor of political science at the University of Houston, Houston, Texas, and research scientist at The Institute of Ecology in Indianapolis, Indiana.

The book was edited by Jo Hinkel and designed by Elsa Williams. The index was prepared by Lorraine and Mark Anderson, and the figures were drawn by George Hager.

Contents

Foreword by Marion Clawson   xi
Preface   xiii

I. INTRODUCTION

1. The Public Lands and the Clash of Conflicting Interests   1
Philosophies of Natural Resource Management   2
Modern Issues in Public Lands Management   10
Interest Group Theory and Public Lands Policy   22
Plan of the Book   29
Notes   31

II. THE NATIONAL CONTEXT/AGENCY HISTORIES AND ADMINISTRATIVE PROCESSES

2. The Forest Service   41
The Federal Lands   41
The Origins of the Forest Service   45
Forest Service Organization and Management   60
Notes   69

3. The Bureau of Land Management   75
    History of the BLM   75
    Formal Organization of the Bureau of Land
        Management   97
    Notes   105

4. Multiple-Use Management Procedures   110
    Timber Management   112
    Grazing Management   115
    Wildlife Management   117
    Recreation Management   119
    Wilderness Management   120
    Minerals Management   122
    Special Uses   123
    The Multiple-Use Philosophy—Tools and
        Constraints   125
    Conclusions   128
    Notes   129

III. GROUP INFLUENCE AND LOCAL PUBLIC LANDS MANAGEMENT

5. Local Land Management/The Actors   135
    The Study Sample   136
    Local Land Managers   145
    Interest Group Affiliations   155
    Industry User Groups   159
    Nonindustry Interests   166
    Group Attitudes About Public Lands Issues   173
    Summary   180
    Notes   181

6. Rangers' and Area Managers' Constituencies   186
    Local Administrators' Group Contacts   187
    Differences in Organization-Sets   195
    Conclusion—Local Constituencies and the "Capture
        Thesis"   204
    Notes   205

7. The Nature of Group Influence/Participants' Views — 208
The Rise of Environmental Influences on Local Land Management   209
Constituency Management—Administrators' Reactions to Environmentalism   218
The Consequences of Constituency Management   219
Conclusions—Group Influence and Conformity   226
Notes   229

8. Public Participation — 232
The Scope of Public Participation   233
New Public Participation Styles   236
Special Cases of Participation—The Grazing Associations and Advisory Boards   246
Conclusions   258
Notes   259

9. The Style of Local Public Lands Policymaking — 263
The Locus of Decision Making   264
The Focus of Pressure Politics   269
Decision-Making Mechanisms   274
Conclusion   283
Notes   285

10. Interest Group Influence and Use Allocation Policies — 289
A Concise Model of Group Influence   290
Group Influence on Policy Output Levels   298
Relative Influence of Groups and Administrators   305
Conclusions—The Group Influence Model and Its Implications   310
Notes   313

IV. CONCLUSIONS

11. Conformity, Capture, Multiple Clientelism, and Multiple Use — 321
The Capture-Conformity Debate   322
Professionalism and Conformity   325
Capture and Clientelism   331
Multiple Clientelism and the Public Interest   339
Notes   341

APPENDIXES

A. Data-Gathering Methodology 349
B. The Unidimensionality of Public Lands Attitudes 357
C. The Group Influence Model/Technical Aspects 364

Index 390

FIGURES AND TABLES

Figures

1-1. Natural resource philosophy dimension	10
2-1. The National Forest System	49
2-2. Line and staff organization of the Forest Service	62
3-1. Public domain administration districts	99
3-2. Bureau of Land Management organization chart	101
5-1. Selected group's positions on E-U scale attitude dimension	179
6-1. Urban areas and rangers' organization-set types on NF1	204
7-1. An Environmentalist view of Forest Service constituency relationships	213
10-1. A general group influence model	291
10-2. The public lands group influence model	297

Tables

2-1. Origins of the Public Domain	42
2-2. Major Federal Public Land Management Agencies	44
3-1. Disposition of the Public Domain, 1781–1977	77
5-1. Levels of Selected Uses, Sample Ranger Districts and Resource Areas, 1973	142
5-2. Administrative Unit Resources, 1973	148
5-3. District Administrators' Prior Employment History	150
5-4. District Administrators' Agency Experience	151
5-5. Group Affiliations of Local Line Officers	152
5-6. Group Affiliations of Interest Group Participants	156

5-7.	Interest Group Resources of Selected Groups, 1973	162
5-8.	The "Environmental-Utilitarian" Attitude Scale	177
5-9.	Environmental-Utilitarian Scale Scores for Selected Groups	178
6-1.	Organization-Set Contacts of Rangers and Area Managers	190
6-2.	Contact and Interaction Rates for Selected Groups	192
6-3.	Organization-Set Type I—Balanced Primary Users Plus Conservationists and Recreationists	196
6-4.	Organization-Set Type II—Range Districts	197
6-5.	Organization-Set Type III—Mining or Oil and Gas District	198
6.6	Organization-Set Type IV—Overbalanced Toward Traditional Users	199
6-7.	Organization-Set Type V—Overbalanced Toward Conservationists and Recreationists	200
6-8.	Summary of Local Administrators' Organization-Sets	201
7-1.	Participants' Beliefs About the Most Important Factors in Forest Service and BLM Policymaking	210
8-1.	Public Participation Events	235
9-1.	Style of Supervision of Rangers and Area Managers	267
9-2.	Indicators of District Administrator-Supervisory Interaction	267
10-1.	Public Lands Group Influence Model	301
10-2.	Summary Tables of Alternative Timber Sales Model	304
10-3.	Relative Influence Indexes of Interests and Administrators in the Group Influence Model	307
A-1.	Response Rates by Selected Categories	351
B-1.	Administrators' and Interest Group Leaders' Attitudes Toward Selected Public Lands Issues	359
B-2.	Local Participants' Perceptions About Interest Group Dominance in Local Public Lands Policymaking	360
B-3.	Correlation Matrix of Selected Attitude Items	361
B-4.	Eigenvalue of Initial Unrotated Factors	362
B-5.	Attitude Factor Matrix	362
C-1.	Group Categories on Which Standardizing of Resources Indicators Was Based, by Resource Category	373
C-2.	Public Participation Event Dominance	375
C-3.	Parameters Used as Substitutes for Nonrespondents and Other Missing Data Cases	378
C-4.	Heuristic Ranger's Livestock Industry Interest Set	379
C-5.	Summary of Results for Alternative Model Versions	382
C-6.	Correlation Matrix, Ratio Outputs, and Optimum Arguments	387

Foreword

Resources for the Future has long had a strong interest in public land management. The organization helped to make possible, and in 1960 published, Herbert Kaufman's classic book, *The Forest Ranger: A Study in Administrative Behavior.* I personally have written several books directly bearing on public land administration, and in recent years, John V. Krutilla has made intensive studies of national forest administration. And there have been others—on the RFF staff or sponsored by RFF—who have been concerned with this general field. Paul Culhane follows very much in this tradition, and with this volume he makes a notable contribution to RFF's bibliography on the subject.

Laws, regulations, and policy at the local level are not necessarily, or perhaps not even usually, the same as these laws, regulations, and policy are perceived at the national (or at the state) capital. This was true during the colonial period of American history, and it was especially the case during the long era of federal land disposal. When I served as a federal land administrator, I became acutely aware of this situation and tried to do something about it. Now that I am a researcher and writer, I am more than ever impressed with the divergence between announced policy and actual results in the field.

The basic problem is that individuals interpret laws and policies to their individual advantage. Their ideals or goals, their strivings for personal advantage, their efforts to use public lands for their own purpose, and even their moral codes greatly affect what actually happens. Some actions may be illegal; more are likely to be legal but different from what was desired and intended by the sponsors of the laws.

Culhane examines carefully the relations among federal agencies, between various private groups and the federal agencies, and among various interest groups in federal land management situations. He has amassed a highly useful body of new information through extensive field research, and he analyzes it carefully to show the relationships inherent in the data. Some of his findings corroborate my own intuitive judgments, hence I think they are sound and incisive; of course, elsewhere he produces evidence to show that some of my guesses were wrong. Regardless, he has assembled solid empirical evidence which now replaces the kind of general and often highly subjective views held by many of us who are not close to the actual present-day working of federal agencies in the field. For those with a background in research and in actual federal land management, Culhane's findings are of particular interest and value.

Culhane shows clearly that the relatively recent public involvement provisions of federal land legislation impose new and unaccustomed burdens on local federal land administrators. The training of most professional land managers has not prepared them to deal with these new responsibilities. Culhane's treatment of this subject is more precise and better documented than most other studies. Although his conclusions are not surprising, Culhane goes beyond other studies, showing that the astute and fully competent federal land manager can use public involvement to obtain sounder decisions and wiser actions and even to enhance his own position. This latter theme is almost wholly original with Culhane.

I commend this book to every person interested in public lands management, and, indeed, to everyone interested in how federal programs operate in the field. I think Culhane provides new and constructive insights. Prediction of a book's life is hazardous, but I judge this one will long remain one of the outstanding contributions to the field.

November 1980

Marion Clawson
Resources for the Future
Washington, D.C.

Preface

During the 1970s, land managers in the U.S. Forest Service and Bureau of Land Management (BLM) often must have felt they were victims of the old Chinese curse "May you live in interesting times." The decade began with the first Earth Day, an event that revealed the increasing strength and militancy of the environmental movement; as it ended, western commercial users of the public lands, disaffected by environmentalist policymaking victories, had launched the "sagebrush rebellion." The conflicting pressures reflected in these movements are as old as the sagebrush itself. However, the 1970s presented land managers with an especially difficult set of problems. Those managers were expected to reconcile often sharply polarized interest group pressures with professional values, as well as with diverse federal statutes and regulations that reflected uneasy compromises among group and professional influences.

Political researchers, in contrast, consider themselves blessed by interesting times. It was this study's good fortune that the 1970s highlighted many of the subtle political tensions that had existed in public lands politics for decades. Although the technical specifics of public lands management differ from those in other fields of natural resources management, the political tensions in public lands policymaking are similar to those in other natural resources fields. Thus, this description of the Forest Service's and BLM's handling of those tensions should be of interest to many in the natural resources management community as a whole.

The study should also be useful to students of public administrative politics generally. When I embarked on the first phase of the research described here, I was prepared to find that industry pressure groups had, as was commonly believed, successfully bent the Forest Service and BLM to their corporate wills. My technical objective was to develop a method for quantitatively measuring interest group influence, and thus for objectively documenting the extent of any group dominance. (The development of such a method has stymied students of public policymaking.) This technical objective was accomplished, but the findings resulting from the method proved my initial expectations incorrect.

Students of American public policymaking have begun to express reservations about the conventional wisdom that industry client groups inevitably "capture" relevant federal administrative agencies. James Q. Wilson, who edited *The Politics of Regulation* (New York, Basic Books, 1980), has recently assembled considerable evidence of the failings of the capture thesis as applied to regulatory policymaking, the policy arena in which this thesis is most widely accepted. The findings presented here also add a powerful caveat to this theory of agency capture.

Resources for the Future assisted this study of public lands management during the important 1970s in many ways. Marion Clawson, a major contributor to the scholarly literature on public lands policy, helped arrange initial financial support for the project and later served as a facilitator and critic of the manuscript at RFF. Roger A. Sedjo and Robert Cameron Mitchell of RFF, Dean E. Mann of the University of California, Santa Barbara, and Perry Hagenstein of Resource Issues, Inc., provided a host of excellent suggestions for refining the text. Jo Hinkel, my excellent editor at RFF, guided the book smoothly through its final stages of production. Finally, Herbert Kaufman's *The Forest Ranger* had a great intellectual influence on this study. Kaufman eschewed treatment of the political and policy aspects of public lands management, but his insights into Forest Service intraagency administrative behavior are as true today as when RFF published them twenty years ago.

Over the years, many Forest Service, BLM, and interest group people have contributed to this study. Space limitations will not permit me to acknowledge each, but I would especially like to thank Jerry O'Callaghan of the BLM and Del Jaquish, Lennart Lundberg, and Bill Ripley of the Forest Service for their cooperation. Paul Friesema introduced me at

Northwestern University to public lands politics and continues to assist me in my efforts to examine natural resources policy. David Brady and Alan Stone, of the University of Houston, provided critically important encouragement and advice on this book. After all this advice, I was blessed with a gracious perfectionist, Bette Cohen, for a manuscript typist.

Finally, Diane Culhane, my wife and a professional editor, has been a part of this project from our first drive West for the beginning of the field research through the many evolutionary stages of this manuscript. No author has ever had a better partner in such an endeavor. This book is lovingly dedicated to her.

Indianapolis, Indiana Paul J. Culhane
November 1980

I
INTRODUCTION

1

The Public Lands and the Clash of Conflicting Interests

As with any other policy arena, public lands politics are marked by confusing crosscurrents of substantive controversies. Throughout the nineteenth century, the history of the growth of the United States consisted largely of the acquisition and disposition of the public domain lands of the frontier. Today, with the frontier settled, the federal government still owns one-third of the nation's land area, and two agencies, the Bureau of Land Management (BLM) and the Forest Service, manage most of that land. The policies guiding Forest Service and BLM management of this huge amount of land have been affected by several divergent philosophies of natural resources management and buffeted by bitter arguments about numerous management issues.

Most of the substantive controversies of public lands politics have been related directly or indirectly to the so-called capture-conformity debate, which has affected evaluations of the public lands agencies for two decades. That debate consists of a variety of positions about whether public lands policies are, or should be, influenced more by interest group pressures or by professional judgment and statutory law. Some commentators argue that any group influence subjects an administrative agency to potential "capture" by its primary clientele, while others support certain forms of group influence, such as public participation. Most observers of public lands politics maintain that a degree of conformity to professional and legal standards is necessary and beneficial, but some charge that the conformity of the agencies' officers has hardened into overbureaucratization.

The capture-conformity debate has been largely shaped by two 1960 publications on local administration in the Forest Service and BLM.[1] One book left the impression that the Forest Service was a highly disciplined, professional agency untainted by special interest influence. The other depicted the BLM as a mediocrity so thoroughly influenced by its clients, the western stockmen, that it could be considered their captive. However, the BLM's defenders believe the latter book's conclusions are at best overstated, and some critics of the Forest Service maintain that that supposedly model conformist agency is as thoroughly corrupted by the special interests as the BLM.

During the 1960s and 1970s, public lands management changed in several significant ways. New statutes were enacted into law. The BLM and Forest Service continued to mature, changing without abandoning their historic roots. Most important, changes in the nature of interest group pressures on the public lands agencies came into full bloom during what President Nixon heralded in 1970 as "the environmental decade." Given such changes, it seems appropriate to inquire again into the role of interest group influence on local public lands management and, in particular, to reexamine the capture-conformity debate.

Philosophies of Natural Resource Management

The origins of the capture-conformity debate lie in the four major philosophies of American natural resource management—utilitarianism, progressive conservation, romantic preservation, and environmentalism. Each philosophy consists of beliefs about natural resource management goals and optimal ecological conditions. Each also reflects an underlying political philosophy, a set of beliefs about how political processes should or do affect those management goals and ecological conditions. The first major natural resource philosophies evolved during the early political struggles over the public lands. Those philosophies, somewhat modified, continue to lend fervor to contemporary arguments about the management of the federal lands.

Utilitarianism

Utilitarianism was the philosophy that seemed to guide Americans' attitudes toward the environment through the nineteenth century. The pure utilitarian acted as if natural resources were inexhaustible and believed that they should be used to raise individual and collective standards of living. Thus, material consumption not only was seen to be gratifying for the individual, but it provided the basis for social and cultural advancement. The seemingly limitless western frontier was viewed as an inexhaustible resource base for the growth of the American economy and society.

Utilitarianism did not have a well-developed intellectual base (in contrast to later philosophies), and it would be difficult to find a modern or historic proponent of the pure utilitarian position. To some extent, in fact, the philosophy of utilitarianism was constructed by conservationists as a "straw man" to attack in condemning utilitarian behavior. According to conservationist critics, utilitarianism included a religious or cosmologic view and a politicoeconomic justification. Roderick Nash, an historian of the American wilderness, notes that rural societies affected by the vagaries of nature take a dual view of nature.[2] Nature is beautiful and the source of human sustenance, but it is also unpredictable and threatening. Because nature is so important to societies, especially primitive societies, the control or conquest of nature takes on moral and religious overtones. In the Judeo-Christian tradition, the moral imperative to control nature is best expressed in the biblical injunction to "subdue the earth," which lent a religious fervor to the taming of the American frontier from the time of the Puritans.

American utilitarianism, however, was based primarily on nineteenth-century conservatism. Laissez-faire conservatism was a blend of classic, free-market, capitalist economic theory and an individualistic interpretation of the libertarian principles of the U.S. Constitution. Viewed by its critics as an attempt to justify privilege, laissez-faire conservatism developed—or degenerated—into social Darwinism, which held that the success of exploiters was a scientifically inevitable result of competition and "survival of the fittest."[3] Thus, both the Judeo-Christian tradition and nineteenth-century conservatism helped transform exploitative materialism into a religiously and politically legitimate—even inevitable—means of economic, cultural, and spiritual growth.

Progressive Conservation

The purely utilitarian position slowly became untenable in the latter part of the nineteenth century. Long before the geographic limits of the supposedly limitless public domain had been reached, Americans had learned not only that natural resources could be exhausted, but that nature abused could turn on mankind. This dual lesson was learned, in large part, in the forests—the gems of the western public domain. American scientists were aware of the findings of their European—especially Swiss and German—counterparts that the danger of flooding was greatly increased by extensive deforestation. The first dramatic American demonstration of another danger occurred in 1871, when logging residues from extensive cut-and-run operations led to a fire that destroyed the town of Pestigo, Wisconsin, killing 1,500 people and burning over one million acres.

The conservationist position arose as a reaction to the destruction caused by the utilitarian plunder economy.[4] The first significant American proponent of this position was George Perkins Marsh, whose wide-ranging synthesis of the scientific literature on physical geography focused on the dangers of disturbing the balance of nature by uncontrolled human economic activity. Like most physical geographers of the time, Marsh was most concerned with the effects of domestic livestock grazing and deforestation—the processes that most contributed to the problems of the public lands of the American West. Equally important, Marsh proposed a replacement for the philosophical-theological basis of utilitarianism, the subdue-the-earth injunction. In one of his most eloquent passages, Marsh called for a sense of mankind's stewardship or usufruct—a sense that man has a right to enjoy the benefits of nature, which belongs ultimately to God, but only in a responsible way:

> Man has too long forgotten that the earth was given to him for usufruct alone, not for consumption, still less for profligate waste. Nature has provided against the absolute destruction of any of her elementary matter, the raw material of her works.... But she has left it within the power of man irreparably to derange the combinations of inorganic matter and organic life, which through the night of aeons she had been proportioning and balancing, to prepare the earth for habitation, when in the fullness of time, his Creator should call him forth to enter into its possession.[5]

The main line of early conservation, however, took a different approach. The progressive conservation movement of the turn of the century was most closely associated with President Theodore Roosevelt and particularly with his natural resources advisor, Gifford Pinchot. Progressive conservation was based on two principles central to the progressive era as a whole: opposition to the domination of economic affairs by narrow "special interests" (that is, large business firms) and a fundamental belief in rationality and science.[6] Grant McConnell pointed out that the real political force of the progressive conservation movement was best expressed by Pinchot's third principle of conservation: "Natural resources must be developed and preserved for the benefit of the many, and not merely for the profit of the few."[7] This principle derived from the populist opposition to institutions like the railroads, and was translated by Pinchot and the progressive conservationists into opposition to the symbols of natural resources exploitation of the day, the timber barons and the cattle barons. Thus, an assertion of the public interest was an important ingredient of progressive conservation.

Much like the environmental movement, whose growth in the 1960s and 1970s was led by natural scientists like biologist Barry Commoner, the early conservation movement was organized by people in the sciences. The first organized conservation effort was the lobbying of the Congress in 1873 by the American Association for the Advancement of Science to establish forest reserves. Pinchot, a forester and silviculturalist, and many of his contemporaries, such as W. J. McGee, John Wesley Powell, and Frederick Newell, were scientists by training or self-perception, or both, and scientific expertise provided the solution to the conservation problem. As Hays pointed out:

> Since resource matters were basically technical in nature, conservationists argued, technicians, rather than legislators, should deal with them. Foresters should determine the desirable annual timber cut; hydraulic engineers should establish the feasible extent of multiple-purpose river development and the specific location of reservoirs; agronomists should decide which forage areas could remain open for grazing without undue damage to water supplies. . . . Conservationists envisaged . . . a political system guided by the ideal of efficiency and dominated by the technicians who could best determine how to achieve it.[8]

The ideal of efficiency, however, was not upheld only by the progressive conservationists; efficiency was a central theorem of the progressive movement as a whole, manifested in such diverse ways as civil service reform, under the Pendleton Act, and the scientific management approach to industrial administrative theory.

The basic principle of conservation was "wise use," with the emphasis on *wise,* for the progressive conservationists were reacting to rapacious, short-term, profit-maximizing, utilitarian exploitation, particularly of the forests. Pinchot recalled vividly his experience in Europe, where earlier generations had, in maximizing consumption, stripped the forests of their ability to continue producing. His missionary zeal in the United States was devoted to ensuring that such overconsumption would not occur in America, at least not in the western forests (since it had already occurred in the Midwest).

Much reaction against conservation was based on the presumption that conservation meant locking up resources. One reason for this reaction was the fact that the forest reserves were withdrawn from use by the Forest Reserve Act of 1891, but management was not authorized until passage of the Organic Act of 1897 and did not actually begin until even later. However, Pinchot argued that conservation meant developing resources for human use while avoiding waste. Progressive conservation was based on Pinchot's principle of providing "the greatest good for the greatest number [of people] in the long run."[9] This principle is embodied in the statutory responsibilities of the Forest Service and the BLM: public lands resources are to be managed for "multiple use," in theory an optimum and high level and mix of uses, and for "sustained yield," the maintenance of those high levels of use "in perpetuity."[10] Natural resources were to be utilized—Pinchot even described the forest as a "tree farm" and a "wood factory"[11]—but in such a way as not to impair future utilization. The principle was also applied to water resources development, the other important natural resources issue of the progressive era, in the belief in the efficacy of multipurpose water resources impoundments.

Romantic Preservation

A third philosophical approach to natural resources—preservationism—developed about the same time as progressive conservationism, but was quite different. Nature, and especially wilderness, was a place of transcendental experience for the romantic preservationists, such as Henry David Thoreau, John Muir, Aldo Leopold, and Edward Abbey.[12] It was a retreat from the artificiality and disharmony of urban, technological culture. Indeed, that culture was itself a violation of nature, the "machine in the garden," as Leo Marx put it.[13] Wild things—wilderness, wild rivers, wildlife—were reminders of mankind's roots in and dependence on the natural order, as well as spiritual retreats from the urban world. The romantic preservationists wanted wild nature preserved from the utilitarians, who valued it only as it could serve human consumption. Wild things were of value *in their own right*. As Justice William O. Douglas argued, natural things ought to be viewed as "persons," in the full legal sense, imbued with inalienable rights irrespective of mankind's use or evaluation of them.[14]

Environmentalism

Conservationism and preservationism were the twin historic predecessors of the fourth natural resources philosophy—environmentalism. The central beliefs of environmentalism are best described in Barry Commoner's *The Closing Circle*.[15] Mankind, Commoner argues, is interrelated with nature, not apart from and superior to it. Humans, like all living things, depend on the biosphere (the shallow skin of the earth and the earth's atmosphere) for existence, and the resources of the biosphere are finite. The stability of the biosphere depends on the maintenance and renewal of those resources. Commoner, a biologist, points out that all species are consumers of the biosphere. In a natural biological system, a species that takes from the biosphere returns what it consumes, in altered form, so there is no net change in the system. A stable species-biosphere relationship is one with what Commoner calls a closed cycle of consumption. Commoner contends that man's relationship with nature has systematically broken this cycle.

Modern environmentalism is most akin to the preservationist position in that environmentalists are biocentric. Nature comes first for the environmentalist, as it does for the preservationist, in any case of conflict between human use and nature's requirements. In one sense, environmentalism is more biocentric than romantic preservationism, since environmentalists see mankind as an inextricable part of nature and biological relationships, whereas the preservationists' transcendent view of nature sees man as apart from them. On the other hand, environmentalists' acceptance of human controlled consumption reflects a more practical and less romantic view of nature than the preservationists'. The kinship of modern environmentalists with the turn-of-the-century preservation movement is most clearly seen, however, in organizational terms. Some of the most important contemporary environmental groups began as preservation groups; the Sierra Club is the most notable example, but preservationist backgrounds can also be found in other groups, ranging from the Audubon Society to the League of Women Voters.

Environmentalists share several characteristics of the progressive conservation movement as well. Like conservationists, environmentalists are interested in a wide variety of human-biosphere relationships. The preservationists, from the 1890s through the 1950s, were often involved in fights to preserve wild lands, especially by their incorporation in the national park system; their participation in other natural resources issues, such as water resources development policy in cases like Hetch-Hetchy and Echo Park,[16] was predicated on the preservation of the wild lands affected by the programs at issue. Modern environmentalists have, however, come out of the wilderness, and are interested and involved in the whole range of natural resources issues: pollution, perhaps the most obvious and striking type of human breaking of the closed cycle; depletion of finite, nonrenewable energy resources, and the biological dangers of nuclear power; the destructive effects on natural systems of some water resources construction projects; as well as the more traditional preservationist issues, such as protection of endangered species and preservation of wilderness.

The similarities and differences between modern environmentalists and traditional conservationists can best be seen by examining their political philosophies. Environmentalists share, to a considerable extent, the political grievance of the progressive conservation movement. Like the progressives, most environmentalists believe uncontrolled exploitation by economic interests is a major cause of natural resources problems; many environmentalists, most prominently Commoner,[17] are basically critics of capitalism and classic economic theory. Environmentalists, like progressive conservationists, are opposed to control of public natural resources by private special interests, whose interests they see as inimical to the broader public interest. Political theorists may have great difficulty defining the public interest,[18] but environmentalists and progressives do not —the public interest is the opposite of the interests of the trusts, barons, and corporate lobbyists.

Environmentalists, however, differ from the progressives in their solution to the problem of utilitarian exploitation. The progressives' two-part solution was to manage natural resources by (1) creating *public* agencies dedicated to the public interest, and (2) using professional management by technical experts. Environmentalists are profoundly skeptical about both approaches. The primary adversaries of modern environmentalists are usually not specific users or user groups, but public agencies—in many cases the very same agencies that were created by the progressive conservation movement, such as Pinchot's Forest Service, Frederick Newland's Bureau of Reclamation, and George Norris's Tennessee Valley Authority (TVA). Perceiving many natural resources agencies as sympathetic to—if not in collusion with—utilitarian interests, environmentalists tend to reject bureaucracy as a solution to resource problems.[19] Environmentalists are equally unimpressed with the progressives' technical-professional solution to resource problems. As was the case with the early conservation movement, many of the luminaries of environmentalism are scientists, particularly biologists: Barry Commoner and Garrett Hardin are two prominent examples. Environmentalist scientists, however, are generally critical of the effects of modern technology. They generally believe in the systems approach to science—the approach of studying the complexity of relationships of whole systems.[20] They thus reject what they see as the reductionism of modern science, the tendency to reduce complex systems of interrelationships to simple one-cause-and-one-effect relationships. According to Commoner, this "linear" nature of modern technology is the root cause of the environmental crisis.[21] However, while environmentalists are critical of the technical-professional position of progressive conservationists, it should be recognized that progressive conservationists themselves made a similar critique of utilitarianism. The deficiencies of single-use exploitation (a linear view of resources) led progressive conservationists to advocate multiple-use management of public lands and multipurpose development of water resources.

The conservationist acceptance of use suggests the major philosophical distinction between conservationists and environmentalists (as well as between conservationists and preservationists). Conservationists of the progressive conservation mold focus first on human needs. The biosphere is important, but only as it is useful to mankind. For the environmentalist, and even more the preservationist, however, the biosphere is primary, human use secondary. This distinction between the conservation and environmental philosophies is one of emphasis: Conservationists worry about a depletion of resources that would affect future human consumption; and environmentalists worry about the future of the biosphere, including the human race.

Thus, one can think of the various philosophical positions on natural resources as forming a continuum (figure 1-1), with varying degrees of emphasis on human consumptive use and biosphere maintenance. A pure utilitarian (which no one will admit to being, but which many behave like) is concerned solely with the human use of natural resources, irrespective of the wider consequences. The conservationist is committed to use, but attempts to reconcile it with biosphere-imposed restraints: to maintain productivity, it is prudent to respect the biosphere. The environmentalist is committed to maintaining the integrity of the biosphere: As a part of

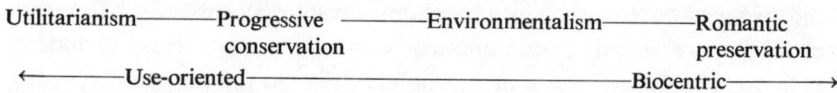

Figure 1-1. Natural resource philosophy dimension.

the biosphere, mankind must not imperil it; maintenance of mankind's existence is a secondary benefit, and the continuation of mankind's ability to use the biosphere is a tertiary benefit. The preservationist wishes to protect parts of the biosphere from human use, irrespective of the possible benefits of that use for humans.

Modern Issues in Public Lands Management

The main philosophies of natural resources management—conservation, preservation, and modern environmentalism—grew out of public lands conflicts, and contemporary public lands conflicts continue to reflect the importance of those philosophies. The issues confronting the larger, multiple-use agencies, the BLM and the Forest Service, are more controversial than those facing the National Park Service and the Fish and Wildlife Service. The last two agencies are not free from controversy, but essentially preservationist land management missions insulate them from a whole range of conflicts. Because of their multiple-use doctrines, however, the BLM and Forest Service are routinely in the midst of fundamental conflicts, since the proponents of various uses take widely divergent philosophical positions on natural resources management.

Three of the basic program areas of multiple-use land management illustrate the substantive conflicts facing public lands agencies. The Forest Service's and BLM's timber, grazing, and wilderness programs are by no means their only controversial program areas, nor are conflicts restricted to broad programs, as opposed to specific projects or cases. But the three programs provide examples of the substantive complexity and political difficulty surrounding public lands policies, and, indeed, natural resources management in general.

Timber Management

Because it has a larger forest inventory than the BLM, the Forest Service has been the major focus of timber management controversy. During much of the service's existence, its timber management policy was rather passive. Private forestlands could provide for the nation's timber demands. Federal policy generally kept federal timber sales at low levels to avoid depressing private timber prices; Forest Service policy was more or less custodial, involving, for example, forest fire prevention and suppression. Thus, less accessible old-growth stands were left relatively uncut. During the 1950s and 1960s, however, cutting practices on private forestlands began to affect national forest timber policies. The large forest products firms had been cutting over their own lands at rates generally exceeding natural annual tree growth. Faced with declining private inventory, the industry began to make increasing demands on the national forests' inventory.

The Forest Service's policy of gradually increasing the harvest of national forest timber in response to these demands has met two basic lines of criticism. Environmentalists criticize the implications, level, logic, and methods of Forest Service timber management.[22] Perhaps their most fundamental dissatisfaction with service attempts to meet rising demands on public timber inventories stems from their belief that the agency is moving toward dominant use management, in which timber considerations outweigh all others (especially recreation uses). Environmentalists are also convinced that proposals to increase the allowable cut on the national forests are excessive. (The *allowable cut* is the presumed maximum volume of timber that can be cut on a given Forest Service administrative unit; it is measured in board-feet, and is usually the average for a period, such as ten years. Under new timber regulations, the allowable cut has been called, more accurately, *allowable sale quantity* since 1979.) Environmentalists feel that the logic of proposals to increase allowable cuts is fatally flawed. Under the influence of advances in silvicultural system planning in the forestry profession, the Forest Service believes that more intensive management could lead to increasing the allowable cut without violating sustained yield principles. The catch is that intensive management requires considerable investment in activities such as reforestation, and those investments are often not made because of emphasis on the current sales program in the service's budget. One of the more persuasive facts bolstering the environmentalist belief that existing allowable cuts are excessive is the large reforestation backlog caused by past increases in logging.

The most violent criticism of Forest Service timber policy surrounds the clear-cutting harvest method. Clear-cutting is a form of *even-aged management,* the goal of which is to produce a forest composed of trees of a single species of the same age. Such a stand, especially when it is composed of a commercially valuable species, has several advantages. The primary silvicultural advantage is that some commercially desirable species are shade intolerant, that is, they will not regenerate if other trees block their sunlight. Thus, to allow for proper regeneration of such trees, all the trees in the area must be cut—hence the term *clear-cutting.* Environmentalists are highly critical of the practice because it results in a very unsightly postharvest landscape. They also point to a substantial body of research that indicates that clear-cutting accelerates erosion, leading to unacceptable siltation of streams and rivers and excessive losses of soil nutrients, which in turn greatly decrease the productivity of clear-cut sites.[23] These effects illustrate, for environmentalists, Commoner's environmental crisis scenario—that is, myopic technology, driven by questionable economics, breaks the closed circle.

Unfortunately for the Forest Service, environmentalists are not the only critics of its timber program. Many nonindustry forest economists argue that the service's timber policies are economically inefficient,[24] a position with which most of the forest products industry agrees. Marion Clawson, a forest economist with Resources for the Future, has made perhaps the most widely cited general critique on the Forest Service's timber management.[25] Clawson argues that the forests do not achieve their full potential because of unsound, even counterproductive management. He argues, for example, that Forest Service timber management expenditures are only minimally related to timber production potential, as measured by actual receipts from timber sales. In fact, timber management costs, by Forest Service region, are *inversely* related to timber value; timber expenditures are higher per unit of timber sold in regions with low receipts per unit sold and lower in regions of high per unit receipts.

Among forest economists, the most controversial service policy involves its long-range criteria for timber harvest scheduling. The Forest Service has interpreted the sustained yield principle of the multiple-use doctrine to require a *nondeclining even-flow policy,* which limits the allowable harvest to the amount of timber that can be removed yearly at a constant or increasing, never declining, rate over the long run. This policy is controversial in regions, such as the Pacific Northwest, with high proportions of old-growth forest. The nondeclining even-flow policy significantly lengthens the period of conversion from old-growth stands, which have little or no annual growth, to managed stands of faster-growing trees. Forest economists argue that this extended conversion period (up to 200 years) is inefficient and unproductive and contributes to high levels of tree mortality. They advocate a more flexible policy allowing accelerated harvest of old-growth stands in the short run and achieving long-run sustained yields much sooner.[26]

The Forest Service disagrees with both its environmentalist and forest economist critics. It defends clear-cutting by arguing that, given the regeneration needs of certain species, no other harvest system is acceptable. In particular, it believes that selective-cutting alternatives to clear-cutting would result in *high grading,* the counterproductive removal of the best-growing stock in the early rounds of harvesting. The Forest Service justifies its conservative timber harvest scheduling policy by pointing out that the uneven-flow policy advocated by some forest economists would lead to a decline in harvest levels after the accelerated liquidation of old-growth timber. The service maintains that its nondeclining policy prudently avoids the dislocations in the timber industry that might be caused by such a decline.

Range Management

Though both the BLM and Forest Service have similar programs for domestic livestock grazing on their lands, the bureau has been the primary target of range management criticism. Perhaps the main reason for this is that its rangelands are in generally poorer condition than the service's. The BLM itself estimates that some 135 million acres of its land—or 83 percent of its land in the eleven western states (excluding Alaska)—is in unsatisfactory condition.[27] Poor range conditions have been common for the BLM's lands in this century. (In fact, as will be shown in chapter 3, poor range conditions provided the impetus for the establishment of the BLM's predecessor.) A number of factors contribute to poor range conditions, including the arid climate in the intermountain West, most of which receives less than 12 inches of precipitation per year. The agency's environmentalist critics, however, unanimously lay the blame for unsatisfactory range conditions on overgrazing by domestic livestock.

The BLM is, of course, aware of the problem of overgrazing. Particularly during the 1960s, it attempted to decrease overgrazing by negotiating a lowering of the number of grazing leases. It has also attempted to institute a number of range management programs, the goal of which is to improve range conditions while maintaining or increasing levels of livestock grazing. The best known of these is the rest-rotation grazing system, developed by the BLM's August Hormay.[28]

A subsidiary issue for many years was the level of fees paid by ranchers to use public domain grazing lands. For many years, BLM grazing fees were set at levels far below market value, 5 cents per animal-unit-month initially and only 33 cents per animal-unit-month in 1968. In 1969 the BLM and Forest Service scheduled increases designed to bring the grazing fee to about $1.95 by 1980.[29] While 1975 fees of $1.14 were still below the figure determined to be the fair market value in 1966 ($1.23), the 1969 fee changes have gone a long way toward redressing the levels of fees.

Raising grazing fees is obviously unattractive to ranchers. Stockmen point out that public lands are significantly less productive, per acre, than private lands and that normal fair market costs per animal-unit-month do not accurately reflect the costs of livestock operations on public lands. Livestock industry opposition to these fee increases (as we shall see in chapter 3, the issue dates back to the 1940s) led to a congressional moratorium on the Forest Service–BLM fee increases beginning in 1976.

Wilderness

The third controversial program, that of designation of Wilderness areas, provides a clear-cut example of a very basic disagreement between the preservationist leanings of environmentalists and the progressive conservationist background of the multiple-use agencies, especially the Forest Service. Environmentalists believe that the service is fundamentally opposed to Wilderness designation of areas of the national forest system. The Forest Service, they say, has dragged its feet on recommending areas for congressional designation.[30] The service's criteria for recommending additional Wilderness areas include, in addition to the basic criteria of the Wilderness Act, "availability," "need," and "strong public support." Availability means that areas are excluded if they are commercial, regulated forest included in existing Forest Service timber harvest plans. The need criterion implies that current recreational demand for backcountry use is unfulfilled. According to preservationists, the availability criterion and the more restrictive use of the need criterion (in comparison with demand calculations for other uses) reflect a Forest

Service bias against Wilderness and in favor of timber production.[31] The Forest Service has, in fact, recommended that only a small portion of what the preservationists call "*de facto* wilderness" be designated as Wilderness. The Forest Service's 1972–73 Roadless Area Review and Evaluation inventory, for example, identified 1,449 roadless areas (the preservationists' *de facto* wilderness), comprising 55.9 million acres, but only 274 areas, totaling 12,289,000 acres, were nominated for further study.[32] The selected wilderness study areas were often high-country, untimbered areas, causing wilderness advocates to charge that the Forest Service had adopted a "rocks and snow" policy of wilderness additions. Preservationists recall Pinchot's utilitarian view of conservation (for example, his view of the forest as a "wood factory"), and allege a production orientation of modern forestry professionals to explain the service's bias against wilderness.

There is some truth to the preservationists' criticisms. However, what the preservationists mean as a criticism, the Forest Service sees as good professional land management in the progressive conservation tradition. Multiple use is the key doctrine in the Forest Service's (and BLM's) philosophy of land management. As will be discussed in later chapters, multiple-use management means more than just accommodating as many uses as possible on a given unit of land, but it does mean that Forest Service officers have a deep-seated aversion—rooted in the progressive conservationist origins of the agency and the philosophy of its founder Pinchot—to single-use management of public lands. Despite the statement in the Multiple Use–Sustained Yield Act of 1960 that "the establishment and maintenance of areas of Wilderness are consistent with . . . the Act,"[33] the service generally views wilderness as single-use management, and thus professionally undesirable (at least on a large scale). Moreover, as trained foresters, Forest Service officers' beliefs about aesthetics and recreational capability differ from the preservationists'. Foresters generally regard a managed forest—that is, a forest ecosystem altered in ways that human managers believe desirable—to be visually and professionally gratifying and suitable for many kinds of rewarding recreation. This is diametrically opposed to the preservationist view, in which a natural ecosystem—nature unmodified by human desires—is both aesthetically pleasing in its own right and a prerequisite for an edifying backcountry recreation experience. Finally, Forest Service managers have an ingrained opposition to overuse of a resource that results in abuse of lands under their jurisdiction. They believe Wilderness designation acts as a magnet, creating excessive backcountry use, which in turn results in soil compaction, trampling of vegetation, and other resource damage in parts of some Wildernesses, destroying the very aesthetic values Wilderness designation was intended to protect. The Forest Service has been forced to respond to these overuse problems with research and wilderness management programs.[34]

While the Forest Service is unenthusiastic about Wilderness designation on philosophical and managerial grounds, other users of public lands are opposed because Wilderness designation threatens some of their tangible interests. The forest products industry, in particular, opposes extensive Wilderness designation in cases in which commercial forests would be removed from the Forest Service's harvest program. (In addition, as professional foresters, most forest industry officials share the service's professional biases against Wilderness.) Many local governments have also opposed Wilderness designation for fiscal reasons. Since federal lands are exempt from local property taxes, Congress provides that a percentage of payments for use of public lands (for example, 12.5 percent of most BLM grazing fees and 25 percent of all national forest receipts) is returned to local governments in lieu of taxes. In counties with large proportions of federal land, in-lieu payments may form a significant part of the local government's revenue base. Since Wilderness designation precludes or inhibits revenue-producing uses, local governments knew in the past that the designation adversely affected their fiscal bases. In 1978 Congress revised the payment-in-lieu-of-taxes formula; now the national forests, for example, pay local governments 75 cents per acre or 25 percent of gross receipts, whichever is greater. This revised formula has eliminated or greatly reduced the potential fiscal penalty of Wilderness designations. However, local officials have also opposed Wilderness designation because many of their constituents, especially in rural counties, are economically dependent on consumptive use of federal lands.

Political Critiques

As was the case with advocates of the basic philosophies of natural resources management, especially progressive conservationists, participants in contemporary public lands controversies criticize the political process involved, as well as substantive issues. Indeed, critics commonly argue that the substantive failings of public land managers are attributable to irresponsible policy-making processes. In the contemporary American mood, bureaucratic statism has fallen prey to both conservative and liberal critics. The process critiques of the BLM and Forest Service reflect this antibureaucracy mood.

Laissez-faire capitalism, the political philosophy of utilitarianism, underlies the most simple political critique. Public bureaucracies, according to this critique, are inherently inefficient because they are not guided by a profit motivation and are excessively influenced by "political" considerations (which apparently means irrational or partisan considerations). Public lands, according to this view, would be better managed if they were all turned over to private enterprise and the control of the free market. However, returning the public lands to the free market has very few serious supporters among those currently interested in federal land management.[35]

The classic economic viewpoint, with which the pure laissez-faire critique is associated, does have serious modern proponents, however. Some critics, generally economists, argue that the public lands could be managed more efficiently through the use of rational decision-making procedures that would give greater weight to cost-effectiveness.[36] The conceptual and practical difficulties with rational decision making—indeed, even the desirability of using the rational decision method in governmental policymaking—have been the subject of a voluminous literature. The premise of this chapter—that there is no consensus on the goals of public lands management—makes rational decision making difficult. (That is, the very first step in the classic model of rational decision making is to identify the agreed-upon goals of the decision process.)

A long-standing, if simplistic, variation on the efficiency critique involves governmental reorganization. The location of the Forest Service in the Department of Agriculture, while the other three land management agencies are in the Department of the Interior, is believed by some to contribute to inefficiency. Efforts to reform public lands management by transferring the Forest Service into Interior—a notion of reform long since discredited by organization theorists—have a long history of failure.[37]

The most fundamental political (and certainly the most widely circulated) critique is that the public lands agencies are excessively influenced by consumptive users. Environmentalists such as Daniel Barney and Jack Shepherd argue that the Forest Service's policies of excessive timber cutting, use of clear-cutting, and opposition to Wilderness are caused by political subservience to the timber industry.[38] Both Barney and Shepherd cite a 1970 decision as support for their argument. After the House of Representatives defeated an industry-supported bill, the National Timber Supply Act, that would have mandated a 50 percent increase in the Forest Service's harvest levels, the industry is alleged to have used presidential assistant Charles Colson to obtain a directive from President Nixon for the Forest Service to increase its allowable cut. Barney's and Shepherd's conspiracy theory is in the best traditions of muckraking: in league with the timber industry and the Nixon White House (surely, by 1974, a place that conspiracy theorists would recognize as sinister), the Forest Service was contributing to the rape of the forests.

Phillip Foss's critique of the pre-1960 BLM is even more pointed.[39] Foss contends that the western livestock industry thoroughly controlled the BLM at all levels. Of particular interest to Foss were the operations of the local grazing advisory boards that were established by the BLM soon after its founding (and later at the state and national levels). These advisory boards were allowed to exercise both formal and informal control over most aspects of BLM range management policy.[40] They succeeded, throughout much of the agency's existence, in preventing BLM officials from reducing livestock use to the carrying-capacity levels indicated by professional range surveys and required by the applicable statutes and regulations. Foss thought this situation particularly pernicious, not just because the stockmen were an obviously self-interested clientele, nor even because board control contributed to overgrazing and poor range conditions, but because the BLM had sown the seeds of its own downfall by creating the boards and handing decision-making power over to them.

The BLM's difficulties were compounded by the political pressures exerted on it by the congressional interior subsystem. Dominated by congressmen from the western, livestock-oriented states, the interior committees gave improvements of range conditions and management a low priority. The Department of the Interior, more dependent on programs such as those of the Bureau of Reclamation, was not able to push hard for the BLM and defend it before the same committee members who controlled the department's more important programs.[41]

Another structural or process critique of the agencies advanced by environmentalists is that the statutes governing the agencies grant excessive, uncontrolled administrative discretion. The best-known expression of this critique is Charles Reich's.[42] Like most in this school of criticism, Reich is a law professor, and his argument is fairly legalistic. His basic point is that the legislation governing the activities of the Forest Service and BLM (as well as the Park Service) is vague, a broad grant of largely uncontrolled authority to the agencies. The very general directions of statutes like the multiple-use acts—"due consideration shall be given to the relative values of the various resources"—are, according to Reich, "mere euphemisms that abdicate all real power" by Congress. Reich's assumption of a virtual absence of formal control by democratic institutions suggests several other questions about the agencies' decision-making processes: Are the agencies open to the public? Are decision processes sufficiently formalized to ensure evenhanded decisions? What is the effect of the professional norms of agency experts? In short, will agency procedures ensure democratic responsiveness? Observers from Reich to Barney have felt that the agencies' decision-making procedures fall short of these criteria of democratic responsiveness.[43]

The capture and discretion arguments are two major criticisms of administrative responsibility that have been leveled against federal bureaucratic politics generally. At first blush the two theses may seem contradictory: if the agencies are captured, how can they be operating under uncontrolled discretion, especially if a key element of capture is White House pressure on the Forest Service or congressional subsystem pressure on the BLM?

Theoretically, broad grants of discretion allow situations to develop in which agencies might become captured. The Congress as a whole—as opposed to the congressional committee subsystems—and the president cannot make all the important basic policy decisions governing agency operations. By giving agencies broad discretionary authority, constitutionally specified institutions free those agencies to respond to whatever other factors become salient in their decisional environment. If the agencies have a constituency, and if their decision procedures are such that only the constituency is allowed access to decision making, then the groundwork has been laid for agency capture.

Reich argues that Forest Service procedures allow *differential* access. These procedures provide a right to appeal a decision ("standing" in a legal-administrative sense) only to materially aggrieved parties, that is, consumptive users; and hearings have a locational bias in favor of local constituents, who are overbalanced in favor of these same users.[44] Thus, the general public is excluded from agency policy processes. In the BLM, the advisory board had the same effect of structurally predisposing the agency to capture by a narrow constituency. The excluded general public would presumably favor policies more in the public interest than policies made in a process favoring a narrower range of clients. Insofar as this general public was identifiable, it was believed (by conservationists and preservationists) to consist of conservationists and preservationists. Cutler, for example, argues that the reason behind the large volume of litigation instituted against the Forest Service was that the agency did not have open "public participation" channels, which would have allowed Wilderness advocates to participate in agency decision making.[45]

The final relevant political process issue involves an *ad hominem* attack on environmentalists, their self-placement in the public interest movement notwithstanding. Because many environmentalists (such as the modal member of the Sierra Club, a symbol of the environmental movement in the eyes of many of its critics) have high educational and occupational status, environmentalism as a whole has been branded an "upper-middle-class social movement," and its policy preferences, consequently, elitist.[46] If one accepts this criticism, environmentalist policies would have no more—and, in the view of such critics, less—right to the halo of the public interest than industry-supported policies, thus defusing the progressivist, anti-special interests line of attack used by environmentalists.

Issues and Ideologies

The importance of the various criticisms of the BLM and Forest Service does not really lie in their logical, theoretical, or factual validity. One can adduce evidence of overcutting, overconservative timber harvest criteria, overgrazing, excessive grazing fees, and a disinclination to designate Wilderness, even though such conclusions are based on judgments advanced by partisans of the how-much-is-too-much variety, and even though issues like clear-cutting and the nondeclining even-flow criterion are classic examples of political issues embedded in scientific-technical debates. One can find evidence of capture, excessive discretion, or environmentalist elitism, even though the evidence is rooted in a dated or flawed body of literature. The clear utility of these critiques lies in their ideological importance in natural resources politics.

Factions in public land management politics tend to operate under ideologies that combine both substantive and political process beliefs and are rooted in the historic philosophies of natural resources management. The Forest Service's and BLM's guiding principles are still almost identical to those of the progressive conservation movement, of which they are products: multiple-use and sustained yield policies produce the "greatest good for the greatest number in the long run," and that outcome is best obtained by entrusting public lands to public agencies staffed by professional land managers. Professional critics of the agencies accept the use and efficiency orientations of the progressives, but argue that bureaucratic statism in federal land management produces inefficient results.

The environmental movement's ideology is perhaps the most succinct of those described earlier, and is certainly the most widely published. With respect to the Forest Service and BLM (as well as other agencies, such as the Army Corps of Engineers and the old Atomic Energy Commission), the environmental ideology holds that (1) the policies of the agencies with respect to timber management, range management, Wilderness, and some other issues are bad (that is, environmentally destructive, nonconservational, and not preferred by environmentalists); (2) the agencies are subservient to user interest group "bad guys," who prefer the bad policies described in item 1; and (3) the agencies are subservient to user interests because representatives of the public interest (that is, environmentalists) are systematically excluded from an agency policymaking process embedded in excessive administrative discretion. This ideology shares several features with the twin historic, philosophical antecedents of modern environmentalism. As did the progressive conservationists, the environmentalists argue that present levels of use are not wise, and that present use patterns are likely to lead to diminished resource productivity over time. Another element of the ideology, the centrality of the Wilderness issue in Forest Service politics, harkens back to the preservationist philosophy of John Muir.

For our purposes, however, it is especially important to note the similarities between the modern environmentalists' critique of public lands management and the political grievance of the progressive conservation movement. As noted earlier, Pinchot's philosophy was part conservation and part populist progressivism. The evil of exploitation of the public lands was not just that the land was being despoiled, but that it was being despoiled for the narrow economic interests of the barons. Modern critics, like "Nader Raider" Barney, echo this grievance, the administrative irresponsibility of agency responsiveness to narrow economic interests in derogation of the public interest.

Interest Group Theory and Public Lands Policy

Interest group theories of politics provide an ideal framework for examining federal public lands management. The wide range of possible uses of the public lands provide tangible potential rewards for contestants in public lands policy processes. Moreover, the wide range of philosophies demonstrate that those contestants have strong and diverse opinions about how the public lands should be managed. Those opinions are ultimately translated into interest group pressures on Forest Service and BLM line officers. The capture-conformity debate boils down to the issue of how and how much those pressures influence public lands policy.

Group Theory as a General Theory of American Politics

The body of literature known as interest group theory includes a variety of studies on the role of groups in the political process. The core of that literature is a set of general treatises, most notably those of Arthur Bentley and David Truman, discussed below. It also includes several secondary, specialized elaborations on such important topics as the formation of groups and styles of group lobbying. The group literature also contains a normative argument, *pluralism,* that defends the propriety and legitimacy of group influence, as well as a large and often persuasive body of normative criticism of pluralism.[47] The form of the overwhelming majority of empirical studies in the group literature—regardless of whether they are dealing with general, specialized, or normative theoretical issues—has been the nonquantitative case study.[48]

Arthur Bentley's *The Process of Government* was the first general treatise on group theory.[49] Bentley forcefully argued that all political processes are manifestations of interest group activity:

> Pressure, as we shall use it, is always a group phenomenon. It indicates the push and resistance between groups. The balance of group pressures *is* the state of society.[50]
>
> All phenomena of government are phenomena of groups pressing one another, forming one another, and pushing out new groups and group representatives (the organs and agencies of government) to mediate the adjustments.[51]

Implicit in Bentley's prose is the core proposition that interest group activity is the key determinant of governmental policymaking. Bentley, however, is never very explicit about which aspects of group activity influence governmental policymaking or how; in fact, he often seems purposely abstract on these points.

David Truman's *The Governmental Process,* one of the most important treatises on group theory, is both more comprehensive and more straightforward than Bentley's opus.[52] Unlike Bentley, Truman covers the broadest possible range of group roles and behavior, including the internal organization of groups and their influence on public opinion, political parties, legislatures, chief executives, administrative agencies, and the courts. Like Bentley, Truman argues that governmental decisions are the products of the activities of competing groups, but he goes on to identify three distinct facets of group activity.

The first facet is a group's *interest,* the set of shared attitudes among members that lead the group to make certain claims on the rest of society. Truman uses a group's interest as its defining characteristic; thus, he would define an environmental group not in terms of its formal-legal characteristics (such as the Sierra Club's structure, specified by its by-laws, consisting of a national board and staff, regional chapters, and local groups), but in terms of its positions on natural resources issues and the actions it takes to translate those positions into governmental policy.[53] Interests are crucial, Truman explains, because they maintain the internal cohesion of the group and define its objectives.

The second facet is the group's "power." Truman, as do some other group theorists, generally uses the term *power* to mean the same thing as influence; in this precise usage, power is not an intrinsic property of a group, but the result of its having imposed its will on society.[54] However, Truman and other group theorists sometimes also use the term loosely to refer to certain group resources that enable a group to operate effectively and influentially. A group's key resources are the skills of its leaders or agents in playing the political game, the amount of money it can devote to political activity, and the number of members it can mobilize for political activity.[55] These resources are often (though not necessarily) interrelated; a group with a large dues-paying membership, for example, can afford to hire an effective professional staff.

The primary utility of group resources is that they can help a group achieve *access,* the third facet of group activity.[56] Access is the necessary link between a group's interest and the resources devoted to pursuing it, on the one hand, and influence or policy impact, on the other hand. Access is necessary for the group to get its message across to decision makers, and much of the tactical skill and activity of groups is directed toward obtaining favorable access. Thus, Truman notes that access is "the facilitating intermediate objective of political interest groups."[57] What access facilitates is group influence. As Truman states, "The product of effective access, of the claims of organized and unorganized interests that achieve access with varying degrees of effectiveness, is a governmental decision."[58]

Truman's elaboration on Bentley's notions of group theory is not wholly faithful to Bentley's approach. Group theorists disagreed on the emphasis to be given to the group as the dominant force in society relative to the emphasis on the individuals in groups and their attitudes and interests. Bentley steadfastly rejects efforts to reify group activity, that is, to break it down into more precise concepts. He refuses to recognize interests as phenomena distinct from group activity, because to do so would tend to support the importance of individuals' preferences and attitudes, rather than a pure group approach. Similarly, he treats group power as identical to group activity: "As the interest is merely a manner of stating the value of group activity, so these factors of dominance are likewise just phases of the statement of the group, not separate from it, nor capable of scientific use as separate things."[59]

Truman, who is very familiar with the politicopsychological and sociopsychological research of the 1930s and 1940s, is not averse, in elaborating Bentley's approach, to making analytical distinctions compatible with the individualistic orientation Bentley rejects. This disagreement is, however, a subtle one. Both theorists agree that group activity is an amalgam of such factors as interests, power, and access.

With the publication of Truman's treatise, the general group theory of politics is fairly complete. Since 1951, group theorists have generally focused on a number of specialized or secondary theoretical topics. Two of these topics, one dealing with the origins of interest groups and the other with the style of group lobbying, illustrate the wide range of group theory.

The group theory treatises assume that groups organize because their members believe they can pursue their interests more effectively through organized groups than individually. Mancur Olson, however, notes that this simple assumption of rationality is paradoxical.[60] Olson demonstrates that no individual who acted rationally would join a group because of the "free-rider" problem: since the group seeks "public goods,"[61] no individual could be denied the fruits of the group's success. Because there is no incentive, short of coercion, to compel group membership, rational self-interest inhibits the formation of organized interest groups.

Group theory provides four common explanations for the existence of interest groups. First, Olson argues that small latent groups (the potential beneficiaries of some policy) can organize for political activity if some member's share of the collective good is larger than the cost of organizing the group; this is often the case for narrow (and especially oligopolistic) sectors of business activity.[62] Second, Olson notes that political activities are secondary responsibilities of many organizations that actively pressure government. A forest products firm, incorporated to earn a profit from harvesting timber, that must spend some time trying to influence the Forest Service illustrates the second explanation, while an association of forest products firms in a region dependent on sales from public lands illustrates the first. Third, people may be motivated to join groups by ideological altruism, not rational self-interest, as Olson presumes. Fourth, Robert Salisbury suggests that group founders play a critical role, persuading initial members to support a group by the prospect of future collective rewards, then later retaining members by introducing selective membership benefits.[63] The Sierra Club illustrates the third and fourth explanations. The club was organized by John Muir in the 1890s to obtain about as public a good as is imaginable, the preservation of the Sierra Nevada high country in California. Today some members join the club because they are ideological environmentalists, but the club's large membership is maintained primarily by such selective benefits as its magazine, *Sierra,* and club hiking outings.

Another major specialized topic in group theory deals with the muckraker myth that interest groups exert strong-armed pressure on decision makers or corrupt them by methods such as bribery. Several major studies in the 1960s painted a portrait of lobbying that was quite different from the pressure-and-corruption myth.[64] Lobbyists were found to act as suppliers of information for legislators who already agreed with their positions. Their function is to heighten interest in specific legislation, cuing legislators' agendas rather than influencing their attitudes. Since most interactions take place between lobbyists and their legislative allies, the notion of pressure is clearly inappropriate and the lobbyists' informational style highly appropriate. Also, since the communication function is the most important part of the lobbyist's role, a lobbyist's credibility, communications skills, and ability to develop personal contacts with decision makers are his most important assets. Jeffrey Berry's study of the strategies and tactics of public interest groups (for example, environmental groups) in the 1970s supports the informational view of lobbyists' operations.[65] Berry found that informational tactics, such as one-to-one presentations and formal participation in public hearings, are the most commonly used. When groups exert pressure, it takes the form of letter-writing campaigns and lobbying by influential members from congressional home districts.

The Group Theory of Bureaucratic Politics

In addition to special theories on topics such as group formation and lobbying style, the body of group theory includes special theories of group influence in the different branches or institutions of government. The most relevant of these special theories, given our focus on the federal public lands agencies, is the theory of bureaucratic politics. That theory is not a simple offshoot of the Truman–Bentley model of group competition. (On the contrary, Truman was significantly influenced by the theory of bureaucratic politics, which predated *The Governmental Process* by two years.) It is instead a product of the evolution of organization theory.

Traditional organization theorists viewed federal administrative agencies—in fact, all formal organizations—as closed, insulated entities. The organization, in the traditionalist view, is a simple, legally defined entity; the Forest Service and Bureau of Land Management, for example, would be seen simply as agencies established by certain federal statutes, composed of people paid from each organization's Treasury funds, and organized or structured according to the formal hierarchical charts shown in chapters 2 and 3. Traditional management theorists are primarily concerned with official relationships (that is, those governed by written rules) within formal hierarchies, and ignore influences on organizations from outside their formal organizational hierarchies. Traditional public organization theory recognizes only one legitimate outside influence—statutory law.[66]

Modern students of public bureaucracy have rejected this rigid, closed view of organizations. Herbert Simon, the founder of the modern approach to organization theory, argues that the critical influences affecting any organization come from its *customers,* those who use its products and provide it, in exchange, with the resources it needs; and its *suppliers,* those whose cooperation is needed to produce products for its customers.⁶⁷ Simon, in fact, defines the *organization* as including both the traditional legal entity (the firm or government agency) and its customers and suppliers. Simon's insights have been developed into what is called the *open systems theory* of organizations, which argues that the external influences acting on an organization are the most important determinant of organizational behavior.⁶⁸ According to the open-systems theorists, administrative units are *focal organizations* within an environment consisting of other organizations, their *organization-set*.⁶⁹

The mainline administrative group theory, developed in 1949–50 as an extension of Simon's modern organization theory by Long, Simon and his colleagues, and Selznick, is *clientelism*.⁷⁰ Long observes that if a bureau is to effectively carry out its mission within the fragmented American governmental system of checks and balances, it must assure its continued survival, and this means it must have its own source of power. Simon and his colleagues argue that, just as a business firm depends on customer satisfaction, so a government bureau survives by developing a satisfied interest group clientele which will support the agency before its legislative and executive superiors. Selznick's classic study of the Tennessee Valley Authority details the ways in which the TVA co-opted potentially hostile local elites into a clientele that supported the agency. The TVA consulted and cooperated with local elites so that they came to think of themselves as a part of the TVA organization. Local elites thus supported the TVA because threats to it were seen as threats to "their" agency. This support allowed the TVA to survive and prosper in a very hostile political environment from the 1930s through the Eisenhower administration.

The Capture-Conformity Debate

Academic commentators on clientelism, however, see the exchange with clienteles as a two-edged sword. Perhaps the most important critics of clientelism generally are Grant McConnell and Theodore Lowi.⁷¹ McConnell describes interest groups as narrow sectors of society with, in most cases, an ideological commitment to localism, and he details the mechanisms by which agencies institutionalize differential clientele group access to and influence on decision-making processes (that is, the co-optive mechanisms described by Selznick). He argues that the institutionalization of narrow group influence—as opposed to simple responsiveness to groups that happen to petition agency officials—tends to defeat broad national policy goals and pervert the democratic process through a transfer of public power to narrow private interests. To McConnell's charge that clientelism is undemocratic, Lowi, who calls clientelism "interest group liberalism," adds the charges that clientelism is based on the faulty political philosophy of pluralism and an unconstitutional and illegal devolution of legislative power to executive agencies, and results in unjust policies and ineffective planning. Because critics like McConnell and Lowi believe clientelism leads to group control of agencies and deflection of the agency from its proper mission, in opposition to clientelism's stated logic of agency manipulation of clientele groups to ensure agency survival and effectiveness, their criticism is commonly referred to as the *capture thesis*.

The theory of clientelist bureaucratic politics, as developed in the 1940s, is a refutation of the traditional model of American public administration. That traditional model, which was dominant in academic circles from 1887 through the 1930s, is based on the assumption that administrative processes should be apolitical. Traditional public administrationists believe that administration is simply a process of applying technical expertise to the execution of public policy and of ensuring that the resulting correct decision is applied uniformly by all administrators in the agency. Both traditional public administration theory and the progressive conservation movement are products of the Progressive era. The apolitical thesis, for example, is to a considerable extent a justification of the progressive reform of the civil service system enacted in the Pendleton Act,[72] and the belief in technical expertise is a central feature of both traditional public administration and progressive conservation.

Both traditional public administration theory and the criticisms of bureaucratic politics are reflected in the two poles of the capture-conformity debate. The capture pole is best expressed in Phillip Foss's 1960 description of the BLM as dominated by its livestock industry clientele. Foss's critique, as noted earlier, is central to environmentalist criticism of the public lands agencies. The word *capture,* however, is somewhat misleading. As we shall see in chapter 3, Foss describes the unsuccessful efforts of the BLM and its predecessor, the Grazing Service, to reform public range management in the face of stockmen's resistance—not the kind of submissiveness or collusion suggested by capture.[73] Nonetheless, the BLM has been frequently used, notably by McConnell,[74] as a prime example of a captured agency.

The *conformity* position is most closely associated with Herbert Kaufman's study of the Forest Service and is usually treated as being consistent with traditional public administration theory.[75] Kaufman argues that the service uses a number of formal and informal practices to obtain an extremely high degree of compliance with central agency policy from its field officers. (These procedures will be discussed in detail in chapter 2.) Largely on the basis of Kaufman's study, the Forest Service enjoys a reputation among students of bureaucracy as one of the most highly disciplined, conformist, well-managed agencies in the federal government.

Students of public bureaucracy have taken different stands on the two poles of the capture-conformity debate when judging national level agency behavior. McConnell and Lowi categorically oppose clientelist behavior as inevitably leading to capture. On the other hand, Emmette Redford, an eminent public administration theorist, defends clientelist-style bureaucratic politics in Washington office agency relationships with Congress and national interest groups as a form of policymaking that is efficient, sophisticated, and responsive to legitimate public preferences.[76] Public administration theorists generally agree, however, that conformist behavior is appropriate for low-level agency officers. Redford, for example, argues that local administration ("micropolitics," as he calls it) should be conducted according to the traditional principles of apolitical, impersonal, technically expert administration.

The capture-conformity debate in public lands management revolves around the actions of local public lands administrators. The focus of Kaufman's study, as indicated by its title, is the district ranger, the lowest-level line officer in the Forest Service, while Foss's study on the BLM's difficulties with its rancher constituents deals extensively with the ways that local managers are supposedly captured by local constituents. Thus, uncaptured conformist administrative behavior is regarded as the ideal for local public lands managers.

Plan of the Book

The purpose of this book is to reexamine the capture-conformity debate as expressed in Kaufman's and Foss's 1960 studies and the contemporary journalistic literature on public lands politics. This requires an examination of the nature and consequences of group influence on local administrators of the Forest Service and BLM. Aside from the fact that the capture-conformity debate focuses largely on local lands management because of studies such as those of Kaufman and Foss, an examination of group influence in local administrative politics is important in its own right. "Policy" is often treated as an abstraction, associated with the dry prose and dusty volumes of government documents. But policy is really what government does for or to citizens, and what the Forest Service and BLM do is done in the field. What local Forest Service and BLM officers do matters more, ultimately, than what is contained in dry documents in Washington, D.C. Much has been written about the influence of groups and their lobbyists on Washington politics. More must be learned about the importance of groups in field administration, at the bottom of the pyramid of the federal apparatus. Since many observers, such as Redford, believe local administration is, or should be, apolitical and bureaucratic, a study of interest groups at the local level provides a litmus test for group theory. If groups are influential in local public lands politics, then group theory may indeed be as widely applicable a general theory of American politics as Bentley has claimed.

A study of local group politics must not, however, ignore the context within which public lands management takes place. Contemporary public lands disputes are only the latest in an unbroken series of struggles over American public lands. As noted earlier, current disputes over public lands issues are rooted in long-standing philosophical differences about natural resources management. Moreover, many current issues have been debated continuously for decades. The public lands agencies and their administrative procedures have been formed in the crucible of these political struggles. Part I of this book thus briefly describes the background behind the relationships that contemporary managers of public lands have with interest groups. Chapter 2 describes the history and organization of the Forest Service and chapter 3 the BLM's history and organization. Chapter 4 outlines the local management practices of the two agencies.

In Part II, the heart of the book, group influence in contemporary public lands management is examined. This examination is based on field research conducted in three regions of the western United States during 1973. That research involved interviews with local agency officials and key interest group leaders in the regions, administration of questionnaires to other group leaders, and collection of documentary material. Chapter 5 describes the administrative and interest group actors in the study sample. Chapter 6 describes the agencies' local organization-sets, that is, the patterns of relationships between local land managers and their group constituents. Chapter 7 examines administrators' and group leaders' beliefs about the influence local constituents have on public lands management, while chapters 8 and 9 investigate the formal and informal public lands agency practices that facilitate group influence. Chapter 10 concludes Part II by using a mathematical model of interest group influence (developed in appendix C) to estimate the extent to which groups really affect key public lands policies.

Finally, in chapter 11, the material on contemporary local public lands politics from Part II, as well as the information on historic developments in public lands management since 1960, discussed in Part I, is used to draw some conclusions about the capture-conformity debate.

NOTES

1. These studies, to be discussed in greater detail below, are Herbert Kaufman's *The Forest Ranger* (Baltimore, Md., Johns Hopkins University Press for Resources for the Future, 1960); and Phillip Foss's *Politics and Grass* (Seattle, University of Washington Press, 1960).
2. Nash, *Wilderness and the American Mind* (New Haven, Conn., Yale University Press, 1967) chap. 1.
3. See, for example, Eric Goldman, *Rendezvous With Destiny* (New York, Knopf, 1956) chap. 5.
4. The best-organized sources on the intellectual history of conservation, as well as the preservation philosophy, are Roderick Nash, ed., *The American Environment: Readings in the History of Conservation* (2 ed., Reading, Mass., Addison-Wesley, 1976); Ian Burton and Robert Kates, eds., *Readings in Resource Management and Conservation* (Chicago, Ill., University of Chicago Press, 1965) pt. II; and Henry Jarrett, ed., *Perspectives on Conservation: Essays on America's Natural Resources* (Baltimore, Md., Johns Hopkins University Press for Resources for the Future, 1958) pt. I.
5. Marsh, *Man and Nature: Or, Physical Geography as Modified by Human Action* (New York, Scribners, 1864) p. 35.
6. Grant McConnell, "The Conservation Movement—Past and Present," *Western Political Quarterly* vol. 7 (September 1954) pp. 463–478; and Samuel Hays, *Conservation and the Gospel of Efficiency* (Cambridge, Mass., Harvard University Press, 1959). While some observers see a divergence between their positions, both describe key points of progressivism: Hays's scientific efficiency was the progressives' solution to the "special interests" political grievance that McConnell focused on.
7. Gifford Pinchot, *The Fight for Conservation* (New York, Doubleday and Page, 1910) p. 46, cited by McConnell, "The Conservation Movement," p. 466.
8. Hays, *Conservation and the Gospel of Efficiency*, p. 3.

9. Letter from James Wilson, secretary of agriculture, to Gifford Pinchot, chief of the Forest Service, dated February 1, 1905, implementing the Transfer Act of 1905 (16 U.S.C. §§472, 524, 554). The letter is generally recognized as having been drafted by Pinchot for Wilson's signature.

10. The Multiple Use–Sustained Yield Act of 1960 (16 U.S.C. §531), the Classification and Multiple Use Act of 1964 (33 U.S.C. §1415), and the Federal Land Policy and Management Act of 1976 (43 U.S.C. §1702). The first act governs the Forest Service, and the service was very active in its passage. The second act governed the BLM from 1964 until 1970, and the third act, the so-called BLM Organic Act, replaced the 1964 act. See page 53, for part of the key text of the 1960 act.

11. See, for example, Gifford Pinchot, *Breaking New Ground* (New York, Harcourt, Brace, 1947) pp. 31 and 77.

12. Thoreau, *Excursions, The Writings of Henry David Thoreau* (Boston, Riverside Press, 1893); Muir, *The Mountains of California* (New York, Century, 1894); Leopold, *A Sand County Almanac* (New York, Oxford University Press, 1949); Abbey, *Desert Solitare: A Season in the Wilderness* (New York, Ballantine, 1968).

13. Marx, *The Machine in the Garden* (New York, Oxford University Press, 1964).

14. Dissent in *Sierra Club* v. *Morton*, 405 U.S. 727 (April 1972).

15. Commoner, *The Closing Circle* (New York, Knopf, 1971).

16. Nash, *Wilderness and the American Mind*, chap. 10; Owen Stratton and Phillip Sirotkin, *The Echo Park Controversy* (Syracuse, N.Y., Inter-University Case Program no. 46, 1959).

17. Commoner, *The Closing Circle*, chap. 12.

18. See Glendon Schubert, "The 'Public Interest' in Administration Decision Making: Theorem, Theosophy or Theory?" *American Political Science Review* vol. 51 (June 1957) pp. 346–368.

19. See David Vogel, "Promoting Pluralism: The Public Interest Movement and the American Reform Tradition," Paper read at a meeting of the American Political Science Association, New York, September 1978.

20. See Ludwig Von Bertalanffy, *General System Theory* (New York, George Braziller, 1968).

21. Commoner, *The Closing Circle*, chap. 9. Commoner argues that linear, nonholistic technology is driven by the imperatives of the economic system and justified by the reductionist nature of modern science.

22. Two primary environmentalist critiques of Forest Service timber policy are found in Daniel Barney's *The Last Stand* (New York, Grossman, 1974); and Jack Shepherd's *The Forest Killers* (New York, Weybright and Talley, 1975).

23. See, for example, G. E. Likens, F. H. Bormann, R. S. Pierce, and W. A. Reiners, "Recovery of a Deforested Ecosystem," *Science* vol. 199 (Feb. 3, 1978) pp. 492–496.

24. One of the best known, but most misconstrued, critiques of clearcutting—the Bolle Report—adopts this position. See Arnold Bolle, chairper-

son, "A University View of the Forest Service: A Select Committee Presents Its Report on the Bitterroot National Forest" (Missoula, University of Montana School of Forestry, Nov. 18, 1970).

25. Clawson, "The National Forests," *Science* vol. 191 (Feb. 20, 1976) pp. 762–767. Clawson argues that the forests are managed at less than full value for all uses, not just timber management.

26. A good example of opposing positions within the forestry profession can be found in the symposium of articles in *Journal of Forestry* vol. 75 (November 1977) pp. 699–723. A good summary of the issue can be found in Samuel Dana and Sally Fairfax, *Forest and Range Policy* (2 ed., New York, McGraw-Hill, 1980) pp. 311–333. Some advocates of an uneven-flow policy would allow medium-run harvests below the long-run sustained yield level; practical considerations on some individual forests might also lead to medium-run harvests below the long-run sustained yield level. Medium-run dips below the sustained yield level are not, however, a necessary consequence of the uneven-flow concept.

27. Bureau of Land Management, *Range Condition Report Prepared for the Senate Committee on Appropriations* (Washington, D.C., U.S. Department of the Interior, Bureau of Land Management, January 1975).

28. Hormay, *Principles of Rest-Rotation Grazing and Multiple Use Management* (Washington, D.C., Bureau of Land Management and Forest Service, September 1970).

29. Forest Service, "Grazing Fees on National Forest Range: Past History and Present Policy" (Washington, D.C., Forest Service, CI no. 3, June 1969).

30. See, for example, Mike Frome, *The Battle for Wilderness* (New York, Praeger, 1974) pp. 149–163; Ralph Nader's "Introduction," in Barney, *The Last Stand* pp. xiv–xvi; and Shepherd, *The Forest Killers*.

31. William Devall, "The Forest Service and Wilderness: A Sociological Interpretation," (Arcata, California State University at Humboldt, 1973) mimeo. Normal usage, which we will follow, is for "Wilderness" (capital "W") to refer only to congressionally designated areas.

32. Forest Service, "New Wilderness Study Areas: Roadless Area Review and Evaluation," (Washington, D.C., Forest Service, CI no. 11, October 1973).

33. 16 U.S.C. §530.

34. See, for example, Robert Lucas, "Wilderness: A Management Framework," *Journal of Soil and Water Conservation* vol. 28 (July 1973) pp. 150–154; John Hendee and George Stankey, "Biocentricity in Wilderness Management," *Bioscience* vol. 23 (September 1973) pp. 535–538; and George Stankey and David Lime, "Recreation Carrying Capacity: An Annotated Bibliography" (Ogden, Utah, Forest Service, Intermountain Forest and Range Experiment Station, INT-3, 1973).

35. Aside from a few individual western ranchers and the most outspoken advocates of the "sagebrush rebellion." Such a private takeover of federal lands was also taken seriously by ranchers in the 1940s. See Harold Steen, *The Forest Service* (Seattle, University of Washington Press, 1976) p. 272.

36. See, for example, Marion Clawson, *Forests: For Whom and For What?* (Baltimore, Md., Johns Hopkins University Press for Resources for the Future, 1975), especially chap. 10 to 12. For an example of the literature on the conceptual and practical difficulties of rational decision making in the public lands field, see Jeanne Nienaber and Aaron Wildavsky, *The Budgeting and Evaluation of Federal Recreation Programs; Or, Money Doesn't Grow on Trees* (New York, Basic Books, 1973).

37. See Paul Culhane and H. Paul Friesema, "Federal Public Lands Reorganization, Deja Vu, 1979," in Frank Convery, Jack Royer, and Gerald Stairs, eds., *Reorganization: Issues, Implications and Opportunities for U.S. Natural Resources Policy* (Durham, N.C., Duke University School of Forestry, 1979) pp. 44–64.

38. See Barney, *The Last Stand*; and Shepherd, *The Forest Killers*.

39. Foss, *Politics and Grass*.

40. Foss's major case in point, the Soldier Creek affair, will be discussed in chapter 3.

41. Foss, *Politics and Grass*. Also see Wesley Calef, *Private Grazing and Public Lands* (Chicago, Ill., University of Chicago Press, 1960).

42. Reich, *Bureaucracy and the Forests* (Santa Barbara, Calif., Center for the Study of Democratic Institutions, 1962).

43. Ibid.; and Barney, *Last Stand*, pp. 122–131.

44. Reich, *Bureaucracy and the Forests*, pp. 54–58.

45. M. Rupert Cutler, "A Study of Litigation Related to Management of Forest Service Administered Lands and Its Effect on Policy Decisions," Ph.D. Dissertation, Michigan State University, Department of Resource Development, East Lansing, 1972). Cutler's point of view is especially interesting because he became in 1977 the Carter administration's assistant secretary of agriculture supervising the Forest Service.

46. See, for example, Joseph Harry, Richard Gale, and John Hendee, "Environmentalism as an Upper Middle Class Social Movement," *Journal of Leisure Research* vol. 1 (Summer 1969) pp. 246–254; and William Tucker, "Environmentalism and the Leisure Class," *Harper's* vol. 255 (December 1977) pp. 49–80. For a critique of the factual premise underlying this thesis, see H. Paul Friesema, "Environmental Group Fragmentation and Administrative Decision Making," Paper read at the meeting of the American Society for Public Administration, Chicago, April 1975.

47. The leading pluralist study is Robert Dahl's *Who Governs?* (New Haven, Conn., Yale University Press, 1961). For a comprehensive critique of pluralism, see G. David Garson, *Group Theories of Politics* (Los Angeles, Calif., Sage, 1978).

48. This methodology stands in marked contrast to the very quantitative methods used in empirical research on almost all other aspects of American politics. The first of the classic interest group case studies was Peter Odegaard's *Pressure Politics* (New York, Columbia University Press, 1928). Most of the dozens of monographs of the Inter-University Case Program are good examples of the case-study approach to group research. Some key examples

from the natural resources field are Stratton and Sirotkin, *Echo Park Controversy;* and Hubert Marshall and Betty Zisk, *The Federal-State Struggle for Offshore Oil* (Syracuse, N.Y., Inter-University Case Program no. 98, 1966).

49. Bentley, *The Process of Government* (Chicago, Ill., University of Chicago Press, 1908).

50. Ibid., p. 259.

51. Ibid., p. 269.

52. Truman, *The Governmental Process* (New York, Knopf, 1951). Truman greatly admired Bentley's work. *The Governmental Process* was intended to elaborate on Bentley's *The Process of Government* and to defend it against attacks by institutionalist works such as Robert MacIver's *The Web of Government* (New York, Macmillan, 1948).

53. Truman, *The Governmental Process,* pp. 33–34.

54. Ibid., p. 505. This usage of the concept of power is similar to that of George Catlin in *A Study in the Principles of Politics* (London, Allen and Unwin, 1930); and of Harold Lasswell in *Politics* (New York, McGraw-Hill, 1936).

55. L. Harmon Zeigler and G. Wayne Peak, *Interest Groups in American Society* (2 ed., Englewood Cliffs, N.J., Prentice-Hall, 1972) p. 76. Truman (*The Governmental Process,* pp. 254–261) adopts a similar position, though he does not subscribe to the extreme version of it, associated with Robert Brady's *Business as a System of Power* (New York, Columbia University Press, 1943), that large corporations' huge economic resources inevitably translate into overwhelming political power.

56. Truman, *The Governmental Process,* pp. 506–507. Truman also notes that access is partly a function of "factors peculiar to . . . government institutions themselves."

57. Ibid., p. 264.

58. Ibid., p. 507. Chapter 10 and appendix C will make further use of the proposition, implicit in this quotation, that influence is a function of group interests, resources, and access.

59. Bentley, *The Process of Government,* p. 215. For a good review of the subtle distinctions between group- and individual-based approaches, see Zeigler and Peak, *Interest Groups in American Society,* pp. 8–21.

60. Olson, *The Logic of Collective Action* (Cambridge, Mass., Harvard University Press, 1965).

61. A public good is one that benefits everyone within its effective jurisdiction equally, or at least one that cannot be denied to anyone because he or she did not pay for it. National defense is the common example of a public good; all citizens are equally defended, regardless of the tax burden they carry.

62. Olson, *The Logic of Collective Action,* pp. 22–25.

63. Salisbury, "An Exchange Theory of Interest Groups," in Robert Salisbury, ed., *Interest Group Politics in America* (New York, Harper & Row, 1970) pp. 32–68.

64. See Raymond Bauer, Ithiel Pool, and Lewis Dexter, *American Business and Public Policy* (Cambridge, Massachusetts Institute of Technology

Press, 1963); Lester Milbrath, *The Washington Lobbyist* (Chicago, Ill., Rand McNally, 1963); and L. Harmon Zeigler and Michael Baer, *Lobbying* (Belmont, Calif., Wadsworth, 1969).

65. Berry, *Lobbying for the People* (Princeton, N.J., Princeton University Press, 1977).

66. The most commonly cited source on the traditional viewpoint is Luther Gulick, "Notes on the Theory of Organization," in Luther Gulick and Lyndall Urwick, eds., *Papers on the Science of Administration* (New York, Institute of Public Administration, 1937) pp. 1–45. Weber's ideal type of bureaucracy is often associated with the closed traditional model, though the association is somewhat simplistic; see Max Weber, *Economy and Society;* Guenther Roth and Claus Wittich, eds., (Berkeley, University of California Press, 1978) vol. II, chap. 11. The closed model is based on traditional public administration's "politics-administration dichotomy," which is commonly (and, again, simplistically) associated with Frank Goodnow, *Politics and Administration* (New York, Macmillan, 1900).

67. Simon, *Administrative Behavior* (New York, Macmillan, 1947) pp. 16–18.

68. See, in particular, Daniel Katz and Robert Kahn, *The Social Psychology of Organizations* (New York, Wiley, 1965), especially chap. 2. The open systems argument is obviously quite compatible with the core proposition of interest group theory.

69. See William Evan, "The Organization-Set: Toward a Theory of Interorganizational Relations," in James Thompson, ed., *Approaches to Organizational Design* (Pittsburgh, Pa., University of Pittsburgh Press, 1966) pp. 175–191. Chapter 6 in this volume draws on Evan's concept to analyze Forest Service and BLM relations with interest groups.

70. Norton Long, "Power and Administration," *Public Administration Review* vol. 9 (Autumn 1949) pp. 257–264; Herbert Simon, Donald Smithburg, and Victor Thompson, *Public Administration* (New York, Knopf, 1950) chap. 18 and 19; Phillip Selznick, *TVA and the Grass Roots* (Berkeley, University of California Press, 1949).

71. McConnell, *Private Power and American Democracy* (New York, Knopf, 1966); Theodore Lowi, *The End of Liberalism* (New York, Norton, 1969).

72. See Woodrow Wilson, "The Study of Administration," *Political Science Quarterly* vol. 2 (June 1887) pp. 197–222.

73. I am indebted to Marion Clawson, of Resources for the Future, who was director of the BLM during the height of the struggles Foss described, for pointing out the contrast between the connotation of the word "capture" and the reality of the bureau's conflicts with stockmen.

74. McConnell, *Private Power and American Democracy,* especially pp. 200–211. McConnell has had a long-standing interest in both conservation and the progressive era; see, for example, McConnell, "The Conservation Movement—Past and Present."

75. Kaufman, *The Forest Ranger.* However, also see note 12, in chapter 11

in this volume, on the considerable intellectual irony in Kaufman's position in the capture-conformity debate.

76. Redford, *Democracy and the Administrative State* (New York, Oxford University Press, 1969). Redford, a past president of the American Political Science Association, refers to political relationships among a bureau's Washington office, its relevant congressional committees, and national interest groups as "subsystems" politics. On the subsystems concept, see also J. Leiper Freeman, *The Political Process* (New York, Random House, 1955).

II
THE NATIONAL CONTEXT
AGENCY HISTORIES AND ADMINISTRATIVE PROCESSES

2

The Forest Service

The history of public lands management can be divided into six overlapping phases: acquisition, 1781 to 1867; disposal, 1812 to 1934; reservation, 1891 to 1934; initial or custodial management, 1905 to 1950; intensive management, 1950 to the present; and extensive preservation, 1964 to the present.[1] The crucial shift in federal land policy occurred between 1891 and 1905, when the reservation and initial management phases began. The Forest Service, now the largest public lands agency in terms of budget and personnel, was established during this period and has been the leading agency in federal lands management ever since.

The Federal Lands

At one time or another, four-fifths of the land area of the United States has been in the public domain. Acquisition of legal title to the public domain began with the cession to the federal government by the original thirteen states (chiefly New York, Virginia, Georgia, North Carolina, South Carolina, Massachusetts, and Connecticut) of lands they claimed between the Appalachian Mountains and the Mississippi River (see table 2-1). Title to 42 percent of what is now the United States was purchased from European monarchies, with the largest acquisitions being the 1803

Table 2-1. Origins of the Public Domain

Date	Acquisition and source	Acres (millions)	Percentage of total U.S. area	Present states and parts of states
1781–1802	Cession by original thirteen states	236.8	10.2	Illinois, Indiana, Ohio, Michigan, Tennessee (Mississippi, Alabama, Minnesota)
1803	Louisiana Purchase (includes basin of the Red River of the North)—France	559.5	24.2	Louisiana, Arkansas, Missouri, Kansas, Nebraska, Iowa (Oklahoma, Colorado, Wyoming, Montana, North Dakota, South Dakota, Minnesota)
1819	Florida cession—Spain	46.1	2.0	Florida (Louisiana)
1846	Oregon Compromise—Great Britain	183.4	7.9	Oregon, Washington, Idaho (Montana, Wyoming)
1848	Mexican War cession—Mexico	338.7	14.6	California, Nevada, Utah (Arizona, New Mexico, Colorado, Wyoming)
1850	Purchase from Texas—Texas (Mexico)	78.9	3.4	(New Mexico, Colorado, Oklahoma, Kansas, Wyoming)
1853	Gadsden Purchase—Mexico	19.0	0.8	(Arizona, New Mexico)
1867	Alaska Purchase—Russia	375.3	16.2	Alaska
	Total	1,837.8[a]	79.4[a]	

Source: Bureau of Land Management, *Public Land Statistics* (Washington, D.C., GPO, 1979) pp. 4–5.
[a] Additions do not equal totals due to rounding off.

Louisiana Purchase from France and the 1867 Alaska Purchase from Russia. Another 8 percent was transferred to the United States by Great Britain in the 1846 border compromise between the United States and Canada. The remainder was acquired from Mexico. The largest portion of that, 14.6 percent, was captured by the United States in the war with Mexico and the title transferred in 1848 by the Treaty of Guadalupe Hidalgo; in 1850 small portions of New Mexico, Oklahoma, Colorado, and Wyoming were purchased from Texas, which had won its independence from Mexico in 1836, as a part of the deal admitting Texas into the Union; and the 1853 Gadsden Purchase was the final acquisition from Mexico. These transactions completed transfer of sovereignty and title according to European–American law. The actual transfer of the land from those who had lived on it to Anglos took place later and in other ways.[2] The largest areas of land that remain in the public domain were obtained in the Oregon Compromise, the Mexican cession, and the Alaska Purchase.

The federal government eventually disposed of 62 percent of the original 1.8 billion acres of public domain lands. The major methods employed by the federal government to transfer lands out of public ownership during the 1812–1934 disposal era were land sales and script locations; land grants to states, local government bodies, and railroads; and homesteading. (Federal disposal policies will be described in chapter 3 since they were administered by the General Land Office, a predecessor of the modern Bureau of Land Management.) Public domain land was disposed of to encourage the settlement of the West, so most of the land the federal government sold or gave away was the more valuable. Land adjacent to water or transportation routes and land that could be cultivated was the first to go, along with mineral-rich land. The land remaining in federal ownership was generally desert and high-country forested land.

Toward the end of the nineteenth century, the federal government began to withdraw portions of the remaining public domain, precluding their transfer into private ownership (except under the Mining Laws). The first such reservation was made in an 1872 act that established Yellowstone as the first national park. National parks have been established ever since to protect areas of special scenic, geologic, or historic significance. The second major withdrawal was made in an 1891 statute that established forest reserves. From 1905 to 1910, major additions to the forest reserves were made by President Theodore Roosevelt. Finally, in 1934, with the passage of the Taylor Grazing Act, most remaining public domain land

Table 2-2. Major Federal Public Land Management Agencies

Agency	Jurisdictions in 1977		Estimated jurisdictions after implementation of Alaska Lands Act of 1980	
	Acres (millions)	Percentage of public lands	Acres (millions)	Percentage of public lands
Bureau of Land Management	450.2	61.0	254.9	40.1
Forest Service	187.5	25.4	189.0	29.7
Fish and Wildlife Service	31.1	4.2	82.9	13.0
National Park Service	26.3	3.6	68.5	10.8
Departments of the Army (except Corps of Engineers), Navy, and Air Force	22.8	3.1	22.1	3.5
Corps of Engineers (civil works)	8.0	1.1	8.2	1.3
Water and Power Resources Service (formerly Bureau of Reclamation)	6.7	0.9	6.6	1.0
Department of Energy (Energy Research and Development Administration in 1977)	2.1	0.3	1.6	0.2
Seven other bureaus managing more than 20,000 acres of public domain land	1.4	0.2	1.4	0.2
Remaining agencies, departments, and bureaus (thirty-nine in 1977; twenty-nine in 1980)	1.3	0.2	1.2	0.2
Totals	737.4	100.0%	636.4	100.0%

Sources: The 1977 jurisdictions are based on the data in Bureau of Land Management, *Public Land Statistics—1977* (Washington, D.C., GPO, 1979) pp. 14–30, as modified by a 1980 correction of an inflated listing of Bureau of Indian Affairs acreage in Alaska. Jurisdictions after implementation of the Alaska Lands Act are estimated by the author based on the agencies' pre-1980 acreages [in Bureau of Land Management, *Public Land Statistics—1979* (Washington, D.C., GPO, 1981) pp. 14–31] and estimates by the Department of the Interior (Denver Service Center, Office of the Secretary, and BLM Alaska Lands Office) of the acreage affected by the Alaska National Interest Lands Conservation Act. The BLM's acreage includes an estimated 79.9 million Alaskan acres remaining after native claims, statehood, and national interest land transfers; this estimate is subject to a potentially significant margin (ca. ± 2–3 million acres) of uncertainty and error. Implementation of the Alaska Lands transfers will require several years.

was closed to entry by land-seekers. (The final and official closing of the public domain occurred in 1976 with the passage of the Federal Land Policy and Management Act.) Most of the 737 million acres remaining in public ownership are located in the twelve states (excluding Hawaii) west of the 100th meridian, a line extending north from the Texas and Oklahoma panhandles through Kansas, Nebraska, and the Dakotas. The average percentage of federal land ownership in these twelve states was 52.2 percent in 1977 (ranging from Washington's 29 percent to Nevada's 88 percent and Alaska's 91 percent, whereas the average in the thirty-seven states to the east, including those bisected by the 100th meridian, was only 4 percent (from New Hampshire's 12 percent to Connecticut's 0.2 percent).

More than four dozen different departments, agencies, or bureaus manage land owned by the federal government. However, only about seventeen are significant public land-managing agencies. The Bureau of Land Management, in the Department of the Interior, and the Forest Service, in the Department of Agriculture, are federal land managers with diverse goals, managing their portions of the public lands for many purposes under the principle of multiple use. The remainder of the agencies manage federal lands primarily for dominant uses: the Fish and Wildlife Service and the National Park Service for wildlife and wild area protection, the Bureau of Reclamation and the Corps of Engineers for multipurpose water impoundments, the defense agencies for military bases, the Energy Research and Development Administration (successor to the old Atomic Energy Commission) for research and testing, and so forth.

The Origins of the Forest Service

The origins of the U.S. Forest Service date back to 1873. In response to the rapacious exploitation of American forests, one result of which was the Pestigo, Wisconsin, fire of 1871, the American Association for the Advancement of Science, led by forester Franklin Hough, took two actions that eventually resulted in the institutionalization of forestry in the United States. First, the association petitioned Congress to pass legislation protecting and providing for proper management of the forests. Second, it organized the American Forestry Association (AFA), the first modern professional forestry organization. In 1876 Congress directed the Department of Agriculture to report on the nation's forests and on prospects for their management and protection. Hough was appointed to head the new forestry office in the department; he worked until 1883 to increase the government's role in forestry. In 1886 the forestry office was expanded to become the Division of Forestry; the division's new head was Bernard Fernow, trained in forestry in Germany, a former officer of the AFA, a silvicultural researcher, and the first dean of Cornell's College of Forestry. Fernow was the driving force behind an act in 1891 that gave the president the authority to establish forest reserves.[3] Between 1891 and 1898, Presidents Harrison and Cleveland set aside 33 million acres for such reserves. Just as Yellowstone had been the first national park in 1871, so the Yellowstone Timber Reserve (presently the Shoshone and Teton National Forests) was the first forest reserve. In 1898 Gifford Pinchot, the leader of the progressive conservation movement, was appointed chief of the Division of Forestry.[4] That same year Pinchot organized the Society of American Foresters (SAF), which became the dominant professional forestry association in the country. Pinchot's close friend President Theodore Roosevelt reserved an additional 132 million acres of forests from 1901 to 1908; added to Harrison's and Cleveland's 33 million acres, Roosevelt's reservations brought the forest reserves to 88 percent of their present size. (That 88 percent constitutes almost all of the major western Forest Service acreage.)

In its early days, the Division of Forestry did not manage the forest reserves. When the first forest reserves were established in 1891—and even after passage of the 1897 Organic Act, which detailed the purposes of the reserves[5]—responsibility for the reserves, as for other public domain lands, rested with the General Land Office (GLO) in the Department of the Interior. The GLO was regarded as rife with scandal and the dupe of western exploitative interests. However, it had a long traditional mission, firmly rooted in statutory law and legislative intent, of disposing of public lands, a mission quite different from that expressed in the Forest Reserve Act of 1891 and the Organic Act of 1897, not to mention the conservation philosophy of Pinchot and Roosevelt. In 1905 Roosevelt, at Pinchot's behest, recommended that management of the forest reserves be transferred from Interior to Agriculture's Division of Forestry. Roosevelt's recommendation led to the passage of the Transfer Act of 1905, and the Division of Forestry became the Forest Service by act of the secretary of agriculture.[6] The forest reserves became national forests under the Act of March 4, 1907.[7]

Pinchot's tenure as chief of the Forest Service ended in 1910, soon after Roosevelt left office. Pinchot became embroiled in a dispute with then

Secretary of the Interior Richard Ballinger. He criticized Ballinger's letting of exploitative coal leases in Alaska in a classic confrontation between development interests and progressive conservation. Pinchot's outspokenness, however, caused President Taft to remove him as chief, which led to a public furor and congressional investigation.[8]

Consolidation—1910–45

The defeat, its attendant publicity, and the loss of the charismatic Pinchot damaged the new Forest Service's prestige, but under new chief Henry Graves, a disciple of Pinchot's and former dean of Yale's Graduate Forestry School, the service retrenched. From 1910 through the tenure of William Greeley as chief (1920–28), the service focused on the relatively noncontroversial issue of fire prevention and control. Fire replaced exploitative and monopolistic interests as the service's chief opponent, and fire had little political support. The fire control program was pursued with zeal, even to the point of squelching research evidence developed by the service's own silvicultural researchers that its programmatic opposition to prescribed burning was in error.[9]

Forest Service policy was not entirely passive after Pinchot's departure from the agency. Since the service's mission was limited to management of the national forests, American forest policy was restricted to the federal government's land management role and made no provision for state or private forestry practices. The public land forests of the West, however, were not the only ones affected by land-management problems. Many forests in the East had been badly abused; moreover, it was widely believed that poor forestry practices adversely affected eastern watersheds, leading to flooding, siltation, and other ills.

The Weeks Act of 1911 addressed the limited nature of federal forestry policy by broadening the Forest Service's mission.[10] The states were authorized to establish programs in cooperation with the service to protect against fires (ostensibly fires that would affect the watersheds of navigable rivers). The Weeks Act also authorized the service to expand the national forest system by acquiring private forestlands, also for the ostensible purpose of protecting watersheds. The Clark–McNary Act of 1924 extended the Weeks Act, allowing the service to purchase lands valuable for timber production in their own right.[11] Under the authority of the Weeks and Clark–McNary acts, the service acquired most of the remainder of its land, adding some 20 million acres to the lands previously reserved from the original public domain. (The last of the service's acquisitions, Plains states' "dustbowl" prairie lands, which have been called national grasslands since 1960, were acquired under the Bankhead–Jones Act of 1937 and later transferred to the service.[12]) The land acquired under the Weeks Act was in deteriorated condition because of overcutting, farming, or fires, and much of it had fallen into tax delinquency. Almost all of the Weeks Act acquisitions were in the eastern states, allowing the service to manage a truly national system. The expansion of the national forest system into the East gave the service at least one designated unit in all but nine states (see figure 2-1). Among other advantages (for example, ecosystem diversity), having a unit in forty-one of the fifty states can be politically very advantageous for an agency.

During the 1920s and 1930s, the service was embroiled in an attempt to obtain authority not only to manage the national forest system, but to regulate forestry practices on private lands as well. This effort, led by Gifford Pinchot (by the 1930s the governor of Pennsylvania) on the outside and by Bob Marshall inside the agency, would have meant a return to the very aggressive progressive conservation role of the Forest Service. In 1920 Pinchot was defeated in an attempt to obtain support for regulation of private timberlands from the SAF, by now the preeminent professional forestry association. Pinchot's resolution was strongly opposed by then Chief Greeley.[13] The Clark–McNary Act of 1924, building on the cooperative fire control features of the Weeks Act, authorized the Forest Service to assist both state and private forest owners with reforestation and other improved forestry practices.[14] The forest regulation issue continued to simmer after passage of the Clark–McNary Act, however. In 1933, with the full support of Forest Service leadership, another serious atttempt was made to give the service regulatory authority over private forestlands, but the proposals failed in Congress. The idea gradually faded into the background with the expansion of the Forest Service's role in New Deal social welfare programs. The Civilian Conservation Corps (CCC), one of the most important New Deal employment programs, was administered in large part by the Forest Service. The CCC put more than 2 million people to work during the Great Depression planting trees (more than half the trees ever planted in the nation were planted by the CCC) and building roads and trails, livestock management developments, campgrounds, and other recreation developments.[15] With the increased wood production responsibilities generated by World War II and the general wartime hiatus in new federal programs, the timber regulation issue faded further.

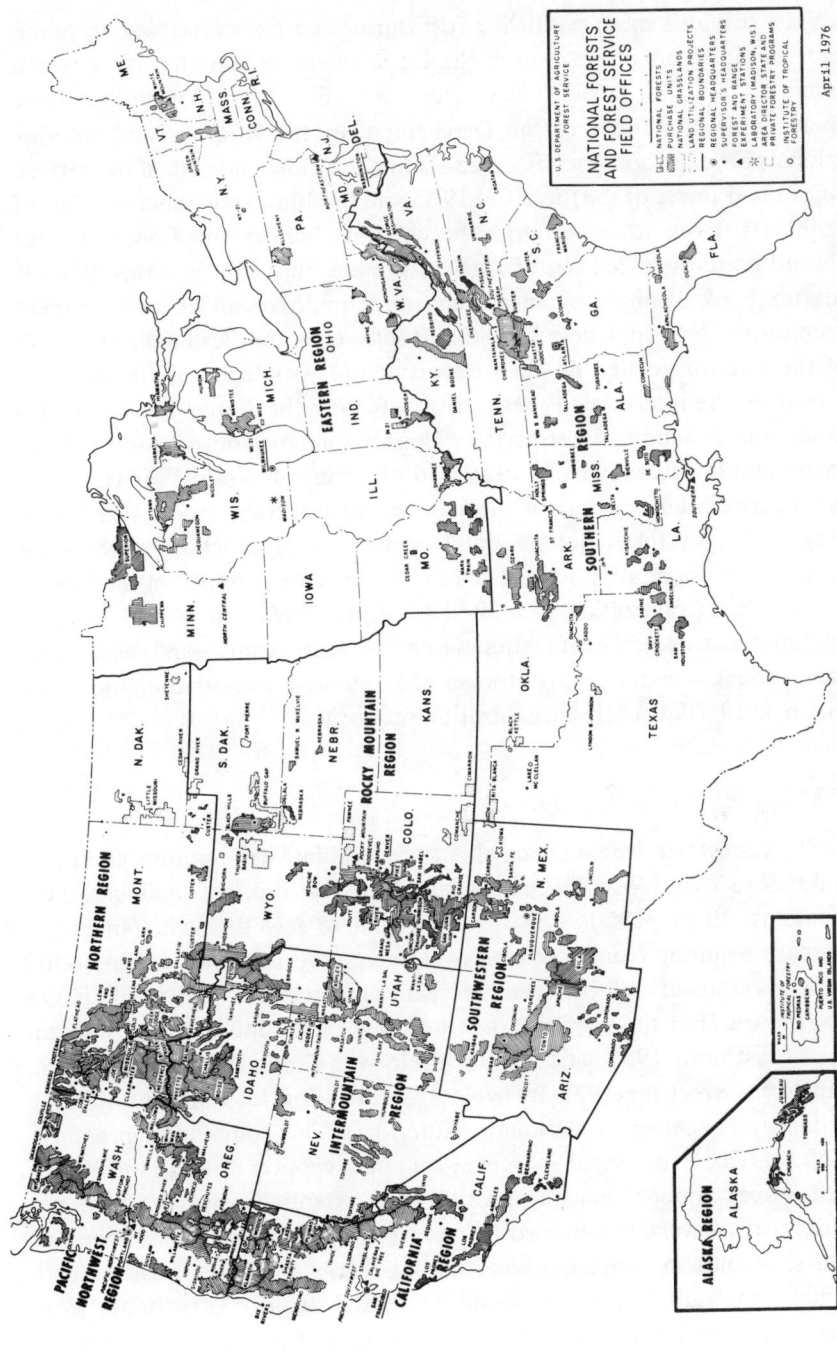

Figure 2-1. The National Forest System. [*Source:* U.S. Department of Agriculture, *Field Offices of the Forest Service* (Washington, D.C., 1976).]

The service's main political effort during the New Deal was to maintain its independent position in the Department of Agriculture, where it operated relatively freely. The service's activities and responsibilities were more similar to those of the Department of the Interior, and Interior officials have harbored a grievance against the independence of the service since the transfer of the forests in 1905 and the Ballinger–Pinchot affair of 1909–10. Even today, Interior bureaucrats believe the Forest Service should be reorganized out of Agriculture and into Interior; this belief is the textbook example of an agency norm imposed on new department secretaries. Harold Ickes, Franklin Roosevelt's and Truman's secretary of the interior needed no such departmental socialization: he was possessed by the interrelated ideas of transferring the Forest Service to Interior and renaming Interior the "Department of Conservation." Ickes carried on his crusade from 1935 until the start of World War II, at one point threatening to resign if the service was not transferred. The Forest Service fought Ickes quietly but forcefully, and Pinchot fought even harder, and not at all quietly. The issue was finally dropped in the face of congressional opposition generated by Pinchot and the Forest Service, though the same reorganization issue surfaced again—and was again beaten back—in the 1950 Hoover Commission Report and the 1971 Nixon and 1979 Carter reorganization proposals.[16]

Mounting Pressure—1945–69

The Forest Service had been able to consolidate its programs and position before World War II, but the end of the war brought significant new problems. In the 1950s, the service began to feel the twin pincers of pressure resulting from postwar economic growth, increased commodity demands coupled with increased recreational demand.[17] (Some old issues dragged on after the war: the private forest regulation question was not put to rest until 1952, and the 1950 Hoover Commission attempted in vain to resurrect the 1936 Brownlow Commission idea of consolidating all land-management functions in Interior.) The commodity pressures on the service had several sources. From its inception through the 1940s, the service's timber management had been essentially custodial; the national forests were maintained in reserve, and little of their timber was sold so as not to depress private timber prices. With the postwar economic expansion, timber demand increased rapidly; sawtimber consumption rose by 49 percent, for example, and pulp and plywood by 235 percent and 475 percent, respectively, from 1940 to 1970.[18] At the same time, private timber inventory was decreasing because the forest industry had generally been harvesting its lands at rates exceeding annual tree growth. The service stood ready, as it had consistently promised, to increase national forest harvests to take up the slack.

During the Eisenhower administration, the whole premise of federal natural resources management, which reflected the progressive conservationism of the New Deal, was called into question. On balance, the Eisenhower administration's position seemed to favor the industry positions on natural resources issues, ranging from opposition to the Tennessee Valley Authority's public power role in the East to support for irrigation projects that benefited private interests, such as Echo Park Dam, in the West.[19] For the Forest Service, Eisenhower free-market Republicanism was reflected in direct threats to the service's management of the national forests themselves: stockmen announced their goal of transferring public rangelands to private ownership, while the forest industry strongly advocated a prohibition against additions to the national forests and even a few schemes to transfer some federal timberlands into private ownership. When these public–private transfer proposals failed, stockmen pushed for vested grazing rights on service (and BLM) rangeland, and the forest products industry mounted a more subtle effort to increase access to and timber harvests on national forests.[20]

Rising recreational use was the second, and countervailing, pressure affecting the service in the 1950s. Many of the people who first made acquaintance with the public lands while working for the CCC during the Great Depression returned after the war to camp in the national forests. Recreation visits to the public lands more than tripled from the 1950s through the 1960s. During the 1950s, conservation groups, with essentially romantic preservationist philosophies and recreationist memberships, also became increasingly active and politically effective. The resurrection of the old-line conservation groups from the inactivity of the 1910–50 period was heralded by the election of the militant David Brower (the founder and current leader of Friends of the Earth, perhaps the most militant contemporary environmental group) as executive director of the Sierra Club and the victory of conservationists, led by the pen of *Harper's* Bernard DeVoto, in the Echo Park *cause célèbre*.[21] The Forest Service had been one of the darlings of the preservation-oriented conservationists because of its criticisms of private timber companies during the decades of private timber regulation conflicts. When the service indicated its plans to open the national forests to increased logging by those same companies, conservationists turned on the agency, opposing its timber policies and advocating increased recreational programs and preservation of wild and primitive areas.

Conservationist and recreationist pressures on the Forest Service were exacerbated by in-fighting with the National Park Service. The Park Service's "Mission '66" proposal, released in 1956, envisioned a significant expansion of park programs. Since the turn of the century, the two services had battled about jurisdiction over especially scenic areas of public lands. The Forest Service generally came out on the short end of these contests, losing a net 4.5 million acres to the Park Service through 1960. Thus, from the Forest Service's point of view, Mission '66 signaled a reintensification of this long-standing jurisdictional duel, and in this duel conservationists would serve as the Park Service's, not the Forest Service's, seconds.[22]

The policy concept that the service used to resist these twin pincers was first manifested in a peripheral issue. The Mining Laws of 1872 granted miners fairly unrestricted rights to claim public lands without demonstrating that significant mineral deposits had been located. The looseness of the mining laws led to a situation in which less than 3 percent of existing claims in the national forests in 1950 were in commercial operation. However, a significant number of "miners" were logging the commercial timber on their mining claims, without, of course, permission from or payments to the Forest Service. The service obtained a broad consensus supporting the reform of these abuses, with support ranging from the timber and organized mining industries, through the AFA, to conservation groups like the Izaak Walton League. The resulting Multiple Use Mining Act of 1955 allowed the service to manage the surface resources on national forest mining claims and eliminate uses (including timber cutting) unrelated to mining.[23] The act was a major breakthrough in the development of the concept of multiple use, which had been debated within the forestry profession since the late 1940s.

The service attempted to use the multiple-use concept to balance the competing pressures on the national forests. In April 1956, Sen. Hubert Humphrey (D., Minn.) introduced a multiple-use bill listing timber, watershed, range, wildlife, recreation, and mining uses as management goals for the service. The bill was strongly supported by the service, especially by Chief Richard McArdle, because the forests' only statutorily authorized uses, under the 1897 Organic Act, were timber and watershed. Thus, the bill would ratify the service's administrative programs of range, wildlife, and recreation use. (Mining was authorized—

or, more properly, given free rein—under the 1872 Mining Laws and subsequent statutes, and was primarily administered by the BLM.) The bill would thus give the service a balanced statutory mission, protecting it from extremist pressures from either consumptive users or preservationists.

The Multiple Use–Sustained Yield Act was passed in 1960.[24] Since the act has become the cornerstone of Forest Service (and later BLM) management, its key sections are worth noting in detail:

> It is the policy of the Congress that the national forests are established and shall be administered for outdoor recreation, range, timber, watershed, and wildlife and fish purposes (§ 528).
>
> The Secretary of Agriculture is authorized and directed to develop and administer the renewable surface resources of the national forests for multiple use and sustained yield of the several products and services obtained therefrom. In the administration of the national forests due consideration shall be given to the relative values of the various resources in particular areas... (§ 529).
>
> "Multiple use" means: the management of all the various renewable surface resources of the national forests so that they are utilized in the combination that will best meet the needs of the American people; making the most judicious use of the land for some or all of these resources or related services over areas large enough to provide sufficient latitude for periodic adjustments in use to conform to changing needs and conditions; that some land will be used for less than all of the resources; and harmonious and coordinated management of the various resources, each with the other, without impairment of the productivity of the land, with consideration being given to the relative values of the various resources, and not necessarily the combination of uses that will give the greatest dollar return or the greatest unit output (§531(a)).
>
> Sustained yield . . . means the achievement and maintenance in perpetuity of a high-level annual or regular periodic output of the various renewable resources of the national forests without impairment of the productivity of the land (§531(b)).

The act has frequently been criticized as an abdication of congressional responsibility over the national forests because it is fairly vague and allows the service to make discretionary judgments among competing uses (for example, ". . . with consideration being given to the relative values of the various resources. . .").[25] It should really be viewed in the context of the 1950s—as a defense against extreme commodity user demands and as a codification of the service's historic conservation mission to promote, as Pinchot put it, "the greatest good of the greatest number over the long run." If the act is also generally regarded as a broad grant of discretionary authority to the Forest Service, so much—from the service's point of view—the better.

At the same time the Multiple Use Act was being passed, the preservationists were mounting a major attack on another front. Since 1919, Forest Service personnel had been leaders in the development of the administrative concept of wilderness. Arthur Carhart, Bob Marshall, and Aldo Leopold were instrumental in setting aside national forest lands from development, first as "primitive" areas, then in 1939 as "wilderness" areas.[26] Since the national park system was established for both preservation and recreation, developments were still permitted within the parks. The Forest Service wilderness system, however, was the first management system upholding pure preservation (with the consistent exception of mining entries).

In the 1950s preservationist groups became increasingly uneasy about the service's administrative, nonstatutory wilderness system. Members of the Wilderness Society (which had been organized by Carhart, Marshall, and Leopold, among others) and the Sierra Club feared administrative protection might be withdrawn, especially given the service's commitment to increasing national forest timber harvests. They also believed the service was increasingly composed of new foresters who were trained in forestry schools in which maximizing wood products output was emphasized, and who were thus unsympathetic to the notion of wilderness.[27] Thus, Senator Humphrey was persuaded to introduce a preservationist-backed wilderness bill in 1956 (the same year he, in a remarkable display of legislative catholicity, introduced the multiple-use bill).

Despite its early leadership in wilderness preservation, the Forest Service was opposed to the Humphrey wilderness bill. Congressional designation of Wilderness areas would decrease the discretion and flexibility of the service's administrative classification system. In addition, the bill threatened the balance the service was seeking to construct through the Multiple Use Act. Foresters in both the service and industry tended to view wilderness as a dominant use (or nonuse), and thus logically inconsistent with multiple use—notwithstanding the observation in the Multiple Use Act, inserted to overcome Sierra Club opposition, that "the establishment and maintenance of areas of wilderness are consistent with ... this Act."[28]

After eight years of Forest Service and industry opposition, Howard Zahniser's Wilderness Society coalition prevailed. The Wilderness Act of 1964 provided for official designation of an area of "primeval character and influence, without permanent improvements or human habitation . . . which (1) generally appears to have been affected primarily by forces of nature, with the imprint of man's work substantially unnoticeable; (2) has outstanding opportunities for solitude or a primitive and unconfined type of recreation; (3) has at least five thousand acres of land or is of sufficient size to make practicable its preservation."[29]

The act designated all areas that had been classified "wilderness" or "wild" areas under the Forest Service's 1939 "U regulations" as statutory "Wilderness."[30] Fifty-four areas, comprising 9.1 million acres, were given Wilderness status immediately under the act. The act also directed the service to review its thirty-four "primitive areas" (5.5 million acres) for possible Wilderness designation, and instructed the Park Service and Fish and Wildlife Service to make similar reviews of their roadless areas.

The "Environmental Decade"—1970–79

The 1970s brought the pressures that began simmering in the 1950s to a boil. The critical factor in natural resources management in the 1970s has been *environmentalism*. As a philosophy, environmentalism is a complex blend of progressive conservationism and romantic preservationism (as noted in chapter 1). As a political force, environmentalism really began with the reawakening of the old-line conservation groups (such as the Sierra Club, Izaak Walton League, National Wildlife Federation, and National Parks and Conservation Association) in the 1950s, particularly by the Echo Park affair. Most observers believe environmentalism captured the interest of the general public through the publication of Rachel Carson's *Silent Spring,* an electrifying indictment of the effects of pesticides and herbicides on humans and their environment.[31] Historian Harold Steen aptly compares Carson's importance to environmentalism with George Perkins Marsh's contribution to the early conservation movement.[32]

Increasing public awareness of environmentalism was, however, best demonstrated by Earth Day I, April 22, 1970, during which a carefully planned nationwide series of media events was held, featuring speeches, environmental workshops, and sideshows such as the sledgehammering of old automobiles. Of more lasting importance than the accompanying frivolity and hoopla, Earth Day marked the beginning of a period during which the number of environmental groups doubled, as did the memberships of many of the old-line conservation-preservation groups such as the Sierra Club, and increased attention was paid to environmental issues by a variety of nonenvironmental groups. Environmentalists of the 1970s have been quite militant, as indicated by their willingness to go to court over a wide variety of issues.

The second major change in natural resources politics (coincident with the growth of environmentalism) was NEPA, the National Environmental Policy Act,[33] signed by President Nixon on January 1, 1970, as the first act in what he called the "Environmental Decade" of the 1970s. On the surface, NEPA was only a vague, hortatory statement of environmental consciousness, rather than a directive that agencies change particular policies in specific ways. The most important section of NEPA was section 102(2)(c), which required agencies to prepare detailed environmental impact statements on "major federal actions significantly affecting the quality of the human environment."

This requirement was a response to several criticisms of the natural resources agencies.[34] First, it formalized agency decisions, requiring a written rationale for agency actions. Second, and more important, the environmental statements were to be public, and subsequent guidelines of the Council on Environmental Quality led to their becoming a major entree for public participation in agency decision making.[35] Some federal agencies, particularly the Forest Service, established public participation programs that went beyond the environmental statement process, including increased numbers of public meetings and informal contacts with previously excluded groups. Uniformly, the agencies claimed these programs were a response to NEPA.[36] In addition, NEPA required agencies to increase their consultations with other agencies, often those that had traditionally opposed their programs, and to diversify their staffs, counteracting some of the problems caused by the domination of some agencies by a single profession, such as foresters in the service. Most important, the large volume of litigation initiated under NEPA forced federal agencies to abide by the act's procedural reforms.

The changes mandated by NEPA have not been implemented in the same way by all federal agencies. However, the Council on Environmental Quality has praised the Forest Service for conscientious implementation of NEPA, implying that the service's performance was the best of all the federal agencies.[37]

The Forest Service's excellent implementation of NEPA did not free it from its long-standing problems. Contemporaneously with the rise of environmentalism, the forest products industry increased its efforts to obtain higher timber harvests from the national forests. In the late 1960s, the industry attempted to obtain congressional authorization for increased logging, under the guise of stimulating low- and moderate-income housing, through a national timber supply act. When the proposed act was soundly beaten in the House, the forest products industry turned to the Nixon administration. Critics of the level of Forest Service logging, such as Daniel Barney and Jack Shepherd,[38] have argued that presidential assistant Charles Colson transformed a task force report, the Forest and Related Resources (FARR) plan, into administration policy with Forest Service concurrence. The FARR plan called for logging an additional 7 billion board-feet of national forest sawtimber, a 50 percent increase over the then-current allowable cut that was identical to the goals of the defeated timber supply act. President Nixon directed the Forest Service to implement the FARR plan in June 1970. In 1973 the service was again instructed, by Secretary of Agriculture Earl Butz, to increase emphasis on logging and sales activities in work planning and budgeting.[39]

Industry efforts to increase national forest timber harvests, however, were overshadowed by the clear-cutting controversy. The issue first became nationally prominent because of criticism of the clear-cutting program on the Bitterroot National Forest in Montana, including the Bolle Report by the University of Montana School of Forestry.[40] Continuing conservationist opposition to clear-cutting led to the Monongahela decision. The Izaak Walton League sued the Forest Service, alleging that clear-cutting on the Monongahela National Forest in West Virginia was illegal because the 1897 Organic Act authorized the sale of only "dead, matured or large growth" trees. When the Izaak Walton League prevailed at both the district and appellate court levels, the entire Forest Service sales program in the Fourth Circuit (West Virginia, Virginia, North Carolina, and South Carolina) and later Alaska was thrown into turmoil.[41] As the court suggested in the Monongahela decision, the Forest Service asked Congress to extricate it from its dilemma. The congressional deliberations became a confrontation between environmentalist critics of clear-cutting and the service, assisted by the forest products industry, which defended the right of foresters to make silvicultural policy.

The bill that eventually passed was a compromise version of a pro-Forest Service bill introduced by Senator Humphrey. The resulting National Forest Management Act of 1976 essentially followed the 1972 clear-cutting guidelines suggested by Sen. Frank Church's Senate oversight subcommittee.[42] The Organic Act was amended, removing the language the Monongahela decision was based on, but the Congress issued a strong mandate for multiple-use timber management, watershed protection, reforestation, and more aesthetic timber sale designs, and prohibited strictly commercial silvicultural methods. All these goals were to be facilitated by tying timber-management planning into a comprehensive multiple-use planning system that provided for public participation.

At the same time the service was working its way through the clearcutting controversy and related timber-management issues, the pace of the wilderness issue picked up appreciably. Since 1964, the major wilderness fights have been over additions to the Wilderness Preservation System, primarily from within the national forests. In the 1970s the wilderness issue began to have precisely the effect the service and user industries had feared in the 1950s—wilderness demands began to complicate Forest Service discretion and affect other multiple uses. Two important court decisions illustrate this.

The Mineral King case has been a *cause célèbre* of the Sierra Club. One of the largest and best known ski area development plans in the past decade was Disney Industries' proposal to build a major alpine ski area in the Mineral King Valley on the Sequoia National Forest in California.[43] Alpine skiing is the major commercial recreational use of national forest lands, and ski areas are thus subject to classic developer-environmentalist confrontations. Preliminary speculation about a Mineral King ski area began as long ago as 1945, but the modern conflict began in 1969, when the Sierra Club filed a suit to block the proposed development. The club alleged the ski area would conflict with the congressionally designated Sequoia Game Range in the valley, and would illegally cross the park for nonpark purposes. In an amended complaint after NEPA was passed, the club also pointed out that no environmental statement had been prepared on the proposal. The Sierra Club suit led to a landmark Supreme Court decision on the legal issue of "standing to sue."[44] Though the decision significantly liberalized the definition of standing to sue, the club technically lost the case. However, it amended its complaint in line with the Court's opinion and refiled in district court, forcing the Forest Service into a lengthy environmental impact statement process that was not completed until 1976, by which time Disney Industries had given up on the development. In 1978 the Carter administration recommended transfer of the Mineral King Valley to the Park Service for inclusion in Sequoia National Park.

2: THE FOREST SERVICE

The second case shows the potential threat that wilderness litigation posed to the Forest Service's timber sales program. In the *Parker* case, a U.S. Court of Appeals enjoined the service from completing the East Meadow timber sale on the White River National Forest, Colorado, in 1971.[45] The East Meadow site was a roadless area adjacent to a designated primitive area regarded as a likely candidate for Wilderness designation. (It subsequently became the Eagles Nest Wilderness. Interestingly, Bob Parker, the pro-wilderness plaintiff, is an officer of Vail Associates, the managers of the Vail Ski area.) The court held that the service's timber management discretion was circumscribed by the Wilderness Act; the service could not take an action that would prohibit Congress from designating qualifying areas as Wilderness. To indicate the magnitude of the problem, the Forest Service's own 1978 wilderness review list (see below) identified some 62 million acres of roadless areas—that is, potentially qualifying areas—which is 36 percent of the Forest Service acreage not already designated as Wilderness.

Controversies such as the *Parker* case gave added impetus to the wilderness reviews mandated by the 1964 Wilderness Act. From 1964 to 1970, only five areas were added to the service's Wilderness system. Since 1970, Wilderness designations have been a constant agenda item. In 1972–73, the Forest Service conducted a massive (and controversial) Roadless Area Review and Evaluation (RARE I), holding hearings on almost all forests in preparation for a major national environmental statement. The hearings and environmental statement received over 54,000 comments. RARE I identified 1,448 roadless areas—*de facto* wilderness to the preservationists—totaling 55.9 million acres. However, the RARE I results did not satisfy environmentalists. The service proposed to recommend 274 new Wilderness study areas (encompassing 12.3 million acres).[46] Nevertheless, environmentalists believed that many important qualifying areas had been left off the new study areas list, and that the service's criteria systematically discriminated against wilderness areas in the East.

Since 1974, environmentalists have been quite successful in obtaining congressional passage of Wilderness designations. Two sets of designations, those dealing with eastern and "endangered" (that is, not on the service's new study areas list) Wildernesses, can be interpreted as rejections of the service's RARE I criteria.[47] By 1978, these and other congressional additions had increased the Forest Service Wilderness system to 106 areas (14.7 million acres). General environmentalist dissatisfaction with RARE I, as well as industry complaints about the uncertainty caused by the piecemeal congressional designation process, led the Carter administration's new assistant secretary of agriculture, M. Rupert Cutler (a former Wilderness Society staffer), to initiate a second roadless area review, RARE II. The 1978–79 RARE II process reviewed 2,919 areas, totaling 62 million acres.[48] Environmentalist dissatisfaction with the service's restrictive alternatives led to compaints of bias when the service recommended "only" 624 areas, totaling 15.1 million acres, for Wilderness designation. The 1979 RARE II recommendations are not likely to be the end of the Forest Service Wilderness issue.

Forest Service Organization and Management

While the Forest Service has frequently been at the center of political maelstroms, it has also been regarded as one of the most professional, best managed agencies in the federal government. (In fact, the management, rather than the politics, of the service has been the focus of most scholarly studies of the agency.[49])

The formal organization of the Forest Service is based on many of the hierarchical and division-of-labor principles of most large, bureaucratized organizations.[50] The largest of the bureaus in the Department of Agriculture, the agency is headed by the chief of the Forest Service, who reports (along with six other bureau chiefs) to the assistant secretary of agriculture for conservation, research, and education. The assistant secretary is, of course, responsible to the secretary of agriculture.

Three basic types of activities form the first level of division of labor in the Forest Service: administration of the national forest system, state and private forestry, and research.

The service's research activities are carried out in eight forest and range experiment stations (with sixty-six subsidiary research locations supervised by the main experiment stations), the Forest Products Laboratory in Madison, Wisconsin, and the Institute of Tropical Forestry in Rio Piedras, Puerto Rico. Research scientists employed by the service are leaders in the field of scientific forestry, including silvicultural, fire control, insect and disease control, forest economics and marketing, watershed, range and wildlife, and recreation research. For example, a recent sample of the *Journal of Forestry,* the profession's leading research journal, contained 153 articles. Forest Service personnel accounted for

35 percent of the authors. All academics, by comparison, accounted for only 43 percent of the authors.[51]

The state and private forestry program—sometimes called cooperative forestry—assists state government forestry bureaus, the forest products industry, and some smaller private forest landowners, primarily in fire and disease control and better conservation, restocking, and management of state and private lands. East of the 100th meridian, state and private forestry activities are administered out of two area offices, one in Upper Darby, Pennsylvania, for the Eastern Region, and the other in Atlanta for the Southern Region (see figure 2-1). In the seventeen western states, where most of the service's field offices are located, state and private forestry is managed through the seven regional foresters' offices in the national forest system.

The heart of the Forest Service is the national forest system administrative structure (see figure 2-2). The basic line administrative unit is the ranger. district. The district ranger, a GS-11 or GS-12 professional forester, has the primary management responsibility for a specific geographic area within a national forest or national grassland. (Some national forests in the East and most national grasslands are quite small. Even though designated as a separate national forest or grassland, each such unit is typically managed as one or two ranger districts.) Rangers, assisted by a few professional staff members and other technical or nonprofessional employees, carry out the primary, on the ground administration of the national forest system. They execute land use and timber plans, develop planning and program recommendations for their districts, supervise resource development and protection activities, manage their own office, and serve as the primary contacts for a wide variety of users of the national forests. The exact distribution of district staff depends on the relative mix of uses on the district. A national grassland district will not have a timber staffer; a district with a major ski area will have a recreation staffer or a snow ranger, or both; some districts, especially in the East, will not have a range staff person. Most commentators, as well as the hortatory official statements of the Forest Service itself, argue that the district ranger is the most important administrative level of the Forest Service.[52]

The four to eight ranger districts on each designated national forest (or the several ranger district-sized national forests or grasslands in the same general area) are supervised by a forest supervisor.[53] The forest supervisor, a GS-13 or GS-14 forester, is responsible for forestwide plan-

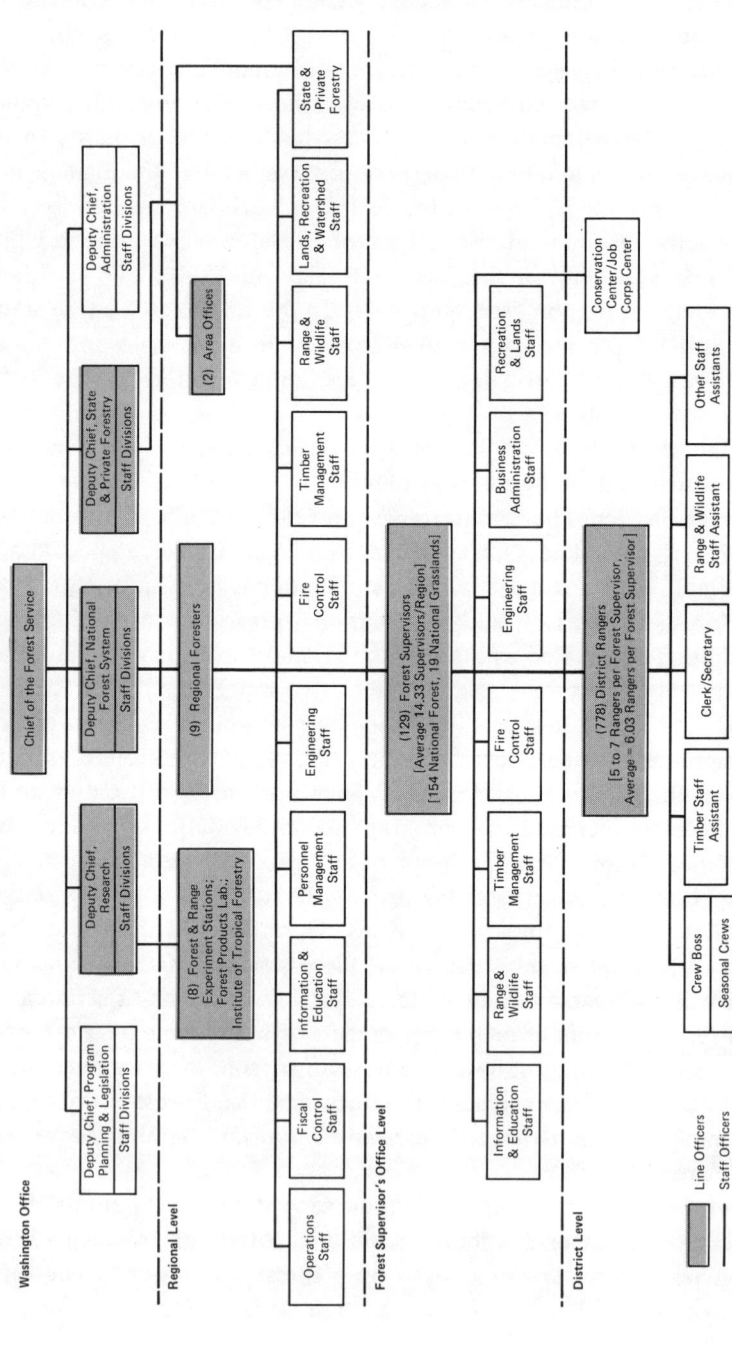

Figure 2-2. Line and staff organization of the Forest Service. Note that there is some variation in staff positions at the ranger district, supervisor's office, and regional office levels. Bold lines indicate line officers and light lines, staff officers.

ning, coordination and control of the ranger districts, and management of the forest office. The supervisor's position is recognized as a policy role, and the supervisor is often a primary contact for interest groups in politically charged local policy matters.[54] Each supervisor's office includes functional staff assistants in resource management (timber, range, and so forth), engineering (for example, road construction), and administration. As with the ranger district, the distribution of staff positions depends on the relative workload of the forest.

Each forest supervisor is, in turn, supervised by one of the nine regional foresters. The regions are labeled by geographic areas, but are also commonly referred to by number, 1 to 10, except 7 (see figure 2-1). The regions vary in size from one state (Region 5, California, and Region 10, Alaska) to twenty states (Region 9, Eastern Region). Each of the regional foresters, except in Alaska, supervises about sixteen forest supervisors; Alaska has three large national forests, but because of its climate it is organized differently from the other regions.

The Washington office of the Forest Service, headed by the chief, is responsible for overall Forest Service policy and supervises the regions, the two state and private forestry area offices, and the research units. Some major national programs, such as the Roadless Area Review discussed earlier in this chapter, are managed out of the Washington office. The service's relationship with the Congress on appropriations, legislation, and oversight, and with formal superiors in the Department of Agriculture and the Office of Management and Budget, is the critical responsibility of the chief and the Washington office.[55]

The set of congressional committees the Forest Service is responsible to is a bit more complicated than that of most federal bureaus. The service deals with two primary subject matter committees in each house of Congress, and several secondary committees. The Senate Energy and Natural Resources Committee (the successor to the old Senate Interior Committee) and the House Interior and Insular Affairs Committee generally have jurisdiction over legislation dealing with the national forests created from the public domain (that is, the western forests). The Senate Agriculture and Forestry Committee and the House Agriculture Committee have jurisdiction over acquired forest lands (mostly in the East) and over forestry generally. The role of the late Senator Humphrey, a member of the Senate Agriculture Committee and sponsor of many of the major pieces of Forest Service legislation discussed above, indicates the importance of the Agriculture Committees' role, even though the

Interior Committees would seem to have more jurisdiction. Most of the service's budget is controlled by the Interior Subcommittees of the House and Senate Appropriations Committees.[56]

As with most hierarchical organizations, responsibility for activities is divided among the various levels of the Forest Service. For example, timber sales decisions are approved by the different line levels on the basis of the size of the sale: rangers are allowed to offer sales, "on their own signature," up to $2,000 in value; sales from $2,000 up to 10 million board-feet require the approval of the forest supervisor;[57] from 10 million to 50 million board-feet, the sale requires approval of the regional forester; sales over 50 million board-feet require the approval of the chief. Planning and decision making for certain types of actions are also allocated among the four line levels. Using timber management as an example again, the ranger is responsible for administering timber sales, ensuring that the timber purchaser lives up to the provisions of the sale contract, such as those regulating treatment of slash (the branches removed from the trunk of a tree); the forest supervisor's timber staff determines the "working circles" for the forest, that is, the areas in which sequential timber sales are planned throughout the very long cutting cycle (for example, 120 years), based on the period of regeneration from seedling to mature tree; and the regional office is responsible for negotiation of the standard provisions of sales contracts between the Forest Service and the forest products industry.

However, almost all actions formally taken at a given level involve considerable influence by both higher and lower levels in the agency. Forest, regional, servicewide, and federal policies influence lower level policy, and lower level line and staff officers set agendas for, and influence the decisions of, their supervisors with reports, recommendations, and the like. For example, a timber sale contract within the range of 10 million to 50 million board-feet would be signed by the ranger, the forest supervisor, and, finally, by the regional forester. As a result, decision making is not a simple matter, but produces a united or merged group decision. The recent hearings on the Crested Butte–Callaway affair provide an excellent example of the indivisibility of Forest Service decision making. During the months preceding the 1976 presidential election, a Senate subcommittee investigated nationally publicized charges that Howard (Bo) Callaway, President Ford's campaign manager, had improperly influenced the service to permit expansion of his Crested Butte ski area in Colorado while he was secretary of the army. Some fifty pages of testimony attempted to determine who made the decision to permit the ski area's expansion. The transcript shows that it was absolutely unclear whether the ranger, the forest supervisor, the regional forester, or the Washington office was the decision maker. *All* had participated in the decision process, but none was singly responsible for the decision. Yet the decision was, the committee concluded, responsible and correct in light of applicable statutory and administrative rules and procedures. (However, it being an election year, the committee Democrats were able to find Secretary Callaway's actions wanting.[58])

The Forest Service's ability to effectively influence its officers' decision making was the subject of Herbert Kaufman's classic study of administrative behavior, *The Forest Ranger*.[59] Kaufman details a long list of "centrifugal" forces contributing to administrative fragmentation and disunity that affect the service more than most other federal bureaus. The large amount of land the service must manage under the multiple-use principle generates a high volume and variety of complex work. Land management involves fairly technical decision criteria on which there may be significant scientific disagreement.[60] Policy intentions are couched generally, but must be applied on the ground by the rangers in specific cases with a variety of special local conditions. Many of the general policy intentions that funnel down to the rangers are inconsistent or may seem so from their perspective. Direct supervisory control is relatively rare because line officers are geographically distant from their superiors; supervisors' offices are often located hundreds of miles, even several states, away from regional offices, and most rangers are 10 to 100 miles away from their forest supervisor's office. (The twenty-eight rangers interviewed in connection with this study were an average of 42 miles from the supervisor's office, from several in the same town to three rangers 99, 102, and 144 miles away, respectively.) Even when a ranger's office is in the same town as the supervisor's (or the supervisor's office in the same city as the regional office), they will be located across town from each other.

Well-known studies of organizational behavior, first and foremost the "Western Electric researches,"[61] have shown that social norms among coworkers can have strong effects in opposition to management policy. Such norms would be a special problem for the service if rangers' personal or professional values were in significant conflict with agency policy. Because rangers' decisions vitally affect important segments of local populations, and because there is a long history of controversial service policies, rangers are subject to possible capture by local interests as a result of sympathy with neighbors and fellow members of local civic groups or capitulation to strong pressures or persuasions. All these centrifugal pressures are magnified by the service's firm institutional belief in delegating responsibility to the rangers, the "backbone of the service."

Kaufman describes three types of managerial mechanisms the Forest Service uses to overcome centrifugal forces. The first includes a variety of procedures that "preform" decisions. These procedures determine in detail the course of action to be taken in a specific type of situation; decision making is thus reduced to a determination of the situation and an application of the predetermined course of action. The preformed decisions take three forms: *authorizations* permit a limited degree of discretion, guaranteeing no organization sanction for taking the action but implying that taking any other action places the ranger at risk; *directives* specify that, if a given situation arises, the specified action must be taken or penalties may be imposed; *prohibitions* prevent certain actions, backed by sanctions. All statutes, executive orders, department regulations, and court decisions are translated into preformed decision rules and incorporated in the Forest Service Manual. The manual is one of the more extensive government documents. Service officers like to measure it in "running feet"—the sum of the thicknesses of the manual binders—currently 25 feet or more, depending on the size of regional supplements. The manual is supplemented by technical handbooks, regional planning guides, and forest resource plans.

A second type of procedure is intended to detect and discourage deviations from the service's preformed decision routines. The service has extensive requirements for reporting what administrative actions have been taken. Ranger-initiated decisions must be cleared, or "signed-off on," by the forest supervisor, and sometimes at an even higher level. Forest supervisors also monitor rangers by arbitrating disputes between rangers and functional staff officers in their offices who make requests or suggestions the rangers do not follow. Although formal disapprovals and adjudications may be relatively rare, rangers can anticipate being overturned if they deviate from the manual's policy directives.

The service has developed an incredibly detailed fiscal and workload planning process as an aid to making budget estimates. Fiscal and workload plans allocate proportions of each employee's and each piece of equipment's time among dozens of specific activities (timber sale administration, range revegetation, soil surveys, forest fire suppression, and so forth). The resulting matrix of employee-equipment time broken down by activities thus contains hundreds of cells. Amounts budgeted to the ranger district for each activity must be accounted for in detail. Rangers, for example, must keep official diaries describing activities in detail, by function, down to the half hour. Such accounting helps ensure that ranger districts emphasize programs preferred by central agency budget policy.

The service regularly conducts six types of inspection that examine ranger, forest supervisor, or regional forester performance in varying degrees of detail. The *general integrating inspection* examines the whole range of land management tasks to determine whether officers are giving proper attention to various activities, the level of performance given available resources, and the degree of adherence to the service's preformed decision policies. A *general functional inspection* examines all aspects of a particular resource management function (for example, timber management or recreation), while a *limited functional inspection* examines a type of task within a function (for example, reforestation) or specific project or area (for example, an individual recreation area). *Fiscal-administrative inspections* examine accounting records, files, and office management, as opposed to field operation. These first four types of inspections are routine and focus on both positive accomplishments and failings. Service administrators maintain they are conducted more for training than for investigatory purposes. The fourth and fifth types of inspection focus on failures: *boards of review* examine major reverses (for example, a large fire), and *investigations* look into charges of professional malfeasance by Forest Service officers. Two final types of review, *appeal hearings* requested by agency clients and *congressional inquiries* for constituents, are similar to inspections but are precipitated by the public rather than by the service itself.

The service also had a policy, at the time of Kaufman's study, of frequent and unanticipatable transfers of officers to new assignments. Frequent transfers meant officers needed to keep their houses in order lest deviations be detected by their successors. Recent revisions in federal government personnel rules governing transfers have supposedly made transfers more costly to the government (for example, by requiring full coverage of moving and residence sales costs), but these changes have merely lengthened assignment periods and not eliminated transfers.

All these mechanisms for detecting deviations from the service's preformed decisions are backed by sanctions. Some sanctions are formal, such as reprimands (oral and informal, or written and placed in the officer's personnel file), suspensions, discharges, and plausibly even cases of criminal prosecution, but formal sanctions are quite rare. Performance ratings are routine and affect officers' opportunities for promotion and assignment to desirable posts. Perhaps most important, reports of significant deviation or failure cause personal embarrassment and guilt feelings. The service's procedures for preforming decisions and detecting and sanctioning deviations are not remarkable, but the detail, complexity, and rigorousness of the procedures are.

Kaufman argues that the third type of managerial control is the key to the conformity of Forest Service officers. The service is able to develop *voluntary* conformity in its officers—both the capacity (technical knowledge and practical skills) and the will (eagerness to carry out preformed decisions) to conform. Development of voluntary conformity begins before entry into the service. A large proportion of Forest Service officers chose the agency as a career at the end of high school. The service actively discourages recruits by describing career and work difficulties more graphically than the vague rewards of forestry, thus obtaining recruits who deeply value the agency's work. All service line officers—indeed, 90 percent of Forest Service professionals—are trained foresters. Forestry education not only gives service officers a common technical knowledge but a common professional value system and appreciation for the history and lore of the profession as well. Some of the recruits who do not fit into the service (15 percent at the time of Kaufman's study) are weeded out during the one-year probationary period; a few are let go but most resign.

After this self-selected body of recruits joins the agency, training and refresher courses inculcate service policy and procedure and socialize recruits to the agency's norms and values. On-the-job supervision by superiors and inspectors, while technically a review of work performed, is also explicitly viewed as training by the service, and it includes information about the agency's philosophy.

Finally, many factors cause the Forest Service officer to identify strongly with the agency. The policy of frequent transfers breaks officers' ties with locales and builds personal friendships with fellow officers. Service officers tend to socialize with each other; Kaufman noted that many rangers look forward to inspections because, in the evening after inspections, they socialize with the inspectors, who are the major carriers of gossip about agency policy, fellow officers, and so forth. There is no lateral entry into the service; all line officers work their way up from the bottom, giving them a common background and point of view. People in the communities in which officers are stationed refer to them not as "Mr. Smith," but as "the Forest Service." Forest Service officers have the same view; it is standard agency parlance to refer to people as "in-service" or "out-service." Forest Service symbols—such as the uniform greens, Smokey-the-Bear hat, badge, and massive wood signs at the entrance to Forest Service offices—further mark service officers as an ingroup.

Finally, officers are encouraged to participate in agency policymaking via polls of field officers, ranger comments to inspectors about policies, informal consultations and formal meetings on policy, and trial runs of new policies on sample ranger districts or national forests in which the local officers' evaluations are crucial. Moreover, local officers, especially rangers, firmly believe they are responsible for their own work and have a great deal of professional latitude in their positions, despite the intricate system of managerial control and directives.

According to Kaufman, self-selection, training, and socialization cause the Forest Service officer to be fiercely dedicated both to the service as an organization and to its mission. The author noted (as did Kaufman a dozen years earlier) the amazing consistency with which ranger interviewees mentioned "multiple use" and Pinchot's "the greatest good of the greatest number over the long run" as the guiding principles in their work. As Kaufman wrote, "They practically merge the individual's identity with the identity of the organization."[62] Thus, service officers voluntarily conform to the service's preformed decisions. In fact, they do not so much conform as they instinctively select the agency's prescribed course of action as the best, most proper decision.[63] This voluntary conformity also contributes to the service's image as a highly professional agency with great *esprit de corps,* and helps explain the Forest Service's tenacious commitment to the principles of progressive conservationism and multiple use.

NOTES

1. On the first five periods, see Marion Clawson and R. Burnell Held, *The Federal Lands* (Baltimore, Md., Johns Hopkins University Press for Resources for the Future, 1957) pp. 16–17; minor instances of acquisition, disposal, reservation, and custodial management continue to the present. For a fuller treatment of the acquisition, disposition, and reservation of the public domain, see Benjamin Hibbard, *A History of the Public Land Policies* (New York, Macmillan, 1924); Paul Gates, *History of Public Land Law Develop-*

ment (Washington, D.C., GPO, 1968); E. Louise Peffer, *The Closing of the Public Domain* (Stanford, Calif., Stanford University Press, 1951); and Samuel Dana and Sally Fairfax, *Forest and Range Policy* (2 ed., New York, McGraw-Hill, 1980).

2. On the acquisition of much of this land from native Americans, see Dee Brown, *Bury My Heart at Wounded Knee* (New York, Holt, Rinehart and Winston, 1971). On the acquisition of land in the Southwest from Spanish land grantees, see Clark Knowlton, "Culture Conflict and Natural Resources," in William Burch, Neil Cheek, Jr., and Lee Taylor, eds., *Social Behavior, Natural Resources and the Environment* (New York, Harper & Row, 1972) pp. 109–145.

3. 16 U.S.C. §§473–483, 551.

4. For more on this central figure in both the progressive conservation movement and the Forest Service, see Harold Pinkett, *Gifford Pinchot: Public and Private Forester* (Urbana, University of Illinois, 1970); Gifford Pinchot, *Breaking New Ground* (New York, Harcourt Brace, 1947); and Gifford Pinchot, *Fight for Conservation* (New York, Doubleday, Page, 1910).

5. 16 U.S.C. §473. The act's goal was "to improve or protect the forests ... or for the purpose of securing favorable conditions of water flow, and to furnish a continuous supply of timber for the use and necessities of the citizens of the United States."

6. Transfer Act of 1905, 16 U.S.C. §§472, 524, 554. Also, letter from James Wilson, secretary of agriculture, to Gifford Pinchot, chief of the Forest Service, of February 1, 1905, implementing the Transfer Act.

7. 34 Stat. 1269 (1907).

8. See James Penick, *Progressive Politics and Conservation: The Ballinger-Pinchot Affair* (Chicago, Ill., University of Chicago, 1968); and Pinchot, *Breaking New Ground*.

9. Ashley Schiff, *Fire and Water* (Cambridge, Mass., Harvard University Press, 1962).

10. 16 U.S.C. §513.

11. 16 U.S.C. §515.

12. 7 U.S.C. §1010.

13. Harold Steen, *The U.S. Forest Service* (Seattle, University of Washington Press, 1977) pp. 175–189; and William Greeley, *Forests and Men* (New York, Doubleday, 1951) pp. 101–111.

14. 43 Stat. 653 (1924), 16 U.S.C. §§471, 499, 505, 515, 564–570. The Clark–McNary policy of Forest Service cooperation with, but not control over, state and private forestry is the cornerstone of the Service's second major program (after national forest management), "cooperative" or "state and private forestry." The third program, forest research, was established by the McSweeney–McNary Act of 1928, 16 U.S.C. §581.

15. Mike Frome, *The Forest Service* (New York, Praeger, 1971) pp. 20–21.

16. Richard Polenberg, *Reorganizing Roosevelt's Government* (Cambridge, Mass., Harvard University Press, 1966) chap. 5. Also see Paul Culhane

and H. Paul Friesema, "Federal Public Lands Reorganization: Deja Vu, 1979," in Frank Convery, Jack Royer, and Gerald Stairs, eds., *Reorganization: Issues, Implications and Opportunities for U.S. Natural Resources Policy* (Durham, N.C., Duke University School of Forestry, 1979) pp. 44–64.

17. The section on the 1950s relies heavily on Steen, *The U.S. Forest Service*, chap. 11.

18. Forest Service, *Outlook for Timber in the United States* (Washington, D.C., U.S. Department of Agriculture, Forest Service, 1973) p. 1.

19. See, for example, Aaron Wildavsky, *Dixon-Yates* (New Haven, Yale University Press, 1962); and Elmo Richardson, *Dams, Parks and Politics* (Lexington, University of Kentucky Press, 1973).

20. Steen, *The U.S. Forest Service*, pp. 272–277 and 284–295. Also see William Voigt, *Public Grazing Lands* (New Brunswick, N.J., Rutgers University Press, 1976).

21. Steen, *The U.S. Forest Service*, pp. 301–303. Also see Grant McConnell, "The Conservation Movement—Past and Present," *Western Political Quarterly* vol. 7 (September 1954) pp. 463–478; Richardson, *Dams, Parks and Politics*, especially chap. 6 and 7; and Owen Stratton and Phillip Sirotkin, *The Echo Park Controversy* (Syracuse, N.Y., Inter-University Case Program 46, 1959).

22. See Dana and Fairfax, *Forest and Range Policy*, pp. 190–204 and 209.

23. 69 Stat. 367 (1955). Also see Steen, *The U.S. Forest Service*, pp. 295–297. The 1872 Mining Laws are codified at 30 U.S.C. §21.

24. 74 Stat. 215 (1960); 16 U.S.C. §528–531.

25. Grant McConnell, "The Multiple Use Concept in Forest Service Policy," *Sierra Club Bulletin* vol. 44 (October 1959) pp. 14–28; Charles Reich, *Bureaucracy and the Forests* (Santa Barbara, Calif., Center for the Study of Democratic Institutions, 1964); and Christopher Curtis, "Managing Federal Lands: Replacing the Multiple Use System," *Yale Law Journal* vol. 82 (March 1973) pp. 787–805.

26. Mike Frome, *The Battle for Wilderness* (New York, Praeger, 1974) chap. 8; and Roderick Nash, *Wilderness and the American Mind* (New Haven, Conn., Yale University Press, 1967) chap. 11.

27. McConnell, "The Multiple Use Concept in Forest Service Policy"; and Frome, *The Battle for Wilderness*, p. 132.

28. 16 U.S.C. §530.

29. 16 U.S.C. §1131(c).

30. For a detailed history of the act, see Frome, *The Battle for Wilderness;* and Nash, *Wilderness and the American Mind*. Normal usage, which will be henceforth followed, is for "Wilderness" (capital W) to refer to congressionally designated areas.

31. Rachel Carson, *Silent Spring* (Greenwich, Conn., Fawcett, 1962).

32. Steen, *The U.S. Forest Service*, pp. 318–320. On George Perkins Marsh, see chap. 1, note 9, plus accompanying text in this volume.

33. 42 U.S.C. §4321.

34. NEPA addresses particularly Charles Reich's major criticisms of the

public lands agencies in *Bureaucracy and the Forests*. See Paul Culhane, "Natural Resources Policy: Procedural Change and Substantive Environmentalism," in Theodore Lowi and Alan Stone, eds., *Nationalizing Government* (Beverly Hills, Calif., Sage, 1978) pp. 211–212.

35. H. Paul Friesema and Paul Culhane, "Social Impacts, Politics, and the Environmental Impact Statement Process," *Natural Resources Journal* vol. 16 (May 1976) pp. 339–356; and Paul Culhane, "Federal Agency Organizational Change in Response to Environmentalism," *Humboldt Journal of Social Relations* vol. 2 (fall 1974) pp. 31–44.

36. See, for example, Forest Service, "Inform and Involve" (Washington, D.C., Forest Service, 1972).

37. Council on Environmental Quality, *Environmental Quality—1974* (Washington, D.C., GPO, December 1974) p. 41. Also see Friesema and Culhane, "Social Impacts, Politics, and the Environmental Impact Statement Process."

38. Daniel Barney, *The Last Stand* (New York, Grossman, 1974); Jack Shepherd, *The Forest Killers* (New York, Weybright and Talley, 1975) chap. 5.

39. This order was greeted with considerable, although subtle, resistance by Forest Service field officers. Several rangers and supervisors criticized the order in interviews. At the same time, a number of national forests revised their allowable cuts downward, apparently as an administrative mechanism to avoid sales levels the field officers felt were excessive.

40. Arnold Bolle, chairperson, "A University View of the Forest Service: A Select Committee Presents Its Report on the Bitterroot National Forest" (Missoula, University of Montana School of Forestry, November 18, 1970). Also see Luke Popovich, "The Bitterroot—Remembrance of Things Past," *Journal of Forestry* vol. 73 (December 1975) pp. 791–793.

41. *West Virginia Division of the Izaak Walton League* v. *Butz,* 522 F. 2d 945 (4th Cir., August 1975). Relying on the Fourth Circuit decision, the court in *Zieski* v. *Butz,* 406 F. Supp. 258 (D. Alaska, December 1975) enjoined clear-cutting on the Tongass National Forest. The section of the Organic Act at issue was 16 U.S.C. §476.

42. 16 U.S.C. §1600–1614. Also see, John McGuire, "National Forest Policy and the 94th Congress," *Journal of Forestry* vol. 74 (December 1976) pp. 800–805; Dennis LeMaster and Luke Popovich, "Development of the National Forest Management Act," *Journal of Forestry* vol. 74 (December 1976) pp. 806–808; and "Major New Public Land Laws Provide Detailed Guidance for Activities of Forest Service and Bureau of Land Management," *Environmental Law Reporter* vol. 6 (November 1976) pp. 10240–10245. The act's major importance lies in its statutory authorization of a formal, comprehensive Forest Service land use planning process. See Paul Culhane and H. Paul Friesema, "Land Use Planning for the Public Lands," *Natural Resources Journal* vol. 19 (January 1979) pp. 43–74. The act was drafted as a series of technical amendments to the 1974 Resources Planning Act, 16 U.S.C. §1601.

43. See Jeanne Nienaber, *Mineral King: Ideological Battleground for Land*

Use Disputes, Ph.D. dissertation, University of California, Department of Political Science, Berkeley 1973; and M. Rupert Cutler, *A Study of Litigation Related to Management of Forest Service Administered Lands and Its Effects on Policy Decisions,* Ph.D. dissertation, Michigan State University, Department of Resource Development, East Lansing, 1972, chap. 4.

44. *Sierra Club* v. *Morton,* 405 U.S. §345 (U.S., April 1972). "Standing to sue" defines which plaintiffs will be allowed to pursue their litigation in the federal courts; standing is a crucial threshold issue in policy-related litigation against government agencies. See Karen Orren, "Standing to Sue: Interest Group Conflict in the Federal Courts," *American Political Science Review* vol. 70 (September 1976) pp. 723–741.

45. *Parker* v. *United States,* 448 F.2d.793 (10th Cir., October 1971), *cert. denied* 405 U.S. §989 (1972).

46. Forest Service, *New Wilderness Study Areas: Roadless Area Review and Evaluation* (Washington, D.C., Forest Service, CI no. 11, October 1973).

47. The acts are the Eastern Wilderness Areas Act, P.L. 93-622 (Jan. 3, 1975), and the Endangered American Wilderness Act, P.L. 95-237 (Feb. 24, 1978).

48. Forest Service, *Roadless Area Review and Evaluation, Final Environmental Statement* (Washington, D.C., Forest Service, January 1979) p. v.

49. See Herbert Kaufman, *The Forest Ranger* (Baltimore, Md., Johns Hopkins University Press for Resources for the Future, 1960); "Planning and Delegation: Forest Service," in R. Joseph Novograd, Marshall Dimock, and Gladys Dimock, eds., *Case Book in Public Administration* (New York, Holt, Rinehart and Winston, 1969); Jeanne Nienaber and Aaron Wildavsky, *The Budgeting and Evaluation of Federal Recreation Programs* (New York, Basic Books, 1973); William McWhinney, *The National Forest: Its Organization and Its Professionals* (Los Angeles and Berkeley, University of California Socio-Technical Systems and Organization Development Research Program and Forest Service MaSS Staff, May 1970); and Luther Gulick, *American Forest Policy* (New York, Institute of Public Administration, 1951).

50. Forest Service, *Organization and Management Systems in the Forest Service,* (Washington, D.C., GPO, July 1970) chap. 3. Students of organization theory will find this chapter fascinating, since it describes the Service's organization in terms of such traditional principles of organization as the "scalar principle," the "span of control principle," and the "territorial jurisdiction principle."

51. The source of the data is *Journal of Forestry* vol. 73 (January 1975) through vol. 74 (April 1976). Joint authorships were counted as fractions; for example, one Forest Service author and one university author of the same article would be counted "1/2 service author" and "1/2 university author." Actual authorships, out of a total of 153 articles, are Forest Service, 53.3, all university authors, 65.3, BLM, 1. A large proportion of the non-Forest Service authors acknowledge Forest Service research assistance, use its photographs, or did fieldwork on national forests.

52. The Forest Service Manual calls the ranger the "backbone of the

Service." Also see, Frome, *The Forest Service,* pp. 37–38; Kaufman, *The Forest Ranger,* pp. 3–4; and Bill Devall, "District Ranger: A Collective Portrait" (Arcata, California State University at Humboldt, 1973) p. 1, mimeo.

53. The largest number of ranger districts on a single forest known to the author is thirteen on the Mark Twain National Forest in Missouri.

54. Forest Service, *Organization and Management Systems in the Forest Service,* p. 13; and McWhinney, *The National Forest,* pp. 22–23.

55. On the importance of bureau relationships with congressional committees, see J. Leiper Freeman, *The Political Process* (New York, Random House, 1955); and sources cited in chapter 1, note 76.

56. Forest Service, *Organization and Management Systems in the Forest Service,* pp. 73–74.

57. A board-foot, the standard unit of measurement of timber volume in the forestry profession, is the cubic volume of a piece of lumber one-foot square and one-inch thick. The Forest Service usually abbreviates thousand board-feet as MBF; thus 10 MMBF is 10 million board-feet.

While people commonly talk about Forest Service "timber sales," it should be recognized that the service offers rights to log trees in specific areas under a specified harvest prescription; the service cannot make a sale unless a logging operator is willing to buy. The service does not harvest its own trees and sell the cut logs.

58. U.S. Senate, Committee on Interior and Insular Affairs, Subcommittee on the Environment and Land Resources, *Inquiry into the Preparation of the East River Unit Plan, Gunnison National Forest, Colorado* (Washington, D.C., GPO (committee print), April–May 1976), 2 vols., especially "Hearing" volume, pp. 114–131 and 214–247; and author's file of correspondence, documents, and newsclippings on Crested Butte, 1973–78.

The model of decision making in which administrators are so thoroughly influenced by other members of the organization that it is impossible to identify the decision maker is described by Herbert Simon, *Administrative Behavior* (New York, Macmillan, 1947) chap. 11.

59. See note 48. The following paragraphs summarize Kaufman's findings. Kaufman's study is a thorough case-study application of Herbert Simon's theory of organizational influence in *Administrative Behavior.*

60. See, for example, Ashley Schiff, *Fire and Water* (Cambridge, Mass., Harvard University Press, 1962), on the conflicts between service researchers and line officers over prescribed burning in southern pine forests and the relationship between forest protection and flood control. Also see the issues discussed in chapter 1.

61. Fritz Roethlisberger and William Dickson, *Management and the Worker* (Cambridge, Mass., Harvard University Press, 1939). Also see Peter Blau, *The Dynamics of Bureaucracy* (Chicago, Ill., University of Chicago Press, 1955).

62. Kaufman, *The Forest Ranger,* p. 197.

63. Ibid., p. 198.

3
The Bureau of Land Management

The modern Bureau of Land Management (BLM) was created by a 1946 reorganization, which combined the General Land Office (GLO) and the Grazing Service. While the BLM is one of the newer federal agencies, its organizational roots in the GLO go back almost to the beginning of the Republic, and its roots in the Grazing Service to the progressive conservation era. Because of controversies surrounding its predecessors, the BLM has retained an unfortunate—and currently inaccurate—image as the Forest Service's embarrassing stepsister.

History of the BLM

From the days of the Confederation through the nineteenth century, the U.S. Treasury sold public lands to individual settlers and land speculators. In 1812 these functions were organized under the new General Land Office in the Department of the Treasury, and in 1849 the GLO was transferred to the newly created Department of the Interior. The GLO was responsible for the disposition of federal public lands during the heyday of land sales, grants, and homesteading.[1] The first major land disposal policy, begun in 1804, involved selling tracts of land (usually 160 acres) to settlers at a price of, by 1820, $1.25 per acre, a substantial sum at the time. The intent was to raise federal revenues by sales to farm families, but the sales did not raise much money, and most of the land was bought by land speculators. Meanwhile, settlers often squatted on the land they had not purchased and then demanded first rights to buy it, rather than having to go through speculators. This right of preemption was first recognized in 1830 (and became a permanent process in 1841). Soldiers and military veterans were granted public land in the form of "bounties" or "script" from the Revolution through the Civil War. Such methods eventually resulted in the disposal of one-fifth of the public domain, much of it good agricultural land in the Midwest and South (see table 3-1).

During the same period, the federal government attempted to stimulate settlement of frontier lands indirectly through grants to states and railroads. The first indirect settlement grants, in 1823, were for construction of wagon roads, canals, and other internal improvements. Land was granted to the states, and then usually given to construction firms as payment for the improvements. Beginning in 1841, more general grants were made to the states. The most important of these grants were for local, or common, schools, and for other institutions, particularly what came to be called land grant colleges. (In several of the western states, these school lands remain in state ownership today, intermingled with unappropriated public domain lands.) Some of the state grant lands were transferred to railroads as an incentive for expanding rail service. The Illinois Central received the first direct railroad land grant in 1850; the largest of the railroad grants, which underwrote the transcontinental routes, were made after the beginning of the Civil War. The railroad grants usually followed a checkerboard pattern of alternating sections along either side of the right-of-way. Finally, beginning in 1849, the federal government began to grant supposed swampland, which was presumably unsuitable for farming, to the states. In truth, the lands granted were usually not swamps in the first place. For example, much of the very fertile farmland in California's Central Valley was disposed of this way. (The Bureau of Reclamation, through its Central Valley Project, is still helping to irrigate this so-called swampland.) Over one-sixth of the public domain was disposed of by these grants to the states and railroads.

The disposal of federal lands is most commonly associated with the homesteading policy. The early federal policy of land sales represented an unsuccessful compromise between the desire to use federal lands to produce revenue and the Jeffersonian concept of agrarian democracy. As it became clear that the land sales and state grants disposal methods re-

Table 3-1. Disposition of the Public Domain, 1781–1977

Type of disposition	Million acres	Percentage of total public domain	Percentage of disposed public domain
Confirmed as prior valid claims	34.0	1.8	3.0
Private, public, and preemption sales; also script locations, mineral entries, and townsite/town lot sales[a]	303.5	16.5	26.5
Veterans' grants (military bounties)	61.0	3.3	5.3
Grants for transportation development:			
Directly to railroad corporations	94.3	5.1	8.2
For railroads, via grants to states	37.1	2.0	3.2
For wagon roads, canals, and rivers, via grants to states	9.5	0.5	0.8
Granted to states for:			
Support of common schools	77.6	4.2	6.8
Support of universities and other state institutions	21.7	1.2	1.9
Reclamation of swampland	64.9	3.5	5.7
Other purposes[b]	117.5	6.4	10.3
Granted or sold to homesteaders	287.5	15.6	25.1
Sold or granted under Timber and Stone, Timber Culture, and Desert Land acts	35.5	1.9	3.1
Subtotals, dispositions	1,144.1	62.3[d]	99.9[d]
Public domain remaining in federal ownership	704.7	38.3	
Original public domain[c]	1,837.8	100.6[d]	

Note: Disposition data are estimated from available records.

Source: Bureau of Land Management, *Public Land Statistics—1977* (Washington, D.C., GPO, 1979) pp. 6–9.

[a] BLM's "disposed of by methods not classified elsewhere" category; may also include very minor miscellaneous categories.

[b] For construction of unspecified public improvements, reclamation of desert lands, water reservoirs, and so forth; most (103.4 million acres) granted by Alaska Statehood Act.

[c] Areas computed in 1912, not adjusted for 1970 recomputation; thus, columns do not total correctly (error = 0.59%).

[d] Round-off error; also see note c.

77

sulted in land speculation, fraud, or both, pressure mounted for direct grants of land to small farmers. Phillip Foss quotes an 1825 oration of Sen. Thomas Benton of Missouri to illustrate the patriotic optimism of the Jeffersonian Democrats' belief in homesteading: "I say give without price to those who are not able to pay; and that which is so given I consider as sold for the best of prices; for a price above gold and silver; a price which cannot be carried away by delinquent officers, nor lost in failing banks, nor stolen by thieves, nor squandered by an improvident and extravagant administration. It brings a price above rubies—a race of virtuous and independent farmers, the true supporters of their country, and the stock from which its best defenders must be drawn.[2]

From 1848 through the beginning of the Civil War, homesteading was a major national issue. It became entangled in the abolition–slavery conflict, and southern congressmen blocked passage of homestead bills until secession. The first Homestead Act was passed in 1862, providing that any head of a household could acquire title to 160 acres of public land by making improvements and residing on the land for five years.[3] Homesteading picked up after the Civil War, with an average of 3.3 million acres of original homestead entries per year from 1866 to 1875; by 1891–1900 the yearly average entries had increased to 6.3 million acres.[4] However, only about one-quarter of all homestead entries initiated during the nineteenth century were patented (that is, title was transferred to the homesteader after five years).

After the Civil War, Congress embarked on several additional disposal methods. The Timber Culture Act of 1873 provided for transfer of title to settlers who promised to plant trees; the impracticability of planting trees in the Prairie and Central Basin states made this act another fraud-prone disposal method of the nineteenth century. The Desert Land Act of 1877 provided for sale of 640 acres of arid land on the condition that irrigation was undertaken. On its face, the Desert Land Act sounds silly—why would a settler pay $1.25 per acre for arid land and install costly irrigation systems when supposedly good land could be homesteaded free? In fact, desert land entries were usually fraudulent acquisitions of land for nonfarming purposes. The act is noteworthy, however, for increasing the size of the disposal parcel from 160 acres to 640 acres; Congress was gradually coming to terms with the arid West. The next disposal method, the Timber and Stone Act of 1878, was the first to provide for transfer of land for nonfarming purposes (that is, for development of timber and stone resources on the land). These three acts eventually disposed of only a small proportion of public land.

After the turn of the century, congressional disposal policies attempted to deal with the realities of the arid West. In 1900, two-thirds of the acreage in the states west of the 100th meridian was still in the public domain, as was 13 percent of the land in the Plains states except Texas (mostly in the Dakotas, Nebraska, and Oklahoma).[5] Congress, despite the failures of the 1862 Homestead Act, clung to the concept of settling the West with virtuous farmers. The Kincaid Act of 1904 was the first act to recognize ranching as a legitimate agricultural use of the public lands. It provided for ranch homesteads of 640 acres, but was limited to Rep. M. P. Kincaid's district in northwest Nebraska. Because of the success of the Kincaid Act, the Homestead Act was amended in 1909 to provide for 320-acre homesteads. This amended act, however, was still limited to farming homesteads. The Stockraising Homestead Act of 1916 finally extended the grazing use and 640-acre provisions of the Kincaid Act to the rest of the public domain. The new federal irrigation program, begun under the Reclamation Act of 1902, plus the enlarged homestead provisions of the 1909 and 1916 acts, led to a great increase in homesteading. (In retrospect, however, even the increases to 320 and 640 acres were unrealistic and inadequate. The 320-acre homesteads on which dry farming methods were to be used, for example, largely became the Dust Bowl of the Great Depression.) While homesteading is commonly thought of as a nineteenth-century phenomenon, there was actually much more homesteading during the early decades of the twentieth century. The yearly totals of homesteading entries from 1871 to 1900 averaged 5.8 million acres; from 1901 to 1920, yearly entries averaged 12.7 million acres. Most of the increased homesteading occurred in the Plains and Intermountain states, extending roughly from Oklahoma to North Dakota to Idaho to Arizona).[6] About 287 million acres—one-sixth of the public domain—was transferred into private ownership under the various homestead acts.

Since the disposal of federal land was a major national policy during much of the nineteenth century, the GLO was an important bureau in the federal government. Both the political background and the prominence of GLO commissioners attest to the agency's importance. Of the twenty-eight commissioners during the nineteenth century, sixteen were former state governors or U.S. Senators or Representatives, one was a former vice president of the United States, and another was a justice of the U.S. Supreme Court.[7]

If the GLO was politically important, its activities were largely clerical. The policy of the federal government was generally to dispose of federal land as fast as possible, not to manage it or ensure its efficient settlement. Thus, the GLO had little need of professional specialists, and was considered relatively maladministered. At its best, local GLO administration was often chaotic during land rushes,[8] in large part because the agency was chronically understaffed and underfunded (even though the agency turned a huge profit over to the Treasury). At its worst, the office was generally regarded as corrupted by land-grabbers who misrepresented claims to acquire public land. It was common for persons who wished to obtain land for purposes other than farming to file homestead or desert land claims and to circulate the claims among friends or relatives without taking a final title to the lands. Often the land was actually used for livestock grazing or logging, not farming. GLO employees and state officials dealing with state land grants sometimes acted in collusion with the land-grabbers. Employees who tried to arrest fraud often saw their cases thrown out of court because local judges and juries in the West were sympathetic to the land-grabbers; sometimes such employees also found themselves fired.[9]

However, the aim of both congressional policy and public sentiment, especially in the West, was to get rid of the public lands. That the GLO did this ineptly and sometimes scandalously was not regarded as a serious matter in the nineteenth century. The problems of GLO administration became more salient with the beginning of the progressive conservation era. The corruption of the GLO was a major reason that Gifford Pinchot, a former GLO official, sought to have new forest reserves administered by his Forest Service in 1905. Five years later, corrupt GLO handling of Alaska coal lease applications, the story of which was leaked to Pinchot by GLO inspector Louis Glavis, precipitated the confrontration with Secretary of the Interior Richard Ballinger that led to Pinchot's firing by President Taft.[10]

GLO land disposal practices had several long-term consequences. Federal land disposal policy had developed in the East, an area of relatively high precipitation. Land was sold in square parcels of 160 acres, more than adequate for farming, in conformance with standard surveying practice. In the arid West, however, these practices had quite different results. The original 160 acres were almost always inadequate for farming. Even when the size of homesteads increased to 320 acres, this was inadequate for economical operations. The land was best suited for range grazing by domestic livestock, but the crucial elements in western livestock operations were water and large tracts of land. Thus, the pattern of settlement that developed was to homestead 160 or 320 acres to obtain those sections that controlled water. Once a rancher obtained control of the water supply in an area, it was pointless for others to obtain the surrounding public land. This left the surrounding land as open range that the ranchers who controlled water could use free, thus providing the second necessary element for successful operations. The public lands near the railroad grants, which were disposed of in a checkerboard pattern, were controlled in the same way: ranchers who bought land from the railroads gained free use of the public land surrounded by the railroad sections. In this manner federal land disposal policies led inadvertently to the settlement of only a fraction of the land in the western range states, with concomitant free use of adjacent public domain rangeland for grazing.[11]

This pattern of land disposal did not, however, lead to completely stable range use. Homesteading and federal laws attempting to prohibit fencing of public land led to overgrazing by local stockmen and nomadic bands of large-herd sheepmen, which in turn led to deteriorated ranges in which grazing capacity was estimated to have been cut in half. The most valuable forage species (those preferred by livestock) were especially overgrazed, leading to a succession of less valuable (or worthless) species. The loss of vegetation cover caused increased erosion, siltation, and soil productivity loss.[12]

The Taylor Grazing Act

As early as 1875, the federal government began to hear warnings of the inappropriateness of its land disposal policies. In that year Commissioner Samuel Burdett of the GLO warned that land west of the 100th meridan was not suited to farming as practiced in the East and that, consequently, title to public land could not be realistically acquired in accord with the intent of the land laws, which was to settle the West with farmers.[13] Burdett's observation was later echoed by Presidents Grant and Hayes and by Maj. John Wesley Powell, the founder of the U.S. Geological Survey, who had made extensive observations of western conditions on an extended tour of the region. Powell noted the inadequacies of existing range use, and proposed expansion of homestead allotments to 2,560 acres and a system of "pasturage districts" to manage public rangeland.[14] As with most radical proposals advanced for the first time, Powell's recommendations were not enacted into law. Through the rest of the century, however, his prediction that the extant pattern of range use would lead to overgrazing and range deterioration came true, as was finally admitted by GLO Commissioner William Richards in 1907.[15] From 1899 to 1927, seventeen bills were introduced in Congress to alleviate range problems by management along the lines of Powell's pasturage districts.[16] Although the national cattlemen's associations and several presidents, including Teddy Roosevelt, weakly supported the bills, all died in committee. The dominant policy supported by Congress remained the traditional homesteading approach. Congress attempted to deal with the problem through the Stockraising Homestead Act of 1916,[17] which raised the homestead acreage to 640 acres, far below Powell's estimate of a minimally economical size.

While Congress remained committed to outmoded homesteading approaches to the public lands, the understanding between the executive branch and stockmen was complicated by the Forest Service. As early as 1903, Pinchot had proposed Forest Service management of grazing on the public domain lands. The service was, of course, the only land management (as opposed to land disposal) agency in the federal government at the time, and the concept of grazing control was congruent with the service's progressive conservation ethos. From 1910 into the 1930s, Interior, which resented its recent loss of the national forests, successfully fought the loss of the public rangelands as well. At the same time, federal control of public domain grazing was made more complicated by opposition to service policy on national forest grazing.

The Forest Service permitted grazing on national forestland from its inception in 1905. The service brought overcompetition for the range under control and charged a nominal grazing fee. The end of overcompetition and overgrazing was generally welcomed by stockmen, and the small fee was accepted. The service, in cooperation with Interior, was behind many of the public domain pasturage district bills introduced in Congress in the 1920s because of concern about the relationships between public domain and national forest grazing. In 1916 the Forest Service had initiated a gradual increase in grazing fees. In 1924, however (after several years of pressure from congressional appropriation committees), the service was forced to propose immediate grazing fee increases up to the fair-market level. At the same time, the service was moving to decrease overgrazing that had occurred during World War I by cutting range use. These actions aroused a storm of protest from stockmen, who had been the service's most supportive clientele. The controversy permanently alienated stockmen from the service, made any proposal that the service administer public domain range politically unfeasible, and soured many stockmen on the whole concept of federal range regulation.[18]

The breakthrough in federal grazing policy grew out of the Mizpah–Pumpkin Creek experiment.[19] In 1926 a stockman, a railroad agricultural agent, and a county extension agent in southeastern Montana organized a cooperative association to regulate use on, consolidate management of, and begin to draw revenue from the hodgepodge of public domain, railroad grant, state school, absentee-owned, and county tax-foreclosure lands. Their plan was sanctioned by a special act of Congress in 1928 that allowed a stockmen's association, under the authority of the Department of the Interior, to manage 108,000 acres, trade state for federal land to consolidate units, pay taxes on private land for the privilege of use, and use public domain for a nominal fee.[20] The Mizpah–Pumpkin Creek association was highly successful, providing revenue for landholders who had previously lost money (by paying taxes on non-revenue-producing land), allowing for improved utilization, and significantly improving range conditions. Of even greater importance, it served as the impetus for the Taylor Grazing Act, which finally brought to fruition Powell's call in 1879 for pasturage districts.

In 1932 a Forest Service grazing district bill (H.R. 11816) passed the House but died in committee in the Senate. Rep. Edward Taylor of Colorado reintroduced the bill in 1933 in the first New Deal session of Congress. Taylor's bill came under a "states' rights" attack in committee and encountered some opposition from stockmen, but most stockmen had come to favor federal regulation of the federal range. The bill was also actively supported by Franklin Roosevelt's new Interior Secretary Harold Ickes. Supported by the Department of Agriculture and the president, Ickes waged one of his famous campaigns, testifying aggressively for the bill, threatening to withhold Civilian Conservation Corps (CCC) camps from the public domain without the bill, and finally (having dredged up a few obscure legal authorities) threatening to withdraw the whole public domain on his own authority. The Taylor Grazing Act was passed June 28, 1934, as a result of Ickes's pressure, Taylor's legislative skill, and the considerable influence of the dust storms of that year.[21] At one point in the debate Taylor referred to the dust swirling east to the very steps of the Capitol as proof of the deterioration of the western ranges and the failure of the homestead acts in the West.

The Taylor Grazing Act had a number of general land management provisions, even though it was primarily a grazing act. Major portions of the act were solely concerned with range management. The act's major provision authorized the establishment of grazing districts and the leasing of forage within the districts to local stockmen with a history of prior use of the range (the so-called section 3 leasing provision). The basic administrative policies were drawn from the Forest Service's range management procedures: confinement of each livestock operator's grazing operations to a specified area; prohibition of trespass by ranchers without permits; and payment of fees for use of a specified number of animal-unit-months (AUMs) of grazing.[22] Section 15 of the act provided for leasing to adjacent ranchers of scattered small tracts of public domain land not included in grazing districts (the so-called section 15 lands). Section 9 was subsequently interpreted as providing authority for the establishment of stockmen's advisory boards, modeled after the Mizpah–Pumpkin Creek association. In addition to its grazing provisions, the act gave the secretary of the interior authority to classify land according to its best use (section 7) and to exchange or sell lands (sections 8 and 14, respectively) with considerable discretion. Entry under the mining laws was still allowed under the act.

The Taylor Grazing Act had two important effects. First, it ended the major era of disposal of federal public domain lands. To prevent a rush of homesteading, President Roosevelt signed an executive order on November 26, 1934, withdrawing for classification (under section 7 of the act) all public lands west of the 100th meridian except in Alaska and Washington. This withdrawal ended homesteading. Second, following passage of the act, a new Division of Grazing—in 1939 renamed the Grazing Service—was established in the Department of the Interior to administer the act's provisions. The establishment of the Division of Grazing ended the nonmanagement of the public domain, although it would be many years before the division's successor, the BLM, began to effectively manage the public domain.

The first years of the Grazing Service were remarkable.[23] Ickes chose as first director of the Grazing Service, Farrington Carpenter, a Republican stockman, graduate of Harvard Law School, former county attorney in the Colorado high country, constituent of Representative Taylor, and key witness in the hearings on the Taylor Grazing Act. Carpenter opened up shop with seventeen people on loan from the Geological Survey and the GLO, plus two graziers pilfered from the Forest Service (without

Ickes's knowledge)—twenty civil servants, most without range management experience or training, to manage millions of acres used by thousands of stockmen. Carpenter's cadre had no organizational history and, in most cases, did not even have comprehensive maps showing where federal rangeland was located. In addition, Carpenter had a personal aversion to bureaucratic, authoritarian administration, based in part on his experience with the Forest Service imposition of range fees and controls. He thus embarked on a policy of using local stockmen, elected by their fellow ranchers to serve on district advisory boards, to make the major local decisions on allocation of permits under the Taylor Grazing Act. Carpenter's primary reasons for this course of action were (1) the stockmen were familiar with the location and prior use of public domain rangeland, whereas Grazing Service personnel were not; and (2) he wished to avoid bureaucratic authoritarianism by giving great weight to local constituents of the Service—"home rule on the range," as Representative Taylor described it. Section 9 of the Taylor Grazing Act contained vague language that Carpenter construed as authorizing the creation of stockmen's advisory boards with considerable authority delegated by the Grazing Service: "The Secretary of the Interior shall provide... for cooperation with local associations of stockmen... interested in the use of the grazing districts." The institution of the advisory boards was subsequently ratified by amendments to the act in 1939.[24]

The basic decision criterion the advisory boards were supposed to use in allocating range permits among stockmen was "commensurability," borrowed from the Forest Service. In the Southwest commensurability was determined by the possession of water rights, while in the more northern of the Intermountain states it was based on land ownership. In both cases commensurate water or land was supposed to determine the number of units of livestock a stockman could run on the public range. (Commensurability, in addition, was a property of the land and could only be transferred with the land.) A second criterion was a rancher's history of use of the range during the "priority period," the five years immediately preceding passage of the Taylor Grazing Act.[25] In practice, however, the initial determination of range rights was through an informal bargaining process, based on a stockman's ability to persuasively allege a certain level of use during the priority period, while facing peers who had some familiarity with his operations.[26] However, the commensurability criterion gave considerable advantage to stockmen with property adjacent to the federal range and was a major factor in the elimination from the federal range of large, nomadic bands of sheep. The Taylor Grazing Act was generally seen as a pro-cow–anti-sheep policy. Carpenter, likewise, was considered to be anti-sheep. The advisory boards, composed of local stockmen, were instrumental in forcing permit criteria that sealed the doom of the nomadic sheepmen. The order of preference for obtaining permits was "(1) applicants with dependent commensurate property with priority of use; (2) applicants with dependent commensurate property but without priority of use; (3) applicants with priority of use but not commensurate property."[27] The relative order of criteria 2 and 3 was the crucial issue. This discrimination in favor of local ranchers was based in part on the generally accepted belief that the nomadic sheepmen were irresponsible graziers, responsible for much of the deterioration of the range. In addition, the sheepmen–cowmen conflict was (and still is) aggravated by chauvinism, suspicion, myth, and folklore.

The Range War—1939–52

In 1939 the Division of Grazing was reorganized and renamed the Grazing Service, and Carpenter was replaced by Richard Rutledge. Like Carpenter's chief aide, Ed Kavanaugh, Rutledge had been brought into Interior from the Forest Service. The Rutledge appointment resulted in part from Secretary Ickes's confrontation with the Forest Service. Soon after passage of the Taylor Grazing Act, the service—assisted from without, as usual, by Gifford Pinchot—had renewed its efforts to wrest control of public domain range from Interior. At the same time Ickes had begun his attempt to force transfer of the Forest Service to his proposed "Department of Conservation."[28] This attempt was not limited to congressional and interagency jousting. Ickes attacked Pinchot personally in a pamphlet defending Richard Ballinger's actions in the 1910 Ballinger–Pinchot Affair.[29] In 1937–38, Ickes attempted to establish a credible Interior forestry program by obtaining congressional authorization to manage GLO timberlands in western Oregon.[30] The appointment of Rutledge, a former Forest Service regional forester and one of its best grazing specialists, answered charges that Interior's Grazing Service was not headed by a competent professional, charges leveled by those who favored placing all public grazing land under the management of the Forest Service. With World War II, the confrontation subsided into a stalemate; the Forest Service stayed in Agriculture and Interior kept the Taylor grazing lands.

Rutledge brought more than just his professional experience from the Forest Service to the Grazing Service. Because of the 1920's grazing fee increases and allotment cuts, stockmen were deeply suspicious of Forest Service grazing policies. Beginning in 1936 and continuing through the 1940s, the Forest Service continued its efforts to increase grazing fees to a realistic level and to reduce the number of livestock on overgrazed and deteriorated ranges. These proposals aroused considerable opposition from western stockmen and several confrontations occurred between the Forest Service and stockmen at both the Washington office and local levels.[31] Rutledge believed, as did most Forest Service graziers, that the federal government should be remunerated for grazing use and that grazing use should be limited in order to conserve range resources. His appointment to head the Grazing Service seemed to signal to stockmen that the industry's easy accommodation with Farrington Carpenter's Division of Grazing had come to an end.

The livestock industry attack was not long in coming. In 1940 Sen. Pat McCarran of Nevada began a series of investigations of the Grazing Service.[32] McCarran was an unreconstructed states' rights Democrat, and was bitterly antagonistic toward Interior in general and Ickes in particular. In addition, his Nevada constituency included the closest thing to the mythical cattle barons using the public lands. Of the fifty largest grazing district operators in 1944, 30 percent (fifteen) were Nevadans, and their average of 9,185 animal units was almost twice as large as the average (4,760) of the other thirty-five large operators. There were also far fewer small stockmen in Nevada than in the other nine grazing district states.[33] McCarran's Senate Resolution 241 of March 1940 demonstrated his belief in minimal Grazing Service management until the public domain could be turned over to private ownership; failing private ownership, public land policy should, McCarran seemed to believe, be subject to the approval of users (that is, stockmen). The first target of McCarran's investigation was the Grazing Service proposal to double grazing fees from their 1940 level of five cents per animal-unit-month. (The Forest Service fee at the time, by way of comparison, was 31 cents.) The investigation—which began in Ely, Nevada, a center of antagonism toward the Grazing Service—turned into a bitter attack on Ickes, Rutledge, and the Grazing Service. The proposed increases were delayed by McCarran's investigation and the uncertainties caused by the outbreak of World War II. In 1944, after constant skirmishing with McCarran, Rutledge retired as director of the Grazing Service for health reasons.

Rutledge was replaced by Clarence Forsling, another former Forest Service professional, who promptly proposed to treble grazing fees, basing his proposal on a range economics study begun in 1941 as a result of the McCarran investigation. McCarran intensified his investigation, and the Grazing Service was placed in an untenable position. McCarran and the livestock industry held increased grazing fees hostage, trying to force Grazing Service recognition of stockmen's rights to control grazing district policy. However, the House Appropriations Committee (with more eastern members than McCarran's committee) questioned Grazing Service expenditures, since the agency was operating at a loss because of its low grazing fees. The House acted in 1946 to drastically cut Grazing Service appropriations. While some western congressmen opposed the cut, McCarran supported it in order to put pressure on the Grazing Service.

The fiscal year 1947 compromise appropriation—which slashed the Grazing Service budget to 53 percent of its 1945 level, thus reducing personnel by 66 percent, barely enough to maintain a skeleton staff—was the principal victory in McCarran's crusade to reduce the Grazing Service to dependence on range users.[34] Local stockmen's advisory boards contributed $200,000 (from the 50 percent of grazing fees returned to the states, and passed on by the states to the stockmen's boards) to the 1947 appropriations of $550,000 to help pay the salaries of local graziers.[35] Grazing Service officials were thus literally paid by the users they were supposed to regulate. Thoroughly cowed, the Grazing Service was led behind the barn and put out of its misery; President Truman's Reorganization Plan Number 2 of 1946 consolidated the Grazing Service and the old GLO to form the Bureau of Land Management.[36]

Fresh on the heels of the grazing fee-appropriations victory, McCarran and the major livestock association leadership laid plans for what William Voigt of the Izaak Walton League has called the Great Land Grab.[37] The stockmen and McCarran began discussions in 1946 leading to a 1947 resolution of the American National Livestock Association favoring legislation providing for sales of public rangeland to the stockmen who grazed it; the sales were to be on terms very favorable to the stockmen (for example, 1.5 percent interest over a thirty-year mortgage, with 90 percent of the revenue returned to the states). The main objective of the stockmen was to transfer BLM lands to private ownership, a goal they believed to be consistent with the Taylor Grazing Act. [The act's preamble mentioned management "of the public lands pending its (*sic.*)

final disposal. . . . ."] The stockmen, however, made the mistake of including national forest and even national park rangeland in their formal proposal. This inclusion aroused a storm of criticism from such conservationists as members of the Izaak Walton League and the Sierra Club and *Harper's* Bernard DeVoto. Conservationist opposition, plus misgivings about the plan among other public lands users and many small ranchers, killed the proposal before it advanced very far in Congress.

The early years of the BLM were no easier than the last year of the Grazing Service. The first director of the BLM, Marion Clawson, had to reorganize the agency's structure to rectify the imbalance between the highly decentralized Grazing Service and the highly centralized GLO. (Clawson has noted that the GLO had become so overbureaucratized that the BLM director had to sign almost every GLO document. He spent many hours every day just signing GLO papers, forms, and correspondence.[38]) More important, the underlying causes of the McCarran attacks had not disappeared since the 1947 appropriations fiasco. Grazing fees were only the stated issue—the real issue was adjudication of range rights.

Before passage of the Taylor Grazing Act, stockmen ran as many livestock as they could on the public range. There was no disincentive to such overgrazing; the only beneficiaries of self-restraint were one's competitors. An example of what Garrett Hardin would later call the "tragedy of the commons,"[39] overgrazing had its predictable effect—gross deterioration of range conditions. The Taylor Act merely institutionalized that high level of use for many years. The Grazing Service under Rutledge and Forsling was committed to reforming the levels of use in conformity with proper carrying capacity as determined by professional range surveys. Stockmen, for their part, wanted their grazing licenses "adjudicated"; that is, they wanted the interim one-year permits issued immediately after passage of the Taylor Act, often at pre-1934 use levels, transformed into permanent (though nominally ten-year) licenses. This issue was central to grazing district policy, and the district advisory boards established by Carpenter played a dominant role in its resolution.

Phillip Foss's famous case study of the Soldier Creek controversy illustrates the obstructionist role played by the advisory boards in the adjudicatory process.[40] From 1936 into the 1950s, a local advisory board in southeastern Oregon resisted all efforts of the Grazing Service, and later the BLM, to set range use on the Soldier Creek grazing unit at the carrying capacity indicated by BLM range surveys in accordance with the provisions of the Federal Range Code. A succession of district managers who opposed the district advisory board and its autocratic chairman were sacked. In 1943 the advisory board established range rights, based solely on base property commensurability, at 77,419 AUMs, but it established the "estimated" carrying capacity at 43,260 AUMs. This violated the 1939 Range Code priority system because equal priority rights were given to class I and class II operators, and rights were assigned in excess of carrying capacity. The board agreed to informally negotiate range use each year down to or below carrying capacity without affecting operators' "paper rights." Actual range use averaged 36,447 AUMs from 1943 to 1951.

In 1949 Director Clawson sent in a new district manager to rectify the situation; the new manager promptly proposed a 44 percent reduction in use. He completed a range survey in 1951 that showed the proper carrying capacity of the unit to be 31,284 AUMs. In the face of board opposition to any cuts, the manager proposed a compromise in 1952: all operators' range rights would be reduced proportionately to the 1943 capacity (43,260 AUMs), more than the actual carrying capacity, but less than the 77,419 AUMs of "paper rights." Since ranchers wanted to graze some 49,000 AUMs, the board refused to accept the compromise. When the manager's very unpopular (but still illegal) compromise was supported by BLM superiors up to Director Clawson, the local operators expanded the conflict to the departmental and congressional levels. The following letter, sent to Interior Secretary McKay and the Oregon congressional delegation during the confrontation, shows the attitude of the livestock industry toward the BLM's local administrators:

> The thing which bothers us the most is that the [District Manager] made the cut against the advice of and contrary to the wishes of the Advisory Board. These men are all experienced stockmen—all are operators—they know the range capabilities—they are interested, even more than the Manager, in a long time operation. Certainly it was never the intention of Congress that this one bureaucrat should override the considered judgment of the cumulated experience of the members of the Advisory Board. *The Manager and his paid personnel should furnish the information and the board should fix the policy.*
> If this is not the theory, it should be.[41]

Bear in mind that this decision was made by an agency of the federal government, the owner of title to the land in question, which was being leased to the stockmen who elected the advisory board. The cut was an attempt to arrive at a level of use consistent with law, after many years of informally negotiated operations conducted by the board in almost total disregard for the provisions of the Taylor Grazing Act and the Federal Range Code. It is hard to imagine a more comprehensive assertion of the right of a self-interested clientele group to control a public agency. For many years Grazing Service, and later BLM, field managers stood in precisely this sort of vassal relationship to the district advisory boards, especially on the only really important issue of local management, grazing lease levels.

Multiple Use—1953–76

Marion Clawson took over the BLM at its low point, but by the time he left the agency in 1953 it had begun to make the transition to a full-fledged conservation agency. BLM appropriations and staffing continued to be complicated during the late 1940s by the so-called Nicholson Plan.[42] Clawson was able to obtain a grazing fee increase (to 12 cents) and an increase in grazing personnel in 1950. In terms of the stockmen's interests, Clawson turned out to be worse than a conservationist; he was an economist who believed the BLM could and should operate as a professional land management agency. His parting shot reflected this belief; in 1952 he initiated a detailed study of grazing fees that concluded fees should be raised to an average of 28 cents per animal-unit-month. After he was eased out by the Eisenhower administration, his successor took three years to raise fees from 12 to 15 cents.

Of even greater importance, the process of adjudication, or professional determination of range carrying capacity and reduction of grazing leases to the capacity level, which Clawson began, continued during the 1950s and was finally completed in 1967. Adjudication was a difficult and little-noticed process.[43] Local district managers were forced to conduct thorough, competent, and reliable range surveys of both public grazing district rangelands and ranchers' base or "commensurate" property. Armed with these surveys, the managers then had to persuade their district advisory boards that the cuts resulting from the surveys were supported by the facts. The facts alone, however, never persuaded local stockmen to accept the cuts. Appeals up through the BLM hierarchy, via the Congress, or to the courts were common. Cuts in range use were a fundamental economic threat to ranchers. A cut obviously decreases ranchers' income flows by decreasing the numbers of livestock they can raise. Moreover, the capitalized value of grazing leases (and Forest

Service permits) is included in the market value of an operator's ranch, so a cut in lease levels directly diminishes the worth of his private property. For these reasons, cuts were never accepted lying down. So the district manager, after marshaling his facts, still had to ride out the resulting appeals. The adjudication of each grazing management unit during this period was thus a small tempest in a teapot.

The infamous Soldier Creek controversy was a case in point. As explained earlier, local stockmen refused to accept the district manager's 1952 proposed compromise (which was itself about 38 percent higher than actual carrying capacity). The district manager who proposed the 1952 compromise resigned from the BLM in 1954 at the height of the political pressure generated by the district advisory board, and the new manager was able to successfully resolve the situation. A 1954 General Accounting Office investigation, and the decision in a 1955 quasi-judicial administrative appeal initiated by some of the class I stockmen in the district, gave the BLM legal support for its position that both carrying capacity *and* range rights should be reduced to the levels indicated by the 1951 survey (31,284 AUMs). Armed with full legal support and a thorough base property survey (plus the 1951 survey of the federal range), the new district manager was able to confront the operators with a solid case in 1956; all the facts were in order and all appeals had been exhausted. The operators were forced (after a bitter three-day protest meeting) to sign an agreement to a 14 percent cut in actual range use, a 28 percent cut in official carrying capacity, and a 60 percent cut in legal range entitlements.[44]

The adjudication process was the most important local level manifestation of the professional maturation of the BLM in the 1950s and 1960s. The Forest Service had earlier grown up side by side—and benefited from its relationship—with the organized forestry profession. But the Grazing Service and early BLM had not enjoyed such an advantage. A well-organized range management profession, represented by the Society for Range Management and supported by strong university range management programs, did not develop until after World War II.[45] Thus, it was not until the 1950s that the field organization of the BLM came to include significant numbers of professional range managers. However, as those professionals became increasingly prominent in the BLM hierarchy in the early 1960s, they represented an important force favoring a redirection of the BLM's key policies and legislative authorities.

Many of the BLM's difficulties with the stockmen were rooted in the ambiguities of the Taylor Grazing Act. Many enabling statutes with a purportedly public interest, regulatory goal may be more accurately characterized as an industry's attempt to have government manage competition within the industry and help the industry attain a stability it could not achieve on its own.[46] The history of passage of the Taylor Grazing Act is consistent with this view; stockmen supported the act because of overcompetition for the federal range, especially between cattlemen and nomadic sheepmen. Section 2 of the Taylor Grazing Act illustrates its ambiguity; it describes the act's purposes as "to preserve the land and its resources from destruction or unnecessary injury, [and] *to provide for the orderly use, improvement and development of the range*" [emphasis added]. While the first purpose can be read as conservation of a resource in the public interest, a regulatory function, the second, which dominated the history of the legislation and was most important to its crucial supporters in the western livestock industry, is a managerial function, supporting the dominant user industry. Thus, the Taylor Grazing Act was a weak basis for conservation-oriented BLM management and tended to put BLM professionals at a disadvantage vis-à-vis their livestock industry clients.

As described earlier, the Forest Service adopted the multiple-use concept in the 1950s as a way of deflecting the dominant use demands of, among others, the timber and livestock industries. With similar motives, the BLM embarked in 1960 on an effort to obtain a similar authorization. Charles Stoddard, the BLM director from 1963 to 1966 and a former official of the Izaak Walton League, and Secretary of the Interior Stewart Udall, also an active conservationist, strongly supported adoption of the multiple-use concept by the bureau. In 1964 a BLM-Interior bill passed as a part of a package deal with a bill creating the Public Land Law Review Commission (PLLRC). The Classification and Multiple Use Act of 1964 gave the secretary of the interior and the BLM the authority to inventory the public domain lands and classify them for either disposal or retention in federal ownership.[47] The authorization to classify public lands for retention was particularly significant because it was the first legal recognition of the fact that most of the public domain would not and could not be disposed of. The BLM was also given a mandate to follow multiple-use principles in planning for and managing lands to be retained in federal ownership.

The PLLRC, created at the time of the 1964 act's passage, was a pet project of the industry-oriented chairman of the House Interior and Insular Affairs Committee, Wayne Aspinall. The PLLRC eventually produced a number of very good studies (notably Paul Gates's massive

1968 volume, *History of Public Land Law Development*). Many of the commission's recommendations appeared to have little impact on federal policy, perhaps because they seemed too pro-industry and out of step with the times when released during the fervent early years of environmentalist activism. However, the PLLRC firmly asserted that the era of disposal of public lands was over and that those lands should, with very minor exceptions, be permanently retained and managed by the federal government.

In supporting the Multiple Use Act, the BLM sought to obtain an "organic act," legislation that would give it a statutory mission and permanent standing. The 1964 act's contemplation of permanent federal management of public domain lands, which the PLLRC seconded, was an important first step in this direction. However, the Classification and Multiple Use Act was not a full-fledged organic act because it was a temporary measure that expired six months after the PLLRC issued its final report in 1970. Nonetheless, Udall and Stoddard implemented the act in the broadest possible manner, and the BLM's officials acted as if their multiple-use mission were permanent, even after the act's technical expiration. From 1970 to 1976, however, the BLM continued to seek a full-fledged, permanent organic act.

That search was complicated by the continuation of several long-standing BLM issues into the 1970s. In 1960 the BLM and Forest Service had again tried to raise grazing fees. A study completed in 1966 concluded that the value of federal grazing permits and leases was $1.23 per animal-unit-month. In 1969 the Interior and Agriculture Departments began a joint program of phased increases to bring fees up to the $1.25 fair-market level.[48] The increase was, of course, controversial. On the one hand, the livestock industry contended, as it had since 1924, that the increase was unreasonable because the cost of the federal permit or lease had already been paid (although not to the federal government) via the capitalized value of the less-than-fair-market permit or lease in the cost of a rancher's base property. On the other hand, environmentalists maintained through the 1970s that the fee increases were too gradual and the $1.25 fee was still less than a fair-market rate (in comparison with the much higher cost of renting an animal-unit-month of grazing on private lands in an open market).

Environmentalists were also active in other BLM policy areas, and, as was typical of environmentalist activism in the 1970s, the BLM was involved in significant litigation. The BLM is responsible for minerals

3: THE BUREAU OF LAND MANAGEMENT

and oil and gas leasing on federal lands, a responsibility that traces back to its roots in the old GLO. In the 1970s leasing and related management programs became fairly controversial, resulting in major environmentalist suits against oil and gas leases on the outer continental shelf.[49] Environmentalists also entered the fray over the BLM's principal program area, grazing leases. As noted in chapter 1, environmentalists believe BLM lands are in such poor condition (and the BLM itself rates 83 percent of its land in the western states in "unsatisfactory" or worse condition) because of overgrazing by domestic livestock. In 1974 the BLM released an environmental impact statement defending its livestock grazing program.[50] The Natural Resources Defense Council (NRDC) sued the BLM, alleging the environmental statement was inadequate; because the key decisions about grazing lease levels are made at the local level, the NRDC argued, the nationwide evaluation avoided the main policy issue of overgrazing and concomitant resource damage. The court-approved settlement in the case required the BLM to prepare environmental statements for each of its grazing allotment management plans on all its grazing districts.[51]

The BLM's situation, in seeking an organic act during the 1970s, was similar to the Forest Service's in the period leading up to the 1960 Multiple Use Act. The livestock industry continued to press its demands (opposing the 1969 fee increases in particular), but environmentalists, who seemed to have forgotten about the BLM after the Great Land Grab proposal fizzled, were exerting increasing pressure upon the BLM from the opposite direction. The Federal Land Policy and Management Act of 1976 was the answer to the BLM's quest for an organic act.[52] The BLM was given statutory status as a permanent federal agency, and its director was made a presidential appointee subject to Senate confirmation. The Federal Land Policy and Management Act also gave the BLM its statutory multiple-use mission, in language almost identical to that in the Forest Service's 1960 multiple-use act.[53] The BLM was authorized to implement its multiple-use mission by conducting comprehensive long-range planning. (The BLM actually began its planning process as one facet of its broad interpretation of its 1964 multiple-use act.) The Federal Land Policy and Management Act also authorized multiple-use advisory councils as a counterbalance to the stockmen's grazing advisory boards and as symbols of the end of the BLM's Taylor Grazing Act era.

In a concession to the livestock industry, the act placed a one-year moratorium on grazing fee increases and directed the BLM and Forest

Service to make yet another study of fees, taking into account ranchers' costs of production and the "reasonableness" of the fees. The bureau and service restudied the matter and concluded, as they had in 1969, that a fair-market value fee was reasonable, so the livestock industry lobbied Congress to overrule a public lands grazing fee study one more time. The Public Rangelands Improvement Act of 1978 established a complicated grazing fee formula, supported by the livestock industry, based on the 1966 fair-market fee of $1.23, average meat prices, and the average stockman's operating costs. Under the formula the 1979 BLM fee would have been $2.03 per animal-unit-month, although it was limited to $1.89 by a provision that yearly fee increases not exceed 25 percent.[54] Given the long history of this controversy, however, the 1978 Rangelands Act is not likely to be the last word on the subject of grazing fees.

The BLM's 1976 act also addressed two preservationist issues. BLM lands had not been included within the purview of the 1964 Wilderness Act. Environmentalists (and officials in the BLM) were especially concerned about severe resource damage to the California desert, which was subjected to heavy use by off-road-vehicle enthusiasts from southern California cities. The Federal Land Policy and Management Act established the California Desert Conservation Area and directed the BLM to conduct a Wilderness study similar to the Forest Service roadless area review.

Finally, the act recodified many of the BLM's responsibilities for land withdrawal, classification, and disposal. Since it terminated the statutory authorizations for routine public land disposals and established the BLM as an agency with a permanent responsibility to manage the remaining public lands, the Federal Land Policy and Management Act of 1976 marked the final closing of the public domain.

Ironically, even though the 1976 act marked the official end of the disposal era in the history of the public domain, the largest land transaction of that era is yet to be consumated. In 1977 the BLM was responsible for 450.2 million acres of federal lands, 19.9 percent of the land surface of the United States. However, 274.2 million of the BLM's acres are in Alaska, and the BLM will soon transfer most of that land to other parties. That transaction hinges on what is rather cryptically termed the *d-2 lands*.[55] The Alaska Statehood Act of 1959 had granted the State of Alaska 104 million acres of federal land, but the transfer was complicated by land claims of Alaska's native Americans. Those claims were settled by the Alaska Native Claims Settlement Act of 1971, which provided for the transfer of 44 million acres of federal land to native corporations. Section 17(d)(2) of the act instructed the Department of the Interior to select 80 million acres of "national interest" lands for consideration as new national parks, wildlife refuges, forests, and wild and scenic rivers. Many of the land transfers to the State of Alaska and native corporations have been held in abeyance pending congressional designation of these d-2 lands as parks, refuges, and so forth.

Congress struggled from 1977 through 1980 with the Alaska National Interest Lands Act, which has been legitimately called the "environmental decision of the century" since it would more than double the sizes of the national park, wildlife refuge, and wilderness preservation systems. A highly organized coalition of environmental groups militantly supported a very preservationist bill, sponsored by Rep. Morris Udall, that passed the House in May 1978 but died in the Senate in the face of industry and local opposition led by Alaska Senators Gravel and Stevens. The Carter administration, which endorsed the bill, then used the Antiquities Act of 1906 and Federal Land Policy Management Act to designate 56 million acres of d-2 lands as national monuments and freeze the status of the rest. In 1980 Udall and the House sent the Senate an even more preservationist bill that would designate 127.5 million acres as parks, wildlife refuges, and so forth. The Senate sent back to the House a somewhat weaker bill that would designate a total of 104.2 million acres in new units, including 43.6 million acres added to the Park system and 53.7 million to the Wildlife Refuge system. In November 1980, following the election of Ronald Reagan, an opponent of the Alaska lands bill, the House acceded to the Senate bill so that outgoing President Carter could sign the Alaska National Interest Lands Conservation Act.[56] An interesting aspect of these struggles over Alaska lands, especially in view of the bitter fights before 1960 over transfers from the Forest Service to the Park Service that totaled less than 5 million acres, is the BLM's relative indifference to the prospect of losing jurisdiction over more than 100 million acres.

Formal Organization of the Bureau of Land Management

The current activities of the BLM reflect its dual organizational history. One of its major functions is to manage, according to multiple-use principles, the public domain lands. The BLM manages 176 million acres located in the lower forty-eight states and, even after the Alaska land transfers, will still manage about 80 million acres in Alaska. BLM multiple-use management of its lands is of three types. First, the huge block of Alaska land is afforded only a very low level of custodial management, and remains essentially wilderness (albeit subjected to periodic mineral "rushes"). Second, the BLM manages 2.6 million acres of prime Douglas fir timberland, spread in a checkerboard pattern through the Coastal Range and Cascade Range of western Oregon. These timberlands reverted to the federal government in 1916–19 when the Oregon and California Railroad and the Coos Bay Wagon Road companies violated terms of their land grants. Because the bulk of these revested lands were part of the Oregon and California grant, they are commonly called the O&C lands. For a variety of reasons—not the least of which are the statutes establishing BLM administration of the revested grants—the O&C lands are managed primarily for timber production.[57] Third, 146.9 million of the 176 million acres of public lands in the lower forty-eight states are managed within grazing districts established under the Taylor Grazing Act. All of these 146.9 million acres are located in the ten states west of the 100th meridian, excluding Washington and Alaska. Figure 3-1 shows the general location of the areas organized into grazing districts, as well as the areas of the O&C lands and the recently created California Desert Conservation Area district. Not all the land within the grazing district (or O&C or California Desert) boundaries is federal land. Typically, private land, state land (especially school grant land), and sometimes land managed by other federal agencies are intermingled with BLM-administered land. The BLM proportion of land within grazing districts ranges from around 90 percent in parts of Nevada and Utah to 25 percent in areas such as eastern Montana. Insofar as land within grazing districts is managed for a dominant use, it is devoted to domestic livestock grazing.

The other major type of BLM management activity is the legacy of the GLO. The BLM still handles much of the land title work on current and former public domain lands, as well as surveys of current public lands. Most of this activity involves the initial leasing work for minerals and oil and gas exploration on public or federal interest lands. The BLM handles activities leading up to leasing. Postlease operations are monitored by the Conservation Division of the U.S. Geological Survey. The BLM's leasing responsibilities apply to its own lands, other federal lands (principally the national forests), and the outer continental shelf (OCS), an area of

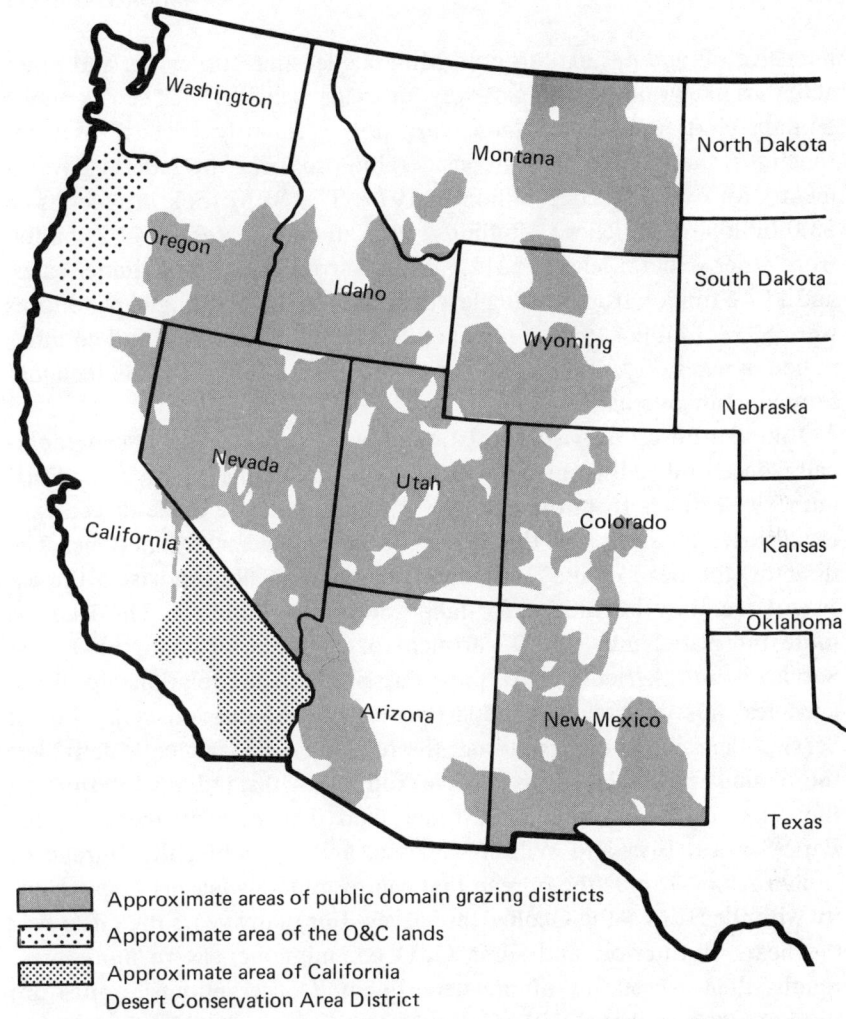

Figure 3-1. Public domain administration districts. (Based on data from Marion Clawson, *Bureau of Land Management*, New York, Praeger, 1971, p. 44; Philip Foss, *Politics and Grass*, Seattle, University of Washington Press, 1960, p. 100; and *BLM California—1980*, Sacramento, BLM, 1980, p. 1.)

intensive oil and gas exploration. Minerals leasing, surveying, and other activities like granting rights-of-way for roads or powerlines across public domain lands are termed *lands functions*. Primarily because of these functions, the BLM makes a considerable profit for the federal government—for example, $2.2 billion in 1977. The BLM took in receipts of $3.0 billion, of which $2.4 billion was from OCS leases, $344.5 million from other mineral leases, $212.1 million from O&C lands timber sales, and $17.6 million from grazing leases. The BLM's operating expenditures were $358.7 million, and it returned $272 million to states and counties in lieu of taxes on federal lands and paid $138.5 million into the reclamation and Indian trust funds.[58]

Like the Forest Service, the BLM's formal organization is geographically decentralized (see figure 3-2). The main line of organizational authority extends from the director, through the state office director, to the district manager for the BLM's land management functions. The director, the head of the Washington office, officially reports to the assistant secretary of interior for land and water resources. The BLM is more integrated into the Department of the Interior than the Forest Service is into Agriculture. In part, this is due to the relationship of the agencies' missions to their departments' general missions: the Forest Service's mission is different from the rest of the department's activities, the tenuous rationale of "trees as a crop" notwithstanding; Interior, on the other hand, contains three other land management agencies (the Park Service, Fish and Wildlife Service, and, arguably, the Bureau of Indian Affairs), plus the bureau that shares minerals leasing responsibility with the BLM—the Geological Survey. For many years the GLO was the heart of Interior, and some GLO commissioners were more prestigious than secretaries of the department. Conservationist critics are fond of asserting that the BLM's integration is due to its "developmentalist" leanings, which fit in well in the developmentalist Department of the Interior. However, this charge of institutional infection blithely ignores the strong preservationist traditions of Interior's other two land management bureaus, the Park Service and Fish and Wildlife Service.

As with most bureaus, the BLM's Washington office is mainly responsible for overall agency policy and relations with Congress and other high-level federal policymakers. Because of the Grazing Service's difficulties with Senator McCarran during the 1940s, the politics of congressional committee–executive bureau subsystems have special historic meaning for the BLM. (During World War II, the Grazing Service's

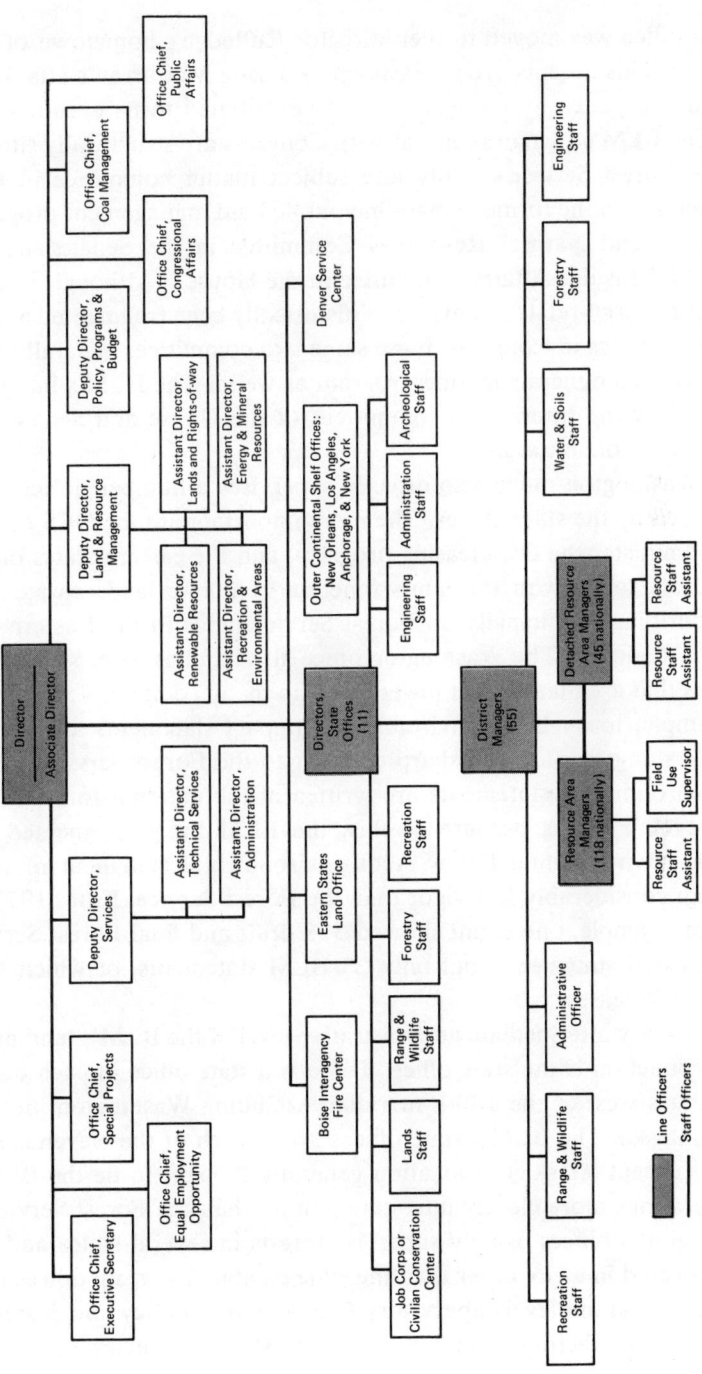

Figure 3-2. Bureau of Land Management organization chart. (Based on BLM, *Managing the Nation's Public Lands*, Washington, D.C, U.S. Department of the Interior, BLM, January 1980, pp. 165–166; and authors' field notes.)

national office was moved to then-director Rutledge's hometown of Salt Lake City. This absence from Washington during McCarran's attacks on the agency is generally thought to have contributed to its eventual gutting.) The BLM's current relations with Congress are structurally simpler than the Forest Service's. Only one subject matter committee in each house deals with the former's mainline public land management program, the Energy and Natural Resources Committee in the Senate and the Interior and Insular Affairs Committee in the House. (Although responsibility for energy-related matters has historically been fragmented among many committees in Congress, these same two committees generally control the BLM's minerals leasing program as well.) The BLM's budget is controlled by the Interior subcommittees of the House and Senate Appropriations Committees.[59]

The Washington office also directly supervises a number of activities not handled by the state offices. The more important are the OCS offices, which administer the OCS leasing program, and the eastern states office, which deals solely with the lands function of public lands east of the 100th meridian (principally on Forest Service lands in the Eastern and Southern Regions). The Washington office also handles other specialized functions that are managed at lower levels in many comparable agencies. For example, many BLM environmental impact statements are written in the Washington office, in sharp contrast to the Forest Service, where most environmental statements are written at the national forest or regional level. Perhaps because of this, the BLM has implemented the National Environmental Policy Act's environmental statement requirement with considerably less vigor than the Forest Service. From 1972 to 1974, for example, one count showed 338 draft and final Forest Service environmental statements, but only 23 BLM statements, of which nine were on OCS leases.[60]

The primary intermediate administrative level of the BLM's land management function is the state office. There is a state office in each of the eleven states west of the 100th meridian excluding Washington, but including Alaska. The BLM's state offices are in each of the eleven states' capitals (except Alaska), a location generally thought to tie the BLM's field operations more closely into state politics than the Forest Service's, whose regional offices usually supervise forests in several states and are usually located in a city other than the state capital. The state offices perform the typical midlevel supervisory functions of a policy and planning nature, ensuring district compliance with BLM policy, reviewing district plans and so forth. They also house a variety of staff specialists who have statewide responsibilities or are available as consultants to the districts. The major special responsibility of the state offices is the lands function; that is, the functions of the old GLO and its district land offices for minerals, right-of-way leasing, and land exchange or sale.

The basic administrative unit of the BLM is the district office. There are fifty-five districts, an average of five per state, ranging from Alaska's two to Oregon's (which handles BLM activities in Washington state) eleven.[61] Most of the districts are organized around grazing districts established under the Taylor Grazing Act, except the two custodial Alaska districts, about half the Oregon districts (which are forestry districts managing the O&C lands) and the new California Desert district. The primary responsibility for management of BLM lands lies with the head of the district office, the district manager.

In addition to specialized staff, the district manager is assisted by a number of resource area managers.[62] The resource areas are a further geographic subdivision of the district. The job of the area manager is similar to that of the Forest Service's district ranger: both are responsible for areas of comparable workload; area managers are GS-11 professionals, while district rangers are GS-11 or GS-12, depending on the district. However, area managers have less formal and informal authority than their Forest Service counterparts. The greater emphasis on the district manager as the basic local manager in the BLM can be seen in the location of the area manager's office. While all rangers have offices separate from the forest supervisor—giving them some independent identity— most area managers' offices are in the same building as the district manager's.[63] Some area managers, referred to as "detached resource area managers," do operate separate offices in areas significantly distant from the district office; three of the nine area managers in this study were in charge of detached resource areas. In-house area managers usually have a small staff, sometimes only a field foreman, while detached area managers usually have one or two professional assistants, equivalent to the situation on a smaller Forest Service district.

While the Forest Service, as a result of studies such as Kaufman's, has been regarded as one of the most professional agencies in the federal bureaucracy, the BLM has been viewed by some as generally less well managed. Part of the problem with its image is caused by alleged understaffing. The average BLM district is staffed at about the level of a small Forest Service national forest. The average professional staff of forest supervisors' offices plus ranger staff professionals—for the forests in this study—numbered 41.5 professionals per forest, while BLM district and resource area professional staff averaged only twenty-one professionals per district.[64] The fifty-three BLM districts (excluding Alaska) manage 175.6 million acres, an average of 3,313,200 acres per district. The 127 non-Alaska forest supervisors' offices in the Forest Service manage 166.5 million acres, or 1,311,302 acres per forest. Thus, with appreciably lower field staffing than the Forest Service, the BLM manages more than twice as much acreage per field administrative unit. However, the acreage it manages represents, on the average district, a lower workload than national forest system land. National forest land is generally much more productive and supports more varied uses at higher output levels (per unit of land area) than the BLM land within grazing districts, which is typically scrub desert. Moreover, certain lands functions that BLM state offices handle (such as right-of-way permits) are handled on the ranger district or forest level by the Forest Service. Thus, the BLM's field staff, relative to workload, is not nearly as understaffed as is commonly believed. Certainly in times past it was understaffed, such as after 1946, when the Grazing Service's budget had been slashed, and district advisory boards often paid BLM district expenses out of the percentage of grazing fees returned via state government to the district. Today, however, BLM field staffing is not out of line in comparison with that of the Forest Service.

A more serious charge against the BLM has been that its field staff members are not as professional as their counterparts in the Forest Service.[65] In the early days of the Grazing Service there were few professional range managers. The few professionals in government service were in the Forest Service (as mentioned above, a number of these men were recruited away from the Forest Service by the Grazing Service). More important, the Grazing Service's first director, Farrington Carpenter (a former stockman), emphasized "practical experience" as a qualification for district graziers. Carpenter's criterion was codified by 1936 amendments to the Taylor Grazing Act, one of which required higher-level Grazing Service (and later BLM) managers to be residents of western states and gave Civil Service hiring preference to people with "practical range experience." As a result, early employees of the Grazing Service tended to be former ranchers or ranchers' sons, not people professionally trained in range management. Later the BLM began hiring professionals, though still under the western residency rule. In the late 1950s, when

Calef and Foss studied the bureau,[66] the older rancher–managers were still dominant at the level of district manager and above, while more professional range managers occupied lower ranks. In part because Calef's and Foss's books were the only field studies of BLM administration, the image of the BLM manager as a "good old boy" rancher has persisted in academic circles.

As Marion Clawson pointed out, the BLM of the 1970s was considerably more professional than it was ten years earlier.[67] All the BLM managers interviewed for this study hold degrees in range management or natural resources management. Eight of the thirteen area managers and district managers interviewed are active in a professional association, usually the Society for Range Management. (One district manager had even been an American Political Science Association congressional fellow.) This is comparable to the educational background of Forest Service rangers and the professional activity of Forest Service line officers who were interviewed for this study.[68]

There is still some sniping between Forest Service and BLM people about the professionalism of each other's agencies. Several of the rangers and area managers interviewed aptly compared this interagency sniping to a college football rivalry. BLM managers tend to have less *esprit de corps,* and to carry themselves with less élan, than do their Forest Service counterparts. However, the BLM has become almost indistinguishable from the service in one critical respect: as professionally trained resource managers, BLM officers have a strong commitment to the principles of multiple-use land management and progressive conservation.

NOTES

1. The best sources on federal land disposition are Benjamin Hibbard, *A History of the Public Land Policies* (New York, Macmillan, 1924); Paul Gates, *History of Public Land Law Development* (Washington, D.C., GPO, 1968); E. Louise Peffer, *The Closing of the Public Domain* (Stanford, Calif., Stanford University Press, 1951); and Samuel Dana and Sally Fairfax, *Forest and Range Policy* (2 ed., New York, McGraw-Hill, 1980). Useful brief accounts can be found in Marion Clawson, *The Bureau of Land Management* (New York, Praeger, 1971) chap. 1 and 2; and Phillip Foss, *Politics and Grass* (Seattle, University of Washington Press, 1960) chap. 1.

2. Cited by Foss, *Politics and Grass,* p. 20, from *Congressional Debates,* 19 Cong., 1 sess. (1826) pp. 727–728.

3. 12 Stat. 605 (1862).
4. Peffer, *The Closing of the Public Domain*, pp. 134–137.
5. Ibid., pp. 10–11.
6. Ibid., p. 137.
7. Vernon Carstensen, ed., *The Public Lands* (Madison, University of Wisconsin Press, 1968) app., pp. 505–509.
8. Clawson (*The Bureau of Land Management*, pp. 27–28) tells of a GLO employee who, because he was the office's "youngest and most agile" person, had the job of opening the office; while the rest of the office staff braced themselves on the other side of the counter, this employee would unlock the door and try to hurdle the counter before being trampled by a mob of land-seekers.
9. Ibid., pp. 15–17 and 30–34. Also see S. A. D. Puter, with Horace Stevens, *Looting of the Public Domain* (Portland, Ore., Portland Printing House Publishers, 1907); Harold Dunham, *Government Handout* (New York, DeCapo, 1970). Puter was a convicted land swindler, and Stevens a former GLO employee.
10. Gifford Pinchot, *Breaking New Ground* (New York, Harcourt Brace, 1947) chap. 29, 43, 69, and 71 through 76.
11. Foss, *Politics and Grass*, pp. 28–29.
12. Ibid., pp. 29–36.
13. *Report of the Commissioner* (Washington, D.C., General Land Office, 1875) pp. 6–9, cited in Foss, *Politics and Grass*, p. 39.
14. John Wesley Powell, *Report on the Lands of the Arid Regions of the United States* (Washington, D.C., GPO, 1979) pp. 24 and 33–36.
15. *Report of the Commissioner* (Washington, D.C., General Land Office, 1907) pp. 79–80, cited in Foss, *Politics and Grass*, p. 42.
16. Foss, *Politics and Grass*, pp. 41–48.
17. 39 Stat. 862 (1916).
18. Peffer, *Closing of the Public Domain*, pp. 170–175 and 181–200; and William Voigt, *Public Grazing Lands* (New Brunswick, N.J., Rutgers University Press, 1976) p. 311.
19. Peffer, *Closing of the Public Domain*, pp. 201 and 214–215; and Foss, *Politics and Grass*, pp. 48–50.
20. 45 Stat. 380 (1928). Also Act of March 1, 1929, 45 Stat. 1430 (1929).
21. 48 Stat. 1269 (1934), 43 U.S.C. §315. For more on the background of the Taylor Grazing Act, see Peffer, *Closing of the Public Domain*, chap. 12; Foss, *Politics and Grass*, chap. 3; Clawson, *The Bureau of Land Management*, pp. 76–78; and Wesley Calef, *Private Grazing and the Public Lands* (Chicago, Ill., University of Chicago Press, 1960) pp. 52–57.
22. An *animal-unit-month* (AUM) is the standard livestock grazing measurement unit. An *animal-unit* is basically one mature cow, one horse, or five sheep or goats. An animal-unit-month is the amount of forage consumed by an animal-unit in a month, about 800 pounds. BLM lands have fairly low productivity, ranging from 6.1 acres per animal-unit-month in Montana to 22 acres per animal-unit-month in Nevada; by comparison, land in states such as Illinois or Indiana can support five times the animal-unit-months per acre of

3: THE BUREAU OF LAND MANAGEMENT

the best BLM districts (Clawson, *The Bureau of Land Management,* pp. 75–76; and Calef, *Private Grazing and the Public Lands,* p. 81).

23. This section is based largely on Clawson, *Bureau of Land Management,* pp. 34–38; and Foss, *Politics and Grass,* pp. 61–85. Foss's account is based primarily on the papers of Farrington Carpenter and Edward Kavanaugh, Carpenter's chief assistant and one of those transferred from the Forest Service.

24. Foss, *Politics and Grass,* pp. 80–82. Readers should note the similarities between Carpenter's philosophy and the grass roots philosophy that led the Tennessee Valley Authority to adopt the co-optive approach during the same period; see Phillip Selznick, *TVA and the Grass Roots* (Berkeley, University of California Press, 1949).

25. Foss, *Politics and Grass,* pp. 83 and 62–63; and Calef, *Private Grazing and the Public Lands,* pp. 60–62.

26. Calef, *Private Grazing and the Public Lands,* pp. 62–70.

27. Foss, *Politics and Grass,* p. 83.

28. Peffer, *Closing of the Public Domain,* chap. 14; and Richard Polenberg, *Reorganizing Roosevelt's Government* (Cambridge, Mass., Harvard University Press, 1966) chap. 5.

29. Harold Ickes, *Not Guilty: An Official Inquiry into the Charges Made by Glavis and Pinchot Against Richard A. Ballinger, Secretary of the Interior, 1909–1911* (Washington, D.C., Department of Interior, Office of the Secretary, 1940).

30. Act of August 28, 1937, 43 U.S.C. §1181. Peffer, *Closing of the Public Domain,* pp. 239–240. These timberlands are commonly referred to as the "O&C lands," and the act as the "O&C Act."

31. Voigt, *Public Grazing Lands,* chap. 7 to 15.

32. Peffer, *Closing of the Public Domain,* chap. 15; Foss, *Politics and Grass,* chap. 8; and Voigt, *Public Grazing Lands,* chap. 21 and 22.

33. Peffer, *Closing of the Public Domain,* pp. 253–256. See note 22 for a definition of animal-unit.

34. Ibid., pp. 266–271. Fiscal year 1945 is used as a comparison base because the House Appropriations Committee made a small cut in FY1946, as a threat, for the same reason.

35. Foss, *Politics and Grass,* pp. 85–86.

36. 11 *Federal Register* 7876 (1946), 60 Stat. 1100 (1946).

37. Voigt, *Public Grazing Lands,* especially chap. 1 and 9; and Peffer, *Closing of the Public Domain,* chap. 16.

38. Marion Clawson, "Reminiscences of the Bureau of Land Management, 1947–48," in Carstensen, ed., *The Public Lands,* pp. 454–455.

39. Hardin, "The Tragedy of the Commons," *Science* vol. 162 (Dec. 12, 1968) pp. 1243–1248. The article is not on overgrazing of public lands per se, but on overgrazing of a "commons" as a metaphor for environmental degradation.

40. Foss, *Politics and Grass,* chap. 7.

41. Letter of February 9, 1954, from Malheur County Court, Vale, Ore-

gon, to Secretary of the Interior McKay, Senator Cordon, and Representatives Norblad, Angell, Ellsworth, and Coon; cited in ibid., p. 165. Emphasis added.

42. Foss, *Politics and Grass*, pp. 187–191.

43. None of the major works on the BLM discuss this very important process thoroughly, with the exception of the Foss narrative on the Soldier Creek adjudication (*Politics and Grass*, pp. 168–170) and Calef's general treatment of the substance of adjudication "cuts" (*Private Grazing and Public Lands*, pp. 135–140). The author's information is based largely on interviewees' recall of the process.

44. Foss, *Politics and Grass*, pp. 166–170. Percentages are derived from the following figures: 1956 use, carrying capacity, and entitlement rights of 31,284 AUMs (the 1951 survey figure); actual use average, 1943–51, of 36,447 AUMs; prior carrying-capacity determination, in 1943, of 43,260 AUMs; and legal entitlements, the 1943 "paper rights," of 77,419 AUMs.

45. Samuel Dana and Sally Fairfax, *Forest and Range Policy* (2 ed., New York, McGraw-Hill, 1980) p. 230.

46. See Gabriel Kolko, *The Triumph of Conservatism* (New York, Free Press, 1963) especially pp. 1–10; and Alan Stone, *Economic Regulation and the Public Interest* (Ithaca, N.Y., Cornell University Press, 1977) pp. 16–17.

47. 33 U.S.C. §1411. On the Classification and Multiple Use Act, see Dana and Fairfax, *Forest and Range Policy*, pp. 230–234; and Voigt, *Public Grazing Lands*, p. 303. On Secretary Udall's views of resource conservation, see Stewart Udall, *The Quiet Crisis* (New York, Avon, 1964).

48. Forest Service, "Grazing Fees on National Forest Range" (Washington, D.C., Forest Service, CI no. 3, June 1969). The $1.25 figure reflected inflation changes from 1966 to 1969.

49. *Natural Resources Defense Council* v. *Morton*, 458 F.2d 827 (D.C. Cir., January 1972); *County of Suffolk* v. *Secretary of the Interior*, 562 F.2d 1368 (2d Cir., August 1977); and *Massachusetts* v. *Andrus*, 8 ELR 20192 (1st Cir., January 1978). Also see Paul Culhane, "Natural Resources Policy: Procedural Change and Substantive Environmentalism," in Theodore Lowi and Alan Stone, eds., *Nationalizing Government: Public Policies in America* (Beverly Hills, Calif., Sage, 1978) pp. 234–236.

50. Bureau of Land Management, *Livestock Grazing Management on National Resource Lands, Final Environmental Statement* (Washington, D.C., BLM, Dec. 31, 1974).

51. *Natural Resources Defense Council* v. *Morton*, 5 ELR 20327 (D.D.C., December 1974).

52. 43 U.S.C., §1701; P.L. 94–579. Also see Paul Culhane and H. Paul Friesema, "Land Use Planning for the Public Lands," *National Resources Journal* vol. 19 (January 1979) pp. 43–74.

53. 43 U.S.C., §§ 1732(a), 1702(c). See chap. 2, note 24, and associated text for the language of the Forest Service's act.

54. *Public Lands News* vol. 3 (Nov. 16, 1978) pp. 4–5. The grazing fee study was required by 43 U.S.C., §1751(a). The formula in the Public Rangelands Improvement Act, P.L. 95–514 (Oct. 25, 1978), is the Forage Value

Index plus the Beef Cattle Price Index minus the (cattle) Price Paid Index, divided by 100, and multiplied by the 1966 base fee of $1.23. The various indexes are regularly computed by government agencies such as the Economic Research Service.

55. Bureau of Land Management, *Public Land Statistics—1977* (Washington, D.C., GPO, 1979) pp. 3 and 20. The d-2 lands are named after section 17(d)(2) of the Alaska Native Claims Settlement Act of 1971, 43 U.S.C. §1601.

56. 94 Stat. 2371 (1980). The act, in addition to the 43.6- and 53.7-million-acre additions to the Park and Wildlife Refuge systems, respectively, adds 3.2 million acres to the National Forest system, 2.2 million to the BLM's National Conservation Area system, and 1.2 million acres to the BLM's Wild and Scenic Rivers system. (Other lands within Park, Refuge, and Forest systems' boundaries are also designated Wild and Scenic Rivers.) The act also designates a total of 56.7 million acres of additions to the National Wilderness Preservation System (within both existing and new units).

57. Bureau of Land Management, *Timber Management, Final Environmental Statement* (Washington, D.C., BLM, September 1976).

58. Bureau of Land Management, *Public Land Statistics—1977*, pp. 166–177.

59. Michael Barone, Grant Ujifusa, and Douglas Matthews, *The Almanac of American Politics—1978* (New York, Dutton, 1977) pp. x–xii.

60. Paul Culhane, "Federal Agency Organizational Change in Response to Environmentalism," *Humboldt Journal of Social Relations*, vol. 2 (fall/winter 1974) p. 41. Also see VTN, Consolidated, Inc., *The National Environmental Policy Act Process Study: An Evaluation of the Implementation and Administration of NEPA by the Forest Service and the Bureau of Land Management* (Irving, Calif., Report by VTN to the Council on Environmental Quality, February 1975).

61. Bureau of Land Management, *Managing the Nation's Public Lands* (Washington, D.C., BLM, January 1980) p. 166.

62. The districts included in this study consisted of two to five resource areas, but the typical BLM districts consisted of three.

63. Office-to-office distance may seem like a trivial point, but there is a practical political effect of the location of line officers: clients of the agency will often go to the highest official in their area, tending to focus more political pressure on the district manager than the area manager. In addition, of course, in-house area managers are more easily subject to district manager supervision and influence, and thus less independent, than detached resource area managers.

64. Author's field interview files.

65. Calef, *Private Grazing and Public Lands*, pp. 261–263.

66. Foss, *Politics and Grass;* Calef, *Private Grazing and the Public Lands*.

67. Clawson, *The Bureau of Land Management*, pp. 41–42.

68. Author's field interview notes.

4

Multiple-Use Management Procedures

Local field officers of the Forest Service and Bureau of Land Management (BLM) are responsible for specific areas of land—national forests or national grasslands and their component ranger districts in the national forest system, and districts and their component resource areas in the BLM's system. The job of the local land manager is to administer the various programs by which the public lands are made available for use by the public. Thus, the national political controversies that envelop the Forest Service and BLM ultimately affect the administrative or decision-making routines of local land managers. Timber, grazing, wilderness, and other benefits are provided not in the halls of the South Agriculture or Interior buildings in Washington, but "on the ground."

The politics of local land management cannot be understood apart from the uses of the public lands, nor can those uses be understood apart from the administrative procedures through with they are provided. As described in previous chapters, multiple use was enshrined as the cardinal doctrine of Forest Service and BLM management by the Multiple Use–Sustained Yield Act, the Classification and Multiple Use Act, and the Federal Land Policy and Management Act. That abstract doctrine is translated into on-the-ground reality by the agencies' standard operating procedures. Those procedures, the subject of this chapter, should really be viewed as independent influences on public lands policymaking because of the central importance of the multiple-use policy.

As multiple-use land management agencies, the Forest Service and BLM produce a variety of tangible goods and services. The multiple-use acts identify numerous goods and services as appropriate uses, including "outdoor recreation, range, timber, watershed, and wildlife and fish purposes."[1] The BLM's multiple-use acts include mining as an acceptable use,[2] and the Forest Service's act defines "establishment and maintenance of wilderness" as consistent with multiple use.[3] In addition to the statutory multiple uses, both agencies permit a variety of special uses. While the BLM and Forest Service manage the resources of their lands, they usually do not produce goods and services directly themselves; they make lands under their jurisdiction available to users, generally through a variety of contractual arrangements.

Most of the primary or direct uses of the public lands also provide secondary benefits. The most commonly cited secondary benefit is jobs and income created by individuals and firms that use public lands directly (as well as by those individuals' and firms' suppliers). (The agencies provide some employment benefits directly. As a carryover from its New Deal Civilian Conservation Corps program, the service administers a large number of Job Corps and Youth Conservation Corps camps on national forests throughout the country, funded by the Department of Labor under the Comprehensive Employment and Training Act.) Although these secondary benefits often play a role in the rhetoric about land use policy—and the jobs argument is used just as much by environmentalist advocates of recreational uses as by industry advocates of consumptive uses—they are incidental to primary management objectives.

Another form of secondary benefit is the payment to local and state governments of portions of receipts from use of federal lands. The proportion returned to local governments varies with the use: in 1974, for example, 25 percent of most Forest Service receipts were returned to local governments, while the BLM's public lands payments ranged from 12.5 percent of section 3 grazing leases to 88.2 percent of Alaskan mineral rents and bonuses, and averaged 37.5 percent of all BLM receipts (except for proceeds of outer continental shelf leases).[4] The percentage payments are basically payments in lieu of taxes, to compensate governments that rely on *ad valorem* property taxes but cannot tax federal lands (which are a large proportion of the land within many local government jurisdictions).

Timber Management

Timber management planning is the most important resource management activity of the Forest Service, accounting for 44 percent of its 1975 appropriations for forest land management and 43 percent of the smaller research and cooperative forestry appropriations. Moreover, a number of other service appropriations (especially for forest roads and trails, forest fire protection, and "general land management" in the national forest management, research, and cooperative forestry parts of the budget) benefit timber management more than other programs.

Although timber sales are sometimes referred to as isolated events, they are actually only one part of a complicated timber management planning sequence. Timber management plans cover ten-year cycles, and are the most technical and complex area of Forest Service management. The first step in the timber planning sequence is an inventory, based on aerial photographs and extrapolation of field sample data, that results in estimates of the volume of timber, species composition, and age composition of the forest.

The second step is calculating the forest's allowable cut. (Allowable cut has undergone several name changes; the most recent—and more accurate—name is "allowable sale quantity," but for convenience, we will use the more familiar term.) An allowable cut is calculated for each national forest; ranger districts' allowables are included in their forests' calculations, and regional and national allowables are sums of the forests' figures. Calculation of allowable cut is a fairly sophisticated process, with most forests using the computerized linear programming model Timber Resources Allocation Method (Timber RAM). Constraints imposed by agency policy—for example, the "nondeclining even flow" definition of sustained yield (which is, as noted in chapter 1, quite controversial)—and professional silvicultural assumptions such as rotation age (the length of time it takes to produce a mature tree) are combined with the inventory data to arrive at the allowable cut. The timber management plan usually includes a schedule of timber harvests to be conducted during the ten years covered by the plan. Thus, the plan specifies both the maximum volume of timber that could be harvested under current sustained yield conditions and a target sales level. Forest Service policy states that sales may not exceed the maximum sustained yield level, the allowable cut, and if sales are less than the allowable cut, local officers should strive to increase those sales.

The third step in the timber sales process is the preparation, by district rangers, of sales action plans. These plans include a schedule of sales on the district, their silvicultural treatments, and associated activity (for example, road construction) over a relatively short period (usually five years). Long-term management considerations predominate at this stage; sales are scheduled to achieve the silvicultural and multiple-use goals for the area, not just to satisfy commercial demands. Silvicultural prescriptions vary from area to area. If, for example, the objective is to obtain an even-aged stand, one of the following prescriptions is used: *clear-cutting,* a one-cut harvest of all trees in a given area; *seed tree cutting,* a two-cut harvest in which the first cut leaves enough trees to naturally reseed the harvest site, with the seed trees cut after the new crop is established; or *shelterwood cutting,* another two-cut harvest in which the first cut leaves enough trees to provide both shade and seed for regeneration. *Selective cutting,* the harvest of individual trees at repeated intervals, is used to produce a mixed-aged stand. Forest Service policy since the 1940s has generally favored even-aged prescriptions.

The fourth stage involves two actions, an environmental analysis report (EAR) on the sale and an appraisal of the timber sale area. The EAR, a smaller version of an environmental impact statement (EIS), is primarily designed to ensure that a sale's impacts on an area's soil, water, wildlife, visual attractiveness, and so forth are considered and its adverse effects mitigated. The EAR is usually prepared by a team composed of the district ranger and supervisor's office specialists in wildlife management, hydrology, landscape architecture, and so forth. The timber appraisal begins with a *cruise* or on-the-ground estimate of the timber volume on the sale site. The appraisers then estimate the market value of the timber products producable from the estimated sale volume. By subtracting the average operator's road, harvesting, and mill costs (plus a profit margin), the appraisers arrive at the *stumpage value,* the minimum price for which the timber should be sold.

The fifth stage is the sale. A sale prospectus is mailed to timber operators on the Forest Service's mailing list for the area. Actual sales are conducted under one of two open bidding methods—sealed bids and oral auction. With the former method, the highest sealed bid is awarded the sale; with the latter, an oral auction follows the opening of sealed bids. (Sales are made to the highest bidder except in fairly unusual situations, such as when the highest bidder has a history of past collusive bidding or breaching of contract.) Bids establish the stumpage price of the standard volume unit, 1,000 board-feet. The volume of the sale is set at the amount estimated by the presale cruise survey or determined by *scaling* (measurement of both volume and quality) of the logs brought out of the sale area after the trees are cut. In old-growth stands the cruise estimate may be inaccurate, so scaling is usually used in these cases (which usually involve western forests). In highly managed forests (generally in the East and South), the cruise is more accurate and is thus used as the sale volume. The more accurate the cruise, the less risk there is to the timber purchaser. At the same time, the scaling method encourages timber operators to leave low-quality logs in the sale area, since logs that are not scaled do not have to be paid for. This creates postharvest cleanup problems and also results in a waste of wood fiber.

The sixth and final step in the timber management process is the harvest itself and postharvest cleanup and reforestation. The timber sale contract awarded to high bidders goes beyond the specification of sale area and type of cut; it specifies in detail road design and construction, logging methods (principally the method used to bring felled trees to the yarding area for loading on trucks[6]), and postharvest cleanup procedures. An important part of postharvest cleanup is the removal or burning of *slash,* the unused residues of logging; excessive slash presents a fire hazard and causes reforestation problems. Most sales contracts (including seed tree and shelterwood prescriptions) provide for reforestation by seeding or planting. The Forest Service may require timber operators to deposit funds for reforestation. These so-called K–V funds, named after the Knutson–Vandenburg Act of 1930,[7] can be used to reforest only the sale area, but they can be applied to a wide variety of tasks, including site preparation, seeding and planting, and thinning and other stand-improvement work once the new stand is established.

The BLM's timber management program is much smaller than the Forest Service's. The BLM manages 24.3 million acres of commercial forestland, but 19.5 million acres of this is in Alaska and receives little, if any, management. The largest share of BLM timber management activities are concentrated in the 2.6 million acres of O&C lands in western Oregon, slightly more than half the BLM's commercial forestland in the lower forty-eight states.[8] The O&C lands are heavily stocked with very valuable stands of Douglas fir; about 84 percent of the BLM's standing timber volume in the lower forty-eight states is on the O&C lands. The few timber programs in BLM districts other than the five O&C districts in Oregon are fairly low level.

4: MULTIPLE-USE MANAGEMENT PROCEDURES

Because of certain characteristics of the O&C lands, BLM timber management differs slightly from that of the Forest Service.[9] Since the O&C lands contain primarily Douglas fir, clear-cutting is the rule, thus simplifying timber management planning. (Douglas fir is a prime candidate for clear-cutting because it is shade-intolerant—that is, it cannot regenerate in shade.) The planning of BLM timber sales is complicated, however, by the landownership pattern in O&C areas; BLM land is intermingled in a checkerboard pattern with private land, making access to BLM timber somewhat complicated. Nonetheless, BLM timber inventory, sales, and harvest procedures are generally similar to the Forest Service's.

Grazing Management

The Forest Service's and BLM's range management procedures are also similar.[10] This similarity stems, in large part, from the fact that most of the current grazing management concepts and procedures were developed by the Forest Service in its early years and later applied to public domain grazing by the Grazing Service; as noted in chapter 3, many of the Grazing Service's early leaders were former Forest Service professionals.

Grazing management is organized around "allotments" in both agencies. Allotments are geographic units within Forest Service ranger or BLM districts, within which a limited number of ranchers run their stock. Although they may conform to physiographic features (for example, a small watershed), they are typically organized around ranchers' historic patterns of range use in an area.

The first step in range management planning is the preparation of a range inventory. The inventory identifies the basic physiographic features of the allotment—vegetative types, soil conditions, average precipitation, topography, and so forth. An important part of the inventory is an estimate of the amount of forage on the allotment; estimates are derived from visual inspection or clipping and weighing of the vegetation on sample plots within the allotment, or both. Surveys are repeated every three to five years to establish long-term range conditions. The product of the inventory and survey is the allotment's carrying capacity, the amount of forage the allotment can supply expressed in animal-unit-months. The forage capacity of public grazing lands is generally quite low. Former BLM Director Marion Clawson notes, for example, that in 1967 BLM lands averaged 13.3 acres per animal-unit-month, or about 60 pounds of forage per acre. By comparison, the least productive farm feed—wild hay—produces about one ton per acre, or thirty-three times the yield of BLM land.[11] Of course, public domain lands are *not* comparable to good farmland—as the disastrous results of homestead farming in the range states amply demonstrated during the Great Depression—because those lands even remotely suitable for farming passed out of federal ownership long ago during the disposal era of public land management.

The second step in range management planning is the allocation of grazing privileges among the stockmen in the allotment (after making some provision, usually small, for wildlife use of the allotment's forage.) Ranchers are issued permits by the Forest Service and licenses by the BLM. The permits and licenses specify the number of stock and seasons of use (that is, the beginning and ending dates for use of the allotment) and are usually issued for ten-year periods. Both agencies also issue special grazing permits (for example, for trailing stock across public lands). Moreover, ranchers are allowed to take nonuse permits if they do not wish to run livestock on federal lands in a given year but wish to retain their grazing privileges. (For example, if a rancher died and a buyer could not be found for the ranch, an estate executor would use a nonuse permit to retain permit privileges, which increase the value of ranch property.) An individual rancher's permit or license is based on his commensurability, or ability to maintain his stock when not on the allotment. The stockman's own ranch is an important factor in his commensurability, of course, but he can also count his BLM lease toward the Forest Service commensurability requirement, and vice versa. Thus, it is quite common for ranchers to have both Forest Service summer range permits and BLM winter range licenses. BLM licenses are technically also allocated on the basis of history of use during the so-called priority period prior to the passage of the Taylor Grazing Act. As noted in chapter 3, priority of use was an important issue during the early years of Grazing Service management, but it has little practical importance today because the process of adjudication settled the issue.

As a practical matter—though not as a matter of law—grazing permits and leases are relatively permanent. The total animal-unit-months permitted on an allotment may not exceed carrying capacity and, on deteriorating ranges, may sometimes need to be reduced. But barring such deterioration, a rancher who obtains a permit or license can expect to have it routinely renewed. Federal permits or leases are also routinely transferred to the buyers of base ranches and livestock. Because of this permanence (and the historic price of grazing fees below market value), federal permits and licenses add to the value of base ranches, and stockmen have sought to have their privileges recognized as permanent legal rights. The Forest Service and BLM have opposed granting legal grazing rights because they oppose the concept of giving away property rights to public lands. Of greater practical significance, permanent legal grazing rights would decrease the agencies' management flexibility (since the proposals would require federal compensation of ranchers if their grazing rights were decreased, for example, to rectify overgrazing), and would make it very difficult for the federal government to ever receive fair-market-value grazing fees (since the capitalized value of the permit or lease "right"—which only acquired value because grazing fees were less than the fair market level historically—would have to be treated as a cost of business and subtracted from the fair market price).[12]

Forest Service grazing management plans (like most of its other plans) are accompanied by an EAR, while the BLM's allotment management plans (AMPs), because of National Resources Defense Council litigation,[13] are accompanied by a full-fledged environmental impact statement (EIS). Grazing management EARs and EISs take into consideration the effects of range use on soil conditions, wildlife, and so forth, but the real focus of the agencies' grazing plans in the 1970s has been on the implementation of intensive, or rest-rotation, grazing systems. Developed by the BLM's August Hormay, rest-rotation is based on the premise that simply decreasing range use does not prevent deterioration—stock merely overgraze preferred vegetation or in preferred locations (for example, near water). The aim of rest-rotation is to maintain good soil and range conditions uniformly throughout allotments and to encourage desirable plant species. Rest-rotation means rotating the degree of grazing permitted on individual pastures within an allotment, from none at all to grazing all vegetation in the pasture, over two- to eight-year cycles.[14] With the rest-rotation policy, the BLM and Forest Service have abandoned the custodial, if politically difficult, approach of cutting range use, and are moving into an era of intensive grazing management designed to improve range conditions and simultaneously *increase* the sustained-yield carrying capacity of grazing allotments.

Wildlife Management

Grazing management is, in theory, only part of the agencies' range responsibility. The other part, wildlife management, often takes second place to livestock grazing in the agencies' field programs.[15] Both agencies manage several types of special wildlife conservation areas, and both are directed to protect the habitats of certain wildlife species. The Endangered Species Act of 1973,[16] which prohibits the capture or killing of endangered species, is also a mandate to protect such species' critical habitats. In addition, and of particular concern to the BLM, the Wild and Free-Roaming Horses and Burros Act of 1971 gives special protection to wild horses.[17] These horses have become distinctly unendangered since the act prohibited their capture or killing by their main predator, man. The explosion in the wild horse and burro population has created significant competition with domestic livestock and other wildlife species. The BLM's response, which has attracted a good deal of whimsical national news coverage, has been a rather unsuccessful effort to place captured wild horses in deserving foster homes throughout the country. Local BLM and Forest Service wildlife management plans are supposed to maintain wildlife habitats generally and, where appropriate, to provide for management of any special wildlife areas, endangered species habitats, and wild horses. (Local officers, of course, are also supposed to consider the effects of other resource programs on wildlife habitats.) These wildlife plans, however, generally pale in comparison with other management plans, such as the Bureau's AMPs or the service's timber management plans.

Perhaps the most important reason wildlife management seems to be a secondary consideration for the agencies is that they do not have full control of the wildlife resources on their lands. According to long-standing U.S. legal doctrine, state governments have authority over wildlife within their boundaries, even if the animals are on federal land. Under English domestic and colonial law, wildlife was the property of the king, and the state governments assumed that prerogative.[18] The major management tool for controlling wildlife populations is hunting. Thus, the number of hunting licenses issued by state fish and game departments represents the major form of human influence on the size of wildlife herds. The BLM and Forest Service may affect wildlife through habitat management, but if either wishes to influence the management of wildlife populations, it must negotiate with state game officials. The BLM and Forest Service also have incomplete jurisdiction over predator species (for example, coyotes); especially at the time of this study's field research, the Fish and Wildlife Service had considerable authority over predator control programs on national forests or BLM lands.

Recreation Management

The multiple-use agencies' recreation programs fall into five general categories: (1) hunting use, (2) wilderness or backcountry use, (3) use or development of public lands for commercial or other generally permanent recreational purposes, (4) development by the agencies of their own recreational facilities, and (5) pleasure driving.[19] With the exception of hunting, these uses are administered according to recreation plans developed by local agency officers.

As noted above, control over hunting and fishing through the granting of licenses is exercised by state fish and game departments. One result of this state control is that the agencies have not thought it feasible to charge hunters and fishermen for the use of public lands. Many observers inside and outside the agencies have argued that lack of revenue from hunting and fishing (and other recreational uses) is the major reason the agencies' recreation budgets are so low.[20] Another result is that the agencies' hunting- and fishing-related efforts at the local level are primarily limited to persuading ranchers—who are generally leery of hunters because of hunters' alleged boorish behavior (littering, leaving stock fence gates open, accidentally shooting livestock, and so forth)—to allow hunters access to public lands across the ranchers' private lands.

The second and third recreational categories, backcountry use and commercial or similar developments, will be discussed later. Since backcountry use is related to the whole wilderness issue, it will be treated under that heading in the next section. Commercial recreation use is generally administered as a special use, and can more conveniently be discussed later, within the context of special use permits.

The most significant of the agencies' recreational developments, the fourth category of recreational programs, are the Forest Service's campgrounds and picnic areas (and associated facilities for swimming, boating, and so forth). Although existing forest campgrounds are excellent, most local service administrators are currently responsible only for maintenance functions (for example, sanitation and site protection, but not new construction) because of limited appropriations. Campground funding has been limited by a weak user fee structure, compounded by unwitting congressional legislative errors from 1972 to 1974 that first effectively barred fees, then reinstated them after considerable revenue loss. Most national forest ranger districts have at least one picnic or campground location, and usually more.

Most people associate professional visitor services with another important federal land management agency, the National Park Service. Most national forests do not have extensive formal visitor information or interpretive services. Vacationers can stop by a local office for a recreation map, of course, and many forests maintain scenic overlooks (and even more have roadside multiple-use public relations displays). But visitor centers can be found on very few forests, and most that exist merely dispense recreational information to tourists. Major Forest Service interpretive programs (such as that at Blanchard Springs Caverns on the Ozark National Forest, a major tourist attraction in the northern Arkansas Ozarks with a large staff of summer seasonal cave guides) are very rare.

The BLM has a relatively underdeveloped recreation program in comparison with the Forest Service. Like the service, it maintains a few scenic overlooks, especially in the spectacular, geologically scenic southwestern desert country. But the BLM's campgrounds are few and far between.

The fifth type of recreation program, highway driving for sight-seeing, makes up a substantial proportion of the official recreation visits to the Forest Service's and BLM's lands. Such a program, of course, involves almost no administrative effort, since the recreation is incidental to the fact that paved roads traverse the public lands. Exceptions to this generalization are found in a number of Forest Service proposals to build scenic roads through undeveloped areas primarily—or sometimes, according to critics, *purportedly*—for sight-seeing.[21]

A much more controversial form of recreation driving is nonhighway, or off-road vehicle (ORV), driving. Such use of the public lands has become popular in the 1970s as a way of getting out into nature in a manner congruent with the vehicle-oriented life of urban Americans. However, ORV can significantly damage resources by compacting soil, destroying vegetation, and hastening erosion, especially when ORVers drive up slopes. As a result, many local Forest Service and BLM units have restricted ORV use to established trails or banned ORVs altogether from certain areas. The BLM's lands are generally more susceptible to ORV damage than the service's because as flat open spaces they attract ORVs, and yet as semidesert they are more fragile. However, the BLM's ORV rules have generally been less strict than the Forest Service's.[22]

Wilderness Management

Most observers of public land management are familiar with Wilderness designations, but it should be noted that the agencies use a variety of designations to formally protect wild areas; primitive and scenic area designations are the most important other wild area designations. Likewise, many observers also believe only the Forest Service is in the wilderness management business because Wilderness has been such a controversial service policy issue in the 1970s. The BLM, however, had a small-scale program of primitive and scenic area designation even before the 1976 Federal Land Policy and Management Act gave it an official Wilderness mandate.

The most visible aspect of preservation management is the designation of areas for special protection. In the case of Wilderness areas, Congress is the ultimate designator; that is, official Wilderness status is conferred by statutory law. The Forest Service's Roadless Area Review and Evaluation (RARE) program, however, has been the crucial predecessor of congressional action.[23] Both the first (1972–73) and second (1978–79) rounds of RARE reviews have been agencywide programs under the official jurisdiction of the Forest Service's chief. Local administrators also play important roles in the RARE process, since the early steps in RARE evaluation are made by forest-level officers.

Three criteria guide local RARE recommendations. The *suitability* criterion deals with a roadless area's conformity to the naturalness standard in the Wilderness Act, which includes the area's scenic and recreational qualities. The *availability* criterion involves the extent to which Wilderness designation would interfere with other important uses, particularly commercial timber harvests. The *need* criterion addresses the demand for wilderness and backcountry recreation in the area's region. The determination of particular areas' ratings on these criteria has been primarily the responsibility of forest-level officers. The forest's recommendations are then reviewed at the regional and Washington office levels; higher-level decisions, in particular, have established minimum levels on the three rating scales necessary for areas to be recommended for Wilderness consideration.

Much of the public participation in RARE processes has also taken place at the local level. During the 1972 RARE process, for example, personnel on almost all national forests held public meetings in conjunction with their roadless area evaluations. After RARE I, the chief listed areas to be studied further for possible recommendation as Wilderness. The resulting studies, which began in 1973 and continued until the beginning of RARE II in 1978, were also conducted by local service administrators.

No matter how contradictory the term *wilderness management* may sound, active Forest Service work does not end when an area has been designated Wilderness. The agency must keep nonconforming uses out of Wilderness areas. The only *development* (if one can use such a term for activities in a Wilderness) permitted in Wilderness areas—as a result of a special provision in the Wilderness Act—is mining. While the Forest Service must allow miners access to claims in Wilderness areas, it can impose restraints on access (requiring access, for example, by helicopters or pack animals) that can be so costly as to preclude mining.

The most significant Wilderness management problem is that backcountry use, especially in very popular Wilderness areas, can exceed the carrying capacity (defined in terms of the solitude backcountry users desire) of the area or even cause soil and vegetative damage. To prevent overuse of Wilderness that ruins the very characteristics the designation was meant to protect, many ranger districts have prepared special management plans for areas under their jurisdiction. These plans often include requirements that Wilderness users obtain permits before entering the area; the permits are used to distribute backcountry users more evenly throughout the Wilderness and, sometimes, to limit total use of the area.

Minerals Management

It is useful to divide federal minerals policies into three programs.[24] So-called hard-rock mining (for example, for metals and uranium ores) falls under the first and is governed by the Mining Law of 1872.[25] This law provides that miners who discover minerals on public land can file a claim that grants them the right to extract the minerals with no payment to the government. The law also allows miners to obtain full title by taking the claim to "patent," which involves surveying and payment of a nominal fee ($2.50 or $5.00 per acre). The second minerals program, under the Mineral Leasing Act of 1920,[26] covers exploration for coal, oil, and gas on the public domain lands, as well as certain other minerals, such as phosphate and potash. Rights to exploit these resources are leased to private developers in return for a nominal annual rental fee and a royalty of one-eighth the value of the minerals produced. In some situations (especially speculative oil and gas leases), leasing is noncompetitive and the first applicant for a tract is issued the lease; in other situations (for example, after oil or gas is discovered in an area), leases are open to competitive bid. The third type of minerals program involves the leasing of oil and gas tracts in the outer continental shelf.[27] Such leasing arrangements, as noted earlier, govern a large proportion of current domestic oil and gas exploration and are major moneymakers for the federal government. They are conducted within a competitive bidding system in which the federal government receives cash bonuses at the time of the bidding, as well as royalties when and if production begins.

Each of these minerals claiming or leasing systems is quite complex, and because of a variety of controversies, each set of policies is in flux.[28] However, local land managers have minimal control over mining uses. Before passage of the Federal Land Policy and Management Act in 1976, miners were not even required to notify the agencies of claims on their lands. (Mining claims have also been used historically for a variety of illegal purposes, including establishment of summer cabins in national forests.) When the agencies have a chance to officially approve mining rights by patenting mining claims or issuing mineral leases, those decisions are the formal responsibility of BLM state offices, not local Forest Service or BLM administrators. Postlease monitoring and administration are conducted by the Conservation Division of the U.S. Geological Survey, not by Forest Service rangers or BLM area managers. The agencies have evolved informal administrative practices for consulting with local land managers over mineral management decisions. BLM state offices forward lease applications to BLM district offices and Forest Service rangers for review and stipulation of conditions to protect surface resources during mining operations. The agencies are often able to negotiate conditions on mining claim operations when they control access across federal lands to the claims. But such procedures are a far cry from the formal control that local BLM and Forest Service officers have over other uses of lands under their jurisdiction.

Special Uses

The Forest Service allows a variety of special uses of national forestland under special use permits; in the BLM, administration of these uses is called the "lands function." (Some of the contracts called "permits" by the Forest Service are called "rights-of-way" by the BLM; for convenience, we will use the simpler Forest Service term.) Most special uses fall into one of two major categories. The first includes a number of transportation or commercial facilities such as roads, gas pipelines, powerlines, or microwave transmitters; permits for these kinds of facilities are issued to state highway departments, natural gas firms, utilities, and telephone companies, respectively. The second general category includes private recreational developments. Almost all the ski areas in the western United States are on national forest lands and are operated under special use permits from the Forest Service. Entrepreneurs for other recreational activities, including backcountry outfitters and guides and river-running guides, need Forest Service or BLM permits to conduct their business on public lands. For many years the Forest Service permitted sylvan summer homes, some of which were originally established as illegal mining claims. Perhaps the most unusual recreational special use with which the author is familiar was obtained for jumping guards over barbed wire cattle fences. A local summer homeowner's favorite sport was to go coyote hunting with her friends English style: red coats, bugles, hounds, English saddles, and afternoon tea. The ranger who had issued the permit admitted this activity caused some bemusement among the local ranchers whose fences were being jumped.

Each type of special use permit has its own peculiarities. Forest Service ski area permits, however, can serve as an example of special use management. Ski area development is a major commercial undertaking requiring considerable capital investment in lifts, restaurants, lodging, and so forth. For obvious climatic and topographical reasons, the best downhill skiing requires mountain sites, which, in the West, are mostly on national forest lands. The service is generally sympathetic to making suitable national forest sites available for this kind of use.

The first step in processing a ski area permit is the preparation of a site suitability study by the regional office staff. Such a study usually is requested by local skiing or business interests, including, but not limited to, prospective permittees.[29] The study compares the site's topography and snowfall to ideal ski area conditions and examines the economic feasibility of the site (considering, for example, regional ski demand, proximity to ski markets, and other competitive or complementary areas in the vicinity).

After the area is identified by the regional forester as a potential winter sports site, the Forest Service issues a prospectus, or invitation to bid and submit development plans on the site. It naturally prefers to receive competitive bids for winter sports sites. (For example, the prospectus on the controversial Mineral King development, discussed in chapter 2, received six bids.) Often competitive bids are not possible, especially for very large ski areas, because one prospective developer already owns the key tracts of private land at the base of the mountain on which support facilities would be built. In any case, acceptance of bids is at the Forest Service's discretion; it may accept the best combination of high bid and acceptable plan, or accept or reject a bid submitted by the only possible developer (in which case no development would occur).

The third step in the process is the issuance of the special use permit. Most ski areas are issued two types of permits. A *term permit* is issued for an area of up to 80 acres for a period of up to thirty years. Term permits cover lands on which facilities such as ski lifts or base buildings will be constructed. However, no significant modern ski area can operate on an area as small as 80 acres, so *terminable permits* are issued for the balance of the site, such as that intended for ski runs and trails on the mountain. Terminable permits are issued annually and, in theory, can be revoked at the Forest Service's discretion. In practice, they are automatically renewed as long as the overall operation of the development is satisfactory and conforms to service requirements. Term and terminable permits are issued on the condition that the service approve the developer's final detailed plans before construction begins. In accepting bids and issuing permits, the Forest Service does not relinquish control over the planning and operation of the development; the annual renewal feature of the terminable permits, in particular, gives the service a good deal of leverage over the management of the ski area.[30]

Once the area is developed and operating, its owner pays the service a fee based on the area's gross sales and fixed assets. The Forest Service also monitors operations to ensure lift and slope safety, adequate maintenance of facilities, and so forth. (With regard to slope safety, the service has the country's best program in the field of avalanche research and management.) On larger areas, the district ranger's staff may even include a snow ranger.

The Multiple-Use Philosophy—Tools and Constraints

Readers familiar with the BLM and Forest Service will notice some conspicuous omissions from the preceding recital of the agencies' multiple uses and management programs. Watershed usage is listed as one of the main statutory multiple uses of both agencies. In addition, both agencies manage significant road-building programs; for example, 13 percent of the service's professional employees in 1973 were engineers, most of whom worked on national forest transportation systems.[31] Watershed use and road programs are treated differently because they are the principle keys to multiple-use management.

As George Hall pointed out in 1963, multiple-use management in actual Forest Service and BLM practice means more than just producing amounts of different goods and services: 5 million board-feet of timber, plus 6,000 animal-unit-months of grazing, plus a new campground, plus a project to improve wildlife habitation in a certain area, and so forth.[32] The philosophy of multiple use—and it is a philosophy, not a precise management formula—is that any use should be carried out to minimize interference with other uses of the same area and, if possible, to complement those other uses. In economists' terms, the goal is to minimize external diseconomies of the use and maximize the use's external economies (net benefits), even if the cost of producing the primary output is increased.[33] The concept of sustained yield reinforces this approach to multiple use; sustained yield is the long-run result of multiple-use management. The optimal level of a use is the highest level sustainable in the long run that does not diminish (and ideally increases) the sustained yield of other resources.

The reality of public land management, however, is that some uses conflict; Wilderness and timber production are common examples of mutually exclusive uses. Land managers must rely on savvy or professional experience to reconcile problems of conflicting uses. In a case study of multiple-use decision making in the Forest Service, Philip Martin suggested that problems of use conflicts are handled by modifications of the planned use to minimize conflict with other uses or resources.[34] He gave two examples to support his argument. The first involved an application for a pipeline special use permit. The application, as submitted by the company, was determined to cause too many conflicts with other uses (fire control, scenic vistas, wildlife habitat, and so forth). Rather than deny the application, though, the local rangers offered the company a different route that would meet the company's needs, but would not produce unacceptable use conflicts. The second example involved the issuance of a mining permit for prospecting to follow up a company's initial indications of the presence of iron ore. Again, the ranger and staff officers were opposed to the original application because they wished to preserve an area of valuable timber, as well as a scenic area and a special wildlife habitat, and were concerned about stripmine reclamation, but they did want to allow the mining operation because of its potential economic benefits.

Martin described the solution as follows: "Prospecting was confined to a relatively remote, but geologically typical, area. There, the mining survey could test the feasibility of mining without significant adverse impact on the inconsistent uses of the forest, and as a side benefit . . . the mining company would cut several new access roads for fire control and future timber cuttings."[35]

In short, Martin's argument was that the level of outputs (either absolute or relative to potential) is not necessarily the most important focus of land management decision making. The conditions under which uses are allowed are more important than the decision whether or not to allow the use.

Watershed and road programs are especially important in the style of multiple-use management that Hall and Martin described. Roads are the primary tool for opening up areas to many uses. As the mining decision noted above indicates, roads built for one purpose make an area accessible for a wide variety of other uses. Thus, roads are the most systematic type of positive externality in multiple-use management; a use for which a road is built benefits other uses by making the area accessible for those uses. Since access to forested areas is more difficult than to open range areas, transportation system planning is a much more important part of local national forest and BLM O&C land management than it is for most BLM grazing districts and national grasslands.

The term *watershed program* is something of a misnomer because it suggests that water yield is the primary goal.[36] To be sure, there are a few minor special uses on public lands, such as an irrigation or water supply structure on a national forest stream, that consume water directly, and the service has for many years conducted research on manipulation of water yields from national forest watersheds. But the primary activities of the agencies' water management programs are really directed at the *land* within the geographic or topographic units called watersheds.

To ensure water quality (that is, to prevent siltation of streams) and to smooth out water flows (that is, to prevent flooding caused by rapid runoff), the agencies attempt to maintain good vegetative cover on their lands. Thus, efforts that prevent erosion and maintain soil quality are justified as protecting the water yields of public lands.[37] Soil stability, in turn, protects the land's capacity to produce timber and range forage for livestock and wildlife and to maintain aesthetically pleasing conditions (which form the basis for the recreational attractiveness of the public lands). Protection of soil systems to protect watersheds may be the most important feature of agency planning for all users. The productivity of almost all uses is based, in the eyes of professional land managers, on the soil, so to prevent one use from decreasing the productivity of others, managers are supposed to ensure first that the use will not adversely affect soil quality and stability. In this way, watershed management is the key constraint on all other uses of public lands and the heart of multiple use management.

The multiple-use philosophy, making public lands available for as many uses as possible while placing constraints on those uses to protect the soil resources of watersheds, is critically important in BLM and Forest Service administration and politics. It was developed largely by federal land managers, and is thus a key part of the agencies' organizational histories. It has also become a central belief of the land management profession. The multiple-use approach is thus the core norm of both the agencies as well as their individual professionals. As Kaufman's classic study, *The Forest Ranger,* showed, the Forest Service has developed a high level of organizational discipline and *esprit de corps* because its officers share a common educational background, professional belief, and identification with the service's history and mission.[38] As the BLM has become increasingly professional, its officers have also come to share common educational and professional norms. The multiple-use philosophy—central to land management training, professional belief, and agency history—is thus the cornerstone of administrative control and authority in the Forest Service and BLM.[39]

Conclusions

Professionals in the field commonly describe the many programs administered by local BLM and Forest Service officials as very complex, for a number of reasons. First, public lands issues often involve basic scientific or technical matters that are subject to dispute. Second, public lands policy emerges from lengthy administrative decision processes that seem arcane and somewhat mystifying to lay people (as well as to a goodly number of natural resources professionals). Third, the multiple-use principle forces public land managers to try to reconcile different and often

4: MULTIPLE-USE MANAGEMENT PROCEDURES 129

conflicting uses of their lands according to decision criteria that are rather vague and imprecise, but are also accepted as legitimate and critically important by the agencies and their professional employees. It is one thing to accept multiple use, sustained yield, and watershed protection in principle, and quite another to practice them in the face of scientific uncertainty and convoluted administrative routines. Fourth, and perhaps most important, the Forest Service's and BLM's local policymaking processes do not take place in a vacuum. The scientific, administrative, and conceptual complexity of public lands policymaking is magnified by a highly charged political environment. Paralleling the set of multiple uses is a spectrum of interest groups affected by and aware of agency policymaking. These groups and their relationships with and influence on local public land managers will be examined in Part III.

NOTES

1. Multiple Use–Sustained Yield Act of 1960, 16 U.S.C. §528. The BLM's multiple-use acts—the Classification and Multiple Use Act of 1964, 33 U.S.C. §1415, and the Federal Land Policy and Management Act of 1976, 43 U.S.C. §1702—list these same principal uses, plus some other minor uses.

2. 43 U.S.C. §1702 (c). Also see 43 U.S.C. §1411 (a). Since the BLM has formal responsibility for mineral claims and leases on Forest Service land, mining is by implication one use of national forest land, although not mentioned as such in the 1960 Multiple Use Act.

3. 16 U.S.C. §529. As noted in chapter 3, the BLM's 1976 act gave it a wilderness review mandate as well; see 43 U.S.C. §1782.

4. Bureau of Land Management, *Public Land Statistics—1974* (Washington, D.C., GPO, 1974) pp. 175–77. Congress periodically increases the percentage of one or another of the thirty-six categories of BLM receipts distributed to states, counties, and other accounts. Despite a major state attempt during the 1978 revision of the outer continental shelf Lands Act to tap OCS revenues, all OCS receipts still go to the federal treasury.

5. Glenn O. Robinson, *The Forest Service* (Baltimore, Md., Johns Hopkins University Press for Resources for the Future, 1975) pp. 61 and 316–317. Chapter 4 of the Robinson book contains an excellent description of the service's timber management procedures. The following treatment parallels Robinson's discussion, with some terms and procedures updated to reflect more recent changes.

6. Principal yarding methods include skidding, or dragging the log (usually behind a tractor), and high-lead yarding, or pulling the log to the yarding area by means of a cable, pulleys, and engine. In some ecologically sensitive areas, the service has experimented with aerial logging (for example, by helicopter).

7. 16 U.S.C. §576.

8. Bureau of Land Management, *Public Land Statistics—1978* (Washington, D.C., GPO, 1980) pp. 62–63. The following discussion of BLM timber management relies upon Marion Clawson, *The Bureau of Land Management* (New York, Praeger, 1971) pp. 89–92.

9. Ibid. On the O&C lands, also see chapter 3, note 30 and accompanying text.

10. See Clawson, *Bureau of Land Management*, chap. 4; and Robinson, *Forest Service*, chap. 7.

11. Clawson, *Bureau of Land Management*, pp. 75–76. According to Robinson, *Forest Service*, p. 200, the service averaged about 13 acres per animal-unit-month in 1972.

12. On the rationale for giving stockmen grazing "rights"—which is unrealistic given the political realities of the use reduction and grazing fees issues—see Robinson, *Forest Service*, pp. 219–220.

13. See chapter 3, note 51 and accompanying text. The NRDC settlement has changed the initial pattern of NEPA implementation (see chapter 3, note 59 and related text) in which the BLM produced few local level EISs.

14. August Hormay, *Principles of Rest-Rotation Grazing and Multiple Use Management* (Washington, D.C., Bureau of Land Management and Forest Service, September 1970).

15. On wildlife management, see Robinson, *Forest Service*, chap. 8; and Clawson, *Bureau of Land Management*, pp. 110–113.

16. 87 Stat. 884 (1973), 16 U.S.C. §668.

17. 85 Stat. 649 (1971), 16 U.S.C. §1331.

18. See Robinson, *Forest Service*, pp. 231–234, and especially note 30 (p. 241), on the legal and administrative deficiencies of this doctrine.

19. On recreation generally, see Robinson, *Forest Service*, chap. 5; and Clawson, *Bureau of Land Management*, pp. 113–120.

20. See, for example, Robinson, *Forest Service*, pp. 238–239.

21. One controversial project on which a good deal of material is available is the so-called Elk Mountain Road case in northern New Mexico. See Jack Shepherd, *The Forest Killers* (New York, Weybright & Talley, 1975) pp. 182–213; Economic Development Administration, *Construction of Road, San Miguel County, New Mexico, Final Environmental Statement* (Washington, D.C., U.S. Department of Commerce, 1973); *Upper Pecos Association v. Stans*, 500 F.2d (10th Cir., July 1974); and H. Paul Friesema and Paul Culhane, "Social Impacts, Politics, and the Environmental Impact Statement Process," *Natural Resources Journal* vol. 16 (May 1976) pp. 344–345 and 353.

22. See, generally, David Sheridan, *Off-Road Vehicles on Public Lands, A Report to the Council on Environmental Quality*, draft report, August 1978. Regulations governing ORV use are based on President Nixon's Executive Order 11644, 37 Federal Register 2877 (February 9, 1972), as amended by E.O. 11989, 3 C.F.R. 120 (1978).

4: MULTIPLE-USE MANAGEMENT PROCEDURES   131

23. See chapter 1, notes 33 to 37, and accompanying text; and chapter 2, notes 25 to 29 and 43 to 47, and accompanying text. On the service's wilderness program generally, see Robinson, *Forest Service,* chap. 6.

24. Clawson's *Bureau of Land Management,* chap. 7, contains a general discussion of mining and mineral leasing.

25. 17 Stat. 91 (1872), 30 U.S.C. §22. So-called common variety minerals, such as sand and gravel, are not subject to mining claims, but are disposed of by competitive bids (Act of July 31, 1947, 61 Stat. 681, 30 U.S.C. §601).

26. Mineral Leasing Act of 1920, 41 Stat. 437, 30 U.S.C. §181.

27. OCS leasing is governed by the Outer Continental Shelf Lands Act Amendments of 1978, 43 U.S.C. §1331.

28. See, for example, Paul Culhane, "Natural Resources Policy: Procedural Change and Substantive Environmentalism," in Theodore Lowi and Alan Stone, eds., *Nationalizing Government: Public Policies in America* (Beverly Hills, Calif., Sage, 1978) pp. 233–236.

29. For a more detailed description of service ski area permitting, see Robinson, *Forest Service,* pp. 126–128. On major political controversy involving a ski area, see ibid., pp. 130–136; and chapter 2, note 42 and accompanying text.

30. The service uses this system of double permits because its statutory authority for long-term recreational permits (16 U.S.C. §497) limits such permits to 80 acres. While the system seems awkward—and some critics of ski areas maintain the use of terminable permits larger than 80 acres is illegal—the leverage that the service gains from using terminable permits seems to be one reason the agency has not pushed to have the 1915 statutory limitation amended to conform to modern conditions.

31. Robinson, *Forest Service,* p. 50.

32. George Hall, "The Myth and Reality of Multiple Use Forestry," *Natural Resources Journal* vol. 3 (October 1963) pp. 276–290.

33. Also see Robinson, *Forest Service,* chapter 3. This criterion is analogous to the concept of Pareto optimality in welfare economics: a use is optimal if one cannot increase its output without decreasing the output or benefits from other uses (including intangibles).

34. Philip Martin, "Conflict Resolution Through the Multiple Use Concept in Forest Service Decision Making," *Natural Resources Journal* vol. 9 (April 1969) pp. 228–236.

35. Ibid., p. 235–236.

36. On watershed generally, see Robinson, *Forest Service,* chap. 9; and Clawson, *Bureau of Land Management* pp. 109–110.

37. The Forest Service indicates the environmentalist nature of its approach by the name for its main watershed program, "environmental management." There are some arcane legal reasons—as well as, of course, some very good hydrological and soil conservation reasons—for the indirect linkage of soil considerations to water management. The Forest Service's 1897 Organic Act (16 U.S.C. §475), stated that the improvement of water flow was one of

the two primary aims of the forest reserves, and the Weeks Act of 1911 (16 U.S.C. §513), stated that the purpose of acquiring national forest lands in the East was to protect watersheds. These acts gave Forest Service management constitutional legitimacy (especially in the Weeks Act's authorization of acquisition of private lands) under the constitutional doctrine of federal powers over navigable waters. Most concepts of federal land management originated with the service, so the BLM has used the same watershed management concepts, even though its authority is ultimately rooted in the federal property clause of the Constitution.

38. Herbert Kaufman, *The Forest Ranger* (Baltimore, Md., Johns Hopkins University Press for Resources for the Future, 1960). Also see above, chapter 2, notes 58 to 62 and accompanying text.

39. On the importance of identification of administrators' beliefs with their organization's goals as the key to organizational influence, see Herbert Simon, *Administrative Behavior* (New York, Macmillan, 1947).

III

GROUP INFLUENCE AND LOCAL PUBLIC LANDS MANAGEMENT

5
Local Land Management / The Actors

Studies of administrative policymaking have invariably focused on national politics and decisions, perhaps because agencies' legal rule-making authority is vested in a department secretary or agency head and because the critical issues of agency policy are rarely resolved before reaching the Washington office. However, as explained in chapter 4, local administrators play a critical role in agency decision making. They influence their superiors by making initial recommendations on the whole range of specific resource plans and often have formal authority to allow or disallow uses. As the action arms of their agency, the people who deal with the agency's public on a day-to-day basis, local administrators are inevitably drawn into the politics of agency policymaking. Chapters 6 to 10 will examine the results of a field study of the local level politics of public land management. This chapter serves to introduce the participants in the study's sample of local public lands politics. It describes, in turn, the sample regions and administrative units studied and the administrators and interest groups involved in public lands policymaking in those regions.[1]

Some romantic and popular notions exist about local public lands management. Local land managers are commonly thought of as hardy officers who spend their days working in the woods or on the range; Forest Service officers refer to this as the "ranger-on-a-horse" image. The popular (especially environmentalist) view also sees these rustic officers as confronted by powerful vested interests such as the cattle barons and timber barons. Both views are largely misconceptions. Local Forest Service and Bureau of Land Management (BLM) officers are actually desk-bound managers of medium-sized offices, and the interest groups involved in local public lands politics are more varied and less powerful than the popular image of the barons suggests. Dozens of different groups actively dealt with the local public lands managers in our sample regions. Very few of these entities were large corporations or well-financed voluntary organizations. Most were local clubs and small, owner-operated businesses.

Despite the fact that a wide variety of organizational entities participated in local public lands politics in these regions, a number of factors contributed to some integration of various groups. Overlapping group memberships, commonality of interests, informal coordinating arrangements, and the like produced two major blocs of interest groups—a local user industry alliance and environmentalists. Because of their official positions and professional interests, Forest Service and BLM managers could be thought of as a third bloc, though one that was also linked by overlapping memberships to both major interest group blocs.

The Study Sample

There are several reasons to focus on local land managers when studying public lands politics. As noted earlier, local officers play key roles in agency policymaking, and the Kaufman and Foss studies of capture and conformity dealt with local land management.[2] In addition, more than two cases are needed for certain kinds of systematic anlysis, and the use of local units provides enough cases for such analysis. After one settles on the local level, the question of which local level to use as a unit of analysis remains. There is a difference in the relative autonomy and authority of the two local line officer levels of the Forest Service and BLM. The lowest levels, the service's ranger district and the BLM's resource area, were chosen as the units of analysis in part because of the need for as many cases as possible, but also because of the service's rhetoric and the observations of scholars such as Kaufman about the importance of rangers. Since district rangers outnumber BLM area managers about three to one, these Forest Service-based selection criteria took precedence. One-third of the BLM area managers in the sample turned out to be detached area managers, who have decision latitude and public visibility comparable to those of Forest Service rangers.

The sample of administrative units included three geographic regions, and all Forest Service and BLM administrative units in the region were included in the sample. The regions selected included four national forests, one national grassland, and three BLM districts and part of a fourth. The sample regions included twenty-eight Forest Service ranger districts and nine BLM resource areas.

The sample was selected to obtain a range of units with the most diverse types of locales and uses. This meant choosing regions with both major commodity uses and some recreation uses. In addition, the selected regions have some useful differences in terms of administrative characteristics. The three are located in different Forest Service regions and different states under different BLM state offices; thus, findings cannot be attributed to properties unique to a single Forest Service region or BLM state regime. The mix of Forest Service and BLM administrative involvement also varies from predominantly Forest Service units in one region to more BLM than Forest Service land in another. The range of Forest Service units includes a national grassland, a major national forest (with a large timber program), and a less active, "backwater" forest. The BLM units are mostly grazing district resource areas, but one is an area with a moderately sized timber program, although not one of the O&C timber districts.[3]

Interviews for the study were conducted under assurances that interview material would not be attributed to individuals by name.[4] Tabular data will, of course, not be attributed to individuals. Some qualitative data, such as the administrative unit descriptions in the next section, may require identification. To facilitate anonymous discussions of administrative units, the following conventions will be used: Forest Service units are identified as NFx, NGx, or RDxx, for national forests, national grasslands, and ranger districts, respectively; BLM units are identified as NRLx, after national resource lands (the term applied to the public domain at the time), or RAxx, for district offices or resource areas. The first digit of the ranger district or resource area code number indicates which national forest, national grassland, or BLM district the unit is a part of. RA71, for example, is a resource area in BLM district NRL7; RD21 is a ranger district on NG2, and so forth.

State A

The geography of the area in State A was primarily prairie plains, with an extensive forested high-country area in one part of the region. The region contained a major national forest, the national grassland, and one BLM resource area. It also contained one of the urban population centers of the state, although, with a population of less than 50,000, it was hardly a major metropolitan area. The region included several units of the National Park System and a major state park; one of the Park Service facilities is among the most heavily visited units in the park system.

NF1 had seven ranger districts, as well as a Job Corps camp. It was the major logging national forest in the sample, with about 80,000 board-feet in timber sales in the fiscal year ending June 1973 and a cut that year over 100 million board-feet; the 1973 cut on NF1 was half again as large as the total of all other administrative units in the sample.[5] NF1 also had a large grazing program, with 100,000 AUM's worth of permits issued per year. The forest did not include any designated Wilderness or Primitive areas, nor any major intensive recreational developments or appreciable mineral or oil and gas activity. In part because of major state and federal park attractions nearby, NF1 did have a fair-sized campground capacity. ORV enthusiasts, especially snowmobiles, were major users of the forest. Because of the forest's major timber program, almost all the rangers on NF1 were GS-12 administrators.

The one national grassland in the study, NG2, was several miles from NF1. There were two ranger districts on NG2, which was supervised by the forest supervisor of a small national forest nearby. The regional population center of NF1 was the same as that of NG2, though the ranger stations were located in towns with populations of less than 1,000. NG2 had no timber program, but conducted a high-volume grazing program of about 180,000 AUMs, comparable to an average BLM grazing district. Dispersed hunting and off-road vehicle (ORV) use were the only significant recreational uses on NG2.

The BLM unit in State A was RA61, a detached resource area under NRL6. Operating in many ways more like a Forest Service ranger district than a BLM resource area, RA61 included a mixed lot of section 15 and special category lands over a large proportion of State A. Because these areas were scattered in small, isolated tracts, effective management of most of RA61's land was impossible. RA61 also had one of the smallest inventories of public land in the BLM, a quarter of a million acres. How-

5: LOCAL LAND MANAGEMENT/THE ACTORS

ever, it contained some of the best BLM grazing land, with some areas supporting more than 1 AUM per acre. RA61's timber program, with sales of about 1 million board-feet in most years, was comparable to programs on some of the twenty-six national forest ranger districts in the sample. RA61 had neither major recreation developments nor, at the time of the field research, any major minerals or oil and gas activity. Because RA61's parent district, NRL6, was in a distant region, with different management activities and problems, RA61 is the only resource area in NRL6 included in this study.

State B

The region in State B was evenly divided between high country and semidesert valley. Much of the mountain area was managed as national forests and a considerable proportion of the semidesert was BLM public domain land. Two national forests and one BLM district were in the region. The region included one large and two medium-sized cities, plus two relatively urban towns and several small rural towns; the BLM district office and the forest supervisors' offices were located in the large city, one of the medium cities, and one of the urban towns. The region also included several interesting, but fairly obscure, units of the National Park System.

NF3 and NF4 were in many ways quite similar. Each had seven ranger districts, and each was divided administratively into two divisions. Both had moderate timber programs, with 1973 sales and cuts of less than 50 million board-feet each. Between them, the forests included three Wilderness areas, one of which was being heavily used. Ranger districts on both forests were the sites of some mining or oil and gas activity, with quite heavy activity in one case. Between them, the forests included several ski areas, one a major area. NF4's range program, with over 100,000 AUMs, was heavier than NF3's; however, many of its permittees were small-time operators, with permits much smaller than those required for a viable occupational livestock operation.

The BLM district in the region, NRL7, was a regular section 3 grazing district that also managed some scattered tracts of section 15 land. NRL7 was administratively divided into three resource areas: two were located in valleys next to NF3 and NF4; the third, a detached resource area, was in a different watershed, with different physiographic, management, and cultural characteristics from NRL7's other resource areas, NF3, or NF4.

NRL7 had a considerable range program, leasing more than 225,000 AUMs, the largest of the supervisory level units in the sample and well above the BLM average. Two of the district's resource areas (including the detached area mentioned above) were sites of mineral activity. The district also had a problem with ORV users in a few areas (primarily close to cities). The district's timber program, at less than 1 million board-feet, was very minor.

State C

The region from State C in our sample was primarily desert, with areas of high country. There were no major urban areas in the region, only small to very small sized towns. Parts of the region had an interesting prospecting history and considerable mining activity. The region had several important park system units, although none was among the highest visitation units in the National Park System. There were two BLM districts and one national forest in the region. The region had the heaviest concentration of public lands of the three regions in the sample, with about 90 percent of the region in concentrated blocks of public lands.

NRL8 was located in half of the region, with its headquarters in a very small, ranching-oriented town. It included three resource areas, one of which was a detached area with offices in the larger town at the other end of the district. NRL8 had a major range program, leasing more than 225,000 AUMs, second only to NRL7 in our sample, and (like NRL7) well above the BLM average. The district supported the most substantial recreation program of the BLM units in the sample, including campgrounds, scenic overlooks, and permitted wild area guides. Most of NRL8's recreation activities complement Park Service programs and facilities (and Park Service headquarters were located in the same towns as the BLM offices). NRL8 included several established mines and considerable oil and gas exploration. During the field research, the district was involved in a controversy over range improvement programs.

The district office for NRL9, in the other half of the region, was located in a small town with a population of less than 10,000. Most of the land managed by NRL9 was extremely arid, and NRL9 was the least productive unit in the sample. The district leased about 50,000 AUMs per year, the lowest in the sample, far below the BLM average, and less than the single section 15 resource area in State A. Its timber and recreation programs were modest. As with NRL8, NRL9 was the site of considerable mineral and oil and gas activity. The district was divided into two resource areas, neither of which was detached.

NF5, the third supervisory level unit in State C's region, was split into two divisions: the two ranger districts of one division were surrounded by NRL8; the other division, composed of three ranger districts, was adjacent to NRL9. NF5 had been heavily cut over; one of its divisions was once a major timber producer, and one of the ranger districts in the other division had had an intensive, short-term clear-cut sale in the 1960s. By the time of the field research, however, NF5's timber program had declined to the 1 million board-feet range. NF5 had a very substantial range program for a national forest, with permits for about 150,000 AUMs. The forest maintained an average recreation program, but had no Wilderness and only minor intensive recreation developments. Two of NF5's ranger districts, one in each division, saw heavy mining activity, and a large proportion of the forest was affected by oil and gas leasing activity. Much of the work of the Forest Service on NF5 focused on restoring forest resources after exploitative levels of use; for example, watershed projects to stabilize overgrazed areas, restocking of clear-cut areas, and so forth.

Sample Ranger Districts and Resource Areas

There was, as indicated, a good deal of variation in the levels of various uses among the sample ranger districts and resource areas. (Table 5-1 presents the ranges and average levels of use for some of the units' more important uses.) The two uses that have been central to the agencies' histories are timber production and livestock grazing. The more evenly distributed of these uses in the study's sample was livestock grazing. All districts saw some livestock grazing, with a minimum of over 2,000 AUMs among the sample districts. The median district had 17,700 AUMs under permits or leases in 1973. The mean carrying capacity of the thirty-seven district-level units in the sample in 1973 was 31,278 AUMs (with a median of 15,725 AUMs and standard deviation of 32,758 AUMs). The agencies' timber programs have two types of output indicators, volume sold and volume cut. Forest Service sales and cut volumes can differ markedly. (Timber sales volume in the sample BLM resource areas always equaled cut volume because they were one-year, cruised sales.) Table 5-1 shows that several districts and areas had no sales or cut; these included NG2 and most of the BLM resource areas.

Table 5-1. Levels of Selected Uses, Sample Ranger Districts and Resource Areas, 1973 ($N = 37$)

Type of use	Minimum value (no. at minimum)	Maximum value	Mean	Median	Standard deviation
Number of grazing permits/leases	12 (2)	400	98	67	92
Grazing permits/leases, AUMs	2,600 (1)	116,100	32,440	17,700	31,308
Timber sale volume, MBF	0 (10)	28,367	4,347	431	6,326
Timber cut volume, MBF	0 (7)	29,174	4,922	1,054	7,369
Wilderness areas					
Considered[a]	0 (28)	4	0.43	b	0.99
Approved[a]	0 (33)	3	0.16	b	0.55
Primitive areas					
Considered[a]	0 (21)	8	0.95	b	1.67
Approved[a]	0 (28)	2	0.27	b	0.51
Natural/scenic areas					
Considered[a]	0 (31)	3	0.24	b	0.64
Approved[a]	0 (32)	3	0.22	b	0.63
Mineral/O&G leases/permits					
Applications	0 (25)	90	6.49	b	20.08
Modifications	0 (32)	60	2.54	b	10.37
Approvals	0 (25)	90	5.81	b	18.12

Transmission line special use permits (SUPs)				
Applications	0 (7)	10	2.38	2.00	2.13
Modifications	0 (23)	5	0.65	[b]	1.06
Approvals	0 (9)	10	2.00	1.71	2.05
Road SUPs				
Applications	0 (15)	8	1.62	0.94	2.11
Modifications	0 (31)	3	0.43	[b]	1.02
Approvals	0 (21)	8	1.03	[b]	1.64
Recreation-related SUPs				
Applications	0 (26)	25	1.57	[b]	4.36
Modifications	−3 (1)	3	0.08	0.03	0.86
Approvals	−3 (1)	25	1.13	0.14	4.28
Irrigation/water SUPs				
Applications	0 (27)	6	0.76	[b]	1.53
Modifications	−1 (1)	1	0.08	0.05	0.36
Approvals	−1 (1)	5	0.49	0.17	1.07

[a] Special reservations decisions involved consideration and recommended approval at the local level (irrespective of action at higher decision levels) of new area designations.

[b] Median, which has a value of 0.0, is meaningless in those cases in which more than half the units have zero as the minimum value.

Mean timber sales were 4,347 thousand board-feet (MBF) among the sample units in 1973, with a cut that year of 4,922 MBF. The mean annual allowable cut of the thirty-seven districts was 6,625 MBF in 1973, with a median of 2,961 MBF, standard deviation of 8,331 MBF, and with six units having an allowable cut of zero.[6]

During the year preceding field research, many of the districts in the sample conducted special reviews of parts of their units for preservationist designation. The most important of these processes was the Forest Service's RARE I wilderness review. Nine administrators considered sixteen potential Wilderness areas in the sample, sixteen administrators considered primitive area designations for another sixty-seven areas, and six administrators considered nine natural, scenic, or similar areas. Only twelve of the thirty-seven administrative units did not consider any special reservations.[7] Thirty-seven percent of the areas considered for Wilderness and 15 percent of those considered for primitive areas were recommended for approval at the local level, although not all were approved at higher levels of the agencies.

The final set of outputs to be discussed are the special uses. Minerals or oil and gas exploration or production, while affecting only one-third of the district units, was the highest-volume special use, with 240 permits or leases acted on in twelve of the thirty-seven units in 1973. Transmission lines (a category including pipelines, electric or telephone lines, and other communication systems like antennae) was the next largest category of special uses and affected the largest number of units (all but seven). Road permits or rights-of-way (excluding Forest Service logging roads) and recreation-related permits were the next largest categories, with sixty and sixty-two actions, respectively; 40 percent of the recreation special use permits involved a BLM resource area that issued a large number of permits to wild area guides.

As pointed out earlier, land management agencies typically modify applications for special use permits, particularly to minimize resource damage or conflicts associated with the contemplated use. Table 4-1 shows, in addition to applications and approvals, the levels of modification of use applications. About 41 percent of special use applications that were eventually approved were modified in some way. Not all special use decisions involved new uses; in the recreation and irrigation categories, there were some net cancellations of special use permits. In the case of recreation-related special uses, net decreases were the result of cancellations of summer home permits. (No modifications and approvals for recreation permits were made on twenty-nine and twenty-six districts, respectively, compared with no modifications on thirty-two districts and no approvals on twenty-six for irrigation permits.)

The average levels of the various outputs are important, but even more important are the widely distributed outputs across the sample units. The timber sales mean was 4,347 MBF, with a very large range. Grazing use also ranged from a few animal-unit-months up to 116,000 AUMs, the equivalent of more than 19,000 head of cattle over a six-month season. The number of special uses and special preservation designations also varied greatly; most districts did not recommend Wilderness designations, but one recommended three. The distribution of outputs was also quite lopsided, with many units at the low end of any particular distribution, but a few districts on the very high end.

Local Land Managers

Information collected on the sample administrative units permits some general statements about local Forest Service and BLM administrators. Two types of characteristics are particularly relevant for this study. The first type—organizational resources—is related to the abilities of local administrators to deal with the variety of responsibilities entrusted to them. The second type—administrators' backgrounds—helps give some sense of the kinds of people in local line officer positions in the agencies.

Local Agency Resources

The average district administrator in the sample operated on a budget of about $150,000 and had a staff of three professionals (including himself), two technical grade assistants, a secretary or two, and a field crew of about six people on a full-time equivalent basis.[8] (See table 5-2.) All the administrators had at least one range-wildlife assistant, usually a professional, and most had at least one professional timber staffer. Some of the BLM resource areas did not make a formal, functional distinction in staff assignments, calling professionals "natural resource specialists" and technicians "use supervisors"; we have labeled the former staff category "generalists," although their duties are usually similar to those of staff people in the range-wildlife categories. There were only two full-time professional recreation staffers on the sample district units: the director of a visitor center, who reported to a nearby ranger even though both he and the ranger were of the same rank, and the top assistant ranger of the urban district of NF1.[9]

The median supervisory administrator's budget was about $650,000, and median professional, technical, and clerical staff sizes were sixteen, five, and six, respectively. Some of the bigger ranger districts had larger budgets than the three smaller supervisory units (NRL8, NRL9, and the forest that supervised NG2). The distribution of resource specialists was proportional to the distribution of district administrators' staffs. The major systematic differences were in the "other" and "administrative" categories in table 5-2. The business administrators were located in supervisory administrative staffs. Most of the specialists in the "other" category were engineers, lands specialists, and fire control officers, although a variety of other specialists, such as hydrologists, landscape architects, and archeologists, were also found on supervisors' staffs. The engineers were mainly found on forest supervisors' office staffs, and worked on the extensive road-building activities of the forest, especially roads built in connection with timber sales. Even though all professional staff members on a forest—both those stationed in supervisors' offices and those on the ranger districts—were part of the fire control organization, the staff fire control specialists were all stationed in supervisors' offices.

There were some systematic differences in the size of administrators' budgets and staffs. District rangers generally had greater resources than BLM area managers: the mean BLM area budget was $102,000, versus $167,785 for ranger districts; the mean number of professional staff members of resource areas was 2.88, versus the ranger districts' 3.55. Forest supervisors also generally had larger budgets and more staff than district managers: the average supervisor's office budget in the sample was $982,000, versus $500,000 for BLM district managers; and professional staff size (not including district administrators or their staffs) averaged 20.2 for forest supervisors and 12 for district managers.

Some differences were the result of agency peculiarities. For example, area managers whose offices were in the district office might have smaller staffs and budgets than detached area managers because they could draw on district staff and because office overhead was not part of their budget.

As another measure of area managers' relatively lower autonomy in comparison with district rangers, some area managers did not even have separate budgets. However, area managers' administrative resources were really a discretionary, organizational prerogative of the district manager, reflecting the relative centralization of the district's administrative structure: the area managers of RA61 and NRL7 all had budgets in the $100,000 range and two to four professional staff assistants, while area managers on NRL8 and NRL9 had budgets in the $60,000 range with, at most, one professional assistant, irrespective of whether the resource area was detached or not. (There was some indication that the relative centralization of the districts and resource areas on NRL8 and NRL9 was the result of the preference of the State C director of the BLM for greater centralization.)

The major determinant of the level of administrative unit resources, however, seems to have had little to do with agency quirks. The Forest Service supervisor's office and ranger district budgets and staff fluctuated as low as the level of the lowest-budget BLM district or resource area. The determinant of budget and staff levels seems to have been timber management responsibility. The big-budget, large-staff forests or ranger districts were timber producers. The supervisory unit with the largest staff and the district administrators with the biggest budgets were all on NF1, the major timber forest in the sample. Conversely, the low-budget, small-staff operations were those without timber programs. The BLM resource area with a moderate timber program had a moderately sized budget and staff. And although none were in our sample, the BLM's O&C districts (with major timber programs) have staffs of 80 to 130, which is equivalent to the staffs of NF3 and NF4.[10]

Local Line Officers' Backgrounds

Most district administrators in the study had similar backgrounds. Almost all had joined the agency after college or, in three cases, after college and military service (see table 5-3). Better than half had had experience with a land management agency before joining the agency, most with the agency that later employed them. (The three who worked for another land management agency during college summers were BLM managers who had worked for the Forest Service.) District administrators had been with the agency an average of thirteen years, and had been

Table 5-2. Administrative Unit Resources, 1973

Type of resource	Minimum (no.)	Maximum	Median	Mean	Standard deviation
District administrators ($N = 37$)					
District budget	$35,000 (1)	$342,000	$151,200	$151,784	$73,586
Professional staff					
Timber	0 (15)	4	0.52	0.89	1.06
Range-wildlife	0 (7)	4	0.96	0.98	0.79
Recreation	0 (31)	1.4	0.01	0.14	0.37
"General"	0 (31)	2	0.10	0.19	0.46
Other	0 (27)	1	0.10	0.19	0.35
Administrative[a]	1 (37)	1	1.00	1.00	0.00
Total professional staff	1 (1)	5	3.22	3.39	1.20
Technical staff, total	1 (10)	8	2.02	2.71	1.94
Clerical staff	0 (6)	3	1.45	1.44	0.88
Other (field crew, seasonals, and others)	0 (7)	22	6.00	6.36	6.01
Total district staff	2 (1)	31	13.30	13.90	7.95

Supervisory administrators ($N = 9$)

Budget[b]	$200,000 (1)	$1,656,000	$650,000	$768,222	$527,145
Professional staff[b]					
Timber	0 (3)	5	1.00	1.28	1.61
Range-wildlife	1 (4)	3.5	1.83	1.83	0.94
Recreation	0 (1)	2	0.97	0.93	0.72
"General"	0 (8)	4	0.25	0.44	1.33
Other	2 (1)	13	6.70	6.96	3.90
Administrative[c]	3 (4)	10	4.00	5.11	2.71
Total professional staff	7 (1)	32	16.00	16.44	7.95
Technical staff, total[b]	2 (1)	25	5.00	10.11	9.35
Clerical staff	3 (1)	24	6.00	8.56	6.42
Other (field crew, seasonals, and others)[b]	0 (5)	6.3	1.20	1.81	2.65
Total supervisor's staff[b]	18 (1)	82	30.00	37.14	22.06
No. of subunits supervised[b]	2 (1)	8	5.25	5.11	2.09

[a] The district ranger or area manager.
[b] Does not include district or resource area budget, staff.
[c] Includes forest supervisor or district manager.

Table 5-3. District Administrators' Prior Employment History

Experience prior to joining agency	No. of administrators	Percentage
College, with		
Summer employment, same agency	15	40.5
Summer employment, other land management agency	3	8.1
No relevant summer employment, but		
Ranch/farm family background	3	8.1
Military	2	5.4
No other relevant background	8	21.6
Military, with		
Prior college, summer employment, same agency	2	5.4
Prior college, no relevant summer employment	1	2.7
Employed by economic user firm, after college	1	2.7
Employed by other land management agency, with		
Prior college, ranch/farm family background	1	2.7
Prior college, no other relevant background	1	2.7
Total	37	99.9[a]

[a] Round-off error.

the ranger or area manager on their unit for three and a half years (see table 5-4). District administrators had been supervised by their current district manager or forest supervisor an average of two and a half years. All the BLM area managers and three-fifths of the eleven GS-12 rangers were stationed on NF1, the heavy timber forest in the sample; the other GS-12 rangers were not disproportionately stationed on the heavier timber districts of their forests.

Another important administrator characteristic, which anticipates the concerns of subsequent chapters, was the line officer's current organizational affiliations (see table 5-5). Most administrators belonged to a professional association, particularly the two most relevant land management associations—the Society of American Foresters (SAF) and the Society for Range Management (SRM). The higher number of SRM affiliations was not attributable solely to BLM or national grassland administrators; even administrators on heavy timber districts were SRM members. Several administrators, when asked about this pattern,[11] expressed dissatisfaction with SAF and the belief that SRM was more useful to lower-level administrators in land management agencies. (Research reports in the *Journal of Forestry,* for example, were more sophisticated,

Table 5-4. District Administrators' Agency Experience

Years with agency, range	No. (%)	Years in position	No. (%)	Years with present supervisor	No. (%)	GS rating	No. (%)
8–10	6 (16.2)	1	6 (16.2)	1	8 (21.6)	GS-11	26 (70.3)
11–12	12 (32.4)	2	9 (24.3)	2	12 (32.4)	GS-12	11 (29.7)
13–14	7 (18.9)	3	8 (21.6)	3	5 (13.5)	Total	37 (100.0)
15–16	7 (18.9)	5	6 (16.2)	4	12 (32.4)		
18–24	5 (13.5)	6	3 (8.1)	Total	37 (100.0)		
Total	37 (99.9)[a]	7	1 (2.7)				
		8	3 (8.1)				
		10	1 (2.7)				
		Total	37 (100.0)				

Mean = 13.3
Median = 12.6
Mode = 11
Std. Dev. = 3.5

Mean = 3.7
Median = 2.9
Std. Dev. = 2.4

Mean = 2.6
Median = 2.4
Std. Dev. = 1.2

Mean = 11.3
Median = 11.2
Std. Dev. = 0.46

[a] Round-off error.

Table 5-5. Group Affiliations of Local Line Officers

	Supervisory administrators		District administrators		Total	
Group type	No.	(No. indirect)[a]	No.	(No. indirect)[a]	No.	%
Local community contacts						
Fraternal (e.g., Lions, Elks)	7		27	(3)	34	18.7
Chambers of commerce	5		9	(2)	13	7.7
Professional associations						
SRM	9	(1)	24	(2)	33	18.1
SAF	5	(1)	17	(3)	22	12.1
Others	2		5		7	3.8
Clientele group organizations						
Wildlife federations	3	(1)	10	(5)	13	7.1
Sportsmen's/hunt and fish clubs	2	(1)	5	(2)	7	3.8
Wilderness/preservation associations	3	(3)	3	(2)	6	3.3
Sierra Club	1	(1)	2	(2)	3	1.6
Stockmen's associations	1	(1)	5	(2)	6	3.3

Recreation business firm/association	1	3	1.6
ORV, other recreational user club	2	1 (1)	1.6
State game and fish agency	0	1 (1)	0.5
Mining engineering association	0	1 (1)	0.5
Regulatory federal agency group	1	0 (1)	0.5
Personal affiliations			
Scouts	0	5	2.7
Church groups	0	6	3.3
Local government	0	4	2.2
Schools	0	3	1.6
Archeology/rockhound clubs	0	2	1.1
Other	1	5	3.3
No group affiliations	0	1	N.A.
Totals	**43**	**(11) 139 (27)**	**181**	**100.7**[b]

[a] "Indirect" affiliations are relevant memberships in a group by a line officer's staff subordinates.
[b] Round-off error.

and thus less practically useful, than research in the SRM journal.) Another interesting pattern was the heavy membership in two groups not directly related to local land management—fraternal organizations and chambers of commerce. When asked about these affiliations, administrators explained that these organizations were good ways to keep abreast of local community sentiment.[12] (The fraternal organizations also served a social function that is especially useful for men in the highly mobile land management profession.) Some administrators also belonged to groups that were part of their major clientele interests. A disproportionately high number of such affiliations were with environmental, conservation, and preservation groups.

However, recorded affiliation totals do not tell the whole story about conservation-type affiliations. Early in the interviewing it became apparent that many affiliations with clientele groups served a clearly understood intelligence function for the agencies. However, in many cases it was not the line officer, the official decision maker, who fulfilled this function by being a member of a clientele group, but his professional assistants. This was particularly true with the more "radical" preservation and environmental groups, the Sierra Club and the Wilderness Society. In some cases there was a close association between the second-ranking official in a district administrator's office and local clientele groups. For example, one assistant ranger was an officer in a local Sierra Club chapter and another was a whitewater canoeing partner of a Sierra Club leader. The conventional wisdom was that the younger rangers were philosophically predisposed to join such organizations and in many cases had been members before joining the Forest Service. More experienced officers joined organizations with the understanding that the affiliations would benefit the agency. One administrator who was on the board of a local recreation organization that had a permittee relationship with the agency explained, "Five years ago my membership would have been considered a conflict of interest; in this particular case I was 'encouraged' to join." In another case, a ranger was an officer of a state wildlife federation.

The only other type of group affiliation that needs elaboration (because of seeming conflict with civil service restrictions, such as those prohibiting partisan political activity) is the local government category, with four administrators' affiliations. Two rangers were active in organizing local, quasi-municipal fire departments, while two other administrators were members of county planning commissions.

Interest Group Affiliations

Local Forest Service and BLM administrators' "publics," as they are called, are composed of a fairly wide range of interest groups. During the fieldwork for this study, it was possible to identify about forty different types of interest groups involved in local federal lands politics in the three sample regions.[13] They included over 350 different formal organizations, which differed widely in size, organizational form, and interests in public land management. Before examining the relationships between these groups and the federal agencies, a brief description of these groups should be helpful.

Table 5-6 shows the group affiliations of those persons who were identified as important participants in local public lands politics in the sample regions (that is, those who were interviewed or sent questionnaires). Almost all 392 interest group people represented organizations. In many cases they represented fairly obvious groups, with constitutions, officers, and the other trappings of formal organizations. Such participants included presidents of local grazing associations composed of Forest Service permittees in given areas, presidents and conservation chairmen of local Sierra Club groups, and presidents of local chambers of commerce. In other cases the organization was not much more than the individual. Examples included owners of small timber mills, family ranches, or backcountry guide services. These individuals were sometimes informal spokesmen for similar firms in their areas. This was particularly true of ranchers. On most ranger districts that had no formally organized stockmens' associations, permittees had informal spokesmen (defined by the permittees, the rangers, and the spokesmen).[14] Only one person, an environmentalist gadfly, did not belong to any formal group.

In most cases the primary affiliation was fairly clear-cut: a timber mill owner would fall into the timber firm category, for example, not into the Society of American Foresters (SAF) category, even though he might also be a member of SAF. In a few cases the definition of a primary affiliation was more difficult. Suppose, for example, an individual were a contact of the Forest Service as a grazing association president and a BLM contact as a member of the district advisory board. In such a case —and this example was the most common—defining either the grazing association or the BLM advisory board as the primary affiliation would be somewhat artificial.[15]

Table 5-6. Group Affiliations of Interest Group Participants

Group type	Primary N	Secondary N	Total N	Total %
Livestock industry				
Grazing associations, individual stockmen	108	103	211	24.6
BLM or FS advisory board members	11	31	42	4.9
Public lands councils	0	6	6	0.7
Farmers organizations	0	6	6	0.7
Timber industry				
Forest products firms, associations	36	39	75	8.8
Other economic interests				
Mineral/O&G firms/associations	32	26	58	6.8
Chambers of commerce, businessmen	25	31	56	6.5
Conservation districts (RC&D, soil conservation, etc.)	5	12	17	2.0
Water/irrigation firms/associations	10	4	14	1.6
Realtors	7	4	11	1.3
Contractors	2	3	5	0.6
Utilities, utility associations	4	1	5	0.6
Other special use permittees	0	5	5	0.6
Environmentalists				
Wildlife federations	9	22	31	3.6
Sierra Club	9	11	20	2.3
Wilderness/preservation groups	3	12	15	1.8
General or local environmental groups	6	18	24	2.8
Animal protection group, garden club	2	2	4	0.5
Recreational interests				
Recreation-related firms/associations	14	12	26	3.0
Sportsmen, NRA, hunt-fish clubs	8	15	23	2.7
Off-road-vehicle clubs	12	4	16	1.9
Tourism/booster associations	3	8	11	1.3
Scouts	3	0	3	0.4
Search and rescue organizations	3	3	6	0.7
Summer home permittees/associations	2	1	3	0.4
Other recreational user clubs	4	3	7	0.8
Other interests				
Government				
Local government	27	21	48	5.6
Schools (and teaching occupation)	9	14	23	2.7
State game and fish agencies	11	2	13	1.5
Federal agency (present/prior employer)	0	8	8	0.9
Political party	0	4	4	0.5

(continued)

Table 5-6. (continued)

Group type	Primary N	Secondary N	Total N	Total %
Professional				
SRM	1	3	4	0.5
SAF	0	2	2	0.2
Historical society, other professional associations	2	8	10	1.2
Professional individuals (e.g., lawyer, physician)	1	5	6	0.7
Archeologists	3	0	3	0.4
Fraternal, social, church/religious organizations	3	8	11	1.3
Media	9	1	10	1.2
Indian tribe, other minority associations	5	0	5	0.6
Poverty/charitable organizations	3	2	5	0.6
Other	0	4	4	0.5
Totals	392	464	856	100.2[a]

[a] Round-off error.

The largest single category of groups was the rancher–grazing associations, with over one-quarter of all participants. When BLM advisory board members, all of whom were ranchers, are included, the importance of the livestock industry in the three regions is evident.[16] The next level of groups, in terms of number of individual affiliations, included the timber industry, minerals or oil and gas firms and associations, local government agencies, and local chambers of commerce and businesses. None of the environmental or recreation organizations had many affiliations: the largest number were in the recreational user categories, particularly recreation-oriented businesses and ORV groups. However, environmentalists, at 7.4 percent of all participants, and recreationists, at 12.5 percent, were represented at levels equivalent to other types of participants. Other groups with significant representation included state game and fish agencies, water or irrigation groups, the media, schools, and realty agencies.

Half of the interest group participants' primary affiliations were their occupations. Those in the occupational affiliation category included almost all participants in the economic user categories except those in the livestock industry whose primary affiliations were grazing associations. Another 28 percent of primary affiliations were *related* to participants' occupations. The largest group in this category was the livestock industry; neither grazing associations nor advisory boards were sources of income for participants for which they were primary affiliations, but the associations' and boards' activities were closely related to the participants' occupation of ranching. Only 21 percent of participants' affiliations were unrelated to their occupations. This included most of the environmental, conservation, preservation, and recreation group participants, but not recreation-related businessmen. Only two voluntary association participants were paid, professional interest group staffers.

Many participants also had secondary group affiliations, including memberships in other groups, occupations that were not their primary affiliations, and other relationships. As the totals indicate, each participant could have more than one secondary affiliation, and participants frequently had two or more secondary affiliations of the same type. For example, one individual had secondary affiliations on district, state, and national BLM advisory boards. However, the data on secondary affiliations are not an accurate reflection of all participants' affiliations. The information on interviewees is fairly complete, but questionnaire respondents treated the affiliation question in a rather haphazard way. A few failed to list important affiliations that were already known from interviews with administrators. In most nonrespondents' cases, only primary affiliations were known.

The pattern of interest group participants' secondary affiliations was very similar to that of their primary affiliations, for the simple reason that their secondary affiliations were usually in the same interest set as their primary. Timber mill operators belonged to forest products associations like the Federal Timber Purchasers Association and the Western Forest Industries Association; grazing association presidents, to state stockmen's associations; local wildlife club officers, to the state or national wildlife federations, and so forth. There were, of course, many cases of secondary affiliations that differed from the primary, including a few ranchers who were members of wildlife federations (an unusual combination, since the wildlife federations are leading critics of livestock grazing programs on the public lands). Perhaps the most unusual combination belonged to the participant whose secondary affiliations included the Farm Bureau and the United Mine Workers union; while these affiliations were perfectly appropriate for the individual, the organizations are rather politically divergent.

Participants with local government secondary affiliations had a special importance. (The local government category included both elective and

5: LOCAL LAND MANAGEMENT/THE ACTORS

administrative or executive positions.) A significant number of these participants, especially in State C, were elected officials, particularly county commissioners, with livestock industry affiliations (BLM advisory boards and grazing associations). The relatively large number of rancher–polticians reflected the one-economy background of many of these areas. Such individuals probably had a bit more clout with the agencies because of the agencies' ethic (or at least rhetoric) of intergovernmental cooperation.

Industry User Groups

The first three sets of groups in table 5-6 share a direct economic interest in public lands management. Groups in the livestock industry, forest products industry, and other economic interests categories are composed of business firms or associations of firms that depend on public land uses to varying degrees. Since many of these groups have played important roles in public lands policymaking for many years, as noted in earlier chapters, it is important to understand their interests and organizational characteristics.

The Livestock Industry

The interest group with the most leaders in the sample, the stockmen, has the longest history of involvement in public lands management. Rancher–Forest Service contacts over range management policy began almost immediately after the agency was established. Relations became heated in the 1920s because of conflicts about range permit cuts and grazing fees, and those conflicts were one reason many ranchers supported management of the public domain range lands by the Department of the Interior in the 1930s. After the Grazing Service was created in 1934, stockmen soon became intimately involved in local grazing district policies via the district grazing advisory boards. More than any other group, contemporary stockmen are aware of their long history of dealings with federal land managers. Stockmen's group leaders often speak about the imposition of federal management of the public range as if it occurred last year (in contrast to some other activists, especially environmentalists, who seem to think of last year's conflicts as ancient history). This well-developed sense of history is understandable, since many current range management issues date back to the earlier era of public land management.

There are two major types of stockmen's organizations active at the local level in public lands politics. The first is the grazing association. Members of local grazing associations are those several dozen permittees on the local Forest Service grazing allotments. The associations are organized to work out the details of local grazing management with local rangers. Although the associations have elected officers, bylaws, and so forth, they are loosely organized, with informal operating styles, since the permittees usually know one another quite well. Association officers are thus best thought of as only slightly formalized spokesmen for their fellow ranchers. (As noted above, stockmen on some allotments are not formally organized into associations; in such cases, it is common for a few permittees to act as informal spokesmen for all the permittees in the area.) The second type of local stockmen's organization is the BLM district grazing advisory board. The boards are established by BLM administrators, but board members are elected by the grazing licensees on a BLM district, and they act as spokesmen for local ranchers. The Forest Service and BLM have played important roles in organizing the grazing associations and advisory boards. For this reason, the relationships between these stockmen's organizations and the agencies will be treated in more detail in the examination of public participation in chapter 8.

State stockmen's associations provide their members with a variety of specialized services and are active in agricultural policymaking at the state level. When the state associations become involved in service or bureau policy, it is usually with Forest Service regional offices or BLM state offices. The state associations are normally uninvolved in local public lands matters. Though many Forest Service permittees and BLM licensees are members of their state stockmen's associations, only two interest group participants in the study sample had primary affiliations with state stockmen's associations; one was a state association executive director with relatively infrequent contacts with local Forest Service officials, and the other was a state association president who was primarily the informal spokesman for permittees who were not organized into a local grazing association.

Most of the stockmen's groups in local public lands politics are very small organizations, popular allusions to cattle barons notwithstanding. (See table 5-7 for a comparison of the size of stockmen's groups with that of other types of interest groups.[17]) Most local grazing associations have very low annual budgets, usually less than $1,000, and memberships of thirty to sixty ranchers. The typical grazing association in the sample employed, at most, a range rider or part-time secretary working three to four hours per week. The indicators of stockmen's organizations' size in table 5-7 are affected by a few large state stockmen's associations with several thousand members and large budgets.[18] The data on the few stockmen who were treated as heads of their ranching businesses show that ranches are one of the smallest categories of firms dealing with the public lands agencies.

Forest Products Industry

Almost all the timber industry organizations in local public lands politics are individual businesses, and in the study sample, almost all were owner-operated. A few of the timber operators in the sample were *gypos,* a term commonly applied by foresters to one-man logging operators.[19] But most operators headed medium-sized businesses with average annual sales of over $1 million dollars (see table 5-7). Local forest products firms usually had their own mills, in which logs were processed into lumber and other products (for example, poles and, in one case, pulp), and employed woods crews to fell trees and transported the logs to the mill. The timber firms in the sample employed an average of about one hundred people and were often the largest employers in the small towns in which they operated. However, only a small number of their staff members (fewer than four, on average) were of professional or managerial level, usually only the owner, business manager, and perhaps a forester.

Most timber firm operators belonged to one or more national or regional industry associations, usually the Federal Timber Purchasers Association, the Western Wood Products Association, or the National Forest Products Association. These are typical trade associations, in the sense that their members are business firms, not individuals. Since these member firms obtain a large proportion of their timber from federal lands, especially those in the Federal Timber Purchasers Association, most are very interested in Forest Service timber policymaking. However, the trade associations in the sample were rarely involved in local rangers' affairs. Only one timber industry participant in the sample was a trade association representative, and he dealt primarily with the Forest Serv-

Table 5-7. Interest Group Resources of Selected Groups, 1973

Group membership

Selected groups[a]	Means
Grazing and stockmen's associations (43)	228
Chambers of commerce (11)	95
Water/irrigation associations (6)	150
Sierra Club chapters/groups (3)	525
Wildlife federations (7)	823
Sportsmen's clubs (4)	73
ORV clubs (6)	47
All groups (107) [median = 39]	306

Firms' gross dollar volume

Selected industry groups[a]	Means
Forest products firms (22)	$1,716,800
Livestock operators (8)	124,125
Mining/oil and gas firms (13)	86,118,000
Recreation-related firms (7)	350,000
Realtors (4)	1,543,250
Water/irrigation firms (2)	145,000
Utilities (2)	25,500,000
Contractors (2)	6,500,000
All firms (65) [median = $440,000]	18,953,000

Group budget

Selected groups[a]	Means
Grazing and stockmen's associations (39)	$20,205
Chambers of commerce (10)	21,610
Water/irrigation associations (3)	32,850
Sierra Club chapters/groups (3)	24,078
General environmental groups (3)	17,533
Wildlife federations (6)	5,275
Sportsmen's clubs (4)	1,931
ORV clubs (5)	350
Local governments (9)	277,425
Schools (3)	421,333
State game and fish agencies	533,419
All groups (107) [median = $4,000]	90,427

Staff size

Selected groups[a]	Professional/managerial staff, means	Other employees, means
Forest products firms/associations (23)	3.8	93.7
Stockmen's associations/firms (24)	1.9	2.9
Mineral/oil and gas firms (14)	42.5	217.6
Recreation-related firms (7)	10.7	27.8
Water/irrigation firms/associations (4)	2.5	7.0
Sierra Club chapters/groups (3)	0.3	0.3
Wildlife, sportsmen, ORV clubs (6)	0.0	0.0
General environmental groups (2)	3.0	0.5
All groups (107) [medians = 2.0, 2.3]	14.9	64.7

[a] Numbers of cases with valid data in parentheses. Data drawn from interview or questionnaire responses of 245 group leaders. Also see note 17.

ice's regional office (which was located very close to one of the sample regions) on general timber sale and contract policy, rather than with district rangers.[20] In only one of the study's three sample regions were individual timber operators organized to deal with local Forest Service officials. The forest products operators in State A met informally once a month to socialize and discuss common concerns; and Forest Service officials were often invited to address these meetings.

Other Economic Interests

Unlike the homogeneous livestock and forest products categories, the other economic interests category contains a set of groups that vary considerably in their interests and organizational size and structure. For convenience, these groups will be described, in decreasing order, according to the degree of direct use they make of the public lands.

Like the livestock and forest products industries, mining and oil and gas companies are direct consumptive users of public lands resources. However, the minerals and oil and gas firms were the largest organizations represented in the sample, with annual gross dollar volumes averaging $86 million and number of employees averaging 260. Even the smaller minerals companies are large by public lands standards; for example, a fairly representative owner-operated coal company had an annual gross volume several times greater than the $1.6 million mean gross of all nonmining firms represented in the sample. Mining operators in the sample regions were engaged in both exploration and extraction; in a few cases, the firms' mills were also located near sample public lands units. Almost all the mining firms represented in the sample were exploring for or extracting so-called energy minerals—oil and gas, coal, and uranium. Some of the mining participants were members of mining trade associations, but these associations were relatively inactive in local public lands management; the only noncorporate mining industry participant was the manager of a state mining association.

Utilities and contracting companies had the fewest representatives in the other economic interests category. Like mining firms, contracting companies and utilities have contractual user relationships with the land management agencies, although their uses are not strictly consumptive and they are not so economically dependent on the public lands as other user groups. The utilities obtain special use permits from the agencies for transmission lines or communication facilities, such as telephone lines and microwave relay stations, while contracting companies do the actual construction work for state highway or county road departments on rights-of-way across federal lands.[21] Utilities' and contractors' special uses are less complicated than other public land uses because they are short term, in contrast to, for example, on-going timber sales programs or long-term mining operations. The utilities in the sample were medium to large firms, such as local electrical cooperatives. The contractors represented in the sample were smaller operators, but were still large in comparison with other public lands users.

The water or irrigation groups were consumptive users, since they used water flowing from watersheds (usually Forest Service). Their use of the public lands was less direct than that of the timber, livestock, and mining industries, however, because it did not require a contractual relationship with the public lands agencies. If water impoundments and other structures were located off the public lands, the users did not need agency permits to consume water flowing from those lands. Water users included those providing water for domestic or industrial use and those providing water for irrigation of agricultural lands. Domestic or industrial water was usually provided by a governmental entity, such as a municipal water department. Irrigation water, in contrast, was provided by private concerns; some were incorporated firms, while others were voluntary associations. Aside from the legal differences and some differences in size (see table 5-7), the irrigation firms and associations were quite similar —both were organized to provide irrigation water to farmer–ranchers in their locales. Many of those irrigation beneficiaries, moreover, were also grazing permittees or licensees of the Forest Service or BLM.

The last three types of groups in the other economic interests category had less direct interests in the public lands. Realtors came in contact with the public lands agencies because their clients were public lands users. In a few areas in which there were many summer homes under federal permit on public lands, the agency, usually the Forest Service, would be involved in sales of such homes. Since the Forest Service was phasing out second-home permits, this was a declining source of business. More importantly, realtors were also involved in ranch transactions. The importance of federal grazing permits to the market value of ranch properties brought realtors into frequent contact with public land managers. Finally, one realtor in a small town in which a forest supervisor's and district ranger's offices were located joked that, because of the service's transfer policy, Forest Service personnel themselves were a major source of business. Although the realty firms in the sample had good annual sales ($1.5 million), they were small, owner-operated firms with few salesmen.

Groups in the next category, conservation districts, had even less direct interests in public lands management. The most common were Rural Conservation and Development (RC&D) and soil conservation districts, and there were twice as many RC&D as soil conservation district participants in the sample. The RC&D program provides federal assistance to local sponsoring groups in multicounty areas. RC&D planning and development projects are funded for a wide variety of purposes, from agricultural or industrial water development, to agricultural marketing and processing, to environmental and soil conservation. The soil conservation districts attempt to prevent erosion and improve agricultural land by encouraging proper agricultural practices, as well as small watershed development projects. Both programs are primarily administered by the Department of Agriculture's Soil Conservation Service.[22] At the time of the field research, the service was involved in the RC&D program primarily because it was a Department of Agriculture program. Since the areas affected by RC&D and soil conservation programs in the sample regions included high proportions of federal lands, the programs frequently affected public as well as private lands and benefited the clients of the public lands agencies. The agencies viewed their dealings with the conservation districts as a form of community relations, since the districts were generally represented by community notables. The large number of secondary affiliations held by participants with conservation districts primary affiliations (table 5-6) shows that many of these participants had other clientele relationships with the agencies.

Local businessmen, the second largest group of participants in the other economic interests category, had the most peripheral relationships with the agencies. This group included individual businessmen, such as bankers and merchants, as well as officers of local chambers of commerce. These participants had no significant direct business dealings with the agencies, but were concerned about agency policy because it affected their customers in those industries that used the public lands directly. The agencies view their relationships with local businessmen and chambers of commerce as another forum for community relations, and (as noted earlier) many local Forest Service and BLM administrators actively participate in chambers of commerce for this reason. With average memberships of ninety-five businesses and annual budgets of $21,610, the chambers are potentially very influential.

Nonindustry Interests

Two characteristics distinguish the remaining groups in public lands politics from most of the groups discussed thus far. Most are not economically oriented organizations, and most are voluntary associations. These groups may conveniently be considered in three categories: conservation or environmental groups, recreation-related organizations, and a diverse set of other groups.

The Environmentalists

As suggested in earlier chapters, several groups of an environmentalist, conservationist, or preservationist character have been involved in public lands politics sporadically since the turn of the century. After a period of relative quiescence during the Great Depression and World War II, the national conservation groups rediscovered the public lands in the 1950s, and they began playing increasingly active roles in local public lands politics, especially after Earth Day 1970.

The oldest and best organized of the environmental groups—and for many the archetypal environmental group—is the Sierra Club. Founded by John Muir in 1892, club members were initially concerned with preservation of scenic areas of the Sierra Nevada mountains of California.[23] More recently, and especially in the 1970s, the club has broadened into a national organization (164,000 members in 1976) involved in the full range of environmental issues, including air and water pollution, water resources development, and nuclear energy, in addition to natural area preservation. Club members, however, have retained their interest in backcountry recreation, especially hiking and backpacking, and many members joined the club to participate in its outings rather than its political programs. The club is well-organized nationally; in addition to its San Francisco headquarters staff, it had (in 1975) a five-person Washington staff, nine regional professional staffers, the Sierra Club Foundation (a tax-deductible organization that finances educational and scientific projects in support of the club's explicitly political programs), and the six-attorney Sierra Club Defense Fund. Locally, the club is organized into forty-five chapters, many of which are further divided into groups; the chapters and groups are the levels most involved in local public lands issues.

While the Sierra Club is often seen as the most "extremist" environmental group, the organization with the most narrowly preservationist goals (and thus the most extreme in terms of the philosophical continuum discussed in chapter 1) is the Wilderness Society. Organized in 1935 —primarily by Forest Service recreational staff professionals—the Wilderness Society had a professional staff of ten in its Washington office, plus twelve regional staffers, in 1975. In contrast with the Sierra Club's hierarchical structure, the Wilderness Society is primarily a national organization (with 90,000 members in 1975). Local wilderness groups, usually called wilderness study committees, have only informal relationships with the national Wilderness Society, although most local committees' members are also members of the national society.

The largest environmental group nationally is the National Wildlife Federation, with a membership of 3.5 million in 1972. Organized in 1936, the federation had a national staff of fifteen in 1975, supplemented by nine regional staff members. The national federation is affiliated with state wildlife federations in every state, plus Puerto Rico, the Virgin Islands, and Guam; many state affiliates also have full-time staff. Since most members of the federation and its affiliates are hunters or fishermen, local federation leaders are usually more narrowly interested in public lands range and wildlife management issues than other environmental activists. (The federation's national staff, however, is involved in the same mix of issues as those of other mainline environmental groups). Since its members are predominantly sportsmen, the federation has a much higher proportion of blue-collar workers among its members than the Sierra Club and Wilderness Society (which are composed largely of college-educated people in professional or managerial positions). The wildlife federations had the most affiliations among the environmental groups in the sample regions.

The "general environmental group" category in table 5-6 includes organizations that were organized about the time environmentalism became a national movement (roughly 1970). Environmental Action and Friends of the Earth are national organizations representative of this type of group. However, the general environmental groups in the sample were local or regional groups, and were usually active in a broad range of environmental issues, not just public lands.[24] Thus, the general environmental groups were comparable to Sierra Club chapters or groups in their interests and the scope of their activities, although they were not formally affiliated with any national environmental group.

One of the "general environmental groups" listed in table 5-6 could more properly be termed a local, *ad hoc* environmental group. Such groups are organized around a specific local issue, and are often composed of homeowners opposed to some controversial project in their vicinity (in the case of the group in our sample, opposition to a Forest Service development). The best-known example of a local, *ad hoc* group is the Scenic Hudson Preservation Conference, which was organized to oppose the Storm King pumped-storage power plant in New York State.[25]

The final two groups in the environmental category were an animal protectionist group and a local garden club. Animal protectionist groups are interested in preserving particular threatened species from human activities; representative national animal protectionist organizations are Friends of Animals and the American Horse Protection Association. These groups are somewhat out of the mainstream of the environmental movement because of their narrow focus on certain species, rather than on the ecosystem of which they are part. Moreover, most animal protectionist groups are strongly opposed to hunting. Garden clubs are, likewise, not active, hard-core environmental interest groups, but social and horticultural organizations.

As can be seen in table 5-7, local environmental groups in the sample had large memberships but modest organizational resources. The Sierra Club and wildlife federation memberships were generally larger than the average for the sample, but their budgets and staffs were smaller. (The Sierra Club budget average was inflated by the presence in one region of a large, atypical Sierra Club entity: the average of the other club chapters' or groups' budgets was $1,117.) In general, environmentalists—as well as the recreationist voluntary associations discussed below—had organizational resources that were significantly inferior to those of the consumptive user groups. However, such a comparison is misleading because most of the resources of large consumptive user firms were devoted to apolitical business activities; millions of a major oil company's dollars were not being funneled into an effort to break some ranger's resistance to the corporate will. Since local environmental groups' resources were more focused on natural resources politics, those groups had more influence per dollar or staff person than industry groups. Administrator and interest group interviewees in the State B city that contained all the full-time professional environmental group staffers in the sample believed the environmentalists were richer and better staffed than their opponents in the region's forest products and livestock industries—even though the industries' dollar and employee totals actually far exceeded those of the environmentalists.

Recreationist Groups

The recreationist set of groups is more heterogeneous than the environmentalist. It contains some business firms as well as voluntary associations, and represents quite diverse interests. The three most important types of recreationist groups are the sportsmen's clubs, recreational businesses, and ORV clubs.

The sportsmen's groups include local rod and gun clubs and an affiliate of the National Rifle Association (NRA). (The NRA's membership in rural areas is, of course, composed largely of hunters.) These groups are not formed for explicitly political purposes, but as outdoor recreation clubs. However, some of their leaders in the sample were also active environmentalists; three were officers of Izaak Walton League affiliates (the Izaak Walton League is a mainline environmental group), and three others were officers of state wildlife federations. In fact, except for the leaders of two remaining rod and gun clubs, the sportsmen's groups might have been appropriately listed with the wildlife federations among the environmental groups. As strictly local organizations, the sportsmen's groups in the sample had small memberships (an average of seventy-three members) and budgets (an average of $1,900) and no paid staff. Except for the one NRA affiliate, the groups had no formal links with national organizations.

The largest set of organizations in the recreationist category is the recreational firms group. There were two major types of recreational firms in the study's sample, ski areas operating under Forest Service permit, ranging from small, local areas to a major, nationally known area, and backcountry or river-running guide and outfitting operations on BLM and Forest Service units. The recreation firms were generally small in terms of annual sales and total employees, but there was a sizable variation among the firms, from large ski areas with annual gross volumes over $1 million down to small owner-operated guide services. There was also a difference in the fundamental interests of the two types of firms. Ski areas are generally caught up in the environmentalist-versus-developer conflicts of natural resources politics, as earlier discussions of the Mineral King controversy, for example, indicate. However, backcountry guides generally depend on the scenic and wilderness character of the public lands for their livelihood, and thus often have as strong an interest in preservation as the Sierra Club or Wilderness Society.

Tourism and booster associations are the recreationist counterparts of chambers of commerce. Tourism associations attempt to promote the interests of their member recreational and tourist firms (for example, motels and cabins); a common service of such associations is the operation of an information booth on a town's main street to refer tourists to member firms. Since many recreational and tourist firms derive their income from the scenic character of nearby public lands, tourism associations are often less stridently prodevelopment than are chambers of commerce. The few local tourism associations in the sample were comparable to local chambers of commerce in terms of membership and budget, however.

The third type of recreationist group, off-road vehicle clubs, is more homogeneous than sportsmen and recreational firm groups. Whether composed of motorcyclists, four-wheelers (four-wheel-drive vehicle operators), or snowmobilers, ORV clubs share an interest in open access to the public lands. Unlike some members of recreation firms and many sportsmen, few ORV club leaders have contacts with conservation groups, and environmentalists are generally hostile to ORV use.[26] ORV groups in the sample were local organizations, with small memberships and budgets.

A mélange of minor types of groups are also included in the recreationist category. Some Boy Scout and Girl Scout leaders have contacts with the Forest Service because some Scout camps are located on national forest land. Search and rescue groups are included in the recreationist category even though they are not recreationist interest groups per se, but volunteer organizations that help rangers or local sheriffs locate people lost on the public lands. Some organizations in the sample represented people with Forest Service permits for second or summer homes on federal lands. There were few such groups in the sample, however, in large part because of the service's phasing out of these permits. Finally, the other recreational user category includes trail riders, snow and water skiers, mountaineers, spelunkers, and rockhounds. In the sample regions, only the first four types of recreationists were formally organized into clubs listed in table 5-6; although spelunkers and rockhounds actively used some public lands in the sample, they had no formal dealings with administrators.

As noted above, the recreationist groups are a diverse lot. In the three sample regions, many recreationists were closely aligned with environmental groups. (In addition, of course, many environmentalists are themselves outdoor recreationists; many public lands administrators, in fact, think of environmentalists as just militant recreationists.) Most sportsmen's group members (as well as a couple of people in the smaller recreationist categories) were formally affiliated with environmentalist groups, and many backcountry guides and outfitters shared certain interests with the preservationist groups. Because of the Mineral King case, the ski industry nationally is widely regarded as an opponent of environmentalists. However, many individual ski area operators are allies of environmentalists; a prominent example is Bob Parker, one of the principals in Vail Associates and a preservationist litigant in a major court test of Forest Service Wilderness policy. The operators of the two largest ski areas in the sample regions had environmentalist views and one, who was among the most vociferously conservation-oriented individuals interviewed for the study, worked closely with environmentalists in his region.[27] Only ORV groups had no common interests or formal ties with environmentalists. However, at the time of the field research, controversy over ORV use was relatively muted (and there were no active conflicts between environmentalists and ORV users in the sample regions). Real confrontation between environmentalists and ORV groups developed after 1973, when the agencies embarked on a policy of closing large tracts of federal land to ORV use.[28] In short, it is often useful to think of recreationists as complementing the environmentalists in the sample, even though recreationist groups (especially ORVers) are not universally allied with environmental groups in national public lands politics.

Other Interests

The last set of groups listed in table 5-6 is a catch-all category of organizations with few common interests or characteristics. The type of organization in this category with the most interest group participants was governmental bodies. Most local government participants were mayors, county commissioners, or state legislators. Local government officials are not interested in the federal lands out of vague commitment to intergovernmental cooperation. As community leaders, they are concerned with the welfare of their constituents in those industries that use the public lands directly. Moreover, local governments have a financial stake in the federal lands because of the payments returned to local governments in lieu of *ad valorem* property taxes.[29] Local school administrators have a similar fiscal interest in public land uses, since school districts also rely on property tax revenue. (In addition, the agencies have an information and education relationship with school districts, since Forest Service and BLM officers occasionally visit local schools to give "Smokey the Bear talks" on fire safety, conservation, and so forth.)

The agencies also deal with a number of state-level administrative agencies. The most important of these are the state fish and game departments, which (as noted in chapter 3) regulate wildlife populations on federal lands through the issuance of hunting permits. Because these departments have a conservationist tradition and a primary interest in wildlife management, as opposed to other public lands uses, they often act in concert with conservationist interest groups, especially sportsmen's clubs and wildlife federations. As shown in table 5-7, the budgets of state government agencies, school districts, and local governments were the largest in the sample and comparable to annual gross dollar volume of the median business firm.

Few interest group participants were affiliated with professional associations, the next "other interests" group. The group with the most participants consisted of archeologists, all of whom were university professors who dealt with public lands officers in charge of areas where the archeologists had active field research projects. The most relevant land management professional associations, the Society of American Foresters (SAF) and the Society for Range Management (SRM), had few members not employed by federal agencies[30]; the only participant whose primary affiliation was with SRM was a state university extension range scientist. The only other professional association participant—listed with a local historical society president in table 5-6—was the chapter president of a mining engineers' association who also worked for a mining company.

A number of group members had contacts with local public land managers as a result of agency public relations efforts. Local fraternal organizations often provide an informal meeting ground for community leaders; in one sample region, the dominant local church served essentially that function. As noted in chapter 4, public land managers are encouraged to join local clubs and church groups to maintain good community relations, just as they are encouraged to join chambers of commerce and cooperate with local government officials. Native American and other minority organizations also provide a special community relations link for public land managers in areas with large minority populations. Finally, local journalists play an important role in local administrators' public relations efforts.

Group Attitudes About Public Lands Issues

It is commonly assumed that members of groups with shared interests in a particular policy arena also share preferences about its policy issues. The preceding sections often make that assumption (as, for example, in referring to the environmentalist position on an issue). During the field research, participants were asked a series of questions to determine their (and by inference their groups') views on public lands policy issues and policy-making processes. Responses of group leaders and agency administrators to those questions help illustrate the relative positions of different interests on the issues that make up the political substance of public lands debates.

Specific Attitudes

The first set of questions dealt with interest group participants' and administrators' views about some controversial practices in public lands management: clear-cutting, designating more Wilderness areas, current mineral exploration practices, unrestricted ORV use, predator controls, increased grazing fees, increased allowable cuts and carrying capacities, and giving preference to local economic considerations in policymaking. The questions called for responses ranging from zero, "strong support," through 8, "strong opposition".[31] The overall responses to these questions are not very instructive in themselves because the questions were intended to measure differences in attitudes, not to poll public opinion about agency policies. Moreover, the average responses to most questions fell at about the midpoints of the attitude scales and the differences between the average responses are neither substantively nor statistically significant. (The distribution of responses is shown in appendix B.) However, because many responses were obtained in interviews, it is possible to elaborate on the reasons for typical responses.

Only the "local economy preference" and ORV use questions produced average responses very different from the scale midpoint. Respondents seemed to view policies that benefited the local economy as "motherhood" types of policies; thus, respondents usually agreed, although often with reservations, with the question. The ORV question, on the other hand, provoked strong opposition. ORV clubs have few friends among other users of public lands: administrators and conservationists fear heavy ORV-caused resource damage; timber operators warn of the danger created by ORVs on logging roads; stockmen allege ORVs scare their cattle; and ORVs offend the sensibilities of preservationists and backcountry hikers. Thus, ORV respondents and those who gave a fair-minded response (by observing that all have an equal right to use public lands) were offset by those who had little or no use for ORVs.

The clear-cutting question usually evoked a professional-technical response, especially from foresters in both the Forest Service and the forest products industry. Foresters usually answered with a "weak favor" or "mixed" response, and invariably elaborated with an explanation of shade-intolerant species' regeneration behavior. Even some conservationist activists, while expressing more reservations about the practice, gave the same sort of professional-technical elaboration to their answer.

The "current mineral exploration practices" item evoked reactions to the problems of the land management agencies dealing with the virtual *carte blanche* given to miners by the 1872 Mining Laws. The modal response ("weak favor") was typically accompanied by an expression of general support for continued mining, along with—especially among administrators—preference for more control over extractive uses, comparable to that over logging or domestic livestock grazing.

The "Wilderness" item produced the most clearly divided set of responses, and few participants were neutral or had no opinion on the question. Participants felt either more Wilderness should be designated or there was too much already. Needless to say, a large proportion of environmentalists fell into the former category and forest products industry participants into the latter.

The first livestock grazing issue among the attitude items concerned predator control programs. At the time of the field research, the use of certain kinds of predator controls—such as compound 1080, a poisoned bait, and "coyote getters," a bait-movement-activated cyanide gun—was quite controversial. Stockmen interviewees claimed the predator control techniques were effective and discriminated among predator species, and complained about the levels of their stock losses. (A National Wool-growers Association bumper sticker of the period reflecting this position urged, "Eat American lamb—five million coyotes can't be wrong.") Opponents often claimed that stock losses were exaggerated because

5: LOCAL LAND MANAGEMENT/THE ACTORS   175

losses to predators were reimbursed by a federal program, while other causes of loss were only a normal business risk, and that compound 1080 and "coyote getters" harmed other species such as eagles. (After the field research was completed, the use of certain predator control practices on federal lands was banned by presidential order.)

Interestingly (considering the history of the issue), ranchers gave fairly moderate responses to the second livestock-related question, that on "grazing fees." The field research took place a few years after the Forest Service and BLM began their phased implementation of the 1969 grazing fee increases. Stockmen generally indicated resignation to those increases.

In addition to the structured (or forced-choice) questions about controversial issues, the interviews and mail questionnaires contained questions designed to elicit in-depth descriptions of local public lands political processes from administrators and group leaders. The full range of responses to these questions will be presented in chapter 7 (especially in table 7-1). However, many individual responses to the questions seemed to reflect more ideological preconceptions than objective observations. Five semiideological patterns of responses were used along with the forced-choice attitude responses in the analysis of interest group participants' attitudes. These five patterns of responses to the question, "What are the most important factors in Forest Service and BLM decision making?" included charges that (*a*) public lands administrators were heavily influenced by environmentalist, conservationist, or recreationist interest group pressure; (*b*) administrators were overcommitted to wildlife or recreational use; (*c*) administrators were unduly influenced by or had capitulated to developmentalist pressure; (*d*) economic factors dominated agency policy considerations; and (*e*) the effect of agency actions favoring consumptive uses was destructive—"environmental rape," as the more colorful and outspoken critics liked to put it.

These responses were almost always offered by interest group leaders, of course, not agency administrators, and usually reflected groups' expressed opposition to aspects of the agencies' policies, rather than real differences in local administrators' policy decisions. Generally the more militant leaders of consumptive user groups saw the Forest Service and BLM as capitulating to conservationists and recreationists, while environmentalists saw the agencies as captured by the consumptive user groups or consumptive use doctrines. Thus, interest group participants mentioned only their opponents' pressure, and that mention was usually expressed as a charge that the pressure was excessive or improper. The five patterns were combined into a single measure of beliefs about "perceived group dominance" of the public lands agencies: patterns (*a*) and (*b*) were treated as one attitude, and patterns (*c*), (*d*), and (*e*) were treated as the opposite attitude.[32]

The Unidimensionality of Public Lands Attitudes

Observers of politics are fond of noting that public policy issues are horribly complex. Natural resources politics is indeed technically and administratively complicated, as earlier chapters have suggested. However, as also suggested earlier, beneath all the technically complex positions in public lands debates is a single continuum of natural resources philosophies extending from utilitarianism to preservationism. The responses of the participants to the questionnaire support this idea of a continuum.[33]

The statistical method of factor analysis was used to determine how many underlying attitudinal dimensions existed in the responses of the interest group participants and administrators to the questions discussed in the preceding section. Factor analysis uses the correlations among a set of variables to identify patterns of interrelationships, or factors, that exist in the data. (For example, if the first and second in a set of four attitude measures were highly related to one another but not to the third and fourth, and the third and fourth were closely related to one another but not to the first and second, then the first and second measures would have one underlying factor or attitudinal dimension, and the third and fourth would have another.) There are several common tests for determining the number of factors in a particular set of variables based on the factors' eigenvalue including: the *discontinuity test,* which retains the factors from the first step in the factor analysis before the point at which there is a clear, discontinuous drop-off in the magnitude of factors' eigenvalue; and the eigenvalue-one criterion, which retains those factors with eigenvalue greater than 1.0. The use of these criteria suggest that the attitude items discussed above are best summarized by only one factor because of the very large discontinuous drop in eigenvalue (2.88 less 1.26, or 1.62) after the first factor. (See table 5-8, especially footnote c. For a more detailed discussion of this factor analysis, see appendix B.) In short, the attitude measures reflect essentially a simple, one-dimensional set of beliefs about public lands issues.

5: LOCAL LAND MANAGEMENT/THE ACTORS

Table 5-8. The "Environmental-Utilitarian" Attitude Scale (Factor Matrix)

Attitude item	"E-U" scale (factor loadings)[a]
Predator control	0.642
Wilderness	0.613
Allowable cut/carrying capacity	0.556
Mineral exploration	0.545
Preference for local economy	0.498
Perceived group dominance[b]	0.463
Clear-cutting	0.378
Grazing fees	0.396
ORV use	0.124
Eigenvalue[c]	2.880

[a] "Factor loadings" are the correlations between the factor or "E-U scale" and the individual items; they are also used to weight the attitude variables in the computation of E-U scale scores for individual cases.

[b] The attitude item constructed from open-ended responses; see table B-2.

[c] Eigenvalue for the first initial unrotated factor; the factor accounts for 32 percent of the variance (9.0) among the nine variables. The second, third, and fourth initial factors had eigenvalue of 1.26, 1.01, and 0.85. For further details, see appendix B.

The relationships between specific attitude measures and the main dimension—which can be called, based on the philosophical continuum described in chapter 1, the Environmental-Utilitarian or E-U scale—are shown in table 5-8. The two attitude items that are most closely related to the E-U scale are the "predator control" and the "Wilderness" items, both highly controversial issues at the time of the field research. The "allowable cut–carrying capacity," "mineral exploration," "local economy preference," and "perceived group dominance" measures are also highly related to the factor, with factor loadings in the .5 range. Because of the controversial nature of the issue, the relatively low relationship of the "clear-cutting" item to the E-U scale is initially somewhat surprising; however, as mentioned earlier, a large number of interviewees—from timber firm owners to Forest Service officers to even Sierrans—gave professional-technical responses to this question. "Grazing fees" also has a low relationship to the E-U scale, and "ORV use" is very weakly related to it; for, as mentioned previously, many stockmen had become resigned to the 1969 fees increases, and ORV use was not a highly controversial issue in the sample regions at the time of the fieldwork.[34]

The E-U scale scores for individual group leaders and administrators provide good insight into the differences in attitudes among groups in the sample. Table 5-9 shows the group mean score on the E-U scale for

Table 5-9. Environmental-Utilitarian Scale Scores for Selected Groups

Group type	No.	Mean E-U scale score	Standard deviation
Forest products industry	26	−0.758	0.542
Grazing association, stockmen	63	−0.575	0.501
BLM advisory board	5	−0.816	0.715
Mineral/O&G firms	18	−0.629	0.537
Chambers of commerce, businessmen	18	−0.354	0.712
Water/irrigation firms/associations	7	−0.142	1.006
Sierra Club	8	+1.496	0.359
Wildlife federations	7	+1.255	0.357
Wilderness, general environmental, *ad hoc* environmental, archeological	8	+1.648	0.478
Sportsmen, hunt and fish clubs	5	+0.461	0.751
ORV clubs	7	−0.146	1.067
State game and fish agencies	8	+0.440	0.376
Recreation firms	9	+0.362	0.910
Local government	13	−0.241	0.629
Schools	6	−0.096	0.582
Media	4	−0.607	0.609
Forest Service	33	+0.513	0.424
BLM	13	+0.511	0.588

groups with more than just a few individuals in the sample. While the mean E-U score is zero (since so-called factor scores are "standardized" to a mean of zero and a standard deviation of 1.0), the real midpoint of the scale is higher: the average of the extreme scores (+2.44 and −1.92) is +.26, and the average of the six extreme group means (three group types with significant numbers of individuals at the two opposite ends of the scale) is +.41. Thus, using the taxonomy of philosophical positions presented in chapter 1, individuals with E-U scale scores less than zero might be called utilitarians, those with scores in the zero to +.7 range, progressive conservationists, and those with E-U scores greater than +1.0, environmentalists or preservationists. (The attitudinal midpoint of the E-U scale is about +.3 rather than zero because there are many more individuals in the −.6 to −.8 range than there are in the +1.0 range.)

The mean group scores on the E-U scale reflect the expected distribution of group attitudes. The major economic user groups have attitude scale scores in the utilitarian range: the forest products industry at −.76, livestock industry people (combining grazing associations, stockmen, and BLM and Forest Service advisory board members) at −.59, and the

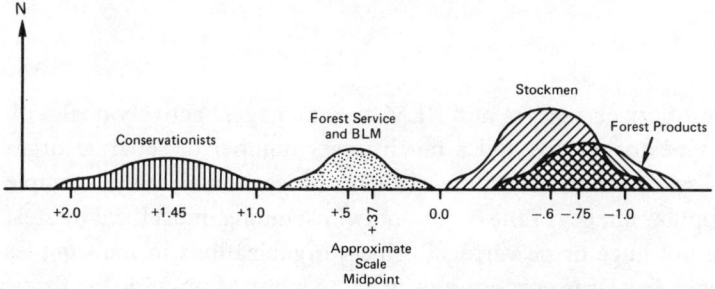

Figure 5-1. Selected groups' positions on E-U scale attitude dimension.

mineral and oil and gas industry at −.63. At the other end of the scale, the mainline environmental groups (Sierrans, wildlife federations, wilderness groups, general environmentalists, and others) have mean E-U scores in the +1.2 to +1.6 range, with several individuals having scores of +2.0 or more. The progressive conservation position at the scale midpoint is occupied by the conservation agencies (the service, the bureau, and state game and fish departments), sportsmen's groups, and recreation-related businessmen. The Forest Service and BLM means are identical, despite the popular image of the BLM as being more "developmentalist" than the service.

Most of the groups have reasonably homogeneous scale scores. Most, especially the major groups, have variance considerably less than 1.0. There are exceptions, of course: the irrigation groups, ORV groups, and recreation operator groups are spread widely, with some individuals in each group occupying environmentalist positions on the scale and some having utilitarian attitudes. One recreation operator had an E-U score in the Sierra Club range, while another had a score in the stockmen's range. However, most major groups have standard deviations in the .4 to .5 range. Figure 5-1 shows the importance of these small standard deviations. With a group mean of about 1.45 and a standard deviation of about .4, the environmentalists fall in the +1.0 to +2.0 range (except for one with a +2.4 score); with a mean of +.5 and a standard deviation of .5, most Forest Service and BLM administrators fall in the 0.0 to +1.0 range; most stockmen between 0.0 and −1.0; most forest products individuals between −.2 and −1.2; and so forth. In short, some of the most important sets of groups in the study occupy distinct spaces on the E-U scale attitudinal dimension.

Summary

Local Forest Service rangers and BLM area managers actively deal with dozens of types of groups and a much larger number of separate organizations—several hundred quite varied entities in only three sample regions. Popular images of the barons notwithstanding, most local interest groups are not huge or powerful. Business organizations in the samples ranged from a few large corporations down to many Mom-and-Pop firms. The active voluntary association ranged from small local clubs up to a few medium-sized groups, and their organizational resources from the modal "none" up to very modest budgets and staffs.

Figure 5-1, however, illustrates an important fact of life in local public lands politics: despite their heterogeneity, the participants in local public lands politics generally fall into three major blocs.

There are a number of important alliances among the consumptive users, and the livestock industry is usually at their center. Stockmen constitute the largest single category of participants in local public lands politics. They have ties to the professional community (including agency professionals) through the SRM. Many local government officials in the three regions, including a number of town mayors and most county commissioners, were stockmen; almost all the irrigation groups, and many of the conservation or RC&D districts, were led by or primarily served stockmen. Finally, stockmen were a primary constituency or customer group for all the local government officials, local businessmen, and realtors in the sample, irrespective of formal affiliations with the livestock industry. At the same time, local government and business leaders formed a bridge to the forest products industry, their other major constituency-customer group and other major traditional public lands user. Altogether, groups that were part of or generally allied with the livestock or forest products industries, or both, were represented by three-fifths (61.2 percent) of the group leaders in the sample.

Environmentalists are the core of the second bloc. Leaders of environmental groups share a number of interests (chiefly reservations about some of the agencies' consumptive use programs), irrespective of their specific public lands priorities. Environmental leaders often belong to several environmental groups, and frequently coordinate their activities. These individuals may accurately be thought of as environmentalists, rather than Sierrans, wildlife federationists, and so forth. Especially because of ties with the wildlife federations, groups like the state game and fish agencies, sportsmen, archeologists, and some recreationist firms and clubs are also linked to the environmentalist constellation.

The third set of participants in local land management, Forest Service and BLM officers, form a very cohesive bloc. Each agency's officers are, of course, formally integrated into tightly knit organizational structures and, as the attitude analysis indicates, the Forest Service's and BLM's officers have nearly identical views about public lands issues. That analysis also demonstrates that local land managers are caught between two polarized blocs of interest groups, with environmentalists in one bloc and the traditional user groups and their allies in the other. The group membership patterns of agency officers show that the officers try to maintain links with both blocs. However, the polarization of the two blocs creates a difficult political environment for local Forest Service and BLM land managers.

NOTES

1. This chapter also includes distributions for the data on administrator and interest group organizational resources and policy preferences that are used in the quantitative analysis presented in chapter 10 of this volume.
2. See Herbert Kaufman's *The Forest Ranger* (Baltimore, Md., Johns Hopkins University Press for Resources for the Future, 1960); Phillip Foss's *Politics and Grass* (Seattle, University of Washington Press, 1960); and chapter 1 of this volume, pp. 27–29.
3. The research was conducted with restricted travel funding, so interviews had to be conducted in a limited number of areas. These sampling criteria are similar to those in two major prior studies of local federal land management—Kaufman's *The Forest Ranger*, and Wesley Calef's *Private Grazing and Public Lands* (Chicago, Ill., University of Chicago Press, 1960). The sample used here included many more ranger districts than Kaufman's five, and about the same number of BLM districts as Calef's four. Phillip Foss's *Politics and Grass* (Seattle, University of Washington Press, 1960), the other major field study of the BLM, examined only one BLM district in detail.

Technically, the samping strategy is a "variance maximization" approach; see Adam Przeworski and Henry Teune, *The Logic of Comparative Social Inquiry* (New York, Wiley-Interscience, 1970) pp. 34–39. The purposive sampling procedure produced a diverse sample and was a practical necessity, but it did not produce a random sample. Thus, results of the study cannot be statistically generalized to the Forest Service or the BLM as a whole, although the sample units are representative. The study units may be treated technically as a population, rather than a sample of all Forest Service and BLM local units.

4. The use of not-for-attribution interviews was based on a belief that such interviews improve interviewee candor.

5. All output figures are from the author's field notes, from information provided by the Forest Service or BLM administrators.

6. Timber and grazing output data for the thirty-seven units were collected for a three-year period—FY1971, FY1972, and FY1973. The distributions of grazing outputs were similar in all three years because the same permittees and licensees received the same number of animal-unit-months year after year, with only occasional adjustments. The mean animal-unit-months for FY1971, FY1972, and FY1973 were 33,203, 33,030, and 32,440, respectively. Timber sales and cuts, however, could fluctuate considerably; year-to-year fluctuations of 6,000 to 9,000 MBF were common, and a few districts fluctuated by 20,000 MBF or more. Mean sales were 3,692 MBF in FY 1971, 5,036 MBF in FY 1972, and 4,347 MBF in FY 1973; the respective yearly cut means were 4,067, 5,272, and 4,922 MBF.

7. Similar categories, in terms of degree of protection, were counted together. For example, wilderness study areas (the bulk of the RARE areas) were counted together with the few pending full Wilderness recommendations. Some BLM areas were included in the primitive category. Administrators also considered four ORV closures or similar designations; counting the ORV category, only eleven administrators considered no special reservations.

8. All staffing figures are "full-time equivalent"; for example, six seasonal employees who worked for the four summer months counted as two full-time-equivalent staff $(6 \times 4/12 = 2)$. Fractional staff figures could be obtained if (1) the full-time-equivalent scoring of some seasonals did not result in a whole number (for example, seven four-month seasonals equals 2.3), or (2) the full-time professional or technical staff who were assigned to more than one functional category were coded as fractional assignments in their respective categories, for example, one whose first assignment was range-wildlife and whose second was recreation would be coded .7 range and .3 recreation). The full-time-equivalent basis qualifier is most relevant for field crews. The agencies, particularly the Forest Service, hire people to do fieldwork during the summer to watch for and fight fires, to construct special developments, to maintain campgrounds, and to perform other resource-related tasks.

9. This district included a major impounded lake that was used for both recreation and water supply. Even districts with major ski areas or major Wilderness did not have full-time, professional recreation staffers. So-called snow rangers, for example, are actually technician-grade employees.

10. Marion Clawson, *The Bureau of Land Management* (New York, Praeger, 1971) p. 56, gives general staffing figures for O&C districts. However, the BLM's five O&C districts sold 1,234,000 MBF in 1974, which is about six times more per BLM timber district than NF3's or NF4's sales.

11. The pattern is unexpected because SAF is the professional association of foresters, and Forest Service professionals (as well as many BLM professionals) are trained in forestry.

12. See the internal Forest Service memorandum "Managerial Development in the Forest," quoted by Kaufman, *Forest Ranger* (p. 174), on the longstanding Forest Service encouragement of rangers to join local "civic, fraternal, and religious organizations."

13. The groups were identified during interviews with local Forest Service and BLM field officers. See appendix A for a description of the methods used to obtain information on interest groups.

14. When there were no organized grazing associations, the names of the more important permittees were requested because of the practical impossibility of contacting all fifty to eighty ranchers in an area. Administrators were asked for spokesmen, however, only when they did not spontaneously identify one.

15. This is not so much a conceptual as a mechnical coding problem. In general, the primary affiliation was defined on the basis of an individual's relationship with the agency with which he had more contacts.

16. All eleven individuals with advisory board primary affiliations in table 5-6 were BLM board members. Eighteen of those with secondary advisory board affiliations sat on BLM boards, and thirteen sat on Forest Service boards. ("Secondary" organizational affiliations are explained on page 158.)

17. The data on which table 5-7 is based were collected on interest group leaders rather than organizations because of the needs of the analysis reported in chapter 10. In some cases, the procedure compromises the use of the data to describe organizational resources. First, for any given individual, some of the organizational resources categories are not applicable. For example, "group membership" and "budget" apply to a grazing association, but not "firms' gross." Thus, the missing cases in table 5-7 are more often "not applicable" than "no answer." Second, ranchers who were not officers in grazing associations were coded as members of organization with a membership of 1. Such coding would be absurd if the ultimate objective were to describe group membership, but it is reasonable when the intent is to use "organization membership" to indicate the contact's "group resources" or "power." Third, in a few cases the same organizational entity may have been coded on several participants' "group resources" categories. In constructing table 5-7, known cases of double listing were eliminated and the summary figures recalculated by hand.

18. As indicated by the large differences between means and medians (across all groups) in the various categories in table 5-7, the same holds true for most of the group types.

19. The etymology of the term *gypo* was unknown to several foresters questioned about the term. The term is a regionalism, perhaps a variation of *jeep-o*, since gypos typically operate with only a jeep or pick-up truck.

20. This staffer had only one or two contacts per year with any given ranger, far fewer than the twenty to fifty contacts of the typical timber operator with his relevant ranger. In truth, this staff man was "smuggled" into the sample; he was invited to sit in on an interview by an impor-

tant timber mill operator who had been included in the sample by the procedure described in appendix A.

21. The Forest Service also uses the term *contractor* to refer to gypo loggers who do silvicultural work (for example precommercial thinning) under contract to the agency. Two such small logging contractors are included within the timber industry category in table 5-6.

22. Some loans for the RC&D program are financed through another Agriculture agency, the Farmers Home Administration. See General Services Administration, *United States Government Manual, 1976–77* (Washington, D.C., GPO, May 1976) pp. 106 and 127–129.

23. Though some research is currently in progress on the subject, very little descriptive information has been published on environmental interest groups. The best overall description is probably still CEQ's survey, *Environmental Quality—1973* (Washington, D.C., GPO, September 1973) chap. 8. Some specific facts cited in this and following paragraphs (such as the founding date of the Sierra Club) come from Gloria Decker, ed., *Conservation Directory—1975* (Washington, D.C., National Wildlife Federation, 1975). Other information comes from group publications (for example, *Sierra*) or the CEQ survey. Specific citations are omitted.

24. A fairly well-known example of such a regional or local general environmental group, although it is better funded and staffed than such groups in the sample, is the Rocky Mountain Center on the Environment, with headquarters in Denver, Colorado.

25. For a critique of the Scenic Hudson group, see William Tucker, "Environmentalism and the Leisure Class," *Harper's* vol. 255 (December 1977) pp. 49–80.

26. For a description of the environmental problems caused by ORVs, see David Sheridan, "Dirt Motorbikes and Dune Buggies Threaten Deserts," *Smithsonian* vol. 9 (September 1978) pp. 66–75.

A story that appeared in an environmental newsletter in one sample region illustrates the general feelings of conservationists toward ORVs. It seems two Sierra Club backpackers came upon a pair of motorcycles while hiking in a Wilderness area. Incensed at this violation of Wilderness regulations, the Sierrans completely dismantled the bikes. On returning, the cyclists found their machines in two neat piles on the ground. They had some trouble reconstructing the bikes, since the parts had been randomly assigned to the two piles. When they finally got the bikes back together, the cyclists found something missing—the sparkplugs. After pushing their machines out of the Wilderness, they went to the local ranger's office to complain, whereupon the ranger handed them their sparkplugs and two $250 citations for having motorized vehicles in a Wilderness area.

27. In addition to the author's interview material, there is published evidence of the latter operator's activities in league with conservationists in an important controversy. Because of the confidential nature of interviews, however, this evidence cannot be cited. The Parker case, *Parker* v. *United States*,

448 F.2d 793 (10th Cir., October 1971), is discussed in chapter 2, note 45, and associated text.

28. The agencies' ORV closure policies were designed to implement Executive Order 11644, 37 *Federal Register* 2877 (Feb. 9, 1972).

29. Ibid., pp. 19 and 110. The few state legislators in the sample were involved in local public lands management for the same reason as town and county officials; in State A, state legislators generally represented their locales in issues involving federal in-lieu payments.

30. Nationally, SAF and SRM have many nonfederal members. Most SAF and SRM members in the sample of participants in local public lands politics, however, were Forest Service or BLM administrators.

31. For a thorough description of the questions, see appendix A. See appendix B on the relationship between the attitude questions and the analysis of group influence on policy reported in chapter 10 (as well as for the distribution of response to the questions).

32. The "perceived group dominance" measure is a trinary (or "dummy") variable in which mentions of response patterns (a) and (b) are coded -1; mentions of patterns (c), (d), and (e), as $+1$; and neither or both responses as zero. This construction was based on the conceptual consistency of the pattern of responses, especially in light of interviewees' elaborations of their responses; a process of statistically tinkering with different combinations of open-ended responses; and the ability to use the resulting trinary variable as an interval measure in later analyses. See appendix B for the distribution of the measure.

33. See appendix B on the relationship among the single philosophical dimension, the corresponding unidimensional attitude structure, and an important assumption in the analysis of group influence on public lands policy to be reported in chapter 10.

34. See appendix B for the reasons the "clear-cutting" and "grazing fees" items which have loadings slightly below the .40 level that is often used as a rule of thumb for deleting variables from a factor analysis) and "ORV use" item (which has a loading significantly less than .40) are included in the E-U scale.

6

Rangers' and Area Managers' Constituencies

As noted earlier, a long-standing criticism of public lands management is that the federal multiple-use agencies have been captured by their major user group clients, the forest products and livestock industries. The capture thesis is commonly applied in academic circles to the Bureau of Land Management (BLM); in fact, the BLM of the 1940s and 1950s has been used as a textbook case of a captured agency. In the popular literature, the capture thesis is at the heart of environmentalists' political criticisms of the Forest Service.[1] The capture critics' argument is, essentially, since the BLM and Forest Service have constituencies composed solely of groups with a prodevelopment bias, and since the nature of an agency's group constituency determines its policies, the BLM's and service's policies are inevitably prodevelopment.

Although the capture critics rarely couch their arguments in the language of organization theory, their attacks on the agencies are clearly applications of open-systems theory analysis of public agencies. Open systems organization theory depicts agencies as "focal organizations" within environments consisting of other organizations, their "organization-sets."[2] Modern open systems organization theorists believe that the pressures emanating from an organization-set are the key determinants of a focal organization's behavior. Open systems theory thus contrasts sharply with the traditional theory of public administration, which posits that organizational behavior is guided primarily by formal rules (especially, in the case of public organizations, by statutory law) and by rational analysis.

The capture thesis is based on a factual assertion about the nature of public lands agencies' organization-sets. It holds that those organization-sets consist of homogeneous alliances of groups favoring consumptive uses. Federal agencies' organization-sets are commonly thought to deal primarily with the agencies' Washington offices. In fact, however, administrative units at each level of the Forest Service and BLM, including ranger districts and resource areas, have their own organization-sets. A systematic examination of rangers' and area managers' local constituencies is thus an important first step in evaluating the application of the capture thesis to the Forest Service and BLM.

Local Administrators' Group Contacts

The distribution of the group affiliations of participants in local public lands politics does not give the best picture of the local constituencies of the Forest Service and BLM. A *participant*, as the term was used in chapter 5, is any person involved in local public lands politics in the sample regions, regardless of whether he is affiliated with an interest group or a state or federal agency. Participants were identified by asking rangers and area managers for the names of the "key men" with whom they dealt outside their own agency. (The term derives from the "key man list,"[3] a list of important non-service leaders the Forest Service required each of its line officers to maintain.) In describing local constituencies, however, it is more accurate to count what we will call *contacts*, rather than participants. A participant is a contact with each administrator with whom he has a relationship. Since any group leader could deal with more than one administrator, he could be counted as more than one contact, and the total number of contacts would thus exceed the number of participants. (Data on contacts are based on both administrators' and group leaders' reports of dealings with each other. See appendix A on the collection and processing of these data.)

The number of contacts in the sample regions far exceeded the number of participants for three reasons. First, and most important, it was quite common for interest group participants to belong to more than one local administrator's organization-set. For example, major timber mill owners typically operated on many, if not all, of the ranger districts (and where there was merchantable timber, resource areas) in a region. The most active conservationist leaders would be in touch with many line officers in a region. When a ranger and area manager were located in the same town, they often had similar sets of contacts: the local chamber of commerce president, ranchers who operated on the BLM winter range and the Forest Service summer range, oil companies exploring on both BLM and Forest Service lands, and others. In all such cases, the participants were counted as multiple contacts.

Second, some administrators listed generic group types as important contacts, even though no single local group leader had frequent, regular dealings with the administrator. Common examples of such contacts included ranchers in areas with many permittees or licensees but no clear or regular spokesman and groups of out-of-town users, such as campers or rockhounds, who individually visited local administrators' offices to seek information or make complaints but were not personally acquainted with the administrators.

Third, administrators often listed federal agency officials, including other federal land managers in the sample, as key contacts. With the exception of Forest Service and BLM officers, federal agency officials had to be classified as a special type of "generic contact." There is a long history of interagency competition among federal natural resources agencies over policy matters.[4] However, it is taboo for agency officials to admit that federal interagency dealings ever involve something that could be called "politics." Thus, officials of federal agencies would not grant interviews or return questionnaires on the politics and policymaking of other federal agencies, and had to be treated differently from other contacts.[5]

The data on agency contacts presented below reflect only the group contacts of rangers and area managers in the sample regions. The line supervisors of local administrators—forest supervisors, regional foresters, district managers, BLM state directors, or their staffs—often dealt with the same interest group contacts. Some contacts, in fact, had more frequent interactions with these higher-level officials than with rangers and area managers, and the higher-level interactions were often frankly described in interviews as roundabout ways of influencing local administrators' actions. In addition, interest group people, especially in the livestock industry, who lived on the periphery of the sample region might be contacts of Forest Service or BLM administrators just outside the sample regions. Information on relationships with supervisory administrators and those outside the sample regions is not presented below since it is peripheral to our concern with rangers' and area managers' organization-sets.

Distribution of Contacts

Local Forest Service and BLM administrators had an average of twenty key contacts (see table 6-1.) The interest group with the most contacts by far was the livestock industry. The average ranger or area manager had about five important stockmen contacts. The second largest group was the forest products industry, with an average of over two contacts per organization-set. The mining industry (including oil and gas firms) had the third largest number of contacts, an average of 1.5 per organization-set. Among the nongovernmental interest groups, the Sierra Club and local businessmen were essentially tied for fourth, with averages of one contact per administrator. The fifth-rank groups, with contacts in about half of the organization-sets, on the average, were wildlife federations, ORV clubs, recreation-related firms (for example, ski areas, backcountry guides), general environmental groups, and water or irrigation groups. The rest of the groups had contacts in a third or fewer of the sample districts' organization-sets.

The largest single group of governmental contacts were local government officials; each ranger and area manager typically had one or two such contacts. State fish and game department officials, who play a major role in wildlife management on federal land, were the second largest group of government contacts, with an average of almost one per organization-set. There were relatively few individual federal agency contacts who dealt with rangers and area managers. (However, if grouped together, the forty-six federal agency contacts would constitute the fifth largest group of contacts.) The largest numbers of Forest Service and BLM federal contacts were in each other's agencies. This occurred, of course, when BLM land was adjacent to Forest Service land. Thus, while fifteen service-bureau contacts may seem like a small number—reflecting little interagency coordination—it was actually a high proportion of the possible number of such contacts based on geographic proximity alone, since twelve ranger districts in the sample were next to BLM land and seven resource areas were next to Forest Service land.

The other federal agencies with more than one or two contacts apiece (though all had fewer than ten contacts) were the National Park Service, the Bureau of Indian Affairs (BIA), the Fish and Wildlife Service

Table 6-1. Organization-Set Contacts of Rangers and Area Managers ($N = 37$)

Group type	Contacts		Interactions	
	No.	%	No.	%
Timber industry				
Forest products industry firms/associations	84	11.5	1,799	21.0
Livestock industry				
Grazing associations, stockmen	169	23.2	1,935	22.6
BLM advisory board members	12	1.6	100	1.2
Forest Service advisory board member	1	0.1	13	0.2
Other economic interests				
Minerals/oil and gas firms/associations	55	7.5	618	7.2
Chambers of commerce, businessmen	35	4.8	359	4.2
Water/irrigation firms/associations	14	1.9	133	1.6
Soil conservation districts	8	1.1	31	0.4
RC&D, other conservation districts	6	0.8	72	0.8
Realtors	10	1.4	196	2.3
Contractors	2	0.3	48	0.6
Utilities	6	0.8	83	1.0
Environmentalists				
Sierra Club	36	4.9	193	2.3
Wildlife federations	17	2.3	116	1.4
Wilderness/preservation societies	6	0.8	28	0.3
General environmental groups	15	2.1	56	0.7
Local *ad hoc* environmental group	1	0.1	4	a
Garden club, animal protectionist group	2	0.3	9	0.1
Archeologists	4	0.5	40	0.5
Private citizen (no known affiliations)	1	0.1	3	a
Recreational interests				
Sportsmen's, hunting and fishing clubs	12	1.6	108	1.3
National Rifle Association affiliate	1	0.1	44	0.5
Off-road vehicle clubs	17	2.3	84	1.0
Scouts	6	0.8	38	0.4
Summer home permittees	3	0.4	13	0.2
Search and rescue organizations	3	0.4	15	0.2
Other recreational user clubs	9	1.2	123	1.4
Recreation-related business firms/associations	15	2.1	169	2.0
Tourism/booster associations	3	0.4	50	0.6
Other interests				
Local government	53	7.3	507	5.9
Schools	11	1.5	81	0.9
State game and fish agencies	34	4.7	356	4.2
Society for Range Management	3	0.4	26	0.3
Historical society, other non-land-management professionals	2	0.3	12	0.1

(*continued*)

Table 6-1. (Continued)

Group type	Contacts		Interactions	
	No.	%	No.	%
Professional individual	1	0.1	12	0.1
Fraternal (for example, Lions, Elks, and others)	4	0.5	72	0.8
Indian tribe, other minority group associations	8	1.1	49	0.6
Poverty organizations	2	0.3	10	0.1
Media	12	1.6	170	2.0
Forest Service (BLM contact)	4	0.5	77	0.9
BLM (Forest Service contact)	11	1.5	220	2.6
National Park Service	9	1.2	207	2.4
Soil Conservation Service	5	0.7	46	0.5
U.S. Geological Survey	4	0.5	116	1.4
Bureau of Indian Affairs	4	0.5	38	0.4
Fish and Wildlife Service (U.S.)	2	0.3	9	0.1
Other federal agencies	7	1.0	64	0.7
Totals	729	99.3[b]	8,552	100.0

[a] Less than 0.1 percent.
[b] Round-off error.

(FWS), the U.S. Geological Survey (USGS), and the Soil Conservation Service (SCS). Two of these agencies, the Park Service and the BIA, managed public lands adjacent to Forest Service or BLM lands. Service and BLM relationships with the BIA—which nominally does not manage public lands, but acts as trustee for Indian tribal lands—involved routine coordination in the sample region.[6] There is a long history of often bitter conflict between the Forest Service and the Park Service over proposals, usually supported by environmentalists, to transfer scenic recreational lands from the national forests to the national park system.[7] More recently, the BLM has been involved in similar jurisdictional disputes with the Park Service. Thus, while most dealings between the Park Service and the Forest Service or BLM involved routine coordination, there was often an underlying tension because of the Park Service's history of expanding its land base at the expense of the other two agencies. Since there were park system units in all three regions, there were several Park Service contacts in the sample.

Contacts from the other three federal agencies generally dealt with specialized programs that overlapped with service or bureau activities. The FWS is another important federal land management agency, but the

FWS contacts in the sample administered predator control programs, not National Wildlife Refuges adjacent to service or BLM lands. The USGS, as noted in chapter 3, is responsible for monitoring mineral and oil and gas leases on public lands after the BLM has issued the leases; thus, rangers' and area managers' dealings with the USGS were usually concerned with ensuring industry compliance with the terms of leases affecting Forest Service or BLM lands. SCS contacts were usually involved in interagency watershed or erosion control projects. Finally, the "other federal agency" contacts listed in table 6-1 were responsible for special local projects or situations—the Army Corps of Engineers for a dam proposal, Federal Aviation Administration officials for an airport special use permit, and so forth.

The distribution of contacts shown in table 6-1 differed somewhat from that of participants (see table 5-6) because, as noted earlier, some groups' contacts had broader relationships with the agencies. The forest products industry, with 11.5 percent of all contacts but only 7.7 percent of all individual participants, is an important example. The reason for the timber industry's higher proportion of contacts than participants is shown more clearly in table 6-2; the average timber operator dealt with 2.41

Table 6-2. Contact and Interaction Rates for Selected Groups

Group type (No. of contacts)	Contact rate[a]	Interaction rate[b]
Forest products industry firms/associations (82)	2.41	21.74
Grazing associations, stockmen, BLM/FS advisory boards (182)	1.53	11.25
Mineral/O&G firms/associations (55)	1.72	11.24
Chambers of commerce, businessmen (35)	1.40	10.26
Water/irrigation firms/associations (14)	1.40	9.50
Sierra Club (36)	4.00	5.36
Wildlife federations (17)	1.89	6.82
General environmental groups (15)	3.75	3.73
Sportsmen, hunting and fishing clubs (12)	1.71	9.00
Off-road vehicle clubs (17)	1.42	4.94
Recreation business firms/associations (15)	1.07	11.27
State and local government (53)	1.96	9.57
State game and fish agencies (34)	2.00	10.47
Total rate, all forty groups excluding federal agency contacts (683)	1.74	11.38

[a] Contact rate = no. of contacts/no. of participants.
[b] Interaction rate = no. of interactions/no. of contacts.

administrators, considerably above the average.[8] The highest contact rates belonged to the Sierra Club and the general environmental groups, with 4.0 and 3.75, respectively. The contacts in some other groups were generally more local; that is, they lived in the same locale as the administrator. Chamber of commerce members, ranchers, ORV club members, and even many wildlife federation representatives were typical local contacts. When a very localized contact dealt with two administrators, they were often the ranger and area manager whose jurisdictions included the contact's locale. Extreme cases of narrow contacts were the recreation businessmen, who in all but one case dealt only with the ranger or area manager who handled their permits.

Frequency of Interaction

The role of the commodity user groups in local Forest Service and BLM constituencies becomes even clearer if one examines the number of interactions—face-to-face meetings, written correspondence, phone conversations, and so forth—between administrators and their group contacts. (See table 6-1, columns 3 and 4. The numbers in table 6-1 are estimates of interactions in the year preceding the field research, approximately mid-1972 to mid-1973. The estimates are based on both administrators' and contacts' reports of number of interactions. See appendix A for a further explanation of the estimating procedure.) The livestock and forest products industries accounted for 24 percent and 21 percent, respectively, of all interactions between district administrators and their key contacts, and the level of forest products industry interactions was almost three times that of the next highest group, the minerals and oil and gas industry. Local administrators generally interacted most frequently with consumptive users and other governmental entities, particularly units of state and local government and state game and fish agencies. Interactions with nonconsumptive clients were less frequent; the conservationist or recreationist group with the most frequent interactions, the Sierra Club, was the tenth-ranked group.

The second column in table 6-2 shows this pattern in a slightly different way. There were basically two patterns of interaction rate (the average number of interactions per contact of a particular group type). The first pattern, with interaction rates in the 10+ range, characterized the economic user groups. The forest products industry, with a rate of almost two interactions per month per contact, had by far the most frequent interactions with the agencies. The other major users—ranchers, mining or oil and gas firms, and watershed users—plus the recreation use permittees, were all in the 9.5 to 11.25 interactions per contact range. The administrators' conservationist group clients interacted less frequently with them, from the wildlife federations' high of 6.8 down to the general environmentalists' low of 3.7.

Interaction rates are indicators of group access to decision makers—a critically important facet of interest group influence—but one should not conclude from table 6-2 that groups in the conservationist and recreationist camps were afforded only half the access of consumptive user groups. First, members of the consumptive user interests tended to deal directly with administrators (with some channeling of interactions by grazing association officers and BLM advisory board members in the livestock industry), while conservationist and recreationist groups dealt with the agencies through leader-activists. If there were five timber mill owners in an area, all five were likely to be contacts of any given ranger. But if there was even a very large and very active Sierra Club group in the area, only one Sierran was likely to be an active contact of any given district ranger. Second, most administrators' interactions with timber operators, ranchers, mining companies' representatives, and recreation operators were routine: a conversation with a rancher about where to place a range fence; a call to a timber mill owner about a temporary shutdown of a timber sale area because of muddy roads; or a conversation with a backcountry guide who came into the office for a fire permit before a trip. Because much of a district administrator's work involves supervising standard uses, many contacts with users have very little political content. No systematic evidence was collected in the interaction data to indicate the proportion of various groups' interactions that were routine, as opposed to explicitly or subtly political. During interviews, however, administrator and group people (especially in the forest products industry) often observed that many agency interactions with direct users were routine. The levels of interaction with indirect-user groups like local businesses and local governments probably represent higher levels of explicit or subtle policy-relevant interaction than the interactions with direct user groups or conservationists and recreationists.

Irrespective of the routine nature of many direct user interactions with rangers and area managers, the fact remains that the organization-sets of district administrators were dominated by the direct user groups. Direct user business groups accounted for 49 percent of all contacts and 57 percent of all interactions. If one adds those groups with an indirect economic interest in consumptive use (for example, chambers of commerce and local government), what might be loosely called the "economic interests" accounted for 65 percent of all contacts and 70 percent of all interactions. However, conservationists and recreationists (including the government recreation-oriented agencies with conservationist clienteles —the state game and fish departments and the National Park Service) accounted for only 24 percent of all contacts and 17 percent of all interactions.

Differences in Organization-Sets

An examination of the average numbers of group contacts in the thirty-seven rangers' and area managers' organization-sets does not reveal the significant differences in administrators' constituencies from various ranger districts and resource areas. Differences in relative concentrations of interest groups types is the key to group influence in public lands politics. The core principle of the open systems theory of organizations is that an organization's environment determines its behavior. Thus, the policies of rangers or area managers with one type of organization-set should be significantly different from those of their colleagues with a different type.

Typology of Organization-Sets

There appeared to be five types of local administrator organization-sets in the sample regions. Within each type there was some variation, and several constituencies were on the borderline between two types, but the types were distinct enough to merit separate discussion. The criterion for assigning a given ranger district or resource area to one type or another was the relative prevalance of four key types of groups—the forest products industry, the livestock industry, the mining industry, and conservationists and recreationists.[9] The roles of livestock, logging, mining, and conservationist contacts in local constituencies were fairly straightforward, but some discretion was used in evaluating recreationist contacts for assigning types to organization-sets. Most recreationists could be treated as complements of conservationists. Many administrators, for example, did not make much distinction between conservationists and recreationists because they saw conservationists primarily as a part of their agency's recreationist clientele. Moreover, certain recreationist groups, notably sportsmen, were generally indistinguishable from conservationist groups (that is, the wildlife federations). However, certain other recreationist groups that were not generally conservationist-oriented, such as most ORV groups, were not given equal weight with conservationists in identifying the type of constituency.

Type I, the most common type of organization-set, was fairly equally balanced on the consumptive user side between forest products and livestock industry contacts and also had substantial representation of conservationists or recreationists, or both. Ranger district 45's organization-set, shown in table 6-3,[10] is a representative Type I district. The ranger had moderately frequent dealings with three timber mill owners, and fewer interactions with a fourth. Livestock industry contacts were a bit fewer than normal for a Type I district (the average number of stockmen contacts for a Type I district was 4.4, with 57.6 interactions). Conservationists were also well represented, particularly by wildlife federation and state wildlife and parks agencies' officials; there were, in fact, slightly more conservationist contacts in RD45 than in most Type I sets. As with most organization-sets, there were miscellaneous contacts, the town manager and a newspaper reporter.

Table 6-3. Organization-Set Type I—Balanced Primary Users Plus Conservationists and Recreationists, (RD45)

Contact	No. of interactions
Medium-sized timber mill owner	24
Medium-sized timber mill owner	13
Large timber company owner	13
State game and fish regional officer	12
State wildlife federation officer	9
NRA state president and county wildlife federation president	7
Grazing association president and national forest grazing advisory board chairman	6
Sheep permittee spokesman	6
Rancher and national forest grazing advisory board member	3
Sierra Club professional staffer	2[a]
Very large timber firm executive	2[a]
Town manager	2
Newspaper reporter	2
State parks commissioner	1[a]
State wildlife federation officer	1[a]

[a] Interactions reported only by the contact.

The second type of organization-set was the livestock-dominated district. There were many contacts among the ranchers, grazing association leaders, and BLM advisory board members, but few or no forest products industry contacts. Most Type II districts had some conservationist or recreationist contacts, although slightly fewer, on average, than in Type I. These were usually people associated with wildlife federations, sportsmen's groups, or ORV clubs. BLM resource area 81, from which the data in table 6-4 are taken, is a good example of a Type II organization-set. The livestock industry, which included the largest group of contacts, was represented primarily by advisory board members. The second largest groups consisted of the wildlife coalition of the rod and gun club leader and the two state wildlife department officials; the State C wildlife agency worked in very close concert with the state's wildlife groups. Interestingly, the BLM advisory board chairman was also a National Wildlife Federation member. Each advisory board was supposed to have a "wildlife representative," although this rule was honored primarily in the breach. This board chairman—a rancher and one of the two most important livestock industry leaders in the area—was the only BLM advisory board key contact in the sample with even a nominal wildlife group affiliation.

Table 6-4. Organization-Set Type II—Range Districts (RA81)

Contact	No. of interactions
Large rancher and Republican party activist	18
Forest Service ranger, same town	17
Rancher-licensee	14
Off-road vehicle club president and sportsman	12
State wildlife department warden	12
National park superintendent	12
BLM advisory board chairman	11
BLM advisory board member	10
BLM advisory board member	10
Mine manager	5
Rod and gun club and wildlife federation officer	4
Mine manager	5
State highway department official	4
State parks department official	3
State wildlife department regional official and wildlife federation member	2
Sierra Club member	2[a]

[a] Interactions reported only by the contact.

The distinguishing characteristic of the third type of organization-set was significant representation by mining or oil and gas interests. Resource area 73, described in table 6-5, is a representative Type III organization-set, with high levels of interactions by several coal and natural gas companies' contacts. Other than the high level of mining contacts, there was some variation in the Type III organization-sets: Some had low to moderate numbers of forest products industry contacts, while others had no such contacts; conservationist and recreationist contacts also varied from few to a relatively large number. All sets had moderate to high numbers of livestock industry contacts. If the criterion of mineral and oil and gas contacts had not been used, the Type III sets would have been classified as Type I or II.

The fourth type of organization-set was biased in favor of the two traditional commodity user groups, the forest products and livestock industries. Conservationists were absent or had almost no interaction with administrators in Type IV sets. Recreationists, when present, tended to be members of ORV, scouts, or other groups out of the conservationist–recreationist mainstream or relatively uninvolved with the central policy issues of public lands management. Ranger district 13, described in table

Table 6-5. Organization-Set Type III—Mining or Oil and Gas District (RA73)

Contact	No. of interactions
Major gas corporation local executive	52
Indian tribal attorney	25
Rancher and BLM advisory board member	24
Major gas corporation local executive	24
Rancher and BLM advisory board member	15
Coal corporation local executive	12
Rancher and BLM advisory board member	12
County manager	12
County wildlife federation president	6
Regional motorcycle club president	6
Small electric co-op manager	4[a]
Rancher and BLM advisory board member	2[a]
O&G corporation local executive	2[a]
BLM advisory board chairman	2[a]
Sierra Club professional staffer	2[a]
State wildlife federation officer	2[a]
Regional general environmental group professional staffer	1[a]
Regional wildlife committee activist	1[a]

[a] Interactions reported only by the contact.

6-6, is an example of an unbalanced, economic group-dominated organization-set, with its heavy forest products industry clientele reinforced by chamber-of-commerce-type contacts. While tourism was an important industry for the town in which the RD 13 office was located, local businessmen, such as the tourism association and chamber of commerce presidents, were generally prodevelopment.

Type V, the last type of organization-set, was the opposite of Type IV. Such sets were unbalanced in favor of conservationists and recreationists. Ranger district 47's set, in table 6-7, was the clearest example of a Type V set. The two ski area managers were the most important user group contacts. (All the Type V districts in the sample included major developed recreation sites.) There were a fairly large number of conservationist contacts; in addition, the more important ski area operator was an informal ally of conservationists in the region. There were no significant forest products industry contacts and relatively few livestock industry contacts. A borderline Type V/I district in the sample had as many

Table 6-6. Organization-Set Type IV—Overbalanced Toward Traditional Users (RD13)

Contact	No. of interactions
Town banker and tourism association president	100
Large timber mill owner	18
Merchant and state commission member	18
Large timber mill owner	18[a]
Chamber of commerce president	12
Large timber mill owner	12[a]
National park superintendent	12
Stockman	12
Stockman	10
Stockman	8
State legislator and businessman in nearby town	6
Trail riding club president and county commissioner	6
State legislator, nearby city	6
Large timber mill owner	6
Scouts, regional director	6
Businessman and stockman, nearby city	5
Realtor, nearby town	2[a]
Medium-sized timber corporation manager	2[a]
Regional RC&D director	1[a]
Rancher	1[a]
Medium-sized timber mill owner	1[a]
State stockmen's association director	1[a]

[a] Interactions reported only by the contact.

Table 6-7. Organization-Set Type V—Overbalanced Toward Conservationists and Recreationists (RD47)

Contact	No. of interactions
Major ski area operator	16
Minor ski area operator	12
Mayor, nearby town	8
Mine manager	7
State game and fish warden	7
Town mayor and rancher-permittee	4
Irrigation association president and permittee	4
Individual permittee	3
Grazing association president	3
Sierra Club member and businessman, nearby town	3
State highway department engineer	3
BLM area manager, same locale	3
State environmental protection agency	3
State forestry department	3
Gypo logger	2
Special use permittee and general environmental group director	1
Regional conservation coordinating committee president	1
Sierra Club group president	1[a]
Regional wilderness study committee president	1

[a] Interactions reported only by the contact.

forest products industry and livestock industry contacts as RD13 (the Type IV district in table 6-6), but it had the highest number of interactions—and the most well developed, if not co-opted, relationship—with conservationists and recreationists of any district in the sample. (This district will be discussed further below.)

The Distribution of Organization-Set Types

The most important characteristic of the sample region's organization-sets was the fairly high degree of balance between industry user groups and conservationists and recreationists. The most common type of set was Type I; almost half the rangers' organization-sets in the sample fell into this equally balanced category (see table 6-8). Another common type, the stockman-oriented Type II set, was also fairly well balanced between its major user group, the livestock industry, and conservationists or recreationists. The second most numerous type, the mining industry-oriented Type III, also had good representation by conservationist and recreationist contacts; except for the high numbers of minerals and

Table 6-8. Summary of Local Administrators' Organization-Sets

Type	Description	No. ranger districts	No. resource areas	Total no. administrative units
I	*Equally balanced:* mixed timber and livestock contacts, with some conservationist/recreationist contacts (two ranger districts are mixed I/IV)	13	1	14
II	*Stockmen-dominated* set, with some conservationist/recreationist contacts (1 ranger district is mixed II/IV)	4	3	7
III	*High mineral/O&G contacts*, with variation on the rest of the set (If not for the mineral/O&G contacts, 3 ranger districts would be Type I, 2 ranger districts + 5 resource areas would be Type II, 1 ranger district would be Type I/IV.)	6	5	11
IV	*Overbalanced, traditional users;* mixed timber and livestock, but little or no interaction with conservationists or activist recreationists	2	0	2
V	*Overbalanced, conservationists or recreationists*, with few timber or stockmen contacts (1 ranger district is mixed V/I)	3	0	3
	Totals	28	9	37

O&G contacts, seven of the Type III districts would have been considered stockmen-oriented, and three would have been equally balanced. Finally, there were very few unbalanced sets. The two Type IV sets dominated by the forest products and livestock industries were offset by the two pure Type V sets dominated by conservationists and recreationists. Though there were four Type I or Type II sets on the margin of being Type IV, there was also a Type V/I district in which important industry groups were more than offset by conservationist and recreationist contacts.

Several factors seemed to affect the composition of rangers' and area managers' local constituencies. First, the physiographic characteristics of administrative units' locales were reflected in potential user industry contacts. Timber mill owners obviously would not establish mills in areas with little or no merchantable timber. The number of a given administrator's potential contacts in the timber industry was not determined solely by the amount of timber on that administrator's unit: A few administrators with very little merchantable timber had many potential contacts in the timber industry because of high-timber-volume units nearby, and a few administrators who could have conducted a timber sales program had no potential buyers in their areas because there were no other units nearby to help supply enough sales to support a mill. Since all the units in the sample had some range or meadowland and long histories of livestock-grazing use, all had many potential livestock industry contacts. Potential mining industry contacts were the most mobile. Mining or oil and gas operators gravitated toward any district with good geological potential for mineral or fossil fuel deposits; most mining industry contacts, however, were in districts near other areas of established mining or oil and gas activity. The physiographic difference between national forest and public domain lands was the main reason for the difference between typical local Forest Service and BLM constituencies. Most national forest ranger districts have merchantable timber and are next to other timbered districts, so that two-thirds of the ranger districts in the sample (thirteen Type I, three Type III/I, two Type IV, and one Type V/I) had significant forest products contacts. Since public domain lands are generally unforested, almost all BLM resource areas had stockmen-dominated constituencies (three Type II and five Type III/II).

The second factor, which influenced the important conservationist and recreationist components of organization sets, was proximity to urban areas. The environmental group activists who dealt with the public lands agencies—the Sierrans, general environmental group people, wilderness committee members, and so forth—generally lived in cities or in towns with urbane, middle-class populations. Several Forest Service officials, for example, attributed the considerable Sierra Club activity in one region to the fact that the economy of one town in the region was based on an advanced research and development center; as one ranger put it, the town had "more Ph.D.s per square mile than any other place on earth." The ranger's observation was echoed by other interviewees: urbane individuals were the activist environmentalists and preservationists because they were interested in the aesthetic and recreational value of the wilderness experience, and were receptive (because of education, reinforced in many cases by current occupation) to the intellectualism and activism of environmental and preservation groups. The same recreational interests underlay many of the sportsmen's groups; sportsmen went to the wilds to escape from their urban, industrial places of work and residence, although with snowmobile or rifle, rather than backpack. Thus, the key to the existence of conservation or recreational groups was the city, the home of the urbane and of urban blue-collar workers who viewed the public lands as a potential recreation area, and the place where one could find enough of both types of individuals to form groups large enough to produce activists.

All three regions conformed to this generalization. In States A and B, where the most active environmentalists could be found, the centers of environmentalist strength were the cities, plus a few urbane small towns like the R&D town. The State C sample region had no real cities, and as a consequence environmentalists were relatively underrepresented, but the few conservationists in the region came from the two more industrialized towns. To illustrate the point, we will use a facsimile of a map of NF1 in State A. (See figure 6-1; the diagram is quite different from a true map of NF1.) There was one major city—by western standards—in NF1's region and a number of small to very small towns on the periphery of or within the forest. NF1 was the focus of most of the recreational activities in the region. Most of the region's environmentalist or conservationist recreational group leaders lived in the major city because of the relative urbanity of its population and the fact that it was where a large proportion of the region's population lived. Most Sierra Club members in the region lived in the city (a proportion of the club's membership considerably greater than the city's proportion of the regional population). The organization-sets of the seven rangers on NF1 were built around this concentration of environmentalists in the major city. Thus, the ranger whose office was located in the city had a disproportionately large number of conservationists and recreationists among his constituents, while the other rangers had relatively balanced sets or sets that tended strongly toward consumptive user dominance. The conservationist contacts that gave the six nonurban rangers some balance were, with one important exception, residents of the major city and primarily contacts of the urban ranger.

The Forest Service consciously took advantage of this concentration of environmentalist and recreationist leaders in State A. NF1's forest supervisor and six nonurban rangers reported that the city ranger coordinated the forest's interactions with environmental and conservation groups. And that ranger was unlike most Forest Service professionals; a GS-12 forester, his personal friends were local intellectual and artistic types, and his forte was "I&E," service terminology for information and education, or what is sometimes pejoratively called public relations.[11]

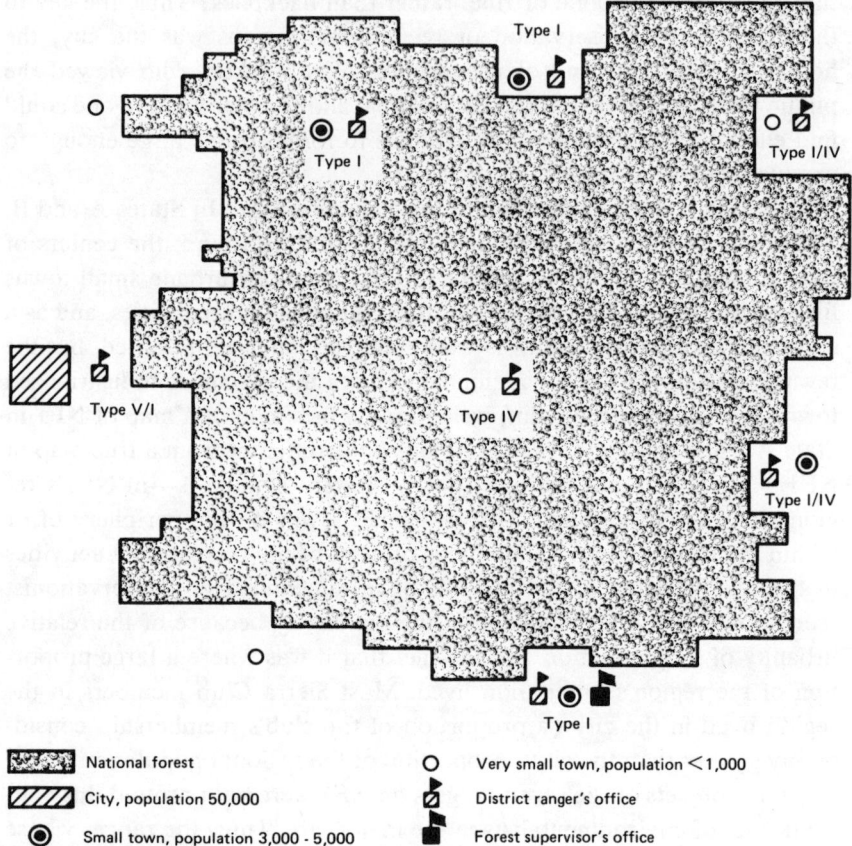

Figure 6-1. Urban areas and rangers' organization-set types on NF1.

Along with his chief assistant—an officer of the local Sierra Club—he cultivated close ties with the city's environmental and recreation groups, particularly the local Sierra Club. NF1 was a model of the efficient division of labor in interest group relations.

Conclusion—Local Constituencies and the "Capture Thesis"

Application of the capture thesis to public lands politics, which is especially popular among environmentalists, is based on two fundamental propositions. First, the critics assume that the agencies have homogeneous local organization-sets dominated by consumptive user industries.

Second, they operate on the theory that a narrow special interest constituency inevitably bends an agency to its will, so the Forest Service's and BLM's developmentalist policies are the inevitable result of their homogeneous developmentalist constituencies. Whatever the capture thesis' deficiencies—and it has its detractors[12]—it has the advantage of being simple and straightforward.

The fundamental premise of the capture thesis critics is not, however, borne out by the facts of local BLM and Forest Service politics. While the industries and their allies constituted a majority of land managers' local contacts, a sizable minority of local conservationist contacts provided a very important counterbalance. As noted in chapter 5 (see for example, table 5-9 and figure 5-1 and accompanying text), conservationists' preferences about public lands policies were diametrically opposed to those of the user industries; thus, they constituted a bona fide opposition bloc. Almost all rangers and area managers had enough conservationist and recreationist contacts to maintain reasonably balanced constituencies.

In particular, the first premise of the capture thesis assumes that most local constituencies are Type IV organization-sets. However, only two of the thirty-seven organization-sets conformed to this assumption of homogeneous, user-dominated constituencies. Moreover, they were offset by two sets dominated by conservationist and recreationist interests. Since the first assumption of the capture thesis, at least as applied to the sample regions, is wrong, the thesis itself must be regarded as suspect.

The nature of agencies' constituencies is merely the first phenomenon examined by proponents of the capture thesis and the more elaborate open systems organization theory. Subsequent and more important questions deal with the ways a constituency influences agency policies. Which groups influence agency policy? How do they influence policy? And how much do they influence policy? It could be, for example, that despite the presence of significant numbers of conservationist group contacts in local rangers' and area managers' constituencies, the administrators actually were influenced only by the user industries. Or it could be that the simple capture thesis is not only oversimplified, but wrong. These issues will be examined in the next four chapters.

NOTES

1. See Phillip Foss, *Politics and Grass* (Seattle, University of Washington Press, 1960); Jack Shepherd, *The Forest Killers* (New York, Weybright and

Talley, 1975); and Daniel Barney, *The Last Stand* (New York, Grossman, 1974). Also see chapter 1, pp. 27–29.

2. See William Evan, "The Organization-Set: Toward a Theory of Interorganizational Relations," in James Thompson, ed., *Approaches to Organizational Design* (Pittsburgh, Pa., University of Pittsburgh Press, 1966) pp. 175–191. The organization-set concept has been used by William Devall to analyze local public lands politics (see "The Forest Service and Its Clients: Input to Forest Service Decision Making," *Environmental Affairs* vol. 2 (Spring 1973) pp. 723–757).

3. This term is rather anachronistic. Despite some recent improvement, however, public lands management has been a fairly male-dominated policy arena: for example, none of the administrators and only 1.5 percent of the group leaders in the sample were women.

4. For two case-study examples of such conflict, see Owen Stratton and Phillip Sirotkin, *The Echo Park Controversy* (Syracuse, N.Y., Inter-University Case Program no. 46, 1959); and Irving Fox and Isabel Picken, *The Upstream-Downstream Controversy in the Arkansas–White–Red Basins Survey* (University, Ala., Inter-University Case Program no. 55, 1960).

5. After it became apparent early in the field research that officials of federal agencies other than the Forest Service and BLM would not participate in the study, these officials were excluded from the list of people to be interviewed or sent questionnaires. When it came to coding reported contacts, other federal agency officials were included in the data as generic contacts and treated as if they had been nonrespondents. On the basis of the early futile attempts to obtain other federal officials' cooperation, it is probable that all would have been nonrespondents anyway.

6. In one sample region there was an important issue involving sacred Indian tribal lands within a national forest. (The particulars of this issue are not given so as to maintain the anonymity of the sample region.) This issue, however, did not directly involve the BIA.

7. For a recent example of an important Forest Service–Park Service jurisdictional controversy, see William Catton, "Decision in the North Cascades: The Proposal as Viewed by a Sociologist," *Journal of Forestry* vol. 66 (July 1968) pp. 540–550.

8. The first column in table 6-2 shows the ratio of contacts to participants for selected group categories, giving a measure of the breadth of a group's contacts. High contact ratios mean more contacts with administrators than the average.

9. Administrative units were assigned to particular types on the basis of visual inspections of tables of the organization-sets. No statistical procedure was used in the assignment.

10. Tables 6-3 through 6-7 show the main group affiliations of each contact in the particular unit's organization-set, along with the adjusted frequency of interaction between the contact and the administrator. Note that some interactions are those reported by the contact but not mentioned by the district administrator.

6: RANGERS' AND AREA MANAGERS' CONSTITUENCIES   207

11. This ranger, the first interviewee of my field research, quickly shattered any stereotypes I might have had about public lands managers. He was attired in a turtleneck and plaid sportsjacket, instead of the expected Forest Service greens and Smokey-the-Bear hat, and had just returned from a speaking engagement at a Jaycees' luncheon.

12. Shepherd's (*The Forest Killers*) and Barney's (*The Last Stand*) views about the capture of the Forest Service are usually regarded as the rhetoric of admitted partisans in public lands debates. More generally, the capture thesis has become one of the most important explanations of regulatory agency failure, but it is also increasingly subject to criticism. See, for example, James Wilson, ed., *The Politics of Regulation* (New York, Basic Books, 1980); and James Anderson, "Economic Regulatory and Consumer Protection Policies," in Theodore Lowi and Alan Stone, eds., *Nationalizing Government* (Beverly Hills, Calif., Sage, 1978) pp. 73–74.

7

The Nature of Group Influence / Participants' Views

The preceding chapters have shown that a large number of groups with widely divergent interests in the public lands regularly deal with local land managers in the Forest Service and Bureau of Land Management (BLM). However, determining the existence of local interest group constituencies only leads to a more important issue—what influence, if any, those groups have on rangers' or area managers' administrative routines and, ultimately, their decisions. This chapter and the remaining chapters in Part III examine constituencies' effects on agency decision making.

An understanding of group influence must begin with an examination of the perceptions that public lands politics participants themselves have about group influence. Group influence is an elusive phenomenon. All participants in politics recognize—or think they recognize—influence when they see it, but students of politics have had some difficulty agreeing on how to define influence and how to see it. The most widely accepted definition of *influence* is the ability of one person to cause another to arrive at the decision preferred by the former. The problem with this definition is that it is often difficult to prove that the influencer's preferences caused, or even affected, the decision.[1] Because of real methodological difficulties in proving influence, some students of politics have compromised and asked political actors which groups they *believe* to be influential. Influence becomes, in effect, the ability to be perceived as the cause of policy.[2] Thus, in dealing with participants' views of local public lands policymaking, we are using this second, subjective definition of influence.

The views of participants in local public lands policy—indeed, all the topics discussed in Part II—also reflect a fundamental ambiguity in the analysis of low-level administrative politics. The analysis of interest group influence focuses attention on the external (or "open systems") relationships of rangers and area managers. Yet these officials are also integral parts of the Forest Service and BLM hierarchical structures and are subject to a host of intraagency influences on their decision making. The open systems approach to organizational analysis, though it contradicts the strictly inward-looking, traditional approach to public administration, does not ignore the importance of internal organizational dynamics. Participants in local public lands politics are also aware of the two types of forces affecting rangers and area managers, external constituency influence and internal hierarchial controls.

The Rise of Environmental Influences on Local Land Management

The administrators and interest group leaders who participated in local public lands politics in the three sample regions held a wide variety of views about the important factors in Forest Service and BLM policymaking. A large number of the responses shown in table 7-1 emphasized intraagency influences on local administrators' decisions.[3] The most frequently mentioned observation was that hierarchical controls—statutes, agency policy, the policies of supervisors, and so forth—were very important in local public lands policymaking. A number of responses alleging that the agencies were overbureaucratized also fell into this category. Such responses (pattern I in table 7-1) were offered first by one-fifth of all participants. Two other internally oriented responses focused on the characteristics of administrators. Pattern J—the observation that administrators' actions were based on their own professional or personal judgments—ranked second among all responses and third among first responses. Less frequently, a major policy influence was attributed to administrators' personalities or character traits (pattern E). Interest group participants usually used this approach to mask their grievances about agency policy. For example, a stockman who was disgruntled with the service's rest-rotation policy said that he did not "get along with this new ranger" who was "inexperienced" and relied on "book learning," when encouragement of rest-rotation was a clear agency policy that the ranger happened to arrive in time to implement.[4] Two final, minor intraagency

Table 7-1. Participants' Beliefs About the Most Important Factors in Forest Service and BLM Policymaking

Response pattern[a]	First response		Second response		Third response		Fourth response		All responses	
	No.	(%)	No.	(%)	No.	(%)	No.	(%)	No.	(%)
Primarily group leaders' responses[b]										
A. Environmental/conservation/recreation interest group pressure	20	(6.9)	21	(7.2)	21	(7.2)	12	(4.1)	74	(8.6)
B. Wildlife/recreation use	2	(0.7)	2	(0.7)	2	(0.7)	0	(0.0)	6	(0.7)
C. Increased regulations/restrictions (effect)	6	(2.1)	6	(2.1)	14	(4.8)	19	(6.5)	45	(5.2)
D. Agency lack of openness	7	(2.4)	11	(3.8)	15	(5.2)	5	(1.7)	38	(4.4)
E. Personal character traits of administrator	8	(2.7)	12	(4.1)	15	(5.2)	15	(5.2)	47	(5.5)
F. Agency lack of resources/authority	1	(0.3)	3	(1.0)	4	(1.4)	5	(1.7)	13	(1.5)
G. Developmentalist philosophy/pressure	9	(3.1)	5	(1.7)	5	(1.7)	2	(0.7)	21	(2.4)
H. Environmental destruction (effect)	2	(0.7)	3	(1.0)	2	(0.7)	0	(0.0)	7	(0.8)
Responses of both administrators and group leaders										
I. Laws, supervisors/agency policy, "bureaucracy"	59	(20.3)	54	(18.6)	31	(10.7)	10	(3.4)	154	(17.9)
J. Administrator's professional/own judgment	28	(9.6)	27	(9.3)	16	(5.5)	16	(5.5)	87	(10.1)
K. Responsiveness, public participation	13	(4.5)	22	(7.6)	27	(9.3)	15	(5.2)	77	(8.9)
L. Ecological/environmentalist/preservationist concern	13	(4.5)	9	(3.1)	6	(2.1)	4	(1.4)	32	(3.7)

Primarily administrators' responses[b]										
M. "What's best for land," soil protection	42	(14.4)	10	(3.4)	4	(1.4)	5	(1.7)	61	(7.1)
N. Multiple-use philosophy	14	(4.8)	14	(4.8)	8	(2.7)	3	(1.0)	39	(4.5)
O. Land use planning policy/process	1	(0.3)	3	(1.0)	7	(2.4)	3	(1.0)	14	(1.6)
P. Interest group pressure, "use conflict," public opinion	13	(4.5)	19	(6.5)	18	(6.2)	7	(2.4)	57	(6.6)
Q. Economic factors/demand/use	22	(7.6)	22	(7.6)	9	(3.1)	2	(0.7)	55	(6.4)
R. "Needs of people"	4	(1.4)	8	(2.7)	4	(1.4)	0	(0.0)	16	(1.9)
Other	7	(2.4)	5	(1.7)	4	(1.4)	3	(1.0)	19	(2.2)
None; no answer; uncodable[c]	20	(6.9)	35	(12.0)	82	(28.2)	165	(56.7)	302	(n.a.)
Totals	291	(100%)	291	(100%)	291	(100%)	291	(100%)	1,164	(100%)

[a] Answers to opening, open-ended interview/questionnaire question, "What are the most important factors in Forest Service and BLM policymaking?"
[b] Response patterns A through H given disproportionately, but not necessarily exclusively, by interest group participants. Responses M through R given disproportionately, but not exclusively, by Forest Service and BLM administrators.
[c] "None" applies to cases with fewer than four responses; for example, if a respondent gave two responses, the third and fourth responses would be "none."

issues were the agencies' lack of personnel or legal resources and the fairly technical (and relatively new in 1973) land use planning processes.

The five intraagency patterns accounted for one-third of all responses.[5] The remaining two-thirds of the responses were related to external constituency influences on the agencies. The central theme of most interviews was that the increased activism of the environmental movement in the 1970s had profoundly affected the Forest Service and BLM. Three basic attitudes about the role of environmentalists in agency policymaking were held by conservationists and recreationists, economic users, and administrators.

Interest Group Perceptions—Capture by the Other Side

Conservationists generally believed that the service and bureau were responsive primarily to economic user interests. These beliefs were manifested in remarks about the developmentalist philosophies of administrators or administrator capitulation to developmentalist interests (pattern G in table 7-1), charges that the effect of policies favoring consumptive users was destructive (pattern H)—"environmental rape," as some conservationists liked to put it—and references to economic use or demand criteria by persons other than administrators (pattern Q). One Sierran attributed the developmentalist philosophy he felt guided the service to administrators' technological orientation and the demise of the conservation values of Pinchot and his contemporaries. Other environmentalists simply saw the service as timber-oriented and lax on controlling timber uses. Sportsmen-conservationists uniformly saw the agencies as favoring domestic livestock use and being hostile to wildlife (figure 7-1). A wildlife federation officer cited his experience on the state game commission to prove the livestock orientation of the agencies: he claimed the representative of the service and bureau consistently voted with the stockmen on the commission and against the wildlife federation and state game department members. Other conservationists argued that it was Forest Service and BLM policy to "keep the locals happy," and since the locals (especially stockmen) had a subdue-the-earth, "pioneer" mentality, the agencies' policies were prodevelopment.

Conservationists also frequently asserted that the dominant use policies the agencies allegedly pursued in response to industry pressure were shortsighted economically. The agencies and the forest products and livestock industries argued that logging and livestock grazing were critical to the health of local economies. However, wildlife and preservation group

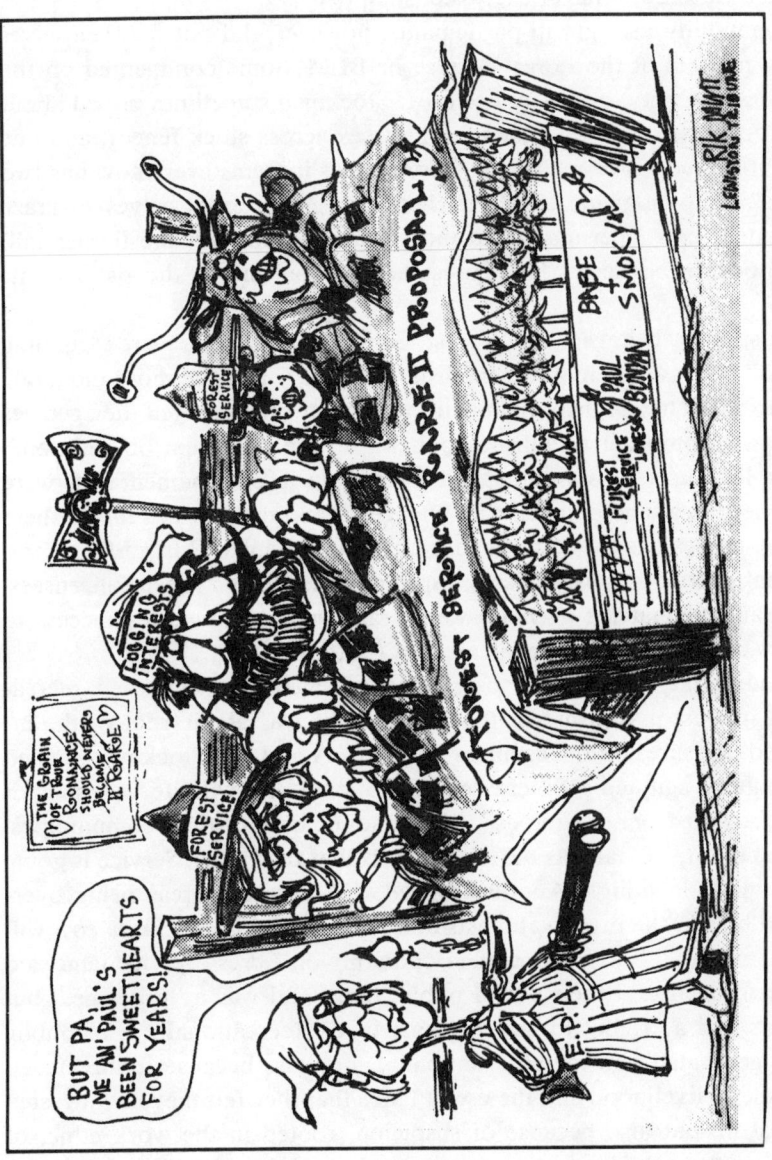

Figure 7-1. An environmentalist view of Forest Service constituency relationships. [Source: Rik Dalvit, *Lewiston (Idaho) Morning Tribune*; reprinted in the Wilderness Society's *Wilderness Report* 16 (February 1979) p. 3.]

leaders often replied that recreation had greater potential economic benefits than additional or excess consumptive uses.

Commodity user group participants, however, did not see themselves as the masters of the Forest Service or BLM. Some commented on the agencies' inability to fully police uses: Stockmen sometimes griped about the sloppiness of woods crews felling trees across stock fences; and one even criticized his peers, noting, "Sometimes it seems every cow has two calves" (implying that some ranchers trucked in extra calves to graze free under cows' permits). But most users agreed with the timber mill operator who sighed, "The Forest Service has me in the palm of its hand."

Most also believed the Forest Service and BLM were "running scared" because of environmentalists (pattern A and the more moderate pattern L). They argued that environmentalist pressures led the agencies to depart from their established policies, to the detriment of traditional public land users. As a timber mill owner put it, environmentalists were "damned vocal and damned well financed," and the service *"thinks* there is a lot of pressure to 'get these loggers out of the hills.' " In addition, traditional commodity-user clients, especially the BLM's rancher-licensees, often argued that the agencies were granting them much less access to agency decision making than in the past (pattern D).

Traditional consumptive users also believed that increased recreational interest in and use of the public lands was at the root of the increased pressures on the agencies (patterns A and B). Stockmen seemed particularly agitated by increased recreational and wildlife use, since it meant a shift from grazing use, the economic base of their communities. As one put it, "What gets me stirred up is that the Forest Service is going in for this fun thing." Another argued, "If there are areas being overgrazed by elk, the preservationists don't get upset, but one extra cow will get them mad." Several stockmen operating on Forest Service land said they had been told their use of public rangeland was a "privilege," but hunters had a "right" to use the same land. Recreational use of public lands generated considerable antipathy, not just because it threatened stockmen's livelihood and the use of lands that they felt they had a vested interest in, but also because of suspicion, rooted in the work ethic, of "this fun thing." This feeling was put clearly, if extremely, by a mining company owner who described Wilderness as "a plot so the rich and weak-minded can play."

The contradictory nature of these two patterns of perceptions—conservationists alleging that the Forest Service and BLM were dominated by consumptive users (patterns G and H) and users arguing that the agencies were dominated by environmentalists and recreationists (patterns A and B)—suggests both sets of groups might have been somewhat paranoid. In fact, these interest group leaders were not really neurotic—they just focused on two different sides of what turned out to be the same coin.

The View from the Middle—Administrators' Perceptions

Forest Service and BLM officers' views of the important factors in their decision making helped reconcile the apparent contradictions in interest group leaders' beliefs. The typical administrator said he tried to both protect his unit's land resources or, as several put it, to do "what's best for the land" (patterns M and L) *and* accommodate economic demands or, in a common euphemism, "the needs of people" (patterns Q and R). These twin goals were the main components of the multiple-use philosophy, which is the cornerstone of these agencies' policies and their officers' professional beliefs.[6]

There was some variation among administrators in the relative emphasis on one or the other of these goals. In State B, for example, extraordinary responsiveness to the needs of local users was incorporated into formal Forest Service policy.[7] A BLM area manager in another area justified his emphasis on economic responsiveness by arguing that it would be morally wrong to destroy stockmen's businesses because past BLM "laxity" had allowed stockmen to build up their operations. Other administrators placed greater emphasis on their resource protection responsibilities; some even noted that their primary responsibility was to rehabilitate their units from the effects of past exploitative practices. But on the whole, local Forest Service and BLM officers believed—as environmentalists charged—that they should make lands under their jurisdiction available to users, including economic users such as forest products and livestock operators. They also firmly believed—as many users complained—that they should place restrictions on permitted uses to protect the land environment.

Forest Service and BLM officers generally viewed their relationships with their local constituencies within a perspective of historical change in public support for these twin multiple-use goals. Before the change, the agencies had only consumptive user constituents: the BLM's constituents were the livestock industry, and the service's were stockmen and, on many districts, the forest products industry. During this time, the agencies had operated in one of two ways, according to administrators. Several BLM managers and some Forest Service rangers said their agencies had been dominated by consumptive user groups, but most service administrators felt, as one ranger put it, that the service "was managing in a vacuum, except for the vested interest groups," and "filled the void" with professionalism, with the *esprit de corps* and capture-avoidance mechanisms described by Kaufman.[8] As another ranger put it, administrators used to manage "by the Manual." Managers in the BLM described a similar pattern. Several recalled the process of adjudications (lowering the levels of grazing leases) in the early 1960s, when the bureau "went it alone" against the stockmen.

One ranger used an interesting example to illustrate the use of professionalism to offset a use-oriented constituency. He had wanted some changes in a Scout camp's design before he would issue a permit. The organization retained, as the ranger described it, a "Wall Street lawyer" who attempted to negotiate tradeoffs with the ranger. When the ranger would not bargain, the lawyer tried to exert congressional pressure through the agriculture secretary's and Forest Service chief's offices. When the Forest Service bureaucracy backed the ranger, the lawyer agreed to the camp design that the ranger wanted, "based on good management practices and the Manual." The lawyer supposedly told the ranger later that he had not believed the service really operated in such a professional-administrative manner.

BLM and Forest Service officers fairly uniformly reported that things were quite different by the 1970s. Many interviewees cited some pivotal event in the transition to a new agency awareness of environmentalism. Some BLM managers suggested the change began in 1965, after the passage of the BLM's Classification and Multiple Use Act. Rangers mentioned "Earth Day," the passage of NEPA, and publication of *Framework for the Future*,[9] a service policy document. Several rangers and some forest product industry interviewees mentioned the Bitterroot clearcutting controversy as the turning point with respect to the service's timber management; one cited the Bitterroot experience as an example of the pitfalls of treating a "vocal minority" of local citizens in a cavalier manner. The key events that reportedly changed the outlook of the service on one national forest were local: a proposal to permit installation of a tramway to the top of a mountain on the forest and a stand conversion program on a ranger district that involved "blading" aspen.[10] Both programs met with considerable public opposition; the local Sierra Club was reportedly organized as a result of the tramway controversy. In another area, a ranger cited a questionable timber sale as the pivotal event. (All these local controversies occurred at about the same time as passage of NEPA, the Bitterroot conflict, and other national events.)

Most of these events, however, were only symbols of the transition from the old order to the new; they illustrated strong public reaction to the agencies' policies or policy changes in response to public opposition. A number of administrators said increased recreational use of the public lands was the real key to change. The increase was dramatic, but it did not occur overnight. Forest Service recreation visitation, for example, grew rapidly, trebling from the 1950s to a 1973 level of 188 million visitor-days; by 1974 the BLM was accommodating 49 million visitor-days of recreation use.[11] The reason for the growth was that the national park system had become increasingly overburdened and the service and the bureau were absorbing the spillover. A district ranger and an area manager both cited as the symbolic change event the issuance of public land maps, which increased the visibility of their lands to the recreational public. Use conflicts involving recreation soon appeared: hunters complained that ranchers would not allow access to public lands; stockmen complained of hunters who littered "their" public rangeland with beer cans; forest cabin owners complained about the effects of timber sales on the view from their cabins. One ranger summed up these conflicts with the story of a "camper who came in to complain about 'the cowshit in my campsite.'"

Administrators saw the increased recreational use of the public lands as the cause of increased environmental pressure on the agencies. Administrators tended to subsume environmental pressures under the heading of "recreational use conflicts." Some administrators saw environmentalists, especially Sierrans or Wilderness Society members, as only a special class of recreationists. By whatever name, "recreationist" or "environmentalist," the effect was the same—the agencies knew they no longer had a homogeneous clientele of consumptive users. Recreationists and environmentalists were seen as a new attentive public of rangers and BLM managers. (Many administrators referred to environmentalists and recreationists as "new" constituents, even though these groups had been around for a long time. Hunters had used the public lands for many years, and the Sierra Club was formally organized many years before the BLM and the Forest Service.)

In short, in the early 1970s, the agencies recognized that a crucial change had occurred in their local constituencies. That change was manifested in balanced interest group pressures, use conflicts (pattern P), and heightened environmental concern (pattern L). Most important, from the agencies' point of view, the new participants were potentially a public constituency that would support the agencies' resource protection goals.

Constituency Management—Administrators' Reactions to Environmentalism

Administrators reacted in two ways to their agencies' new environmental and recreational clients. Many administrators reported that they now tried to consider a variety of additional factors relevant to their new clientele in making decisions, such as the effects on wildlife or the aesthetic quality of an area. This passive reaction represented a vaguely expressed form of environmental consciousness. The more interesting response, however, was active. A number of administrators said that their new environmental clients helped them deal with other users. No longer was the agency alone in trying to convert consumptive users to good land management practices, as had been the case in the old days. One ranger said he had "taken advantage of environmental groups by using them as a hammer on other users." A BLM manager thought of environmentalists as "allies" because he could "work one group off against another to come up with a manageable situation."

Administrators cited many examples of using the environmentalist threat to intimidate consumptive users. A ranger said he was trying to "educate" users to the pressure of environmentalists; because of an article on overgrazing on the forest by the environmental reporter of the major state newspaper, he said, "It seems the stockmen are coming around to the Forest Service position defensively, out of fear of the preservationists." Another ranger reported he had a clipping on exploration damage from a local paper that he liked to pull out while negotiating with oil and gas operators in order to remind them that their operations were under public scrutiny. Yet another ranger said the forest products and oil and gas industries were "a hell of a lot easier to deal with" because of environmentalists: when the oil and gas firms tried to "play the energy crisis" off against the service, he told them they had to "shape up to avoid litigation from the Sierra Club." He claimed to use the same specter to get forest products operators to conform to service preferences on slash disposal. A national grassland ranger recalled the "shocked looks on the ranchers' faces" at a public meeting "when they found out someone else was interested in the public lands." Several rangers and stockmen noted a quote attributed to former representative Wayne Aspinall, that the "Cowboys had better not fight grazing fee increases, but fight to keep grazing" in the face of the environmental threat.[12]

Sometimes the use of the environmental specter went beyond a verbal warning. One ranger recalled how he had taken a local newspaper reporter on a tour of a timber sale area when he was having a few problems with the sale operator and pointed out all the damage in the sale site in an effort to get a critical (and thus useful) story about the service. Another ranger's major problem at the time of the field interviewing was a proposed residential-recreational development on a withinholding (private land inside the forest) that needed a Forest Service road permit for access. Local environmentalists and recreationists were trying to get the developer to sign a contract specifying the environmental constraints on the development. Asked about the Forest Service's position on all this, the ranger smiled, "Oh, we are just sitting back and watching."

As mentioned above, not all local administrators claimed to make active use of their new environmental constituency. Roughly half the administrators suggested they defined their role in a professional-technical way; they saw the new environmental constituency as affecting overall agency policy. These administrators reacted passively to environmentalists, considering environmental values along with economic factors because that approach was agency policy. But the results were similar with both approaches: the service and bureau allowed their "new" environmentalist and recreationist clients to affect their decisions.

The Consequences of Constituency Management

Participants in local public lands politics had greater difficulty identifying effects of interest group activity on specific local policy decisions than expressing their general sense of group influence. This was true for several reasons. First, interest group leaders and many administrators did not have personal knowledge of all factors that entered into specific decision processes. Second, participants understandably had greater difficulty describing influences in specific cases precisely because of their divergent generalizations about influence (the conservationist generalization about industry capture, the industry generalization about environmentalist capture, and administrators' dual constituency generalization); it is difficult to apply three very different generalizations to the same set of facts. Third, as chapter 9 will show in greater detail, group influence, especially in low-level administrative settings, is a nebulous phenomenon—not a direct, visible, cause-and-effect sequence like a logger with a chain saw felling a tree. Thus (as chapter 9 will also suggest) it is fairly easy to fail to preceive influence when it exists.

Local public lands decision processes, as outlined in chapter 4 (pages 110–125), are usually sequences of decisions about specific projects or actions (for example, the six-stage sequence from inventory through reforestation in timber management). However, it is useful to artificially divide the decision process into two parts in discussing the observations of local participants about the effects of interest groups on specific decisions. Participants generally believed groups were less influential in the beginning of the decision process (those steps in the sequence leading up to decisions to allocate lands to certain uses or allow certain levels of uses) than at the end (the steps implementing or monitoring the levels-of-use decisions). These observations about differential influence, shared by administrators and group contacts, were a logical extension of administrators' perceptions of their dual constituencies and manipulations of those constituencies.

Group Influence and the Front End of the Decision Process

The early stages in agency decision processes lead up to the decisions that are presumably of greatest interest to client groups. The volume of timber sold by the agencies, the number of animal-unit-months of grazing permits or leases issued, the numbers and boundaries of Wilderness area designations recommended, and so forth, are the bottom line in public lands policy for the forest products and livestock industries, preservationists, and other clients of the Forest Service and BLM. Thus, explicit group demands for these primary goods and services should, in theory, be the nub of interest group activities.

Both interest group contacts and administrators, however, reported that such explicit group demands had little effect on local agency decisions. Major timber sale contracts were offered by the service according to its professional silvicultural criteria and as a result of its complicated and technical timber management planning process. Forest Service and forest products industry sources argued that industry pressure in any form, implicit or explicit, was almost never involved in major timber sale decisions. Several rangers said they might respond to a request for a small "ranger sale" ($2,500 or less in value) from a gypo logger who was a "good operator" and who had not been able to obtain sales from his usual sources, but only two rangers could recall an instance of persistent industry demands for more sales than the Forest Service had planned. Furthermore, these demands were balanced by two cases reported by different rangers of opposition to planned timber sales: one by local environmentalists and a nearby city government and the other by an irate homeowner near the sale.

Interviewees claimed that users who did explicitly demand increased agency output were usually unsuccessful. The forest products industry struck out in all the cases noted above: The service did not offer the additional requested sales, and the sale volume was lowered significantly in both sales involving public opposition. Ranchers, like small gypo loggers, did not hesitate to request more animal-unit-months. But administrators reported such requests received relatively short shrift. An area manager noted that, in the past, ranchers who wanted to run extra stock "got the increase as a matter of course, just by signing a form, but now we go out, look at the land, and say, 'What about watershed? What about wildlife?' And he doesn't get the increase." Most permittees agreed that they could not obtain increased stock use by request, pressure, or any other means. In fact, their main concern was to avoid "the cut," the administrative decision to lower their permitted allotment of animal-unit-months.

When groups seemed to benefit from local decisions on output levels, their success was usually attributed to administrative factors beyond their control. In an area in which national forest campgrounds were being systematically closed, the president of a strong local private campground association (whose members stood to benefit from the decision because of decreased competition) and Forest Service officers maintained no pressure was involved, that the service was forced into the closing by curtailed recreation budgets. Mining industry officials reported they had no difficulties with basic use rights decisions because, as noted in chapter 4, local rangers and area managers did not have formal control over mineral lease, claim, or patent issuances.

The belief of local participants that groups—or at least *their* groups—played a minimal role in the agencies' local front-end decisions helps explain the beliefs of those same participants about group influence. It was not surprising that group contacts felt the agencies must be captured by their opponents because, on bottom-line policy decisions, they never seemed to successfully make demands for the goods and services they were most interested in.

The Back End of the Decision Sequence—Use Administration

Timber sale contracts, grazing permits or leases, special use permits, and other results of agency decisions usually place conditions on uses, in addition to allowing certain levels of use. *Use administration* involves specifying these conditions and monitoring users to ensure the conditions are met.

Most participants in the sample regions, particularly administrators and user group participants, agreed that the rise of environmentalists as constituents of the public lands agencies was felt most clearly in local use administration decisions. Forest products contacts and rangers almost unanimously reported that the major impact of environmentalists was on increased Forest Service restrictions on timber sales. Rangers were compelling timber operators to do a better job of treating slash (the material left on a sale site after trees are felled, branches cut away, and the main stems hauled away for milling). Treatment requirements included adhering to height limits on stumps and slash piles, gathering and burning slash, and following other procedures made necessary by specific site conditions. The service was also imposing stricter requirements on roads built in connection with timber sales, requiring the closing of sale operations during wet periods, construction of roads built to higher standards, installation of water bars after temporary roads had been used, and other measures. These restrictions were not examples of *ad hoc* decision making, but, as several rangers put it, of "holding operators' feet to the fire" in enforcing the provisions of standard timber sales contracts.

Participants from mining or oil and gas firms (as well as rangers and area managers) said the same sort of restrictions were the main consequence of environmental pressures on their operations at the local level. Administrators were increasingly strict, modifying permits to decrease the adverse effects of exploration or related activities. Typical restrictions involved siting of roads to minimize erosion; reseeding or water barring of roads after use, or both; prohibiting all but four-wheel-drive vehicles in areas where roads were inadvisable; modifying pipeline design to minimize interference with wildlife; and requiring improved fire control equipment. Administrators' goals were to decrease erosion, interference with wildlife (and sometimes livestock), and aesthetic damage. Administrators usually emphasized the erosion aspect, while mineral and O&G contacts (perhaps in a subtle depreciation of agency policy) emphasized aesthetics.

Major range management issues also involved use administration. Perhaps the most important use conflict that local administrators dealt with routinely involved recreation access to public lands through ranchers' property or allotments. Gates locked by stockmen caused many complaints by hunters and off-road vehicle (ORV) users. Stockmen, in turn, were critical of allegedly boorish behavior by hunters and ORV enthusiasts. The major programmatic relationship between the agencies and the livestock industry involved the implementation of rest-rotation grazing management (see pages 14 and 117). While rest-rotation can be very closely related to levels-of-use policies, its immediate management activities involve establishing extensive conditions on stock movement and ancillary improvements (fences, salt blocks, and so forth), so it is largely a use administration type of activity.

Use administration restrictions were even applied to some recreational activities. Excessive ORV and Wilderness backcountry use can damage soil and vegetation in fragile areas. Few incremental restrictions can decrease ORV damage, so ORV restrictions have involved closure of sensitive areas to ORV use. Though they have encountered much opposition recently, especially in California, ORV closures were not controversial in the sample regions in 1973. (Only on a forest with a wet-season closure policy and a BLM district that was in the preliminary stages of considering a closure was ORV use a minor issue.) The Forest Service has also restricted backcountry use of some overused areas with Wilderness permit systems. NF3 and NF4 had such a system at the time of the field research, but since it had been established in consultation with local preservationist groups, it was not controversial.

Use administration restrictions were not recent additions to the BLM or Forest Service policy repertoire. In fact, such restrictions were the substance of the basic compromises in multiple-use management that had evolved prior to the 1970s.[13] Though the restrictions were justified by administrators' references to environmental considerations, they usually involved benefits that were long-standing BLM or Forest Service objectives. Slash controls, for example, might be palmed off as aesthetic requirements, but the rangers' real concerns seemed to be the contribution of slash to hazardous forest fire conditions—a historic and legitimate concern of the Smokey Bears, but hardly a *cause célèbre* of the environmental movement. Nonetheless, all user groups claimed that, because of environmentalists, the agencies became much stricter in the early 1970s.

Most users recognized that some restrictions were good management practices. One timber mill owner, discussing slash requirements, noted, "We should have been doing this all along, but nobody fussed at us before." And a mining firm contact pointed out that mining operation restrictions were the result of "chips coming due from the past when greed outweighed cleanliness." However, though very few users opposed control per se, they generally had some complaint about the agencies' increased regulation of uses. (Note response pattern C in table 7-1.)

A few controls were opposed because users believed they were unnecessary or counterproductive. For example, the major issue on NF1 at the time of the fieldwork was the service's proposal to significantly upgrade the standards to which logging roads were to be built. All the timber operators in the region felt the roads were being overbuilt and did not think the higher-standard roads significantly improved logging operations or erosion control. The industry position was supported by local environmentalists (who thought higher-standard roads paved the way for other development affecting the natural character of the forest) and ORV club members (who preferred to ride rough roads). Moreover, economic self-interest was not a major reason for industry opposition. Because road costs were deducted from the calculation of the stumpage price that the Forest Service received from a sale, the costs of higher-standard roads would not come out of operators' pockets directly. Increased road costs had a very minor effect on the operator's profit margin, since the road contractor's profit increase slightly lowered the timber operator's share of total profit on the sale. The road standards' opponents believed that the service used such standards to force the timber industry to subsidize forest road system improvements (as deductions from stumpage prices) for which it could not obtain direct funding.

A Sierran whose family had a summer cabin under Forest Service permit had another example of agency controls that seemed unrelated to clear resource management principles. He claimed his family had been forced to repaint its cabin roof four times in ten years because each new ranger had a different professional judgment about roof colors.

Apart from disagreements with specific controls, users had three general complaints about increased agency restrictiveness. First, some operators agreed with particular controls but were dissatisfied when controls were not applied uniformly. Several loggers on one forest complained about a ranger who temporarily closed down logging operations in his district during the rainy season while other rangers left their competitors' sales open with, as one put it, "trucks driving through mud up to their axles." The cost of increased controls was, of course, a second complaint. One mining company official claimed, "Sometimes it costs as much to camouflage a powerline as it does to build it." Such costs were often only a minor part of users' dissatisfaction with control, as with the issue of logging road standards described above, but one forest products operator in the sample had been driven out of business when a ranger closed down his sale because of noncompliance with contract provisions. The third general complaint, which was the most common and the most annoying for users, was that the new environmental concern and controls unduly delayed agency decision making. A number of mining and O&G industry officials repeated a common argument: They had a right to their leases and permits; and they would "do whatever they [the BLM] tell us," but the delay involved in deciding what restrictions to impose was "something the industry can't live with." A stockman told of waiting eight years for Forest Service approval of a drift fence. Another rancher reported that he had been negotiating for three years over recreation use conflicts, soil samples, and management responsibilities for a small water impoundment for livestock use.

Such delays were typical results of the combination of restrictive use administration, environmentalist concerns, and the long-standing commitment of public land managers to multiple-use controls. Most of the delays that bothered traditional users were caused by the requirement that administrators prepare environmental analyses on an increasing number of agency actions. An *environmental analysis* or *environmental analysis report* (EAR) is an in-house report, not a NEPA environmental impact statement. An EAR is one stage in what has come to be called the NEPA process of environmental assessment, and a NEPA environmental statement is almost always preceded by an EAR, although most EARS do not lead to full-fledged environmental statements.[14] By 1973, EARs had become the standard decision-making document of the service's and BLM's local administrators.

Administrators recognized the problem of delays in approving uses and stipulating conditions of use, but pointed out that delay was the logical concomitant of EAR's fuller consideration of projects' effects on soils, aesthetics, wildlife, and so forth. They also noted that delays could hinder some beneficial projects, but the need to prepare an EAR could be, as one put it, "another leg to stand on to deny a bad project." That is, the EAR focused on environmental concerns, but it was an additional tool for accomplishing long-standing agency objectives—not a procedure foisted on the agencies out of the clear blue sky of the environmental decade. The Forest Service's EAR, for example, was a renamed and expanded version of a document called a "multiple-use report" in the 1960s.

Conclusions—Group Influence and Conformity

The potential for agency capture, a central theme of some major studies of the Forest Service and BLM, arose from the fact that land managers operated at a great distance from their line supervisors in an organizational environment that was believed to be dominated by dependent, economic user clienteles, the forest products and livestock industries. Philip Foss, in particular, argued that these pressures led the BLM to be captured by its rancher clients.[15] However, Herbert Kaufman argued that the Forest Service was able to avoid capture and foster conformity by a variety of administrative techniques, such as selective recruitment, post-entry socialization, formal control processes (use of the extensive Manual, inspections, and so forth), and frequent transfer of rangers.[16] As noted in chapter 6, the assumption of the simple capture thesis—that the agencies have a homogeneous organizational environment of economic user groups—is not borne out by the realities of the 1970s. The observations of participants about the nature of group influence in local public lands politics adds an ironic twist to the capture–conformity debate.

At first glance, participants' views seemed conflicting. On the one hand, interest group leaders generally thought the service and bureau were captured, albeit not by themselves. To these leaders, the agencies seemed to be single-mindedly pursuing policies favored by their opponents. Environmentalists believed the agencies were subservient to industry interests, while industry leaders felt the agencies were on an environmentalist binge. Forest Service and BLM administrators, on the other hand, did not see themselves as captured. However, their uncaptured state was not the result of the professional-bureaucratic conformity described by Kaufman.

The service's old transfer policy is an interesting case in point. The transfer policy is a good example of the service's mixture of informal and formal management techniques, as described by Kaufman: By breaking rangers' interpersonal ties to the communities in which they were stationed, the service fostered identification with other agency officers as a peer group; by leaving rangers vulnerable to detection of departures from agency policies, transfers sharpened effectiveness of the service's formal control procedures.[17]

However, in the 1970s rangers were being left on their districts for longer periods of time as a matter of conscious agency policy; thirteen of the twenty-eight rangers in the sample had been in their districts for at least five years. There was a significant benefit to longer tenure. Rangers became more familiar with the physiographic characteristics of the areas under their jurisdiction and could make better judgments about the applicability of different management practices without excessive reliance on district staff, particularly less experienced junior foresters. Interest group participants thought this point was particularly important, noting that frequent turnover of rangers disrupted district programs.

One reason for longer ranger tenure was a revision in federal personnel practices. Federal employees who were transferred were more fully reimbursed for their moving and realty costs in the 1970s than before. Thus, the administrative costs of playing, as one Forest Service officer put it, "musical rangers" to avoid capture had become very high. The service also faced an age lump problem; with several years of stable personnel levels and a policy of shifting staff down to field levels in the agency, there were not enough higher-level openings into which GS-11 and GS-12 officers could be transferred.

Primarily, however, ranger tenure no longer involved potential capture because line officers were now subject to multiple pressures. The agency's more balanced clientele eliminated the capture threat. Recreationists and environmentalists now kept rangers objective, and served the same purpose for the BLM. One district manager noted that both the Forest Service and BLM "have a unique opportunity among federal agencies to avoid capture by their users because they have multiple users."

The constituency balance provided by environmentalists resulted in patterns of apparent group influence that were conveniently consistent with agency policy. The policy of both agencies, as reflected in the very general guidelines of the multiple-use acts (and more recent statutes such as the Federal Land Policy and Management Act), was that administrators should attempt to provide goods and services to local clients, while protecting the land resources under their stewardship. As interpreted by administrators, group influences reinforced both parts of this policy. The traditional economic users had needs that created a market for the goods and services the agencies' multiple-use policy said should be provided. In the past, an agency administrators' professionalism or commitment to agency policy was the sole impetus to carry out the second half of the multiple-use goal, resource protection. But in the agencies' current constituencies, environmentalists were seen as an even stronger and more useful reason to effectively protect the land's resources.

The environmental movement of the 1970s constituted a powerful tool that the service and bureau used to reinforce the resource-protection half of the multiple-use policy. Environmentalists' criticisms of past land management mistakes and warnings of possible adverse environmental effects of contemplated agency projects were visible public pressures that agency officers could use to justify increasingly stringent restrictions on consumptive users' activities. The militant preservationist demands of many environmentalists added punch to such pressures because the demands confronted traditional users with a choice between complying with the agencies' restrictions or defending themselves against efforts to place more and more federal land off-limits to the "despoilers." Administrators consciously manipulated this environmentalist threat to obtain user compliance with the restrictions the agencies wished to impose.

Administrators' active use of their dual constituencies resulted in the appearance of very different levels of group influence in the two parts of the policy cycle. Groups were believed to play a significant role in the back end, or use administration part, of the decision cycle, but in the front end of the cycle, leading up to use allocation decisions, most participants believed groups had minimal influence. Participants may not have perceived environmentalist influence on timber sales, but that influence clearly affected slash requirements. Environmentalists did not appear to have any influence over mining or oil and gas lease decisions, but because of environmentalists, mining and energy companies were much more cooperative with Forest Service and BLM preferences concerning exploitation roads, pipeline designs, and so forth.

Administrators' multiple use of their constituencies helps explain the diverging views of capture held by conservationists and economic users. Interest group contacts were not blinded by their own ideologies; they were just looking at different sides of the same coin. Economic users compared their present relationship with the BLM or the Forest Service to the good old days. They were, as administrators confirmed, beset by the environmentalists (and administrators' use of the environmentalist threat). Environmentalists, on the other hand, were not fully aware of past service and bureau relationships with their user clients, or were aware only of those occasions on which the agencies had lost out to users. Some environmental group activists were relatively young, and most were new to environmental activism. Most line administrators, however, had been with their agencies for fifteen years or more, and economic users had dealt with the agencies for even longer—some forty to fifty years in the case of some stockmen. Moreover, administrators did not respond to environmentalists by giving them what they most wanted—Wilderness, wildlife, or whatever (especially the first)—but by playing them off against users. Forest Service and BLM officials had a real commitment to accommodating economic uses of the public lands or "economic demands" or the "needs of people".[18] They were not committed to recreation or Wilderness as primary uses of the public lands. Thus, the environmentalists' belief that the agencies failed to respond to their key explicit demands had some validity.

Capture and conformity, as evaluations of public lands management, are theoretically opposites: capture involves responding to interest groups, while conformity involves the professional use of formal agency procedures to resist group pressure. Thus, it is interesting that the agencies' response to interest groups seemed so thoroughly in conformity with the central multiple-use policies of the Forest Service and BLM. This blurring of the distinction between group influence and conformity with agency policy will be examined further in chapter 8.

NOTES

1. It is easy to show that an influencer preferred a policy and that a decision maker pursued that policy; such a relationship is called *contemporaneous correlation*. Lawyers and scientists, however, require more evidence to prove that the influencer caused the decision. One way to demonstrate cause would be to show that, had the influencer not been part of the decision process, a different policy would have been pursued. Such a demonstration is difficult because one cannot experiment on real political processes (that is, make the decision once with the influencer involved and then repeat it without the influencer). In chapter 10 we will use a formal mathematical model to overcome these difficulties in measuring group influence on policy.

2. The pure form of the so-called reputational approach—pioneered by Floyd Hunter in *Community Power Structure* (Chapel Hill, University of North Carolina Press, 1953)—consists of surveying community notables about whom they believe to be the most powerful people in their community. While there are several differences between the reputational approach and the approach used in this chapter, the latter has many of the same weaknesses (for example, participants' statements may reflect only the myths, not the realities, of influence) and strengths (for example, such myths affect political behavior, serving, for example, as a form of self-fulfilling prophesy).

3. Table 7-1 presents the results of a content analysis coding of the interviewees' responses to the open-ended question that began the interview protocol, and the questionnaire respondents' answers to a similar question on the mail questionnaire. The question was phrased, with slight variation for the type of participant (district administrator, supervisor, or interest group contact), "What are the most important factors in Forest Service and BLM policymaking?" The question was designed to elicit interviewees' objective descriptions of local public land policy processes, but sometimes the answers also reflected attitudinal reactions. Response patterns A, B, G, H, and Q were used in the analysis of participants' attitudes discussed on text pages 175–177. Also see appendix A.

4. Quotations appearing in this chapter are from the open-ended section of the field interviews; see appendix A. Interviews were recorded in longhand, so only the key words in the quotes are exact. The original sentence structure was sometimes altered to fit the text. The primary reason for including the quotations is to convey connotations of interviewees' statements. Readers should be cautious in accepting some of the quotations as statements of fact; they are presented as graphic examples of interviewee beliefs, even though some stories may be apocryphal or exaggerated.

5. Patterns E, F, I, J, and O included 36.5 percent of all responses. As noted below, most Primarily Administrators' Responses in table 7-1, when thoroughly analyzed, are agency policy responses as well.

6. See text pages 125–128. Responses directly reflecting the multiple-use policy or philosophy (pattern N) were frequently given. The four responses related to the multiple-use philosophy (patterns M, N, Q, and R) constituted 71 percent of all responses in the Primarily Administrators' Responses category. Kaufman also noted the extraordinary degree to which low-level Forest Service officers pledge allegiance to the concept of multiple use [*The Forest Ranger* (Baltimore, Md., Johns Hopkins University Press for Resources for the Future, 1960) p. 207].

7. This policy was set forth in the Forest Service Manual addendum for the region; exact citation not given because of the convention of not identifying the sample regions.

8. Kaufman, *The Forest Ranger*. See also text pages 65–69.

9. *Framework for the Future* (Washington, D.C., Forest Service, February 1970).

10. In the process of *aspen blading* a bulldozer blade is used to knock down stands of aspen before planting more commercially valuable species of trees.

11. Glen O. Robinson, *The Forest Service* (Baltimore, Md., Johns Hopkins University Press for Resources for the Future, 1975) p. 119; and BLM, *Public Lands Statistics—1974* (Washington, D.C., GPO, 1974).

12. Chairman of the Public Land Law Review Commission and, until his defeat (at the hands of, among others, the League of Conservation Voters), chairman of the House Interior Committee, Aspinall, a Colorado Democrat, was widely regarded as the western livestock industry's most powerful friend in Congress.

13. See, for example, the discussion above, and pp. 126–127, of Philip Martin, "Conflict Resolution Through the Multiple-Use Concept in Forest Service Decision Making," *Natural Resources Journal* vol. 9 (April 1969) pp. 228–236.

14. An environmental impact statement is required for "major federal actions significantly affecting the quality of the human environment" by section 102(2)(c) of the National Environmental Policy Act, 43 U.S.C. 4321. EARs (or similar documents with different names) are required by department- and bureau-level rules and procedures. Such rules and procedures were usually formally codified as implementations of the Council on Environmental Quality's guidelines interpreting NEPA. For a detailed discussion of NEPA's environmental statement criteria and procedures, see Frederick Anderson, *NEPA in the Courts* (Baltimore, Md., Johns Hopkins University Press for Resources for the Future, 1973).

15. Philip Foss, *Politics and Grass* (Seattle, Washington University Press, 1960). Also see Wesley Calef, *Private Grazing and Public Lands* (Chicago, Ill., University of Chicago Press, 1960).

16. Kaufman, *The Forest Ranger*. Also see text pages 28–29 and 68–69. A study conducted slightly prior to this study's field research concluded that the Forest Service still maintained a high degree of conformity on the part of its field officers; see Gordon Bultena and John Hendee, "Foresters' Views of Interest Group Positions on Forest Policy," *Journal of Forestry* vol. 70 (June 1970) pp. 337–343.

17. Kaufman, *The Forest Ranger*, pp. 155–156 and 176–179.

18. Bultena and Hendee, in "Foresters' Views," also report a high level of commitment by local administrators to resource use.

8

Public Participation

One major effect on the natural resources agencies of the National Environmental Policy Act (NEPA) of 1970 was the increase in formal public participation in agency decision making. NEPA's environmental impact statement (EIS) process has been one very important means by which the public, particularly environmentalists, have participated in natural resources decision making.[1] Beginning with the poverty agencies' "maximum feasible participation" programs in the 1960s, public participation spread to a variety of other policy areas, and as NEPA was being passed, several natural resources agencies were experimenting with citizen participation. The Army Corps of Engineers was among the first to develop public participation programs, and it still has one of the better programs, even though its efforts have not always been fully effective.[2] Public participation has been official Forest Service policy since 1970, falling under the "Inform and Involve" program established in 1972.[3] While not so well publicized, the Bureau of Land Management's (BLM's) public participation program is comparable in form and scope to the Forest Service's.

In one sense, public participation was nothing new for land management agencies. The institution of the BLM advisory board, for example, was a mechanism for permitting participation in agency decision making by a public, although a rather narrow one. But when critics argued that the public lands agencies did not afford the public access to decision making, they were reacting to precisely such patterns of participation as the BLM's advisory boards, the supposed mechanism of its capture by the livestock industry.[4] As environmental groups' political action manuals reveal, the groups with the greatest commitment to public participation saw themselves as excluded from agency decision making before 1970.[5] Thus, *public participation* can mean any mechanism that allows access to agency officials by groups beyond those that traditionally participated intimately in agency policymaking.

Public participation is a euphonious, democratic-sounding term. The public lands belong to the public, so the argument goes, and the public has a right to participate in decisions about its lands. But public participation theorists maintain that participation should not give the public simply a *sense* of participation, but real influence in agency decision making.[6] Thus, public participation should be recognized as a procedure to channel and legitimatize interest group access to administrative decision making. And access, as David Truman, the leading theorist of group influence, put it, "is the facilitating intermediate objective of political interest groups."[7]

The Scope of Public Participation

Agency public participation programs take many forms. Most participants in the public lands policy system think of the public meeting as the primary mode of public participation. These are typically formal affairs, usually confined to a single topic and conducted with a standard structure of introduction of a proposal by agency administrators and reactions by individuals, usually interest group leaders, in a question-and-answer or prepared-statement format. There is some variation on this standard structure. One BLM resource area in the sample held a county fair-style public meeting on a Management Framework Plan (a land use plan for part of the resource area), at which the district staff set up booths around a large room and attendees went from booth to booth to express their views on different aspects of the plan. It is not uncommon for the agencies (especially at land use plan public meetings) to pass out folders with fact sheets, maps, and other material to participants.

Public meetings are supposed to attract a random cross section of the population, the so-called general public, to provide input for the agencies' decision-making processes. Many administrators interviewed, Forest Service and BLM alike, were frustrated that "only the special interests" showed up at public meetings. This frustration usually seemed naive, since administrators' local attentive public *was* the special interests. Sometimes, however, concern about the representativeness of public participation input was valid. One assistant ranger, suspicious of the volume of mail comments on a proposal, traced the large majority back to a stimulated letter campaign organized by the developers who proposed the project. Rangers, like congressmen, devalue such input.

Some administrators also had unrealistic expectations about the nature of the input that public participation was supposed to produce. Forest Service administrators, in particular, expected public participation to be professional; that is, they expected comments in public participation forums to present new information about the subject under consideration that they had overlooked. Thus, when public participation events produced primarily expressions of preferences about management decisions, the Forest Service people were sometimes frustrated. The BLM representatives had more realistic expectations and accepted the preference content of public meetings. (The BLM's realism was the subject of interagency sniping by some Forest Service officers. They argued that the BLM's approach was unprofessional because it allowed laymen to provide information at the inventory stage of planning processes that professional managers should identify for themselves. BLM officers countered that the service's approach to participation was often overprofessional and stuffy.) Frustration with the new public meeting participation forum was common in both agencies and all three sample regions.[8]

Public meetings are not the only medium of participation. Land managers recognize that their relationships with local contacts (discussed in chapter 6) are part of their public participation program. Individual, one-to-one interactions may not sound sophisticated as a public participation plan, but they are often a more effective mode of participation than a public meeting, where the public aspect tends to discourage candor, encourage tactical overstatements of positions, and inhibit two-way conversation.

Agency administrators sometimes attend meetings of relevant groups, including user groups (such as local stockmen's associations or chapters of the Society of American Foresters), conservationists, or more peripherally interested groups, such as chambers of commerce. Local agency officers, especially staff officers, often join some of these groups as a public participation activity (even though the administrator is participating in the public's activity, rather than vice versa).

The Forest Service also takes groups of interested persons on tours of areas of the forest where some agency action is the source of local interest or controversy; the service considers these tours "information and education" (I&E) events. A ranger might give a tour to the site of a recent clear-cut timber sale to show critics how well the sale turned out. One Sierra Club interviewee observed that such tours, especially on horseback, were excellent lobbying opportunities because he could "wait until we are three hours out in the backcountry, and then bend the ranger's ear all the way back." The rangers, who spend most of their time riding a swivel chair, also seem to like this form of public participation, despite being the captive audience.

Local administrators spent a good deal of time in public participation activities. The thirty-seven rangers and area managers in the sample were involved in a total of 556 public participation events in the year preceding the fieldwork (roughly mid-1972 through mid-1973); the number of events per district ranged from three to forty-seven, with an average of fifteen. Table 8-1 shows the distribution of events by type. The most com-

Table 8-1. Public Participation Events

	Category		Subcategory	
Type of event	No.	(%)	No.	(%)
Public meetings, by major subject	153	(27.5)		
Wilderness			29	(5.2)
Land use plan			69	(12.4)
Timber-related function			8	(1.4)
Range-related function			15	(2.7)
Recreation/wildlife-related			4	(0.7)
ORV use			5	(0.9)
Land's function (for example, roads, and so forth)			14	(2.5)
General set of topics			3	(0.5)
Other			6	(1.1)
Agency-initiated meetings with interest groups	279	(50.2)		
Grazing association meetings			214	(38.5)
Grazing advisory board (BLM or Forest Service)			43	(7.7)
NF multiple-use advisory board meeting			2	(0.4)
Other interest group meetings			20	(3.6)
"I&E" and "show me" tours, and so forth	74	(13.3)		
Other	50	(9.0)		
Total	556	(100%)		

Note: Participation events held by the thirty-seven district rangers or area managers in the sample, or related to their districts or resource areas. The mean number of events per district/area was 15.0, the median, 12.0, and the Standard Deviation, 10.8.

mon was the grazing association meeting; almost all of these occurred on ranger districts, and over half were held on four districts with twenty to forty meetings. When the BLM advisory board, Forest Service grazing advisory board, and range-related public meetings are added to the grazing association meetings, livestock-oriented events make up almost half of all public participation events (48.9 percent).

The largest of the nonrange event categories were related to Wilderness and the land use planning process. During the year preceding the field interviewing the Forest Service conducted the Roadless Area Review (RARE I), and most of the twenty-nine Wilderness-related public meetings were held in connection with this process. Also during that year, both the service and the bureau were beginning to implement their agency-wide, comprehensive land use planning processes.[9] The BLM's included public meetings at each of its three stages, and the Forest Service's included public meetings at two of its three stages.

New Public Participation Styles

Public participation was an important concern of many participants in local public lands politics at the time of the fieldwork. In the early 1970s the programs were fairly new, so their successes and failures were fresh in many participants' minds. In addition, public participation began in earnest at the same time environmentalists and recreationists emerged as local clients of the Forest Service and BLM, and these groups strongly supported it. Indeed, the public participation programs clearly illustrated the shift in public lands politics from user-dominated local constituencies to balanced environmentalist-user constituencies.

There appeared to be three styles of public participation in the sample regions during the early 1970s. These styles were influenced by several interrelated factors:[10] administrators' attitudes toward public participation, variations among the local organization-sets of the agencies, the use of informal participation to supplement formal public meetings, and the reactions of group leaders to the agencies' public participation efforts. There was variation from one district administrative unit to another, but public participation style generally seemed similar among most agency units in a sample region. The three styles were (1) relatively underdeveloped public participation in BLM and Forest Service units in State C, (2) polarized public participation in Forest Service units in State B, and

(3) well-developed public participation in Forest Service units in State A and BLM units in State B.

The Underdeveloped Public Participation Style

All hallmarks of well-developed public participation were conspicuously absent from State C sample units. First, the agencies held few public meetings, and those were poorly attended. One ranger reported that only seventeen people attended his two RARE I public meetings. Another ranger's idea of public participation was to meet with local garden clubs or Scout troops. As one ranger put it, both administrators and the local public were "infants" at public participation.

Second, and more important, administrators almost universally approached public meetings as a forum at which to "sell" their positions. There was even the suggestion in some administrators' interviews that public meetings were administrative hoops that they and the meeting attendees had to jump through. This attitude came through very clearly to the agencies' local constituents. One rancher said that, at the public meetings he had attended, "It seemed the BLM had its mind made up already." Another rancher said the BLM and Forest Service "like to have their ducks all lined up, and then hit you with them." A local government official said the service presented its plans with a "take it or leave it" attitude. Another local government official described a meeting in which there was complete opposition to the Forest Service's proposal, after which the service implemented it anyway; the official observed, "I can't figure out why they even bothered with the public meeting if they had their minds made up."[11] The problem with this approach to public meetings is that it engenders an image of the agency and its administrators as authoritarian and close-minded; one mining company official referred to it as the "Smokey-the-Bear attitude."

The underdeveloped state of public participation in State C was only partly because of administrator inexperience with the new forms of participation. Several administrators pointed out that their constituents were primarily traditional user groups. State C, especially the sample region in the state, was hardly a hotbed of environmentalism. (One State B Sierra Club officer said of State C environmentalists, "I can name them all.") In such a situation, public meetings were of questionable value, if not counterproductive. The agencies were already familiar with the viewpoints of their traditional user group clients, so a public meeting in which traditional users vastly outnumbered conservationists and recreationists gave the agencies no new information. Moreover, a public meeting with few or no environmentalists did not allow administrators to "educate" users to environmental demands. Because "the other [environmental] side is just not there," as a Forest Service officer put it, the service deemphasized public participation. So, as a district manager put it, "You have to take the sell-your-plan approach." In short, the system was little changed from the past, when the agencies used a bureaucratic and professional approach against a homogeneous user constituency.

Administrators in the State C sample region did have some contacts with local conservationists. Several Forest Service administrators and a BLM district manager had effective contacts with a wildlife federation officer that involved informal consultation in the early stages of decision making. In addition, BLM, Forest Service, wildlife federation, stockmen, and state game department interviewees reported that the State C game department played a major role, as the representative of the wildlife federations (the major conservation groups in the region), in dealings with the service and bureau. The forest supervisor of NF5 and the district manager of NRL9 both described an informal "interagency board," composed of themselves and the regional state game department director, which convened every month or so during fishing trips.

The Polarized Public Participation Style

Many Forest Service administrators in State B also approached the new public participation mandate reluctantly. When asked about public participation, many rangers damned it by faint praise. Participation made them "take a closer look at" management practices, or it was a "limiting factor" that made them think things through. One ranger conceded that, while the rangers used to be the experts, now there were citizens with more expertise on wildlife, and "this makes it slower to get things done." Another thought the service had increased its efforts to involve the public "by a thousand percent," but felt the public response had not matched these efforts. The service's reluctant effort at participation was reflected in one forest's information and education (I&E) plan, a skimpy and uninspired document on the use of press releases. (The plan's skimpiness was understandable; as the forest's I&E officer put it, "I spend 110 percent of my time on timber management, and the rest on I&E.") Another ranger argued that public participation was Congress's responsibility, not his.[12]

Several other Forest Service officers were more candid about their reservations about public participation. They felt public participation events were too polarized to be productive. As one ranger put it, RARE I public meetings produced "a fifty-fifty split," with user groups "100 percent against and not bashful about saying so, and the preservationists 100 percent the other way." Another ranger cringed as he recalled a meeting of opposing claques: "An ecologist would make a point and the ecologists would all applaud; then a logger or rancher would make a point and their side would cheer."

Environmentalist and user (particularly forest products) contacts confirmed the polarity of this region's Forest Service constituents. The opposing sides were a strong forest products industry and an active, numerous, very well organized set of preservation and environmental groups strongly advocating Wilderness designation and opposing timber sales and a variety of other developments. The two sides' worst confrontation occurred in public meetings held as part of the RARE I process. (The region contained a relatively high number of prime areas for Wilderness designation.) Interest group interviewees in State B complained most bitterly about the other side's domination of the service. A Sierran complained about user "domination" of public meetings, while a timber operator denounced public meetings as "group therapy" in response to the new environmental "delirium."

There were several consequences of this polarized situation. For one thing, personal relationships could get rather nasty. One Forest Service officer expressed open and profane antagonism toward environmentalists throughout his interview. An environmentalist, aware of the service's unhappiness with the polarization, said the service was not adept at communication or preliminary consultation to defuse conflict, gave the impression it resented "meddling," and was "paranoid." A forest products industry source characterized a public meeting as having attracted "environmental freaks who think wilderness is neat, and haven't the vaguest idea about what good resource management is." This same man later turned on the service, saying that rangers were typically "nasty, unbusinesslike, and surly." One other area, a town in State C with a ranger and detached resource area manager, also had a polarized style. A vocal environmentalist there described the agencies as "in bed together with the cowboys." Administrators accused this man of being an "extremist," and a mining company official predicted he was "going to get run out of town someday."

Clearly, some of the people in these public lands systems did not like each other very much. Such personal antagonism did not involve all agency officers or group leaders in the polarized areas to the same extent. However, participants tended to generalize on the basis of a few animosities.

The polarized public participation style had other, less personalistic consequences. Both sides in State B became more extreme. Forest products industry people, for example, reported that environmental "extremism" caused them to react extremely. Because the division brought public participation to a standstill, other agency constituents who were not part of the conflict were affected. One moderate wildlife federation officer commented on the "untouchable" professional image of the service's rangers: "You don't go in and sit on the old boy's desk—you write a letter." Some rangers were able to develop reasonable public relations. One who appreciated the culture of local stockmen, for example, got high marks from local ranchers as a good communicator. An environmental group professional staffer who generally avoided personal recriminations was reportedly used as a receiver of leaks as a pressure-generating tactic in connection with an in-service controversy. And service and environmentalist sources could recall at least one case of prior consultation of environmentalists by the agency, with beneficial results (a plan to restrict overuse of a Wilderness area). But these were exceptions.

Forest Service interviewees claimed that, since it was in the middle of a sharply polarized situation, the service could effectively ignore public participation input. Public participation produced two extreme positions, so the service was free to implement any position in between on the basis of its professional judgment. Some rangers noted that the environmentalist position was less likely to prevail when a polarized participation system allowed the service full flexibility because its policies, and its administrators' professional values, favored more utilitarian decisions. In particular, several rangers complained that polarized situations precluded helpful environmental pressure on timber sale contract enforcement.

In summary, a polarized situation led to understandable agency reluctance to pursue a meaningful public participation program; administrators were gun-shy. This reinforced the existing polarity, lack of communication between the service and both extremes, and general feelings among clients of inefficacy. However, Forest Service administrators reported that extreme polarity allowed them to pursue their preferred policies because of a lack of consensus.

The Well-Developed Public Participation Style

The Forest Service units in State A and the BLM units in State B conducted public participation in ways radically different from their colleagues in the other sample regions. The primary manifestation of the difference was not just more public participation events, but a different attitude toward public participation on the part of administrators, a belief that they should obtain diverse opinions and treat those opinions seriously. Forest Service officers in State A explained that the old style was symbolized by I&E (information and education) and the attitude underlying it was that the service demonstrated to people (especially its critics) why its position was correct. The new approach has been best summarized by the service's 1972 Washington office directive *Inform and Involve* (I&I). Key quotes from the directive illustrate the I&I approach:[13]

> Broaden contacts with groups, associations, and organizations to better inform and involve a wide range of the public on current programs, projects and issues.
> The key . . . is "awareness," and the key to awareness is "listening." . . . It means seeking out and listening to individuals and groups which may have traditionally opposed certain aspects of Forest Service management.
> Recognize that public involvement is an essential part of decision making since it can enable the decision maker to render a better decision.
> Discard any notion that actions which will affect environmental quality or the public interest can be judged only by professionals.
> Keep in mind that all interest groups are champions of some aspects of good resource management. Disregarding the concern of specific groups on one issue because of extreme controversy may well weaken their desire to get involved on other issues in which they could make valuable contributions.
> Recognize that public involvement requires that it must be sought out *before* a decision has been reached.

In short, the change lay in a substitution of "involvement" for "education," from handing the public the service's decision to finding out what the public wanted before reaching a decision. And the public explicitly included "groups which . . . traditionally opposed [the] Forest Service," that is, environmentalists and recreationists.

State A Forest Service officers noted some initial resistance to the change to I&I. As one ranger put it, "Relating to people was not a Forest Service long suit; we related much better to trees." But then the State A rangers accepted participation; a forest supervisor even noted, "Some of them went overboard and wanted to hold public meetings on everything." Most Forest Service officers described the change as part of a shift to a new managerial style. A ranger could no longer be "an old-time ranger who gets on his horse and rides into the sunset," or "a guy who marks his own trees." Not only did a ranger have to manage a fair-sized organization and be a planner, but he had to manage his organizational environment as well. As one ranger put it, "Just as you can tell about a rancher by the gates he keeps, you can tell about a ranger by his public relations." Public participation was no longer, in these rangers' minds, a countervailing force to their professional expertise; I&I skills, rather, were new professional skills.

The sense of public participation professionalism affected the service's conduct of public meetings. NF1's rangers took considerable pride in their ability to organize and conduct public meetings. Several rangers went to some lengths during interviews to describe how a proper public meeting should be held, and several proudly dragged out their public meeting props, particularly their massive map displays.[14] On one occasion during the fieldwork, the author observed several Forest Service officers at a Park Service public meeting. During the meeting, several of the Forest Service officers pointed out deficiencies in the Park Service meeting structure, explained how the degeneration of the meeting into an uncontrolled event was related to its organization, and observed that *they* never made *those* kinds of mistakes. The running commentary indicated that these foresters' viewed public participation skills as professional skills. And their comments were not based on mere hubris; several interest group leaders contrasted the same meeting's deficiencies with the Forest Service's skilled handling of similar meetings.

The most notable feature of the public participation program in the well-developed style, and the feature that most clearly distinguished that style from the other two, was the use of informal as well as formal means of participation. Informal participation was not new to the service or BLM; in the past stockmen and forest products people, as well as other users, had regular informal access to land managers as an adjunct to their normal business contacts. The differences were that the service actively sought to establish informal participation channels, and the primary target of its efforts was its new constituency of environmentalists and recreationists.[15]

The ranger on NF1's city ranger district was the main contact for the service's new clients. His most frequent contact (other than timber operators with active sales, but at a contact frequency equivalent to theirs) was the leader of the local Sierra Club. The ranger and his staff also dealt with other environmental, recreational, and civic groups by attending their meetings and often joining the groups. Where most rangers were members of local fraternal organizations or chambers of commerce, the urban ranger's staff belonged to environmental and recreation groups. One member of the district staff was an officer of the local Sierra Club and a member of the Izaak Walton League. The ranger attended the meetings of several groups on a regular basis. An ORV club president recalled that, after club members attended a public meeting and said some complimentary things about a Forest Service proposal, a district staff representative showed up at their next meeting to ask about joining the club.

Even though much of the district's I&I work was directed at the agency's new clientele, the district did not neglect more traditional contacts: the ranger was a SAF chapter chairman, and one of the assistant rangers was a member of the city chamber of commerce. This approach to public participation represented a very heavy commitment to informal public participation; as the ranger involved put it, "Sometimes there are more words in the mouth than the butt can absorb." This ranger carried a much heavier participation load than those in other districts in State A because of the concentration of environmental and recreation groups in the city, but the same informal participation pattern was found on the rest of the NF1 and NG2 ranger districts.

Informal participation took place in one-to-one situations, over the telephone, on neutral ground (for example, at a meeting of another organization), as well as at meetings of the target interest group. It had two main objectives. The first was to consult interest groups before formal meetings or announcements of proposals. Prior consultation involved pretesting a proposal to determine what, if any, aspects were controversial (allowing the agency, if possible, to eliminate controversial but peripheral aspects of the proposal) and sometimes gathering intelligence on problems before the agency knew what its proposal would be. Informal consultation often took place before formal public meetings. Another purpose of prior consultation, according to some rangers, was to build up a reserve of personal acquaintances and goodwill that could be drawn on in the future.

The Forest Service units in State A were manifestly successful in achieving goodwill. Time and again, interest group interviewees in State A commented on the new, open style of Forest Service public relations. There, the word most often used to describe the service was "cooperative." These positive evaluations were not restricted to one end of the local interest group spectrum. A chamber of commerce interviewee described the Forest Service as "one of the few government agencies which is close to the people," and contrasted the Forest Service openness to the aloofness of the Park Service's local administrators. This interviewee was not the first chamber of commerce person to depreciate the Park Service, but a leader of the local Sierra Club—which nationally is one of the Park Service's strongest supporters and often in conflict with the Forest Service —made a similar observation. Nor were positive evaluations based on feelings that the service capitulated to the interviewees' preferences. Many interviewees expressed some variation on the theme, "They don't always do what you want, but at least they listen."

The service's approach to public participation in State A was not the only aspect of the State A system affecting the efficacy of participation. Many interviewees characterized local environmentalists as "moderates." Local Sierrans supported logging on NF1, agreeing with the Forest Service and forest products industry interviewees that NF1's timber stands were too heavy. As long as the service did not clear-cut, timber sales were acceptable.[16] Also, local environmentalists felt no areas qualified as Wilderness, so the controversial Wilderness issue was not raised. As noted in chapter 7, the forest products industry, environmentalists, major local recreationist groups, and ORV clubs were united in their opposition to the service's policy of upgrading forest road standards. In short, the interest groups with passionately held and mutually exclusive preferences that were found in the other regions did not exist in State A. As a timber mill operator put it, "Somebody must have done a good job of brainwashing these people [environmentalists]." The same could have been said of him and his colleagues in the forest products and livestock industries.

State B's sample BLM district, NRL7, showed many of the same characteristics. BLM administrators expressed the same basic attitude toward public participation, one manager arguing that it was not real public involvement when administrators formulated a plan and then tried to "sell" it. The district practiced informal consultation as a major participation tool, especially with conservationists. During one of the interviews, a Sierran was rummaging through the district files with the full approval of BLM personnel, preparing for a public meeting on land use planning. And the district's relationships with both users and conservationists were well regarded. The oil and gas people had worked out an arrangement whereby BLM staff and the companies' personnel made preliminary inspections of sites to work out problems before formal applications were made. Stockmen thought the bureau was more responsive than the service. One board member characterized the ranger as "haughty," and said of the area manager, "He will listen, even though he may not do what you want." A Sierran described the BLM as better at public participation than the service, as "seeking truth," while participation was a formality with the latter. He said that the BLM was the "most enlightened land management agency" in the state, that the BLM "thinks fifty to one hundred years ahead, while the Forest Service only thinks to the next timber sale," and even stated that the BLM's district manager was more knowledgeable, intellectual, and widely read than his counterparts in the service. Moreover, in a controversy between the Park Service and NRL7 over which agency would administer a scenic area, local environmentalists suported the BLM. The environmental groups that got along so famously with the BLM in State B were viewed as "extremists" by the Forest Service. Thus, the "moderate environmentalist" theme in State A did not apply in State B. However, State B environmentalists did not generally view the BLM as the main focus of the Wilderness issue, which was a major part of their conflict with the Forest Service.

Comparison of the Three Participation Styles

The three styles of participation seemed related to two factors. One was the nature of the local interest group constituency of the agency. When the constituency included few conservationists or recreationists, public participation was underdeveloped. This was understandable, since the participation programs were designed to accommodate the new constituents and to provide a forum for offsetting the traditional commodity users in the agencies' clienteles. If there were not enough conservationists, the new participation approaches were pointless. In those areas in which there was a substantial local environmental clientele, the public participation style was either polarized or well developed. The style of participation seemed based, at least in part, on the perceived extremism of environmentalists vis-à-vis the agencies' policies. The second factor, to which interest group interviewees ascribed more importance, was the perceived commitment of administrators to open participation. The nature of the local constituency seemed to the author, however, to play a much more important role in determining the style of participation.

There seemed to be two types of consequences of the different styles of participation. One involved the feelings of efficacy on the part of the agencies' local constituents. In both the underdeveloped and polarized styles, group constituents did not feel very effective. They viewed the agencies as authoritarian and aloof. Participants in the polarized situation even expressed personal hostility. With the cooperative or well-developed participation style, however, group interviewees had positive feelings about the agencies. The effect of the cooperative style bordered on co-optation. It should be noted that the Forest Service's program in State A was not an *ad hoc* program; the agency in State A did exactly what *Inform and Involve* told it to do, and did it in an efficient and effective manner.

In terms of the effect of different participation styles on what the agencies ultimately decided, it was much more difficult to find a difference. In the underdeveloped participation style, administrators reported that the "sell-the-agency-position" approach allowed them to do things their own way. In the well-developed, consensual style, administrators reported that cooperative participation helped them arrive at the outcomes they wanted. To the extent that interest group interviewees touched on this point, they confirmed the administrators' versions of the effects of participation on decisions. In short, under each participation style, administrators managed the situations to suit their own objectives.[17]

Special Cases of Participation—
The Grazing Associations and Advisory Boards

Public meetings and related aspects of the agencies' new programs were only part of what could be broadly defined as their public participation programs. Using a broad definition of participation, events that targeted only the agencies' livestock industry clientele made up the largest category of public participation events (46.2 percent of all events in the sample units, versus public meetings' 27.5 percent). Thus, in terms of quantity alone, the grazing associations or advisory boards merit discussion. But the grazing-related events were also important for substantive reasons. First, the BLM grazing advisory boards have a central place in the literature on public lands politics because they were supposedly the mechanism by which stockmen maintained their hegemony over the bureau.[18] By the 1970s, however, the role of the BLM's grazing advisory boards had changed considerably. Second, both the BLM's grazing advisory boards and the service's grazing associations illustrate the current relationships between the agencies and their traditional user clienteles.

The Demise of BLM Advisory Board Influence

The grazing advisory boards in the first two decades of the bureau's existence (first as the Grazing Service and later as the BLM) were a dominant influence on local management of the public domain grazing districts. The boards maintained veto power over the most important policy decisions of local managers, the level of livestock grazing leases. Local BLM managers were dominated by the boards after Senator McCarran succeeded in slashing its grazing management budget, and the boards even funded a substantial share of local BLM management. As Foss put it, "Congressman Taylor's use of the term 'home *rule*' was more accurate than he realized."[19]

The consensus among participants in modern BLM management was that the advisory boards were shadows of their former selves. BLM managers unanimously reported that the influence of the boards was vastly diminished in comparison with the boards of the 1950s, which Foss described. The BLM had "moved far away from the attitude that you don't do anything you can't get through the advisory board," according to one district manager. A long-time advisory board member noted, "It used to be that the advisory board was law—but not now." The primary reason for the decline of advisory board influence was that the BLM had taken on the boards over the central issue of levels of grazing leases in the 1950s and early 1960s and won. The central role of the old advisory boards was to stave off administrators' efforts to cut range use down to the BLM's definition of carrying capacity. When the BLM succeeded in lowering the level of range use through the long and difficult process of adjudications, the advisory boards lost on their primary issue, and their power was undermined. A district manager said the board was not as powerful in the 1970s because "the grazing management problem is not as pressing" as it had been. And an area manager who had joined the BLM after the adjudication fights claimed that he had never encountered a strong advisory board.

A second reason offered by several BLM managers and a few advisory board members for the decline of the boards' power was the broadening of the bureau's constituency and management responsibilities. The boards were still composed mostly of stockmen and one pseudo-wildlife representative. (All the advisory board members identified as key contacts by BLM managers were stockmen, and none of the wildlife federation contacts were advisory board members. The wildlife representatives on these boards were either not important enough to have been key contacts or were ranchers who had joined a wildlife federation to qualify as the "wildlife representative."[20]) An area manager noted that the boards' biased composition "has not kept pace with the work of the bureau," and he guessed that, while an area manager used to spend 90 percent of his time on range management, he now spent only 10 percent. The BLM's new conservation and recreation interests, plus additional consumptive interests such as mining and oil and gas, served as a counterbalance to the agency's traditional stockmen's constituency. A district manager noted that the ranchers were only concerned with the BLM's range program, but "not interested in all the problems I deal with"; and he added, "What I need now is a real multiple-use advisory board." Another rancher, a member of the BLM state advisory board, said that the state board rarely even discussed livestock grazing at its meetings, only environment, recreation, land use planning, and so forth. (The state advisory board meeting minutes confirmed this.)

Finally, stockmen and some BLM managers observed that the bureau now had an information advantage over the boards. An important reason for the early advisory board's influence was that the fledgling, understaffed Grazing Service had few professional local managers and no real knowledge of local conditions. By 1960 the BLM's staff was becoming increasingly professionalized and knew the districts as well as or better than the ranchers. Advisory board members recognized that, by the early 1970s, BLM managers had much better information than they did and that the BLM recommendations were usually right. One powerful rancher compared the advisory board to an inactive corporate board of directors: the BLM set the agenda and provided the board with its factual informa-

8: PUBLIC PARTICIPATION   249

tion. In this confrontation of, as he put it, "the BLM's pseudo-expertise versus the ranchers' intuition," the ranchers lost. Another board member said the BLM managers "have the facts," which the board members did not have time (or did not bother) to get, and consequently the board was a "rubber stamp" for bureau decisions.

The rubber stamp characterization was probably extreme. The boards did, as a formal procedure, vote on changes in leases. In many cases board members were strong-willed, powerful individuals. Several members were also local elected officials (particularly county commissioners), and thus persons the BLM had to treat with respect because of their stature in the community and the agency norm of intergovernmental cooperation. Most advisory board members and BLM managers reported that they felt the BLM's managers approved a high proportion of board recommendations. As one area manager put it, the board "keeps the bureau honest," and ensured that managers "have done their homework" on grazing management. But the boards' recommendations rarely involved controversial issues. One board member's notion of a major issue was change in "class of use" (changing animal-unit-months from sheep to cattle use or vice-versa). Another member thought the major role of the board was to ensure that licensees knew that, when they gave up a license, they were giving up their right to that license as well. One-third thought that, aside from routine business, the BLM's main use of the board was to "pass the buck to the board on the dirty decisions," such as those involving disputes between two ranchers. Finally, several managers and board members noted that an important use of the boards was a mechanism for the BLM to sell stockmen on intensive management practices and the bureau's allotment management plans.

On the real gut issue of past BLM–licensee relations—levels of use and particularly cuts in license levels—the boards' weaknesses were apparent. One district manager reported that he did not even consult the board on decisions to cut range significantly. Another said his board was actually a help on permit reductions and adjudications because "They know their neighbors are bullshitting." Board members said the boards had "come around to see the BLM's point of view" on reduced allotments; they only tried to soften the blow to licensees whose allotments were being cut by recommending phased cuts or letting the licensee make up part of the cut on another allotment where a rancher had taken temporary nonuse. The license-level situation had become stable, by the 1970s, and the boards' functions were routine. One district manager summarized the place of the advisory board by saying, "I have my people go to the wildlife federation meetings, I go to the county commissioners' meetings, but *I have* the advisory board meetings."

The Role of Grazing Associations and Advisory Boards in Forest Service Range Management

The Forest Service dealt formally with stockmen through two types of organizations, grazing advisory boards and grazing associations. The former were committees of ranchers established at the discretion of the service for consulting purposes; but, unlike the BLM advisory boards, the Forest Service boards had no statutory mandate or formal decision-making power. Grazing advisory boards were usually established at the forest level or for divisions of the forest (a division being a number of contiguous ranger districts geographically separate from the rest of the forest). Three of the national forests in the sample had forest or division grazing advisory boards. While the advisory boards were committees established by forest officers, the grazing associations were, in theory, voluntary associations formed by stockmen-permittees to act as intermediaries between permittees and the local ranger. (As we shall see, the notion that the associations were primarily organized by permittees to further their own interests was something of a fiction.) Typically there were several grazing associations per ranger district, and they usually dealt with only one district ranger.

The forest or division grazing advisory boards were usually less important mechanisms for dealing with local permittees than the grazing associations.[21] Advisory boards were just what their name implied. However, they were not so much forums for stockmen to offer advice to the forest supervisor or the rangers as forums for the Forest Service, particularly the supervisor's staff, to advise stockmen of changes in policy or procedure. Quite frequently it seemed that an even more important Forest Service goal was to proselytize stockmen on its gospel of multiple use; in the context of the grazing boards, that meant carrying to stockmen the message that the service was managing the forests for recreation, wildlife, environmental, and other values, and that stockmen were not the agency's only customers. The stockmen on the boards were not shy about responding to this message, but most communications in the boards involved Forest Service presentations to or proselytizing of ranchers. In a few instances, advisory boards were reportedly used for mediation when a ranger could not arrive at a compromise with a permittee or settle a dispute between permittees. In these situations, the Forest Service used the board to deflect antagonism away from itself. (These were the same sort of "dirty decisions" that the BLM advisory board member quoted earlier referred to.) One permittee and board member felt these mediation situations reflected stockmen's preferences to "air their personal gripe in front of their peers," rather than settle with the administrators directly. The boards reportedly supported the rangers on some occasions and the stockmen on others, and forest supervisors reportedly usually accepted the board's recommendations insofar as they were within the bounds of Forest Service policy. But such displacements of personal conflicts had little general policy impact.

The ranger district-level grazing associations played a more important role in Forest Service range management than the advisory boards. Most of the grazing associations ought not be considered full-fledged voluntary associations, as most were organized around historic grazing allotments, which the Forest Service defined early in the century on the basis of traditional use patterns. It took the lead in organizing grazing associations where they did not exist. As one indication of the service's role, many of the associations met in the district ranger's conference room.

The Forest Service had several motives in organizing the grazing associations. First, grazing associations decreased the rangers' contacts with stockmen; instead of dealing with all permittees individually, rangers could deal primarily with grazing association presidents or with the association as a whole in meetings.

Second, grazing associations facilitated range improvements that would not have been economically feasible if permittees had operated individually. In addition, the service could enter into cooperative arrangements and cost-sharing agreements on range developments, such as providing fencing material that permittees then installed. (Such cooperative agreements were particularly important to the Forest Service because the budgetary thinking at the time was to deemphasize the use of "force account," that is, the service's own standing field crews, for projects like range developments.) The cooperative agreements benefited both stockmen's operations and the service's management objectives. Not surprisingly, permittees were not averse to the cost-sharing advantages of the grazing associations.

The third objective in organizing the grazing associations was to socialize the permittees to Forest Service norms, especially the multiple-use message. In particular, as with the grazing advisory boards, the agency used the associations to point out that, if they were to avoid threats to their grazing rights, stockmen ought to allow access to public lands, support wildlife use of the public lands, and so forth. At the verbal level, at least, the Forest Service seemed to be succeeding. Stockmen professed, in interview after interview, to be deeply committed to multiple use, arguing that their improved range management led to increased wildlife populations and other benefits.

The fourth Forest Service objective was perhaps the most important. Both the service and the bureau had an official policy goal of implementing intensive range management systems on public grazing allotments. In particular, the service tried to get as many of its allotments under the rest-rotation system as possible. Rest-rotation required more organization among permittees and usually utilized physical range developments to fence off the various treatment pastures in the allotment and, if necessary, to provide water and salt throughout the pastures. Intensive management was a response to deteriorated range conditions, an alternative to cutting range use; in fact, August Hormay, the originator of rest-rotation, argued that simply cutting range use could not eliminate range deterioration.[22]

However, implementing rest-rotation was not easy for the service (or the bureau) because of the stockmens' initial resistance. In some areas the initial phase of rest-rotation involved decreasing the animal-unit-months grazed on the allotment until the range responded. The service promised that intensive management would lead to future increases, a suspicious promise from the ranchers' point of view and one that did not ease the short-term loss. Intensive management also required some investments in range developments that were difficult for ranchers with small, sometimes part-time stock operations, and especially unattractive when coupled with cuts. But primarily stockmen resisted intensive management because of their inbred reservations about the new system. Rest-rotation involved combining two treatments that were anathema to prudent stockmen— leaving some areas ungrazed and grazing other pastures down to the ground. (The former, of course, is more disliked than the latter.) In addition, running both sheep and cattle on the same pasture was a recommended practice under rest-rotation, but violated a strong taboo of western stockmen. One interviewee (a neutral observer, not a stockman or administrator) felt some ranchers' resistance was based on antiintellectualism. Rancher interviewees, particularly the long-time ranchers, often complained about "inexperienced" rangers who "didn't understand local conditions" trying to force them to change the way they had run livestock for years because of "book learning."

Not all stockmen opposed rest-rotation. Some were familiar with the practice; one stockman, for example, pulled out his file of correspondence with Hormay during the interview to document his disagreement with the details of the local ranger's recommended rest-rotation system. Several ranchers supported intensive management programs that had been in effect for several years. They were amazed at an outcome that combined improved range conditions *and* increases in their permit levels. As one stockman put it, "There is an old saying that 'you never get it back,' but the Forest Service has proved that [to be] wrong."

The service made even greater use of grazing associations on the national grassland districts than it did on national forests. The national grasslands, originally acquired under the Bankhead–Jones Act of 1937,[23] were designed to return to federal ownership and range use those lands that had been improperly homesteaded, leading to the dust bowl conditions of the 1930s. The grasslands were administered under a different set of policies from other Forest Service rangelands. For our purposes, the most notable difference was in the service's use of stockmen's cooperative grazing associations.[24]

The national grassland in the sample, NG2, had evolved to the point where most of its allotments were administered by the cooperative grazing associations; two-thirds of the permits on one ranger district and all the permits on the other were under grazing association administration. The grazing association's basic policies for administering its part of the national grassland were contained in a contract between the service and the association. The contracts were individually negotiated, so there was some variation from association to association. However, the typical contract included the following provisions:

1. The Forest Service made available a certain portion of the grassland to the association.
2. The Forest Service notified the association each year of its grazing fee.
3. The Forest Service determined the amount of use, "in cooperation with the association."

4. The Forest Service "assist[ed] the association in the preparation of its management plan."
5. The association board of directors issued permits to ranchers for grazing use and improvements.
6. The association implemented, with Forest Service technical assistance, the range plan agreed upon by the service and the association.
7. The association collected fees from its permittees and paid its grazing fees to the Forest Service after deducting its administrative and maintenance costs.
8. The association tried to accommodate public hunting and fishing use on the nonfederal lands under its control.
9. The association provided fire prevention, detection, and suppression services on its allotment.[25]

In short, the Forest Service replaced its permittee relationship with several dozen operators with a contractual relationship among a few cooperative grazing associations.

To those familiar with the history of public lands range management, the relationship between the Forest Service and the national grassland's grazing associations has a familiar ring. It was similar to the old relationship between the BLM and its section 3 grazing district advisory boards. The Forest Service actually cajoled permittees into a relationship similar to the one that allegedly led the BLM to be captured by its stockmen's constituency. The service had several reasons for encouraging the associations to enter into the contractual relationship. As with regular national forest grazing associations, efficiency was one motive; for not only did the associations decrease the rangers' contacts with their permittees, but they did a substantial amount of the rangers' paperwork (a feature the rangers noted approvingly). More important, the Forest Service saw the associations as a means of gaining the cooperation of stockmen. The agency's management objective on the grasslands was to promote "good grasslands agriculture" on private as well as public lands. The service tried to involve the stockmen in the management of the grasslands to induce them to practice what it felt was good range management. In discussing the sort of stockmen's attitude the Forest Service was attempting to change, one ranger told of a permittee whose public lands allotment was grazed to the ground, but who proudly showed the ranger how the grass on his own ranch was "knee-high." The service tried to get stockmen to view their public lands allotment with the same concern as their own rangeland, and to get the grass knee-high on both. In short, the Forest Service used the grazing associations to co-opt local stockmen.

The results of the service's strategy were as different from those of the pre-1960's BLM–licensee relationship as the structures of the grazing association and the advisory board were similar. The primary difference between the two agencies' experience was that the Forest Service began the relationship from a position of strength. Its administrators were fully professional. It had established its authority over stockmen's use of the grasslands before embarking on the grazing association policy. (Stockmen put this more strongly—they described early Forest Service administrators of the grasslands as "dictatorial.") The gut issue of range management, the level of permitted animal-unit-months of use, had been settled. And the Forest Service maintained, at a minimum, veto power over association activities. Whereas BLM advisory boards in the old days had felt they could "fix the policy" and have the BLM manager carry it out,[26] the rangers set policy and had the *stockmen* carry it out. Stockmen strongly preferred the association system. It made them feel effective; unlike the old authoritarian relationship, the association relationship was uniformly described as "cooperative." The Forest Service was also gaining good acceptance for rest-rotation; an association director reported his association's members were "beaming" over the results of rest-rotation. Ranchers even reported a real, if grudging, acceptance of recreationists, particularly hunters and ORV users, as legitimate users of their national grassland.

Perhaps the most important factor that allowed the Forest Service on NG2 to effectively use the grazing asociations was the phenomenon cited throughout this chapter—the existence of an environmental constituency interested in the grasslands. Both Forest Service and livestock industry interviewees felt that conservationist interest in the public lands, which historically only ranchers had known or cared about, was a major force moving the stockmen closer to the Forest Service's position. Even though NG2 had less public visibility than its neighbor NF1, the rangers and supervisor on NG2 had taken pains to include NF1's conservationists in NG2's organization-set. Rangers reported informal preliminary consultations with key environmental leaders on proposals, consultations that were confirmed by the conservationists. The forest supervisor also included several environmental leaders on his forest multiple-use advisory board, along with the key grazing association leaders, making NG2's committee much more representative than the typical forest multiple-use advisory committee. The Forest Service seemed to have adopted a "high–low" strategy in placing environmentalists on the committee. One environmentalist was a vocal, "radical" individual who provided a shock effect. The other, the president of the local Sierra Club group, had a more moderate image, demonstrating that environmentalists could be reasonable, cooperative, and not committed to the economic ruin of ranchers. The environmentalists on the advisory committee provided the stockmen's leadership with a proximate reminder of conservationist and recreationist interest in the national grasslands.

Advisory Boards and the Federal Advisory Committee Act

The specialized advisory board type of public participation has been under some attack nationally in recent years. The advisory boards' role as an institutionalized means of interest group access to agency decision processes is one source of dissatisfaction with the boards. However, the standard explicit reason for attacks on advisory boards has been that they are manifestations of the proliferation of the federal bureaucracy; advisory boards have thus been targets of those who wish to "control the bureaucracy" by reducing the number of federal agencies. (Of course, an advisory board is not an "agency," unless one takes extreme liberty with the legal, administrative, and commonsensical meanings of the word.) A major attack on the use of advisory boards by federal agencies was made by the Federal Advisory Committee Act of 1973,[27] which attempted to terminate as many boards as possible and make it difficult to establish new ones. More recently, President Carter's effort to reorganize the federal bureaucracy included a renewed attempt to reduce the number of advisory boards.

At the same time that the Advisory Committee Act was attempting to change national policy on advisory boards generally, the public lands advisory boards were at the center of important currents in public lands policy. The roles of the BLM and Forest Service grazing boards were representative of the policy changes in public lands management since the early 1960s. The advisory boards' roles revealed the decreased relative influence of traditional users, especially stockmen, and the agencies' use of balanced constituencies to try to influence traditional users to adhere to the agency line. As such, the advisory boards were symbols of the changes in public lands politics in the 1970s, and there were some interesting changes when the agencies were forced to implement the Advisory Committee Act.

The BLM's grazing district advisory boards had been important tools of livestock industry influence over the bureau in the days before adjudications, multiple use, and professionalism brought the industry to heel. Several BLM field officers argued in 1973 that the stockmen-dominated boards were anachronistic and that the bureau needed advisory bodies that better reflected its balanced constituency. The 1973 Advisory Committee Act provided the means to accomplish these ends; the BLM's grazing district advisory boards were terminated, effective January 1975, under the act. In place of the old grazing boards, the BLM established new multiple-use advisory boards by administrative action. These multiple-use committees, with their diverse representations, were attacked by stockmen as the symbolic final nail in the coffin of their boards' influence. However, the new boards were upheld by the U.S. District Court for Nevada when stockmen sued the BLM, alleging that the new boards violated the Taylor Grazing Act.[28]

The resurrection of the old grazing advisory board was also a minor controversy in debate over the Federal Lands Policy and Management Act (FLPMA) of 1976.[29] The act equivocated on the issue of whether the advisory boards it provided for would be dominated by stockmen or represent the contemporary BLM's diverse constituency. Section 305 of the act authorized the establishment of multiple-use councils, which were the successors of the multiple-use boards established during implementation of the Advisory Committee Act. (The 1978 Rangelands Improvement Act made the multiple-use councils mandatory.) Section 403 of the FLPMA required the reestablishment of the old district grazing boards, but limited their role to advising BLM managers solely on "the development of allotment management plans and the utilization of range betterment funds"; this responsibility was consistent with the diminished role of the grazing boards in the early 1970s and with the Forest Service's use of its grazing associations.

The Forest Service's advisory boards were also affected by the Advisory Committee Act, but in the opposite way. The Forest Service, which had had an established multiple-use statutory mandate since 1960 (and an effective administrative multiple-use policy since 1905) felt little need for multiple-use advisory boards. Forest Service field officers characterized most multiple-use boards in the sample regions as being composed of "yes-men." Only NG2's board functioned effectively, and it was really a hybrid grazing-and-multiple-use board. After passage of the Advisory Committee Act, the service allowed its multiple-use boards to terminate; there were only one regional and five forest-level multiple-use boards left nationwide by August 1976. Just as the FLPMA had tinkered with the BLM's advisory board policies, so the 1976 National Forest Management Act authorized the Forest Service to reestablish multiple-use advisory boards.[30]

In implementing the Advisory Committee Act, however, the Forest Service reestablished all its existing *grazing* advisory boards by administrative action. It had fifty-eight such boards in June 1973; in August 1976, after implementing the Advisory Committee Act, it still had fifty-eight grazing advisory boards.[31] This implementation pattern was, of course, fully consistent with the Forest Service's more effective use (at least for its own purposes) of grazing associations and advisory boards than of multiple-use bodies.

Conclusions

Public participation programs were remarkably representative of public lands policies in the 1970s. The agencies provided a wide variety of opportunities for their local publics to participate in agency decision making. The Forest Service has had a well-developed reputation for an excellent participation program—a program supported early by its Washington office leadership and a cadre of service researchers particularly committed to participation.[32] The Forest Service has been a leader, among natural resources agencies—and, arguably, within the federal government as a whole—in developing public participation programs. This study's findings suggest that the BLM's field implementation of public participation has been quite similar to that of the Forest Service.

The fact that the agencies conducted serious, good faith participation programs highlights the emerging dilemma in evaluating public participation. Advocates of participation argue that participation should lead to real citizen influence, not just a sense of efficacy. But an emerging body of studies has suggested that the most demonstrable effect of even good participation programs is an increase in citizens' beliefs in their own efficacy, not clearly identifiable policy change.[33] In the case of the public lands agencies, the major difference among the different styles of public participation was the degree of good feeling among the agencies' constituents. However, there was no indication that participants believed that better public participation led to greater direct influence on local land managers' decisions. The main uses of public participation were to accommodate new clients' (especially environmentalists') demands for better access to the policy process and to clearly demonstrate to traditional user clients that those new groups were, in fact, parts of the agencies' clienteles. Such uses, while very important, are more subtle than the simple notion of group-to-agency influence commonly associated with public participation.

Public participation is, thus, another example of the differences between the complex real world and the simple capture-conformity debate. Public participation programs establish procedures for groups presumably to influence agency officials, that is, to subject them to potentially "capturing" pressures. Yet public participation is in conformance with explicit—and, in the case of the Forest Service's *Inform and Involve,* very forceful—agency directives. And it often assists rangers, area managers, and other agency officials in implementing a variety of the agencies' objectives, from the inclusion of new clients who form a constituency for the agencies' resource protection goals to the selling of intensive rest-rotation grazing programs.

NOTES

1. See H. Paul Friesema and Paul Culhane, "Social Impacts, Politics and the Environmental Impact Statement Process," *Natural Resources Journal* vol. 16 (May 1976) pp. 339–356. For a round of debate on this aspect of NEPA, see Sally Fairfax, "A Disaster in the Environmental Movement," *Science* vol. 199 (Feb. 17, 1978) pp. 743–748; and Paul Culhane, Richard Liroff, and Sally Fairfax, letters, *Science* vol. 202 (Dec. 8, 1978) pp. 1034–1041.

2. On the Army Corps of Engineers' public participation program, see Daniel Mazmanian and Jeanne Nienaber, *Can Organizations Change?* (Washington, D.C., Brookings Institution, 1979); and Robert Wolff, *Involving the Public and the Hierarchy in Corps of Engineers Survey Investigations* (Stanford, Calif., Stanford University Report no. EEP-45, 1971).

3. Two important official public participation documents are Forest Service, *Framework for the Future* (Washington, D.C., Forest Service, February 1970); and Forest Service, *Inform and Involve* (Washington, D.C., Forest Service, February 1972). An important in-service investigation of public participation is John Hendee, Robert Lucas, Robert Tracy, Tony Staed, Roger

Clark, George Stankey, and Ronald Yarnell, *Public Involvement and the Forest Service* (Seattle, Wash., Pacific Northwest Forest and Range Experiment Station, U.S. Forest Service Administration Study of Public Involvement, May 1973).

4. See Charles Reich, *Bureaucracy and the Forests* (Santa Barbara, Calif., Center for the Study of Democratic Institutions, 1962). On the role of the BLM boards, see Philip Foss, *Politics and Grass* (Seattle, Washington University Press, 1960).

5. A good example is John Mitchell and Constance Stallings, eds., *Ecotactics: The Sierra Club Handbook for Environmental Activists* (New York, Simon & Schuster, 1970).

6. Sherry Arnstein, "A Ladder of Citizen Participation," *Journal of the American Institute of Planners* vol. 35 (July 1969) pp. 216–224.

7. David Truman, *The Governmental Process* (New York, Knopf, 1951) p. 264.

8. Hendee and coauthors, *Public Involvement and the Forest Service*, pp. 15–17 and 151; and Sally Fairfax, "Public Involvement and the Forest Service," *Journal of Forestry* vol. 73 (October 1975) pp. 657–659, both note several of the reactions discussed in the last two paragraphs.

9. These processes, and their relationship to public participation, will be discussed in chapter 9. Also see Paul Culhane and H. Paul Friesema, "Land Use Planning for the Public Lands," *Natural Resources Journal* vol. 19 (January 1979) pp. 43–74.

10. The use of the vague terms *style* and *interrelated factors* is caused by the fact that the interview data allow only subjective conclusions about how the factors are related.

11. These observations were double-checked with administrators, who confirmed that the meeting that was the subject of the last quote was pointless. It concerned a proposed administrative reorganization that the regional office had instructed the Forest Service staff to implement, even though the staff had promised local leaders a meeting would be held on the subject.

12. According to traditional public administration's so-called politics-administration dichotomy, this ranger's comment was particularly apt. See Woodrow Wilson, "The Study of Administration," *Political Science Quarterly* (1887), reprinted in *Political Science Quarterly* vol. 56 (December 1941) pp. 481–506.

13. Forest Service, *Inform and Involve*, pp. 5, 18, 19, and 20 (emphasis in the original in the last passage).

14. These displays were large maps of the district with plastic overlays showing watersheds, roads, grazing allotments, timber sales, and so forth. The overlays gave meeting participants a tangible object to react to, providing focus and concreteness. The fondness of NF1's rangers for such displays as props for public meetings was matched, in the author's experience, only by the Army Corps of Engineers' love of slide shows.

15. See Forest Service, *Inform and Involve*, p. 9, on the importance of environmentalists and recreationists as target groups of service I&I efforts.

16. The common silvicultural prescription on NF1 was overstory removal, in which about 70 percent of the basal area of the sale area, comprised of the largest trees, was logged on the first entry, with the remainder logged at a subsequent entry. The *basal area* is the sum of the areas of the cross sections of the trees in the area, measured at the base for units of one acre.

17. The finding that good public participation has a clearer effect on participants' feelings of efficacy than on agency policymaking is becoming common. See, for example, Mazmanian and Nienaber, *Can Organizations Change?*, especially chapter 7.

18. See Foss, *Politics and Grass*, chap. 6 and 7.

19. Ibid., p. 117 (emphasis in the original).

20. See the discussion of Type II organization-sets on page 1971.

21. In addition to interview data, information on Forest Service grazing advisory boards is drawn from a file of grazing advisory board meeting minutes at the Public Lands Project, Northwestern University, as well as field observation of a board meeting.

22. See August Hormay, *Principles of Rest-Rotation Grazing and Multiple Use Management* (Washington, D.C., Bureau of Land Management and Forest Service, September 1970).

23. 50 Stat. 525.

24. The Forest Service's policy of forming the relationships described on page 253 was not required by the laws governing the national grasslands, but the Bankhead–Jones Act implicitly recognized livestock grazing as the dominant use of the grasslands. Thus, the Forest Service was in the difficult position of trying to manage the grasslands under both the Multiple Use Act and a dominant use act.

25. From a typical grazing agreement contract. The exact citation has not been given for reasons of confidentiality. The contracts also contained other minor or boilerplate provisions, or both.

26. See chapter 3, p. 90.

27. Federal Advisory Committee Act of 1973, 86 Stat. 770, 5 U.S.C. §1, *et seq.*, App. I.

28. See "Bureau of Land Management Advisory Committees," 43 C.F.R. 1784; *Carpenter* v. *Morton*, 424 F.Supp. 603 (D. Nevada, June 1976). Implementation of the Advisory Committee Act took place subsequent to the fieldwork for this study; information on the act's implementation is based, in part, on a telephone interview with Jerry O'Callaghan, chief of the Division of Cooperative Relations, BLM, August 10, 1976.

29. 43 U.S.C. 1701. FLPMA, the "BLM organic act," is discussed on pages 94–96.

30. NFMA, 16 U.S.C. 1600, dealt primarily with timber harvesting (discussed on pages 57–58) and land use planning (discussed on pages 274–278).

31. Information on multiple-use and grazing advisory board data and Advisory Committee Act implementation based on telephone interview with Lennart Lundberg, Division of Administrative Management, Forest Service,

August 10, 1976. Also see, Forest Service, "Grazing Advisory Boards: Intent to Establish," 40 *Federal Register* 5382 (February 5, 1975).

32. Agency leadership support is seen in the Forest Service's *Framework for the Future* and *Inform and Involve*. The research group, centered around John Hendee, is best known for their *Public Involvement and the Forest Service*, and the CODINVOLVE content analysis procedure for analyzing public input to formal decision processes, first published in Forest Service, *A Guide to Public Involvement in the Forest Service* (Washington, D.C., Forest Service, January 1971).

33. See especially, since it deals with the program of the Army Corps of Engineers (the other leading public participation agency), Mazmanian and Nienaber, *Can Organizations Change?*

9

The Style of Local Public Lands Policymaking

The preceding discussions of public participation and the nature of group influence provide some insights into the interaction of external constituency and internal agency policy influences on local Forest Service and BLM policymaking. Participants in local public lands politics portrayed agency officials as responding to different elements in their constituencies and facilitating constituency input into agency decision making by extensive formal public participation programs. However, the uses to which constituencies and public participation were put by local administrators always seemed to inexorably lead to support for central agency policies, especially the core multiple-use policy. To some extent administrators must operate within the bounds of agency policy, but terms such as *influence* and *responsiveness* imply that constituent groups' interests or preferences affect administrators' actions, that administrators are influenced *by* groups and respond *to* groups. The extent of administration conformance to agency goals, as identified in chapters 7 and 8, gives little evidence of such influence or responsiveness.

Any demonstration of real influence of group activities on rangers' or area managers' policies should satisfy three conditions. First, rangers and area managers must be a major locus of decision-making authority. Second, rangers and area managers must be the focus of the kind of interest group activity that could be thought of as political pressure. Third, there must be some systematic means—preferably sanctioned by agency policy—by which rangers and area managers can be forced to respond to group pressures in making their decisions.

The Locus of Decision Making

According to one point of view, it is unnecessary to ask whether local level administrators, such as rangers and area managers, are significant participants in agency decision making. For some observers, all administrative acts involve making decisions[1]; thus, rangers and area managers are definitionally decision makers. As a result of this definition of administration, however, since everyone in an administrative organization is a decision maker, no individual can ever be singled out as the sole decision maker; for out of the web of individual decisions—supervisors' (and their staffs') decisions on instructions moving down through the hierarchy and subordinates' decisions on recommendations moving up— emerges *the* decision.

Viewed in this way, the question of whether low-level public lands managers are important decision makers becomes, instead, Do rangers and area managers make decisions that constitute most of *the* decision, for each of the important decisions about the uses of lands under their jurisdictions? More specifically, Do rangers and area managers have sufficient latitude to make the key decisions about public land use, the front-end decisions about the levels of various uses allowed on their units? There are no truly objective answers to these questions (discernible, for example, by inspecting official agency rules and procedures) because of the complexities of agency decision processes. The answers largely depend on the understandings of the participants in those processes.

Some observers hold that official policy—represented by hundreds of pages of statutory law, the twenty-five "running feet" of the Forest Service Manual and other publications—is so extensive that it surely constrains local administrators. Because of the volume of such policies and the control exercised by superiors to ensure compliance with such policies, rangers and area managers are effectively restricted to simple execution of predetermined agency policy. Others hold that, because of the large volume of agency regulations and the fact that many of them are couched in fairly broad terms, rangers have considerable freedom to choose among different policies or different interpretations of broad policies for specific situations. As was also the case with local participants' views of group influence (discussed in chapter 7), the participants in local public lands politics held widely different views on the locus of decision making.

Interest Group Perceptions of Local Decision Latitude

Interest group leaders generally believed that ranger districts and resource areas were not the primary sites of Forest Service and BLM decision making. Most believed that significant decisions were made at higher levels in the agencies, and that rangers and area managers were left to implement these higher-level decisions and make minor local decisions. As one BLM advisory board member put it, "The only big local decisions are things like whether a gas well site is left open to stock use." One very influential local contact, a rancher and county commissioner, noted, "If you don't solve your problem locally, you don't solve your problem. I've never seen a ranger's decision reversed, unless the ranger reversed himself." Another local contact argued, "If they want to stop you, they can find a regulation." But these were definitely minority opinions.

While the interest group consensus was that rangers and area managers did not control major policy choices, group contacts placed great weight on the personal skills of local officials. The contacts rarely argued that an administrator's personal policy predilections influenced his decisions, but they believed that an administrator's ability to communicate with people was a major asset in effectively explaining and implementing agency policy. Such interpersonal skills could have an important independent effect on users', especially stockmen's, general evaluations of the agency: positive evaluations of the Forest Service or its policy were often conveyed by approval of "this new ranger," while negative appraisals were expressed as complaints that a ranger was "inexperienced." However, the importance ascribed to rangers' and area managers' skills did not imply that group contacts believed local officials were significant independent decision makers.

Local Latitude—Administrators' Views

In marked contrast to group contacts, Forest Service and BLM administrators believed rangers and area managers did play significant decision-making roles. The rangers' job, according to one ranger, was primarily structured around the district work plan, which determined the types and amounts of outputs the district produced, and which the ranger himself planned. Another ranger said that programs were planned and executed primarily at the district level: using timber sales as an example, he noted that rangers made the initial determination of where and how much to sell, did the inventory, the sale layout, and the site preparation, and even influenced the major constraint on timber sales—the allowable cut—through the district inventory. BLM area managers noted that the critical resource area policies involved the allotment management plans and the (multiple-use) management framework plans, the preparation of which was primarily the area manager's responsibility. Furthermore, both rangers and area managers noted that they were the agenda-setters for projects that became public issues. One ranger noted, "The usual pattern is that service feels a need, for example, for a road, and goes public with the idea; we stir it up ourselves." The key to ranger or area manager latitude was that supervisors relied on their recommendations and backed them up when they made decisions or recommendations.

Forest supervisors and district managers generally supported the rangers' and area managers' views of their own latitude. As a formal matter, the authority to sign most decision documents rested with the forest supervisor or district manager, and sometimes even higher, such as with the regional forester or BLM state director. But, while rangers and area managers could make very few formal decisions solely on their own authority, their plans and proposals significantly structured their superiors' options and, as one forest supervisor put it, "The ranger has a veto if he uses it." In fact, many forest supervisors thought rangers made too few decisions. They argued that many decisions resolved at the forest level resulted from rangers' not being sufficiently assertive and decisive, "not doing their jobs," and not adapting fast enough from "the old ranger-on-a-horse role." One noted, "You can tell the difference with (Ranger 46) and (Ranger 47)—you don't get appeals over their heads." Another complained, "I see more decisions than I should."

There was some variation in rangers' and area managers' perceptions of their decision-making latitude. As shown in table 9-1, their perception ranged from very loose supervision to very tight, but on the whole, they believed they had a great deal of autonomy. The most frequently mentioned style of supervision was the most autonomous (which many described as being "allowed to do their own work"). Five out of six

Table 9-1. Style of Supervision of Rangers and Area Managers

Reported style	No. of administrators	Percentage	Cumulative percentage
District administrator allowed to do own work	14	37.8	37.8
Consensual decision-making style	5	13.5	51.4
Only informal supervision	6	16.2	67.6
Formal supervision on surface, but real decision making informal	1	2.7	70.3
Moderate supervisory constraints	5	13.5	83.8
Supervisor's staff given real authority	3	8.1	91.9
Little authority delegated to district administrator	2	5.4	97.3
Tight supervisory control	1	2.7	100.0
Totals	37	99.9%[a]	

[a] Round-off error.

claimed they were subject to moderate or less supervision, and only one felt tightly controlled by his supervisor.

Rangers' and area managers' reports of the frequency of important interactions with their supervisors also suggest considerable independence. Administrators reported relatively few supervisory interactions, with a median twenty-five consultations with, seven reports to, and six instructions from their supervisors per year (see table 9-2). Again, there was variation in the degree to which local officials felt consultations, reports, and instructions constituted supervisory control. For example, the frequency of instructions ranged from none, reported by two officials, to semiweekly for two others. To a considerable extent, the degree of supervisory control was a matter of individual rangers' and area managers' self-perceptions.

Table 9-2. Indicators of District Administrator–Supervisor Interaction

Indicator	Minimum	Maximum	Mean	Median	Standard deviation
No. consultations per year	2	Daily	44.6	24.8	35.4
No. formal reports per year	0	Twice a week	19.0	7.4	27.3
No. instructions per year	0	Twice a week	17.7	6.2	25.5
Interoffice distance (miles)[a]	0	154	41.3	34.0	42.3

[a] Straight line distance from district administrator's office to supervisor's office.

An extreme example of an idiosyncratic view of supervision was the ranger who claimed (even after cross-examination) that monthly vehicle use reports were of importance to his supervisor. Reported levels of supervisory interactions could vary widely within the same national forest or BLM district and were unrelated to the administrator's level of experience or GS rank. However, the strength of supervision was related to the distance of the local administrator's office from his supervisor's headquarters.[2] The average distance was 41 miles. Six area managers were located in the district office (the "zero" listing in table 9-2) and four rangers across town from the supervisor's office (counted as "1 mile"), while other officers were located in different towns from their supervisors, in one case 154 miles away. Not surprisingly, BLM area managers, most of whose offices were just down the hall from their district managers' offices, reported many more supervisory interactions, especially consultations, than did rangers. But on the whole, local level administrators seemed to be subject to fairly loose supervision.

In the early 1970s, local rangers' and, to a slightly lesser extent, area managers' independence appeared to be increasing. The visibility of local land managers was one reason for this increase. Most district rangers and detached resource area managers, because of their position as the agency representative in their community, already had high visibility. The public participation program of the agencies, especially as related to the agencies' comprehensive land use planning processes (to be discussed below), increasingly projected rangers and area managers to the general public as the salient agency policymakers. In addition, in the early 1970s the Forest Service was attempting to gradually increase local officers' shares of agency personnel to help meet the needs of new programs, such as public participation and land use planning.

The latitude reported by local administrators was far from absolute. Statutory laws and national, regional, and state agency policies set very definite bounds within which rangers and area managers had to work. Indeed, the key to understanding the reported absence of strict supervisory controls was that most supervision over local administrators is anticipatory. As Kaufman noted two decades ago, Forest Service officers are recruited, socialized, and advanced in the agency before becoming rangers so as to develop persons who can be trusted to voluntarily conform to agency policy in the field without direct supervision. Many of these same factors, especially similar professional training and values, operate to fit BLM officers into a common mold. Informal and anticipatory supervision, together with a strong sense of social identification with agency peers, produces a supervisory style that is much more collegial than authoritarian.[3]

In addition to agency policy and the structure of informal controls, there were two other, less obvious constraints on local administrators. First, both administrators and interest group leaders noted that staff assistants were becoming increasingly important in decision making at the ranger and area manager levels. Interdisciplinary planning teams, in particular, were becoming most important in planning programs from comprehensive land use to individual timber sales. The need to incorporate the points of view of diverse specialists—which is beneficial in terms of the varieties of consequences thoroughly considered in decision making—cuts into a line officer's decision-making latitude. Some rangers and area managers viewed this development favorably: one ranger even arranged to have a small planning team on hand the day of the interview in order to demonstrate how interdisciplinary planning worked. Other administrators, such as one ranger who referred to supervisor's office staff specialists as "the lesser Pharisees," were less enthusiastic about staff encroachment on their autonomy.

The second unusual constraining factor was that administrators were often routed to their assignments on the basis of their background, skills, or policy preferences. The Forest Service, in particular, tended to assign rangers with a ranching background or range management education to districts with predominantly grazing use. More conservation-oriented rangers were assigned to environmentally sensitive districts (for example, an urban influence district or district with heavy recreation or wilderness management responsibilities). Efficient, production-oriented rangers were usually found on districts with good timber potential and few countervailing pressures. The significance of latitude is diminished if agency supervisors match an administrator's characteristics to his district's sociopolitical and physiographic characteristics; thus, if fairly wide latitude allowed factors such as administrators' predilections to surface and affect their decisions, that effect would suit agency purposes.

The Focus of Pressure Politics

Even though rangers and area managers played very important decision-making roles, activity that could be called "politics" or "political pressure" was generally not directed at them, but at higher levels in the Forest Service and BLM hierarchies. Some of the most highly charged conflicts between groups affected local land managers only after a resolution had been reached at the national or regional and state level and the resulting policies had filtered down to the ranger or area manager for implementation. Typical examples of this process involved basic environmental protection and Forest Service timber sales policies. Administrators and their group constituents, particularly economic users, saw the major impact of environmentalists in terms of national policy changes, such as the NEPA mandate to prepare environmental statements and analyses of local projects and actions. A BLM manager's paraphrase of a state office directive on the implementation of the Wild Horses Act,[4] which many ranchers opposed, is another example of such national influence: "Some people don't like wild horses. From now on, the BLM attitude is that wild horses are good, and a part of the public lands, and we like them." A few rangers and many conservationists felt the forest products industry focused most of its pressure on the national level. One ranger argued that the industry's influence was most clearly reflected in changes in line items in the Forest Service's budget that increased funding for timber sale administration and decreased it for other activities, particularly recreation. This policy filtered down to the local level as these budget amounts were apportioned among regions, forests, and ranger districts.

Individual rangers and area managers recognized that almost all highly charged national or regional conflicts originated someplace else. When a very controversial problem did arise at the local level, it would be passed up the agency hierarchy so that the official decision would be made at—and the inevitable reaction focused on—the forest supervisor's, BLM district manager's, or a higher-level office. (Because rangers and area managers were the primary conduits for stockmen's demands on the agencies, range management cases were the most common example of local controversies that rose up through the agency hierarchy.) Indeed, some rangers and area managers were stationed so close to their line supervisors that local interests might interact directly with the forest supervisor or district manager on particularly controversial issues. Even though the resulting decision might be identical to the local administrator's recommendation, the appearance was one of politics at the higher agency level and local administrator implementation.

9: THE STYLE OF LOCAL PUBLIC LANDS POLICYMAKING 271

This notion of higher-level politics and local level implementation might be called the "trickle-down" theory of political influence on local managers. It is consistent with the belief that low-level officers should act in a neutral, administrative, rather than political, manner. As a result of this notion, rangers and area managers believed they were rarely placed in situations that involved pressure. A half-dozen local officers said that a congressional inquiry was the only kind of pressure to which they were exposed. A congressional inquiry is a request from a congressman to an agency for an explanation in response to a constituent's grievance with that agency. In the case of the Forest Service or BLM, the inquiry is usually made to the Washington office and passed down to the ranger or area manager. (The detached resource area manager of RA61, however, often received direct congressional inquiries because he was the only BLM official in the congressional district.) Although it usually results from an attempt by a dissatisfied agency client to use a politician to put pressure on an administrator, a congressional inquiry is regarded by most observers of American bureaucracy as a fairly routine and innocuous event. But rangers and area managers treated them with inordinate respect, perhaps because their replies to the inquiries took considerable time to prepare and had to be approved at the forest–district, regional–state, and Washington office levels. One ranger complained, "We will get a rubber-stamped form inquiry, with boxes checked off by some congressional staffer, and spend a week jumping through hoops." Other than those resulting from congressional inquiries, rangers and area managers reported few instances of pressure.

One reason local administrators felt unpressured was that they defined pressure as something that occurred in connection with public controversy. Since they spent little time on decisions involving significant public controversies, they logically felt that pressures (or politics or interest group demands) had little effect on their decisions. Moreover, many of the real public controversies they dealt with did not clearly involve front-end decisions about the primary goods and services delivered by the agencies. There were, for example, very few controversies about specific timber sales. More common controversies in the sample regions were the issues of "aspen blading" stand conversion and forest roads standards in State A and a "chaining" range development project in State C.[5] These issues were only indirectly related to primary, front-end decisions (for example, about the levels of timber sales or grazing leases). Furthermore, they were not classic political conflicts in which one set of interests sponsored a policy it would materially benefit from, while another set opposed that policy; rather, they were scientific-technical disputes about the advisability of executing programs the agencies had proposed.[6]

In summary, the consensus among both administrators and interest group participants was that local public lands management was fairly apolitical. Rangers' and area managers' interactions with their clients were characterized as usually nonpolitical, routine, or informational (such as processing a request for a fire permit); explicit political pressure was rare and usually directed at higher-level officials in the agencies; and the relatively infrequent controversies were usually portrayed as administrative rather than political. However, participants were sometimes conservative in defining what constituted local pressure or a political situation.

Many examples could be cited of the reluctance of some administrators and group contacts to think of local groups' strongly held positions as instances of pressure or political demands. Opposition to the chaining project in State C—the most controversial issue in the area at the time of the fieldwork—was cited by several user group contacts as an example of outside pressure when actually it was organized by the leader of a local environmental group. It is unlikely that the contacts were unaware of the activities of this local environmentalist, a very outspoken man. But in this and similar cases, attributing pressure to outside forces seemed to be a way of questioning the legitimacy of the pressure (especially since consumptive users often coupled such claims with the assertion that the policies resulting from outside pressures did not apply to local conditions).

Furthermore, not a single ranger mentioned environmentalist activity for Wilderness designations at RARE public meetings as an example of a group demand. This was true even for rangers who described the bitter, polarized nature of RARE public meetings. Administrators depicted environmentalists (and their opponents') activities not as legitimate expressions of group demands or pressure, but as perversions of the public meeting process.

A third example involved the timber sales program on NF1. All participants—rangers, forest products sources, environmentalists, and neutral observers—agreed the NF1 sales program was not an issue. However, during interviews it became clear that the Forest Service had fallen behind on its own timber sales schedule because of delays in front-end planning and preparation of environmental analyses; that the fall-off in sales disrupted the local forest products market (for example, forcing operators who could not bid on planned sales to overbid on sales out of their normal area); that all operators in the area were perturbed that the rangers had fallen behind on sales, and had told the rangers and the forest staff so; that the rangers knew the industry was unhappy; and that the service had made special efforts to offer extra sale volume to take up the slack. But this situation was not called an issue and was not thought to involve pressure; rangers and forest products sources alike characterized it merely as administrative inefficiency.

Yet another example involved a forest with several of the most conservation-oriented Forest Service officers in the sample. The forest staff and the forest products industry appeared to be conducting a running battle, with the service closing down sales and several mills eventually going out of business, at least one directly at the agency's hands. Participants, however, did not see their relationship in terms of group–agency conflict. Forest Service and forest products interviewees instead discussed the ramifications of "overinstalled mill capacity," stumpage price miscalculation, "contract enforcement," and the like. The forest supervisor spent over an hour during his interview explaining all the technical reasons for the service's imminent reduction in the forest's annual allowable cut (for example, "travel influence zones," "loggable by current technology," and so forth). When the forest's timber management plan was released for public comment, its allowable-cut computation was extensively (yet technically and professionally) criticized by opponents in the forest products industry and supported by local environmentalists.[7] Amid all the technical discourse, one would have never suspected that the Forest Service believed too many loggers were cutting too many trees, and that it was thus playing games with sales prices, slash requirements, and the allowable cut to decrease the pressure.

Finally, in one of the sample regions a classic confrontation took place between environmentalists and the agency regarding a project desired by local development interests. It resulted in two rounds of appellate-level court cases, two sets of environmental impact statements, and, finally, the intervention of the state's governor. The district ranger said the issue did not involve pressure, but "input" based largely on "misinformation."

There is no reason to feel interviewees (many of whom were quite blunt about other things) were being less than honest in these observations. However, if it is correct to see pressure in opposing claques at public meetings, complaints from irate forest products industry clients, and environmentalist litigation, then it becomes difficult to accept at face value participants' statements that rangers and area managers were rarely subjected to political pressure in connection with their front-end decisions on basic agency policies. In fact, the apolitical image of local public lands management appeared to be based in large part on the belief shared by administrators and group leaders that their involvement in important, complicated issues they passionately cared about was something more edifying than "politics."

Decision-Making Mechanisms

Since the style of local public lands policymaking was not manifestly political in participants' minds, it is necessary to identify mechanisms by which group preferences or influences directly affected administrators' decisions. Administrators and group contacts recognized two methods by which administrators incorporated constituents' wants, needs, and interests into their decision making. These mechanisms were not seen as devices of group pressure (or influence, demand, or any other concept connoting explicit group compulsion of administrators to reach certain decisions). In fact, both were in conformity with agency policies and professional land managers' values.

Land Use Planning

A primary contemporary mechanism for group influence in agency policymaking is the intermingling of public participation with decision processes, such as comprehensive land use planning and very closely related functional planning, that result in fundamental allocations of public lands to specific uses.[8] Statutory mandates for comprehensive land use planning were the cornerstones of the two major public lands acts of 1976, the service's National Forest Management Act (NFMA) and the bureau's Federal Land Policy and Management Act (FLPMA).[9] However, the planning processes established under these acts were essentially refinements of administratively initiated planning processes begun in 1969 by the BLM and (as a revision of an earlier process) in 1971 by the Forest Service.

9: THE STYLE OF LOCAL PUBLIC LANDS POLICYMAKING

Forest Service land use planning began with *multiple-use plans,* an administrative device designed as a part of the implementation of the 1960 Multiple Use Act. Each forest prepared a multiple-use plan, which provided a general (and usually fairly vague) framework within which plans for specific resources could be coordinated; ranger districts then prepared their own multiple-use plans based on the plan for the forest.[10] In 1971 the Forest Service changed its planning system, substituting *unit plans* for the multiple-use plans. Each national forest was divided into an average of eight ecologically defined land units, the boundaries of which were generally not the same as ranger district boundaries. As a formal matter, the forest plan was a collection of individual unit plans, but the major focus of the planning process was on the unit plans. Unit plan policies, called *management directions,* identified, for areas of land within the unit, the uses (for example, timber, recreation) to be allowed, and often the relative intensity of use (for example, "dispersed" versus "developed" recreation, the former connoting wildernesslike management and the latter campgrounds, ski areas, and other recreational facilities). While these management directions were much more specific and effective than the vague frameworks of the multiple-use planning process, they were not very clearly integrated into either forest functional resource plans or regional and national plans. The new land management plans established under the 1976 NFMA are designed to correct this problem by more clearly linking comprehensive plans to functional plans (especially timber management plans) and regional and national comprehensive plans.[11]

The BLM's comprehensive planning process, which produces documents called *management framework plans* (MFPs), was begun in 1969. As the Forest Service's early plans were designed to implement the Multiple Use Act, so the MFP process was an administrative vehicle for reconciling conflicting pressures on the BLM following passage of the 1964 Classification and Multiple Use Act. MFPs are prepared for *planning units* or, if one plan is prepared for a combination of planning units, *planning areas.* MFP's policies have varied in scope a bit more than unit plan management directions, containing very specific decisions, as well as broader recommendations for use of areas within planning units. Like the Forest Service's unit plans, the bureau's MFPs are not fully integrated with functional plans, particularly the important grazing-allotment management plans. By 1979 the BLM had not radically altered the MFP process, since regulations implementing the planning sections of the

FLPMA had not been issued. There has been no official indication the MFP process will be significantly altered before all planning units complete plans under the existing MFP process (scheduled for 1981).

Despite some differences in terminology, the Forest Service and BLM planning processes were remarkably similar. The service's unit planning process consisted of eight steps:

1. "Identify public involvement needs and begin public involvement."
2. "Document the planning objectives relevant to the Planning Unit" (based on forest, regional and national policy goals).
3. Inventory "land use potentials, current resources, and public needs."
4. "Formulate resource activity possibilities" (that is, maximum possible productivity of the land for individual uses, irrespective of constraints).
5. "Formulate alternative plans which resolve various activity conflicts and achieve varying levels of contributions to the planning objectives."
6. "Analyze the differences among alternative plans to show tradeoffs among various planning objectives."
7. "Select a recommended proposal from among the alternatives based upon an evaluation of how well each alternative satisfies the various objectives for the unit and the Forest," and prepare a draft environment impact statement.
8. Review comments on the draft environmental impact statement (EIS), reevaluate the plan, write and release a final EIS, and "document the decision on implementing the appropriate unit plan alternative."[12]

The bureau's MFP process consisted of three stages. In the first, or background, stage, BLM planners prepared a *planning area analysis* (an examination of the issues to be dealt with in the planning unit, similar to the Forest Service's step 2), a public participation plan (service step 1), and a *unit resource analysis* or inventory (service step 3). The second stage was the development of the MFP itself. District program specialists prepared program possibilities for the use of each resource (range, minerals, wildlife, and so forth), ignoring conflicts among uses (service step 4); then conflicts were identified and reconciled (a combination of service steps 5 and 6). The MFP was the product of this reconciliation (service steps 7 and 8, except environmental statements were almost never prepared on MFPs). In the third, or implementation, stage, specific plans were formulated for each resource (range, minerals, and so forth); preparation of these resources or implementation plans was, however, a separate process. By far the most important of these resource plans were the grazing *allotment management plans* (AMPs); unlike the MFPs, AMPs had to be accompanied by full environmental impact statements. This requirement was a result of the settlement of an environmentalist court suit.[13]

Land use planning clearly involved fundamental decision making by local land managers. The plans were formally the responsibility of forest supervisors and district managers, as usual, but rangers and area managers were the key line officers on planning teams for units in their jurisdictions. Though comprehensive in scope, the MFPs and unit plans had some weaknesses. Administrators recognized that the plans often did not contain specific programs for implementing the broad planning policies. For example, their management directions usually consisted of broad phrases like "manage for recreation" or "manage for timber production"; "recreation" was not specified as X number of campgrounds or Y ski areas, and "timber production" was not pinned down to projected levels of timber sales and associated silvicultural prescriptions. Such problems are common with plans, and it is not realistic to expect a ranger's planning team, over a six-month period, to do the work of his successors for the next ten years. Rectifying this lack of detail, as noted earlier, has been one objective of the current revision of the Forest Service's planning process. The key to the policy significance of comprehensive plans is that the planning decision to emphasize a use on a given area of land represents a fundamental allocation of land to that use, an allocation that gives the planned use a significant priority over other potential uses. Such allocation should, in theory, significantly structure and influence subsequent decisions about levels of uses allowed on the planning unit. In any case, by the time of the field research in 1973, it was clear that land use planning was becoming the centerpiece of local public lands policymaking.

As important as it has been, land use planning has been an uneasy combination of two very different types of decision making. Many aspects of both agencies' land use planning processes involved highly professional, rational decision-making techniques. The agencies' planning sequences had all the hallmarks of the classic rational decision model: planning objectives were agreed upon in advance (for example, service step 2), a wide variety of alternative plans were formulated (service steps 3, 4, and 5), the consequences of each alternative were analyzed (service step 6), and (service steps 7 and 8) the optimum plan was selected.[14] A key element of the agencies' processes was that planning was performed by interdisciplinary teams; the interdisciplinary approach, a hallmark of the planning profession, is designed to ensure thorough consideration of relevant alternatives and consequences by avoiding the biases inherent in decision making dominated by a single profession. Indeed, comprehensive planning is the epitome of rational decision making.

At the same time, both agencies' planning processes were deeply embedded in public participation programs. Development of public participation strategies was an early step in both agencies' planning processes, and those strategies were supposed to allow for varying degrees of participation at each step. Participation was supposed to make planners aware of the public's preferences about the management of the planning units. The Forest Service, for example, instructed its line officers to "consider the *priorities and preferences expressed by the public,* the capabilities of the lands, and the contributions [of the selected alternative] to meeting Regional and National targets" in making land use plan decisions.[15] (Both the explicitness of this directive and the ordering of decision criteria are noteworthy.) A BLM district manager argued that public input and preferences "set the parameters" in MFP decision making. Several area managers described the MFP process as a formalized method for integrating group demands and "getting around haphazard pressures." The level of public participation was generally regarded as the major difference between Forest Service and BLM planning. Local participants from all types of groups believed the bureau's MFP process was more open to the public; some service officers even quibbled that there was too much public involvement in the bureau's inventory stage. However, the Forest Service's practice of using EISs, which are circulated to the public and government agencies in draft form, opened the unit plans up to participation by a broad and important public (chiefly regional, well-organized groups and government agencies), and one which is different from the agencies' usual local organization-sets.

Rational decision making is theoretically a technical and expert implementation of established policy, a process whose style is supposedly the opposite of a political decision style.[16] But the public participation requirement in land use planning is a result of a recognition that response to group demands is a proper criterion for making decisions in the planning process—that is, that planners should make decisions on political as well as expert-professional grounds.

Comprehensive land use planning is not the only type of agency policymaking that intertwines public participation with highly professionalized decision making on fundamental land use decisions. The Forest Service's RARE I and RARE II processes—which, since they resulted in allocations of areas to wilderness and multiple-use management were very fundamental decision-making processes—included perhaps the two most extensive participation efforts in the service's history.[17] In addition, major functional plans that embody basic levels-of-use decisions, particularly the bureau's AMPs and the service's timber management plans, were normally accompanied by NEPA environmental statements. The EIS was itself a formalized public participation process, and was usually accompanied by full-fledged public participation efforts at the forest or BLM district level. Furthermore, Wilderness reviews, AMPs, and timber management plans were formally parts of the agencies' comprehensive land use planning processes: AMPs and timber plans were implementations of the comprehensive plans (and timber plans will be formally integrated with the Forest Service's new land management plans), and during 1973–78, Wilderness studies were made as part of the unit planning process.

Formal planning processes, whether comprehensive land use planning or the closely related functional planning, thus provided Forest Service and BLM administrators with a specific means of receiving and processing group demands into policy decisions. Insofar as public participation was a serious influence on the planning process—as agency policy required—the planning processes were logical and seemingly legitimate mechanisms for translating group preferences into basic use allocation decisions at the ranger and area manager levels.[18]

The Rule of Anticipated Reactions

The second mechanism for integrating group interests into local administrators' decision making was based more on administrators' intuition and experience than on the direct articulation of group preferences in the planning process. The mechanism also affected all agency processes, from those deeply enmeshed in public participation, such as land use planning, to those in which public participation played no part. Administrators reported that they tried to consider group needs and preferences in their decision making, based on their own intuition and experiential understanding of client group positions and interests. That is, interest groups influenced them through the mechanism that Carl Friedrich termed "the rule of anticipated reactions."[19]

Decision making based on *anticipated reactions* stems from the very human desire to avoid conflict. The negative reactions that public land managers tried to avoid took many forms. For example, an area manager mentioned adverse stories in the news media; and another said it was easier to do a good public relations job locally than to answer a congressional inquiry. A ranger mentioned litigation: "Any individual can stop the show if he finds a judge." Several Forest Service officers in one region even mentioned arson, and they were neither joking nor exaggerating.

Administrators regarded adverse reactions to their decisions as an indication of poor performance. Several even used the same term to describe poor performance: a BLM manager described a project on which special wildlife precautions were being taken, even though there had been no direct messages from wildlife groups, because "We know if we screwed up, we would hear from them," whereas a Forest supervisor said the service was responding to conservationist critics because "If we screw up, the Congress might turn all the national forests into Wilderness." Most administrators did not fear extreme reactions, but expressed feelings similar to those of the BLM manager who noted, "Retrenchment is expensive in terms of prestige and expended resources."

The agencies anticipated the reactions of all types of clients. One BLM manager said the environmentalists' main function was "keeping the land manager honest"; another said the district advisory board did the same thing. One ranger included the tourist passing through the area as a "group" that kept him "honest." A second ranger explained he was not reducing an overstocked range because he knew it would cause a furor locally, and he did not have the data to back up such a reduction. A third said possible adverse reaction even affected his personnel practices (he hired only people from the dominant local social group).

To use anticipated reductions in their decision making, administrators had to be able to accurately identify group preferences and predict what group reactions to their decisions would be. Every interaction between an agency official and a client could tell the official something about that client's views regarding public land management (though many such interactions were so routine that their message content would be subtle, at best). Public participation was a particularly useful learning forum for administrators who based their decisions on anticipated reactions. Group preferences and their intensity were well displayed in public meetings as well as in more informal participation efforts. Participation served to educate administrators about group preferences and how strongly groups felt about those preferences. Some administrators pointed out that the educational value of public participation was particularly important with respect to their new clienteles, whom administrators did not know as well as their traditional clients, and whose preferences many administrators admitted they did not share. One area manager, however, noted that public participation did not help him understand the needs of tourist recreationists (a significant management concern for his resource area) because public meetings were generally held on MFPs in the winter, when tourists were not around; during the summer, managers had to concentrate on field projects.

Administrators suggested that they relied primarily on their own experience, developed from their own and their colleagues' past successes and failures, in anticipating group reactions. One ranger said, in discussing needs people might complain were neglected, "Public participation identifies some, but we identify more ourselves." A BLM manager described the ability to recognize potential problems as just as much a professional skill as the ability to do a range survey or mark trees for sale. Reliance on experience seems unsystematic and fraught with possibilities for error, bias, and miscalculation, but it was probably the most cost-effective means of determining group needs and wants, particularly for those administrators with that sought-after quality, good judgment.

If anticipated reactions were, as administrators said, an important part of their decision-making style, then some of the earlier patterns of participants' observations become less confusing. The anticipated reactions style of decision making helps to explain the reports that environmental group and user group interests were important factors in land management, even though land managers rarely were directly pressured. Also, administrators and user group contacts felt that the agencies responded to environmental and economic pressures, but often that those pressures did not originate locally, even though local administrators clearly had active interest group contacts in their local organization-sets. However, administrators did not need to be directly pressured by groups for anticipated reactions to affect their decisions. Subtle messages—conveyed through the organization-set network, public participation, awareness of past and present conflicts on their own or other administrators' units, and other factors—conveyed group demands to administrators. The pressure was implicit: respond to the demands or conflict will occur. Pressure, in an anticipated reactions context, is both amorphous and ubiquitous, not a set of explicit demands articulated during each discrete decision process.

An anticipated reactions-style response to interest groups was also legitimate and professional: administrators were not being pressured, but were responsive; they were not captured, only prudently avoiding unseemly, counterproductive, and time-consuming conflict. Moreover, an anticipated reactions response to group interests was condoned, if not required, by agency policy. Response to economic users was implicit in the doctrine of multiple use. Response to environmentalists was also implicit in the resource protection aspect of the multiple-use doctrine and other agency policies and traditions; some response to Wilderness demands was even consistent with agency policy. And response to both kinds of groups was agency policy, as demonstrated by public participation programs. The spare sentence structure of the Forest Service's *Inform and Involve* connotes not speculative discourse or interesting hypothesis but central office directive: "[Ranger, you *must*] involve a wide range of the public on current programs, projects, and issues."[20] To conform, a local land manager had to be a little captured.

Traditional economic user clients of the agencies also seemed to be affected by an anticipated reactions process, though the threat they faced was more fundamental than the conflict that administrators tried to avoid. Many stockmen expressed the fear that their continued use of the public lands was threatened. Loggers feared they would lose their sales program. Mining and oil and gas people were leery of restrictions that would make it unprofitable to explore on public lands. These fears arose not from explicit demands articulated to local rangers or area managers, but from subtle environmentalist opposition to commodity use. One stockman, a sophisticated young Republican party activist, noted, "The real fights are below the surface." Given the environmentalist position that recreation was potentially a more profitable use of public lands than ranching or logging, the fears of traditional users were not groundless.

On a superficial level, traditional users often moderated their rhetoric in response to this fundamental threat to their interests. Administrators wryly noted the way in which their consumptive user clients, as an area manager put it, "All come in and tell me what good conservationists they are." The author found this same pattern: stockmen and those in the forest products industry professed dedication to multiple use, including the wildlife, recreation, and resource protection norms of the multiple-use philosophy. Administrators recognized this rhetoric as a defensive reaction, but it proved useful nonetheless. More important, economic users modified their actions in response to environmental pressure on the agencies. Timber operators claimed they were trying to do a better job on logging sites, as one put it, "to save the sales program." Administrators of mining and O&G districts reported that their problems with unauthorized (and damaging) exploration were vastly diminished, that mining and oil and gas operators and landmen were "coming in to see us first." A ski area operator reported telling developers in a related venture to "do a nice job and you'll make lots of money—but they just won't listen." (They should have listened—they lost when they tried to tough it out against the Forest Service and environmentalists.) In short, the environmental threat caused users to anticipate reactions also, and to cooperate more with the agencies' resource protection policies.

Conclusion

It is not a simple, straightforward exercise to show that ranger district and resource area constituencies influence local Forest Service and BLM policies. At the lowest level of public lands management, interest group clients face a mixture of administrative and political motivations behind agency officials' actions. The result of that mixture is a very fundamental obfuscation of the political aspects of local officials' decision making.

The local rangers and area managers in the study were important decision makers. Within the bounds of agency policy and the commonly held beliefs of agency professionals,[21] they appeared to have considerable *de facto* authority in matters of agency policy within their administrative units. Formal authority for agency decisions, however, was usually vested in their superiors, particularly forest supervisors and district managers. Rangers and managers of detached resource areas generally had greater latitude and authority than those BLM area managers stationed in the same offices as their district managers. And, as noted in chapter 7, rangers and area managers had a more visible impact on use administration restrictions in the second half of the decision cycle than on basic use allocations in the first half. But because their superiors tended to back up local officers' decisions and afford them an informal veto over decisions affecting their units, rangers and area managers appeared to control most of the decisions affecting their units.

While local officers were a crucial locus of decision making, they were not the focal points of interest group pressure. Group clients believed politics swirled around higher levels of the agencies' hierarchies—forest supervisors, regional foresters, BLM district managers, and so forth. At least partially, the movement of politics up the agencies' hierarchies resulted from group leaders' beliefs that the most important agency decisions were made above the ranger district and resource area levels. Local administrators maintained a bureaucratic image (some—such as the ranger described above who thought vehicle use reports were a critical supervisory control—more than others) that left interest group clients with the impression that real decision making occurred at a higher level. So while rangers and area managers made significant decisions, their supervisors took the political heat. From the agencies' point of view, this arrangement was beneficial, for rangers and area managers, who (along with supervisors and BLM district office staff specialists) were responsible for the technical and professional work of the agencies, were thus shielded from the full brunt of political controversies.[22]

Though sheltered from some aspects of political conflict, rangers and area managers were still required to be responsive to their group constituents. In the 1970s, rangers and area managers were drawn into fundamental decision processes—the unit and MFP land use planning, RARE, and AMP processes, for example—whose public participation requirements clearly confronted them with the interests and preferences of their group constituents. Even in the absence of combined planning-participation processes and clearly articulated pressure on individual decisions, the concept of anticipated reactions provided a mechanism for linking constituency interests with local administrators' decision making. Administrators were not constantly pressured because they did not require—or treat as legitimate—explicit political pressure. All that decision making based on anticipated reactions required was the administrator's desire to prevent differences of opinion with clients from escalating into conflicts that landed on their supervisors' desks, plus general information on their organization-sets' group interests. The wide range of constituency contacts and the various formal public participation programs certainly provided adequate information on client needs and wants (as well as serving other agency purposes, as noted in chapters 6 through 8).

Though public participation requirements and anticipated reactions style of decision making are logical mechanisms of group influence, that influence needs to be thought of in more neutral terms than "demands" and "pressure." "Responsiveness" to "public input" is consistent with the reputation for the nonpolitical, professional administration the service has maintained since its inception and the bureau has sought to attain since the difficult years of the 1940s. (Indeed, all public bureaucracies find such a reputation beneficial.) Nor is it surprising that low-level professional administrators escape heavy-handed interest group pressure. Perhaps because government decision makers prefer to be treated as rational and well-intentioned, the most legitimate and effective style of lobbying, even congressional lobbying, is the low-keyed, nonthreatening, "informational" strategy, notwithstanding the muckraking image of Washington lobbyists as arm-twisting wheeler-dealers.[23]

Reports of the anticipated reactions style of decision making and statements by administrators that they considered the effects of their decisions on all their local publics, however, might merely mask some other kind of decision making, such as authoritarian professionalism. Given the lack of clear consensus about influence based on the subjective observations of the participants in local public lands politics, we need some concrete evidence that groups really did affect agency policy through such mechanisms as the intuitive anticipated reactions process.

NOTES

1. See Herbert Simon, *Administrative Behavior* (New York, Macmillan, 1947) pp. 1–8.

2. The four indicators in table 9-2 were factor-analyzed along with the administrative experience indicators (years with agency and so forth) discussed on page 147, and in table 5-4. The first factor, "strength of supervision" (eigenvalue = 2.60), consisted of consultation (loading = .90), reports (.84), instructions (.73), and distance from supervisor (−.72). The second factor, "experience" (eigenvalue = 1.97), included years in agency (loading = .61), years in position (.87), and years with present supervisor (.83). The factor matrix was quite simple, with the supervision variables loading low on the experience factor and vice versa. For full statistics and a discussion of this factor analysis, see Paul Culhane, *Politics and the Public Lands*, Ph.D. dissertation, Northwestern University, Evanston, Ill., June 1977, pp. 172–173 (University Microfilms no. 77-32292).

3. See Herbert Kaufman, *The Forest Ranger* (Baltimore, Md., Johns Hopkins University Press for Resources for the Future, 1960) chap. 6. Because of this collegial style, two-thirds of the rangers and area managers in the sample could report they were either personal friends or fairly friendly with their supervisors; one ranger's friendship with his forest supervisor went back to their college "drinking buddy" days.

4. Wild Free-Roaming Horses and Burros Act, 85 Stat. 649 (1971), 16 U.S.C. §1331.

5. On the State A issues, see chapter 7, pages 216 and 224. "Chaining" involves using a heavy chain pulled by two tractors to uproot vegetation, such as piñon and juniper, that is not useful for livestock grazing; the chaining prepares the area for reseeding with forage grasses.

6. As such, these issues were actually fairly typical of the environmental controversies of the 1970s. See, for example, Dorothy Nelkin, ed., *Controversy: The Politics of Technical Decisions* (Beverly Hills, Calif., Sage Publications, 1979), especially p. 16.

7. The sources for this statement are public comments on the environmental impact statement written on the Forest's timber management plan; the exact citation is not given, as usual, so as not to identify the sample region.

8. For a detailed discussion of the history and processes of land use planning by the Forest Service, BLM, and National Park Service, see Paul Culhane and H. Paul Friesema, "Land Use Planning for the Public Lands," *Natural Resources Journal* vol. 19 (January 1979) pp. 43–74, and references cited therein. "Functional" plans deal with a specific use or resource (such as timber, grazing, or Wilderness) and describe when, how, and how much the specific resource will be used. "Comprehensive" plans deal with the whole range of uses or resources on a given area of the public lands.

9. National Forest Management Act, 16 U.S.C. §1600; and Federal Land Policy and Management Act, 43 U.S.C. § 1701. Also see pages 57–58 and 95–96.

10. The use of functional plans for specific resources predated the development of comprehensive multiple-use plans; see Kaufman, *The Forest Ranger*, pp. 98–101. The multiple-use planning system also provided for "multiple-use guides," prepared by each service regional office; these evolved into the regional "area guides" in the 1971 planning system.

11. Timber management issues, especially the harvest scheduling or "nondeclining evenflow" issues discussed on text pages 12–13, dominated the process of drafting planning regulations under the NFMA. Final regulations implementing the NFMA planning mandate were subject to lengthy delays, largely because of controversies over clear-cutting and nondeclining evenflow, which, because of the logic of NFMA, were intertwined with the comprehensive land management planning process. See Forest Service, "National Forest System Land and Resource Management Planning," 44 *Federal Register* 53928–53999 (September 17, 1979).

12. Forest Service Manual, §8226.1 (1975); steps in the original were

consolidated and renumbered. Based on early indications (the September 1979 planning regulations cited in note 11), the structure of the new land management planning process under NFMA will not be significantly different from that of the older unit planning process.

13. *Natural Resources Defense Council v. Morton*, 388 F.Supp. 829 (D.DC, December 1974). On the difficulties caused by complying with NEPA's environmental statement at the implementation—rather than the comprehensive planning—stage, see Culhane and Friesema, "Land Use Planning for the Public Lands," pp. 65–67.

14. The classic rational decision model consists of four steps: (1) identification of goals, (2) identification of all alternative means of achieving the goals, (3) consideration of all relevant consequences of each alternative, and (4) selection of the alternative that maximizes one's goal attainment in light of the alternatives' consequences. See (though he is *not* a proponent of classic rationalism) Simon, *Administrative Behavior*, p. 67.

15. Forest Service Manual, §8812 (1975); emphasis added.

16. For a comparison of, and review of the theoretical literature on rational and political bargaining decision models, see Graham Allison, *Essence of Decision* (Boston, Mass., Little, Brown, 1971), especially chap. 1 and 5.

17. RARE I, which took place at the time of the field research, received over 54,000 inputs (hearing statements, letters, and so forth), and RARE II, in 1977–78, received over 314,000 inputs. See *New Wilderness Study Areas* (Washington, D.C., Forest Service, CI no. 11, October 1973) p. 3; and *Roadless Area Review and Evaluation, Final Environmental Statement* (Washington, D.C., Forest Service, January 1979) pp. 99–100.

18. At the time of the field research, land use plans had been completed on only a small proportion of the planning units in the sample regions. Thus, land use planning did not explain group influence on most of the basic policies in the sample. This caveat is related to the application of the planning mechanism to the results of the quantitative analysis of group influence to be discussed in chapter 10.

19. Carl Friedrich, *Constitutional Government and Politics* (New York, Harper & Brothers, 1937) pp. 16–18. The rule was first described as important in low-level administrative policymaking by Paul Appleby, *Policy and Administration* (University, Ala., University of Alabama Press, 1949) pp. 10–22, and 40–45, and especially pp. 12–13. A variation on the rule of anticipated reactions was also described by Kaufman in *The Forest Ranger* (pp. 106–107) as an important form of influence among officers within the same agency (for example, between rangers and supervisory office staff officers).

20. *Inform and Involve* (Washington, D.C., Forest Service, February 1972) p. 5. Also see text pages 241–242.

21. It should be understood that these are very important bounds indeed. But insofar as we are interested in the differences among many individual decisions, the constants of agency policy and professional beliefs do not explain real variation from one decision to the next.

22. On the technique of buffering an organization's "technical core" from external presures, see James Thompson, *Organizations in Action* (New York, McGraw-Hill, 1967), especially pp. 20–21.

23. The "informational" lobbying style is based on the premise that congressmen (and other government decision makers) are objective, responsible legislators who will act in the public interest when presented the true facts (as a particular group sees them). See Jeffrey Berry, *Lobbying for the People* (Princeton, N.J., Princeton University Press, 1977); Lester Milbrath, *The Washington Lobbyists* (Chicago, Ill., Rand McNally, 1963); Raymond Bauer, Ithel Pool, and Lewis Dexter, *American Business and Public Policy* (Cambridge, Massachusetts Institute of Technology Press, 1963). Also see text pages 25–26.

10

Interest Group Influence and Use Allocation Policies

Local officers of the Forest Service and Bureau of Land Management (BLM) steadfastly maintained they took the interests of their clients into account when making decisions. As noted earlier, local officers' decisions can be analytically divided into front-end decisions allocating lands to certain uses or levels of use and back-end decisions on the administration of those uses. Participants in local public lands politics generally believed interest group politics primarily affected the service's and bureau's back-end use administration policies (see chapter 7, especially pages 222–226. Essentially, the historical change in local public lands constituencies during the late 1960s and early 1970s, when environmentalists emerged as a counterbalance to traditional economic users, resulted in increased restrictions on use administration. It is difficult, however, to ascribe changes over time in use administration restrictions solely to environmentalist influence. Environmentalists were certainly sympathetic with, and sometimes even explicitly called for, increased controls on uses to protect land resources, but the controls were so consistent with long-standing agency methods of operation that local administrators appeared to be using environmentalist and recreationalist pressures to achieve agency goals.

Despite local participants' preoccupation with use-administration policies, front-end decisions about levels of goods and services provided by the agencies' lands were the policy decisions in which local interest group clients had the most fundamental stake. Local rangers and area managers, moreover, routinely included "economic needs" (that is, demands for economic uses) among the most important considerations they tried to be responsive to. If the anticipated reactions style of decision making (plus comprehensive planning and public participation) provided a logical mechanism linking constituency interests and local administrators' decision making, the central questions in local public lands politics are, Can such influence be empirically demonstrated and, if so, how much do constituency interests influence local policies?

To answer these questions, a model of group influence was developed. That model is simply an abstraction of interest group theory in a form that can be readily tested against real-world behavior. The model of group influence used in this study is mathematical in the sense that group theory is abstracted as an equation that can be easily examined with standard statistical tools. This examination of group influence on Forest Service and BLM use-allocation policies—based on objective data, rather than subjective opinions—thus should provide a litmus test of administrators' claims that they were responsive to their local constituents.

A Concise Model of Group Influence

During the past half-century, interest group influence has been examined in a wide variety of ways, ranging from general expositions of group theory—notably Arthur Bentley's *The Process of Government* and David Truman's *The Governmental Process*—to specialized case studies of interest groups and to critiques of group influence.[1] The core argument in all these studies has been that group influence is the primary—and according to some arguments the *only*—explanation for the policies pursued by government. Group theory is essentially an elaboration on the premise that public policies are the products of interest group pressures.

A General Group Influence Model

Group influence is very difficult to define, as the complex beliefs of participants in public lands politics amply demonstrate. Influence is not a readily observable property of an interest group or a public policy, but the effect or consequence of group activity on a policy. Observers of interest group activity have suggested, however, that a number of reasonably observable properties of groups contribute to group influence. One key property is a group's set of interests or preferences—the direction, in a sense, in which it wishes to see governmental policy move.[2] A second is a group's "power," or organizational ability to force its policy preferences on decision makers.[3] A group's size, legitimacy (often defined in terms of the proportion of people in society who share its interests or views), financial resources, and the political skills of its leaders are commonly believed to be important contributors to its power. Finally, a group's access to decision makers is an important resource that facilitates the exercise of group influence.[4]

A model of group influence would thus be a mathematical representation of the group theorists' contention that any policy is a function of the power, value preferences, and access of the groups involved in the policy process. Each group's value preferences give direction and intensity to the exercise of group power, and access is a measure of the degree to which group power and values reach decision makers. In mathematical terms, the relationship between group power, values, and access is interactive, that is, a multiplicative product; a group with twice the power of another group presumably has twice the impact of that group, while a group with half the access has half the effect. The effect of the whole set of groups, however, is additive. Two groups with equal power and access but opposite value preferences should offset one another.

If each group's power, value preferences, and access all significantly affect a policy, then group influence can be modeled as shown in figure 10-1. A group's influence is its relative effect on policy, taking into account the effects of the other groups affecting that policy. The i terms in the general group influence model represent the effect of various groups'

$$O = i_1 APV_1 + i_2 APV_2 + i_3 APV_3 + i_4 APV_4 + \ldots + i_n APV_n$$

Where
  O is a policy output,
  i is the particular group's relative influence index,
  A is the group's access to decision makers,
  P is the group's power,
  V is the group's value preferences, and
  n is the total number of groups in the policy process.

Figure 10-1. A general group influence model.

power, values, and access products on the policy, O. Thus, $i_1, i_2, i_3, \ldots,$ i_n are indexes of the first, second, third, and nth groups' influence on the policy. (See appendix C for a detailed discussion of the derivation of figure 10-1.)

The Public Lands Group Influence Model

To use the general model to estimate the influence of Forest Service and BLM constituencies, we need only substitute data on the policies and interest groups peculiar to public lands politics for the arguments given in the general model. The interest group activity terms in the public lands version of the model are products of scales based on group characteristics discussed earlier; the values or V term is the E–U scale described in chapter 5, for example; and the standardized number of interactions reported in chapter 6 is one measure of access. The public lands version of the group influence model uses seven categories of interest groups (for example, the forest products industry and the livestock industry) and four types of policy outputs (for example, relative timber sales and grazing lease levels).

Timber sales are the major end-product decisions of the agencies' timber management programs. For any administrative unit, the total volume of timber sold (expressed in 1,000 board-feet, or MBF) is the measure of the absolute level of timber output in a given year.[5] The analogous measure of grazing policy products is the number of animal-unit-months (AUMs) of stock use allowed under Forest Service permits or BLM leases on the ranger district or resource area. The third type of economic use examined in the model is the number of permits related to mining, oil and gas exploration or development. It should be remembered that the agencies do not produce timber, livestock, or mineral products themselves, but make their lands available—through timber sales contracts, leases, permits, and other means—to private users. The agencies rely on timber operators to bid on sales and on mining firms to apply for permits on specific tracts; without such bids and applications, there can be no contracts or permits.

Unlike the timber sales, grazing lease or permit, and mineral lease or permit programs, the preservation programs of the agencies do not produce annual decision outputs. The initial preservation designation of an area generally stands for many years—permanently, for all practical purposes. In most years, decisions on Wilderness designation are on the agendas of only a small proportion of administrative units. In 1973, however, the Forest Service was conducting its first roadless area review (RARE I), so wilderness decisions were on the agendas of almost all Forest Service units. The BLM did not engage in a similar systematic Wilderness review (because it did not come under the provisions of the Wilderness Act until 1976), but BLM officers in the sample did review a number of areas for administrative classifications (for example, primitive area designation) that afford wild areas protection similar to that of a Wilderness designation. Thus, a variety of classifications that restrict uses of areas are here considered wilderness actions on the part of the agencies. The measure of preservation decisions is the number of areas designated or recommended by local officers for designation or further study.[6]

While the objects of group competition are the actual levels of goods and services produced by the public lands agencies (the thousands of board-feet of timber sold, number of Wilderness or similar areas designated, and so on), the potential levels of such outputs are not determined by group demands alone. Irrespective of interest group influence, a high level of timber sale contracts cannot be let on a ranger district or resource area with a very low or nonexistent inventory of merchantable timber, nor can Wilderness areas be designated in an area that is heavily roaded, recently logged, or otherwise not even minimally approximating the Wilderness Act's criteria. In short, physiographic characteristics influence the potential of an administrative unit to provide various levels of outputs.

The agencies provide estimates of an area's potential output. Each administrative unit in the Forest Service and BLM has a technically determined range carrying capacity, the supposed maximum level of animal-unit-months of domestic livestock grazing that can be sustained over time at present types of operation. The analogous limit for the timber management program is annual allowable cut, the volume of timber, in thousands of board-feet, that can be harvested while maintaining sustained yield. With respect to Wilderness designation, Forest Service administrators consider all roadless areas (that is, potential Wilderness or, as preservationists like to call it, "*de facto* wilderness"), but recommend only some for further study. In the case of mineral permits, users apply for the use to the agency, giving another measure of potential uses.

The analysis of the model therefore expresses outputs as proportions of potential levels of use—for example, the ratio of timber sold over the annual allowable cut, the ratio of animal-unit-months grazed to carrying capacity, and so forth. Such a measure of outputs has two advantages over the use of absolute levels of outputs. The ratio or proportional measure best reflects the decisions administrators have to make because it takes into account the maximum level of use (for example, how many roadless areas in the ranger district should be recommended for inclusion on the chief's list of new study areas?). Moreover, the ratio measure is more congruent with the political controversies surrounding agency programs; environmentalists complain of overcutting of national forest timber and overgrazing of BLM rangeland (the criterion for too much cutting and grazing being that which exceeds sustained yield levels), economic interest groups point to too many Wilderness designations (with "too many" meaning too high a proportion of inventoried roadless areas), and so forth.[7]

A minor problem with the use of administrative determinations of potential outputs is that those determinations are products of agency decision processes, not just objective, technical indicators of areas' potentials. The national level determination of the service's allowable cut, for example, has been a source of disagreement from the Forest and Related Resources plan controversies in the early 1970s through the recent nondeclining evenflow debate. Similarly, the long-standing debate over the level of grazing involves the adjudication of carrying capacities.[8] At the same time, while allowable-cut and carrying-capacity determinations may be affected by political as well as strictly technical factors, they are still useful indicators of use potentials. Allowable cut and carrying capacities had been established prior to the sample period in all units in the sample, so they were givens in rangers' and area managers' decision making. Local debates about output levels often centered on comparisons against administrative maximum levels: the forest products industry, for example, complained about low timber sales by arguing that the Forest Service was not "meeting its commitment" (that is, the commitment implied by the allowable cut), and livestock industry pressure was directed at staving off reductions to carrying capacity. Thus, local administrators faced incremental choices about how much of the allowable cut or carrying capacity—determined mostly on physiographic grounds and perhaps somewhat on political[9]—could be sold or leased.

To simplify the analysis of group influence on agency outputs, the various types of groups that participated in local public lands politics are combined into five sets, which will be called *interests*.[10] The five interests are the livestock industry, the forest products industry, conservationists and recreationists, economic interests other than the livestock and forest products industries, and other local contacts or entities. Most of the groups fall fairly easily into these interest categories. The livestock interest includes individual ranchers, grazing association and advisory board members, and the one contact from the Society for Range Management (SRM) in the sample. The forest products firms and one industry association staffer are in the forest products category. Various local businessmen and economic users are in the fourth set; the largest group in this "economic interests" set (and the one that has the most influence in the analysis of the model) is the mining industry. Similarly, while a number of miscellaneous groups are included in the fifth, "other interests" set, the largest and most important groups in the set consist of local government officials and school district contacts.

The combination of conservationists and recreationists requires some discussion. Government agencies, such as the National Park Service and state fish and game departments, with a strong conservationist tradition and interests similar to those of conservation groups, were included in the same set of interests as conservationists. For several reasons, recreationists were also combined with conservationists. Most conservationists are actually outdoor recreationists, and their political views about land management complement their interests as recreationists in preserving resources. On most issues administrators and other users tended to treat conservationists and recreationists as having similar interests and playing similar roles in local agency constituencies. In addition, many recreationist groups in the study sample were allied with conservationists. Sportsmen's group leaders often had conservationist philosophies, and many were also members of environmental groups such as wildlife federations or the Izaak Walton League. Most recreation business operators in the sample (the backcountry guides and two ski area operators) had very material interests in wild area preservation, plus environmentalist leanings. However, some recreationist groups do not share conservationists' interests. In particular, off-road vehicle (ORV) groups oppose environmentalists on such issues as wild area preservation, with the California desert controversy being a major case in point. For this reason, ORV groups were deleted from the consevationist–recreationist set in the analysis of preservation policies.[11]

Administrators were also included in the model as two additional groups. A persistent criticism of group theory has been that it assigns government decision makers too neutral and passive a role. Certainly the histories of the agencies and earlier descriptions of local public lands management processes do not suggest that local Forest Service and BLM officers have been straws blown in the winds of interest group pressure. To allow for the possibility that individual administrators may have had some significant independent effect on policy, local administrators (rangers and area managers) and their immediate superiors (Forest supervisors and district managers) are treated as the sixth and seventh entities in the model.

Each term in the model is constructed from data on individual participants' access to local administrators, attitudes, and organizational resources. The indicators of group power are the number of group members, group budget, gross dollar volume (if a business firm), and size of organizational staff; administrative unit budget and staff size are used as indicators of administrators' resources. The indicator of value preferences is the administrator's or group contact's score on the E-U attitude scale (discussed in chapter 5). There are two indicators of group access —the number of interactions between an interest group contact and the administrator of the local ranger district or resource area, and the relative dominance by an interest set of public participation events held in the ranger district or resource area. The indicators of supervisors' access to local administrators are the various measures of strength of supervision—number of reports, instructions, and so forth—discussed in chapter 9.

The two administrator terms in the model are simple products, power times value (PV) in the case of rangers and area managers, and power times value times strength of supervision (RPV) in the case of supervisors. Each interest group contact's power, values, and number of interactions scores are multiplied. Next, the products for all the contacts in each interest set are added and then multiplied by the interest set's public participation dominance score. The resulting products are used as the basic interest group variables in the model.[12]

Assuming that the various ratio policy outputs are not related to one another,[13] the public lands group influence model is the fairly straightforward set of four functions shown in figure 10-2. The functions estimate the effects of the five interest sets' power-values-access characteristics, plus the corresponding administrator characteristics, on grazing, timber sales, preservation designations, and mining or oil and gas permits ratios.

$$\text{AUMs}\% = a_1 + i_{11}\text{StockRNPV} + i_{12}\text{ForPrRNPV} + i_{13}\text{CnRcRNPV} + i_{14}\text{EcoRNPV} + i_{15}\text{OthRNPV} + i_{16}\text{SAdmRPV} + i_{17}\text{DAdmPV} + e_1$$

$$\text{MBF}\% = a_2 + i_{21}\text{StockRNPV} + i_{22}\text{ForPrRNPV} + i_{23}\text{CnRcRNPV} + i_{24}\text{EcoRNPV} + i_{25}\text{OthRNPV} + i_{26}\text{SAdmRPV} + i_{27}\text{DAdmPV} + e_2$$

$$\text{Wild-Prim}\% = a_3 + i_{31}\text{StockRNPV} + i_{32}\text{ForPrRNPV} + i_{33}\text{CnRcRNPV} + i_{34}\text{EcoRNPV} + i_{35}\text{OthRNPV} + i_{36}\text{SAdmRPV} + i_{37}\text{DAdmPV} + e_3$$

$$\text{Min/O\&G}\% = a_4 + i_{41}\text{StockRNPV} + i_{42}\text{ForPrRNPV} + i_{43}\text{CnRcRNPV} + i_{44}\text{EcoRNPV} + i_{45}\text{OthRNPV} + i_{46}\text{SAdmRPV} + i_{47}\text{DAdmPV} + e_4$$

Where
AUMs% is grazing use, in animal-unit-months, as proportion of carrying capacity,
MBF% is timber sold, in 1,000 board-feet, as proportion of allowable cut,
Wild-Prim% is wilderness, primitive, and other areas approved, as proportion of areas considered,
Min/O&G% is mining or oil and gas leases/permits approved, as proportion of applications,
Stock is livestock industry,
ForPr is forest products industry,
CnRc is conservationists and recreationists,
Eco is economic users other that the livestock and timber industries,
Oth is other interest group contacts,
SAdm is forest supervisors and BLM district managers,
DAdm is forest rangers and BLM area managers,
RNPV, RPV, PV are products of power, values, and access, as defined in text,
i is influence indices, and
a is intercepts.

Figure 10-2. The public lands group influence model.

In evaluating these functions, we will be interested in two types of findings, the relative influence (i_{11}, and so forth) of the various interests on policy outputs, and the total effect of all groups on local public lands policies. The second finding should allow us to judge how responsive administrators are to their constituencies.

Group Influence on Policy Output Levels

The model was applied to data from the thirty-seven ranger districts and resource areas in the sample. The data were analyzed using ordinary least squares regression.[14] In the process of analysis, the model was refined in two ways.

First, some groups do not have a significant effect on particular output functions. For example, taking the full timber sales function shown in the public lands group influence model (with all seven terms on the right-hand side of the equation, and full RNPV arguments), the correlation or total effect of all interests is .51. But almost all of that correlation is attributable to three interests (forest products, livestock, and conservation-recreationists) that alone produce a correlation of .49. On the preservation function, four interests produce a .53 correlation alone, whereas the correlation is only .54 when all seven interests are included. The results of the analysis could be more parsimoniously presented if the interests with insignificant effects on particular outputs were deleted from the functions. The technical-statistical criterion for allowing interests into the functions was that terms were deleted from a particular function if their addition resulted in a decrease in the adjusted R^2 statistic or in the statistical significance of the whole function (measured by the F statistic) dropping below the 5 percent significance level.[15] The adjusted-R^2 criterion (but not the whole function's significance criterion) was even relaxed in a few cases for the purpose of exposition, permitting the inclusion of administrators or some interest that, in the substantive debates in public lands politics, was generally thought to have an important effect on a particular type of policy. Each function in the model could be easily reduced to three or four terms using even these very liberal inclusion criteria.

Second, the terms in the model were examined to determine if interest sets' influence did not depend on all four components of the full RNPV arguments shown in figure 10-2. It seemed plausible that, for example, public participation access would not be an important part of the influence style of certain interests or that organization resources would not be important for other groups. Including the nonsignificant characteristics would thus depress the effects of the more relevant components of the interest's argument in the model. The arguments were analyzed to produce a set of "optimum arguments."[16] The objective of this analysis was to maximize the relationship between the interest's optimum argument and the set of outputs (that is, to eliminate components that dampened the interest's effects); if different combinations worked better on different functions, an entity's optimum argument was selected so it performed better on the functions of the policies for which the entity was a major clientele group (for example, timber sales in the case of the forest products industry), yet did not perform anomalously on other functions. As a definitional matter, the attitude V term was always included in optimum arguments. The optimum arguments were stockmen's and conservationists-recreationists' values times participation access (RV), forest products industry and "economic users" power times values (PV), and the "other interests" interactions times power times values (NPV). Only in the case of administrators were the full original arguments used (for example, supervisors' RPV.

Results of the Optimum Predictors, Ratio Outputs Model

As noted earlier, in applying the group influence model to the ranger districts and resource areas in the sample regions, we are interested in two issues. The first issue involves the extent to which all group influences affect particular policies. The multiple correlation (the R statistic in the tables) measures the total effect of predictor variables in a regression equation on the criterion or dependent variable; thus it serves as a measure of the total effect of groups on policy outputs in the model. By this measure, there is a fairly strong relationship, by normal social science standards, between the nature of rangers' and area managers' organization-sets and timber, grazing, and preservation policies. Groups have the strongest effect on the timber sales function (with an R of .61). Groups have slightly less, but still strong effects on Wilderness-primitive areas recommendations ($R = .55$) and grazing lease or permit ($R = .53$) ratios. The output that seems least affected by local level group influence is mining or oil and gas leases or permits ($R = .40$); this low relationship is not surprising because local administrators have less formal authority

—and the mining claims and leasing laws give the agencies generally less discretion—over mining decisions than any other public lands use.[17] Each of the functions is statistically significant at the 5 percent probability level, though the mineral/O&G ratio function is just barely so.[18]

The second aspect of the analysis involves the relative influence of different interests on policy outputs. The influence indexes (the standardized beta from the regression analysis) are used as measures of each group's relative influence on the various outputs. All the influence indexes shown in table 10-1 are in the correct direction. Because of the scaling of the V term in the model, negative indexes are expected on the timber, grazing, and mining functions; more utilitarian attitudes are more negative on the E-U scale, so as attitudes times power or access become more negative, consumptive uses would be expected to increase, resulting in a negative slope coefficient i. The opposite (that is, positive coefficients) is expected on the Wilderness-primitive function.

The most interesting, if predictable, aspect of the influence indexes in table 10-1 is that the groups that were most affected by and interested in a particular policy output have the greatest relative influence on the level of that output. Stockmen have the highest index on the animal-unit-months ratio function, as does the forest products industry on the timber sales function. The economic user interest set has its greatest effect on the mineral/O&G ratio function; high scores on the EcoPV term occur in Type III organization-sets, those with many mining industry operators.

Conservationist-recreationist influence on preservation decisions is a slight exception to this rule; this influence index, .41, is second to the "others" interest set's .53 on the Wilderness-primitive function. The major element in the "others" interest set is local government officials, who have been generally regarded as opposed to Wilderness designations because of local governments' fiscal stake in in-lieu shares of commodity use receipts (such receipts could be decreased if areas were placed off-limits to commodity use by preservation designations). A close inspection of the data (using scatterplots) suggests that when there is a strong negative "others" set, the preservation decision ratio is low, but when the "others" set is more neutral other factors take over. Strong conservationist interests are especially associated with high preservation ratios. The major reason for conservationists' slightly weaker showing on the preservation function is that conservationists' public participation has more influence on preservation decisions than their organization-set contacts.[20] If conservationst-recreationist participation access had been used with-

Table 10-1. Public Lands Group Influence Model (Ratio Outputs, Optimum Predictors)

Predictor variables	Output function for grazing animal-unit-months as % carrying capacity		
	Influence index (beta)[a]	Significance (F of b)[b]	Adjusted R^2 at entry
Stockmen's RV	−0.461	7.60	0.114
Forest products' PV	−0.379	4.91	0.242
Supervisory administrators' RPV	−0.129	0.66	0.235
$R = 0.53$	$R^2 = 0.28$	$F_{3,33} = 4.22$	

Predictor variables	Output function for MBF timber sold as % allowable cut		
	Influence index (beta)[a]	Significance (F of b)[b]	Adjusted R^2 at entry
Forest products' PV	−0.641	19.40	0.317
Economic users' PV	−0.245	2.82	0.350
Conservationists-recreationists' RV	−0.096	0.49	0.340
$R = 0.61$	$R^2 = 0.38$	$F_{3,33} = 6.66$	

Predictor variables	Output function for Wilderness-primitive approved as % considered		
	Influence index (beta)[a]	Significance (F of b)[b]	Adjusted R^2 at entry
Conservationists-recreationists RV[c]	0.406	6.67	0.054
Other interests' NPV[c]	0.527	9.80	0.243
Forest products' PV	0.142	0.76	0.247
Supervisory administrators' RPV	0.093	0.37	0.233
$R = 0.55$	$R^2 = 0.30$	$F_{4,32} = 3.38$	

Predictor variables	Output function for mineral/O&G approvals as % applications		
	Influence index (beta)[a]	Significance (F of b)[b]	Adjusted R^2 at entry
Economic users' PV	−0.398	5.74	0.093
Forest products' PV	−0.282	2.88	0.140
$R = 0.40$	$R^2 = 0.16$	$F_{2,34} = 3.31$	

Note: $N = 37$.

[a] Standardized regression coefficient beta is influence index i. (Regression b and standard error of b are not reported since, because of the group variables' scaling procedures, b has no clear intuitive interpretation.)

[b] F of $b > 4.16$ statistically significant at a 5 percent level.

[c] ORV groups deleted from conservationist-recreationist variable and added to "others" variable for the Wilderness-primitive regression only.

out the attitude V term in the Wilderness-primitive function, conservationists would have had an influence score of .50; the "others" interest set index would have dropped to .44, the timber industry's would have stayed at .13, and the overall multiple correlation would have increased to .62 (with $F = 6.81$).

Public participation effectiveness was quite important in the service's RARE I Wilderness review process (which affected most of the areas considered in the preservation function). RARE I was more of a one-shot decision process than was the case with timber, grazing, or mining policymaking, and public meetings were designed to be the primary avenue for public influence in Wilderness decisions. In fact, public support was one of the three key factors that Forest Service decision makers were supposed to consider in reviewing roadless areas. This made it advisable for groups to mobilize their rank and file for RARE I meetings. (Nationally, the service received over 54,000 hearing statements, letters, and so forth, in conjunction with RARE I.) While the use of conservationist-recreationist public participation access alone might have been more consistent with the real dynamics of the RARE I process, the model used the RV argument because it was consistent with the conservationist arguments used in the other functions (as well as with the convention of always including the V component in the model).

Some of the relatively low influence scores are as instructive as the high scores. Conservationist-recreationist influence on the timber sales function is not statistically significant and the normal inclusion criteria (for example, increasing adjusted R^2) had to be relaxed to add conservationists-recreationists to the equation. Even more important, none of the administrators' terms had significant influence on the model. The inclusion criteria had to be relaxed to add forest supervisors and BLM district managers to the grazing and preservation functions because their influence indexes were very statistically insignificant.[20] Rangers' and area managers' influence scores are even lower, and these officials could not legitimately be included in any output function.

Alternative Interpretations of the Model's Results

The group influence model produces good results, but it is always wise to regard statistical analyses with caution. Since public lands management is a very professional, as well as political, process, the model's results may make some readers uncomfortable because the model includes only interest group pressures, ignoring such factors as physiographic, scientific-technical, and managerial influences. The model's results do not rule out nongroup influences, of course. For example, a healthy proportion of the variation in policy output ratios remains unexplained by the group influence model. Within the limits of the information collected for this study, two of the more obvious alternative explanations of the results were examined.

One alternative to the group theory explanation of local policy output variation is that a unit's physiographic characteristics are the real cause of policy outputs, not group influences. This explanation assumes that a unit's uses flow naturally from its physiographic characteristics and potential users are attracted by those characteristics, so any relationship between user characteristics and levels of use is spurious. The ratio outputs measure was designed to address this alternative explanation. (In fact, a verbal explanation of how physical potential could influence the *proportion* of that potential actually used is rather tenuous.) However, to verify that group influence on ratio-level outputs was not an artifact of physiographic factors, an analysis was performed including the measure of physiographic potential in the relevant functions.

Table 10-2 shows the results of this analysis for the timber sales ratio function. The size of the forest products interest set is indeed related to the magnitude of an administrative unit's annual allowable cut, though not as much as might have been suspected. However, the influence of the forest products industry is undiminished by the inclusion of allowable cut in the model; in fact, the forest products PV's influence index improves from −.64 (in table 10-1) to −.72. The addition of allowable cut increases the function's correlation, but the allowable-cut relationship is in the wrong direction (and probably mostly artifactual).[21] Almost identical results were obtained for the other commodity function, the grazing animal-unit-month's ratio. Since the best available indicators of physiographic potential do not diminish the various interests' indexes, we can assume that the physiographic explanation does not invalidate the results of the model.

Another explanation of the results can be inferred from the literature on forestry economics and from some of the interviews conducted for the study. The variables used in the model as indicators of interest group activity might be interpreted as indicators of economic market, rather than political, characteristics. The market explanation seems most applicable to timber sales. Recall that participants steadfastly maintained that little

Table 10-2. Summary Tables of Alternative Timber Sales Model

Predictor variable	Dependent variable, forest products' PV		
	Beta[a]	Significance (F of b)[b]	Adjusted R^2 at entry
Annual allowable cut	−0.349	4.88	0.122
$R = 0.35$	$R^2 = 0.12$	$F_{1,35} = 4.88$	

Predictor variables	Output function for MBF sold as % allowable cut		
	Influence index (beta)[a]	Significance (F of b)[b]	Adjusted R^2 at entry
Forest products' PV	−0.721	24.59	0.317
Economic users' PV	−0.174	1.45	0.349
Conservationists-recreationists' RV	−0.182	1.72	0.340
Annual allowable cut	−0.361	3.87	0.394
$R = 0.68$	$R^2 = 0.44$	$F_{4,32} = 6.40$	

Note: This alternate hypothesis assumes that the allowable cut's effect on timber sales is causally prior to the forest products-timber sales relationship; thus, ordinary least squares suffices.

[a] Standardized regression coefficient beta is the influence index i.
[b] F of $b > 4.16$ statistically significant at 5 percent level.

pressure was placed on local land managers to offer sales, and that the Forest Service had a strong commitment to sell national forest timber not only to supply consumers with forest products, but to complement other agency resource management goals. A market explanation could account for the report that timber firms only respond to service sales initiatives, but forest products industry characteristics are related to the level of timber sales. In addition, the Forest Service's allowable cut in certain areas might not support a developed market of local timber mills. In such cases no sales would even be planned or offered for sale. This seemed to be the case on NF5, whose allowable cut was so low that there were no real local mills on one division of the forest and only a small local mill on the other.

In some respects this market argument resembles the physiographic hypothesis. The analysis of that hypothesis suggests that the market effect is not a significant consideration (since the market indicator, annual allowable cut, did not eliminate the effect of the forest products industry PV on ratio level outputs). Another (but limited) way to examine the market hypothesis is by inspecting plots of the data; for example, a sharp discontinuity at some threshold point could indicate a market effect, as could clusters around the origin (no timber mills and a zero timber sales ratio) and along a line perpendicular to the timber sales ratio axis (a variable number of mills, but roughly a 100 percent timber sales ratio). No such patterns were found: the plot of forest products industry PV on timber sales ratio is one of the most monotonic (a straight band of data points) in the analysis, with no discontinuities; the only origin cluster is the six national grassland ranger districts and BLM resource areas with a zero allowable cut.

Two quasi-market criteria, used by the service to determine whether to recommend Wilderness designations for roadless areas during the RARE I process, were that there must be a need for additional Wilderness and the designation must have significant local support.[22] Although the Forest Service characterized these criteria as analogous to market demand, they were clearly different from explicitly political interest group demand in name only.

There is no reason to suspect that any market effects were relevant for grazing outputs. Ranchers were present on all administrative units, and were ready, willing, and able to absorb as many animal-unit-months as possible.

Relative Influence of Groups and Administrators

The results of the model offer a number of insights into the nature and distribution of group influence in public lands policymaking. Although the differences among various combinations of group characteristics are sometimes marginal, the nature of the optimum arguments suggests that public participation access, frequency of interaction with decision makers, and organizational resources are not equally important for all sets of interests. Organizational power, for example, does not play a significant role in the amount of influence exercised by stockmen or conservationists-recreationists. Both interest sets are composed of voluntary associations whose resources are usually quite small. It is difficult to tell what effect the slight variations among local groups could have, or whether the huge power variance introduced by an official of a state stockmen's association has more impact than a twenty-rancher grazing association composed of the ranger's or area manager's neighbors.

The different interests also seem to have different access styles. The basic form of access reflected in all terms in the model is the interest set's number of contacts.[23] Only in the case of conservationist-recreationist influence on preservation decisions is this kind of access arguably unimportant. For the forest products and economic users, the number of contacts is a sufficient form of access, unamplified by measures of public participation or frequency of interactions access. Frequency of interactions seems the least important contributor to group influence, being a part of only one interest set's optimum argument. That set, "other interests," is one of the two sets whose interactions with local administrators were generally policy-oriented (the other set is conservationists and recreationists, with low frequencies of interactions). This confirms participants' reports that many interactions between administrators and group contacts, especially user group contacts, were routine and nonpolitical.

Finally, the different effects of public participation access are noteworthy. The average levels of the public participation measures for the economic users and "other interest" sets are very low, and almost nil for the forest products industry,[24] and participation access is not part of their optimum arguments. But participation access is an important contributor to the influence of conservationists-recreationists and stockmen. As noted in chapter 8, the agencies' new recreationist and environmentalist clients were the primary targets of the public participation programs that received such emphasis in the 1970s, and stockmen-oriented participation forums accounted for the largest share of the agencies' public participation events. The effectiveness of public participation has been questioned generally,[25] and participants in local public lands politics, while appreciative of participation programs that were well implemented, were not sure of the programs' effects on substantive agency policy. The results of the analysis of the model, particularly the effect of conservationist public participation access alone on Wilderness-primitive area decisions, support the assumption that public participation programs can foster some groups' influence.

In addition to providing insights into the importance of different components of group influence, the model's results serve as rough estimates of the overall influence of different sets of interest groups. The influence indexes in the four functions are measures of group influence on each output; to provide a heuristic summary of group influence, the absolute values of these indexes can be summed across the four functions. Table 10-3 uses the influence indexes from a regression analysis in which interests were not excluded from the functions on the basis of statistical significance.[26] The forest products industry has the highest total influence across all four policy areas. As noted earlier, each major commodity interest has the highest influence score on the function most relevant to its use of the public lands, and the forest products industry has the highest score on its timber sales function. In addition, the forest products industry seems to have an important secondary influence on the other commodity-use functions. (No odd or artifactual data distributions are apparent in scatterplots or intercorrelations that seem to explain away these secondary forest products industry scores.) The presence of a strong forest products industry, everything else being equal, seems to reinforce higher levels of economic uses across the board.

The total scores in table 10-3 (including part of the forest products industry total score) should be read with some caution, however, because the results of the substantively and statistically less significant mineral-O&G function are included in the totals.[27] If the mineral-O&G function's scores are devalued somewhat, the four nontimber interests (stockmen,

Table 10-3. Relative Influence Indexes of Interests and Administrators in the Group Influence Model

Interest/administrator set	Indexes on specific outputs[a]				Total[b]
	AUMs% (0.54)	MBF% (0.63)	Wild% (0.56)	Min% (0.42)	
Forest products industry (PV)	−0.39	−0.64	0.14	−0.32	1.49
Economic users, not forest products or livestock (PV)	(+0.10)[c]	−0.23	0.00	−0.40	0.63
Others (NPV)	−0.04	−0.01	0.50	−0.03	0.58
Conservationists and recreationists (RV)	(+0.03)[c]	−0.10	0.41	(+0.01)[c]	0.51
Livestock industry (RV)	−0.45	(+0.12)[c]	(−0.10)[c]	−0.06	0.51
Supervisory administrators (RPV)	−0.12	(+0.05)[c]	0.09	(+0.08)[c]	0.21
District administrators (PV)	−0.07	−0.05	0.09	(+0.06)[c]	0.21

[a] Influence indexes (betas) from regression analyses in which all entities were included in the functions, irrespective of significance. Multiple correlation (R) for the function in parentheses under function abbreviation. Also see note 27, page 317.

[b] Totals of the absolute values of the interest sets' indexes across all four functions.

[c] Indexes (betas) in the wrong direction deleted from the function and totals (beta of interest set, if forced into function, shown in parentheses).

conservationists-recreationists, economic users, and others) appear to have, for all practical purposes, equivalent total influence.

Perhaps the most glaring numbers in table 10-3 are the very low total influence scores for administrators. For all practical purposes, the results of the analysis suggest that rangers, area managers, and their supervisors have no influence on the relative levels of policy outputs; the average administrator influence index on any function was .05, which is not significantly (on either a statistical or intuitive basis) different from zero. At first glance, these results seem to support the claim of some hard-core group theorists that government decision makers are mere ciphers who simply implement the resultant of group pressures. For several reasons, however, such a conclusion is unwarranted.

First, there is a technical explanation for the poor performance of administrator variables in the statistical analysis. There is no real variation in the key component of administrator variables, administrators' attitudes or preferences. As noted earlier (see, for example, figure 5-1), administrators have very homogeneous scores on the E–U attitude scale. Other interest sets also have homogeneous attitudes, but the variances of their interest set variables are not dependent solely on variation in attitudes (or power or access times attitudes), but on the number of contacts in the interest set as well. The number of individuals in the district administrator or supervisory administrator sets for any given case is constant: one. Even though the variation across the whole range of the E–U attitude scale is systematic, the variation within the administrators' narrow part of the attitude spectrum is more random. The attitude scale merely serves to fix the essentially professional attitudes of administrators —attitudes the agencies try to develop through selective recruitment, advancement, and socialization of line officers—near the midpoint of the scale. Thus, the random variation in the administrators' terms in the model is understandably not related to the real variation in policy outputs.[28]

Second, some salient characteristics of rangers and area managers, in particular, seem closely related to the characteristics of the officials' constituencies. As noted in chapter 9, an administrator with a ranch background would normally be assigned to a unit with a stockmen-oriented constituency, and rangers with recreationist sympathies were usually stationed on districts with heavy recreation use. (Such characteristics are not necessarily measured directly in constructing the administrator variables in the model.) But since the variation in constituency characteristics is more pronounced, the effects, if any, of these administrator characteristics would be washed out by the computational procedures (that is, the "partial correlation") of the statistical analysis.

Third, differences between administrators may have had a significant marginal effect over time in an incremental decision-making process that does not show up in an analysis of cross-sectional data. This seems quite likely with respect to grazing policy, since grazing levels vary little from one year to the next. Administrators over the years may have significantly affected grazing lease or permit levels, but their effects would not have registered because those administrators had been transferred from the district. Similarly, the current administrator might have made important changes, but the effects would not be large enough, in comparison with the full range of variation in grazing levels, to register in a cross-sectional design. Because of the unique nature of the RARE I process, the incremental argument does not seem to apply to Wilderness and primitive area decisions.

Fourth, and most important, the absence of individual administrators' effects in the model does not mean that administrators as a whole—as part of the complicated structure of agency policymaking—are unimportant in the policy-making process. Chapters 7 and 8 document the ways in which Forest Service and BLM policies, as implemented by local administrators, are crucial factors in local public lands politics and management independent of, and usually more important than, constituency influence. In the area of use administration policy, administrators were not reconciling agency and professional values with environmentalists demands, arriving at a compromise; environmentalist pressures were used to legitimate and augment agency policies and administrators' professional norms. Environmentalists may have wanted more Wilderness and fewer timber sales but the Forest Service gave them improved timber sale administration. In the area of range management, administrators pursued a policy of implementing rest-rotation grazing systems for professional, scientific, and technical reasons. Stockmen's interest in increased animal-unit-months and conservationists' concerns about overgrazing provided group interest reinforcement for the agencies' policy, but neither group demanded rest-rotation on its own initiative. Public participation, while probably improving administrators' understanding of the interests and preferences of their constituents in connection with an anticipated reactions style of decision making, was also pursued by administrators with clear agency goals in mind. Well-developed new public participation facilitated the integration of new conservationist and recreationist clients into local constituencies (where they could counterbalance traditional user clients) and improved the agencies' images of responsiveness generally, while well-organized grazing associations helped the service implement rest-rotation and reduce rangers' paperwork. These patterns of activity involved much more than passive balancing of group pressures.

Overall agency policies on matters such as use administration, rest–rotation, and public participation may have been important, even determinative, factors in local public lands decision making, but the group influence model cannot measure the effects of such policies. National agency policy is a constant for the model; it cannot account for policy variation among administrators in the same agency.[29] The one agency policy the model can assess is the policy that local administrators should be responsive to their constituencies. But that policy does not license administrators, while responding to their clients, to follow their own personal inclinations. In this respect, the finding that local officials' terms in the model are unrelated to their policy decisions is a very positive sign. It indicates that administrators conformed to agency policies in a disciplined way—responding to constituency interests without noticeably interjecting their personal preferences into their policymaking.

Conclusions—The Group Influence Model and Its Implications

In chapter 7, we noted that students of interest groups have generally relied on subjective, "reputational" methods of identifying interest group influence. Group influence, defined as the real effect of a group on policy, was thought to be methodologically impossible to isolate or measure. The model used in this chapter is free of many of the problems of such a reputational approach. By formalizing group theory's central proposition into a set of functions and analyzing data on interest groups and policy outputs from a specific policy system, using common statistical procedures, it is possible to obtain some concrete measure of group influence. Based on the high multiple correlations reported above, interest groups appear to have a major systematic influence on local public lands policymaking.

The results reported in this chapter do not conclusively confirm group theory, of course. They involve a small, nonrandom sample, and apply to public lands policy only. Group theory makes quite sweeping claims about group influence on a wide variety of substantive policy areas; such claims cannot be proved by an analysis of group influence on thirty-seven district rangers and area managers.

On the other hand, this study did examine group influence in local level administrative systems. Group theorists have been confident in asserting that interests influence policy at the highest levels of government, especially legislative. There has been a persistent myth, although less in vogue these days than earlier in the century, that administration (especially local) is less susceptible than other political processes to group influence. The Forest Service, in particular, has even been thought of as a model of apolitical administration.[30] To find fairly strong evidence of group influence at even the lowest levels of public lands management is startling support for group theory.

From its earliest days, interest group theory has been beset by a fundamental disagreement about the nature of group influence. One side, associated with Arthur Bentley, has argued that group influence results from group activity, and that group activity cannot be precisely defined. Other group theorists, notably David Truman, have refined the concept of group activity, specifying that power, interests or preferences, and access are the key components of group activity.[31] The group influence model described here had to ignore Bentley's warning (because a statistical model requires measurable variables) and used indicators of group power, values, and access. The analysis of the public lands group influence model, while not sufficient to resolve the debate about the nature of group influence, can offer some insights into that debate.

The argument, presented in chapter 9, that anticipated reactions decision making is the link between interest groups and policy raises questions about the relevance of sharply defined concepts of access, power, and group interest. Access is important only if one posits that group activity almost always involves repetitive and explicit interest articulation. Insofar as local public lands politics involves minimal overt pressure and interest articulation and relies primarily on covert linkages like anticipated reactions mechanisms, differences among levels of access do not seem to be critical. Similarly, the concept of interests—reflected in explicit messages about group preferences and attitudes—is not clearly relevant in an anticipated reactions style of decision making. If interests are not articulated clearly and in detail, it is questionable to make fine distinctions among group values a crucial component of the model of group influence. Finally, since anticipated reactions decision making involves a low-key, outwardly apolitical style of influence, it is not at all clear how additional increments of organizational power resources translate into more group influence. The quantitative analysis, in fact, suggests that power and access often do not contribute significantly to group influence. The power component is part of only three interests' optimum arguments, public participation access part of two, and frequency of interaction part of one. (As a matter of convention, attitude "values" was included in all interests' optimum arguments, though its deletion from the conservationist-recreationist term in the preservation function would have markedly improved that set's influence score.) The most important underlying reality seems to be the number of contacts in an interest set—that is, group activity broadly—and not the conceptually and mathematically more complicated variables used in the model.

Several considerations support Truman's position on the importance of access and interests. First, groups that were included in the model's analysis did have access; they were formally defined by the district administrators as key contacts. Perhaps variation beyond this fundamental access threshold is of marginal significance, but the study's research design does not allow rejection of the concept of access altogether. Second, even though overt and repetitious interest articulation may not take place, the logic of anticipated reactions mechanisms still relies on the decision-maker's familiarity with group interests. A ranger might not have to be told at each timber sale about the forest products industry's preferences or the Sierra Club's attitudes, but he would have to know (from prior experience, previous conversations, and other means) what those preferences and attitudes were for those interest groups to affect his decision. Finally, power is a complex, elusive quality, and it is undoubtedly more than the simple organizational resources of membership, budget, and staff that this study has used as indicators. Legitimacy, leaders' tactical skills, group cohesion, and interest specificity have all been suggested by group theorists as other important components of power.

On balance, however, Bentley's more nebulous conceptualization describes local public lands politics better than does Truman's: group activity—not the more precise qualities of access, power, and interest—seemed to be the key characteristic of group influence. Rangers and area managers seemed to focus more on the distribution of interest groups in their constituencies than on the precise properties of those groups.

Leaving aside the nuances in interpretation of the indicators of group activity, the model's results form the crucial link in the investigation of group influence in local public lands politics. In earlier chapters a detailed, but incomplete description of group influence was set forth. The service's rangers and the BLM's area managers had clearly established local organization sets. Formal public participation afforded local constituents an access to local decision makers that was clearly condoned, even required, by agency policy. Participants believed groups were influential in local policymaking, but that belief was sufficiently uncertain or contradictory, and the reported group effects on policy were so consistent with the agencies' policies, that real local group influence—as opposed to convenient support for aspects of the agencies' multiple-use goals—seemed ambiguous. In spite of the compelling logic of anticipated reactions-style decision making, administrators' professions that they were responsive to their local constituencies could well have been self-serving rhetoric. The strong influence on the agencies' most basic policies found in the public lands group influence model lends considerable credence to local Forest Service and BLM officers' claims of responsiveness.

NOTES

1. Arthur Bentley, *The Process of Government* (Chicago, Ill., University of Chicago Press, 1908); and David Truman, *The Governmental Process* (New York, Knopf, 1951). Also see text pages 22–25.

2. Group theorists, as noted on text page 24, have engaged in considerable debate over whether a group's interests are equivalent to the preferences of its members. Some policy, for example, might benefit a group even though its members might not have any feelings for or against it. (There is also the subsidiary question of whether anyone has polled group members to determine their attitudes.) We will sidestep this debate and treat group interests and preferences as similar.

3. "Power," like "influence," is often used to describe the effect, rather than an intrinsic property, of a group. Power will refer here only to properties of groups. As will be shown, all the indicators of power used in the model are clearly properties of groups.

4. Access is arguably also not a property of groups. Group leaders often say they have good access to decision makers, but access is better thought of as something decision makers give to group leaders (as the discussion of public participation programs in chapter 8 demonstrates). The formalization of the group model described in appendix C clarifies this point. In any case, a group's access, unlike influence, is readily observable, regardless of whether it is solely a property of the group.

5. The actual end product is the volume of timber cut, but the agencies, especially the Forest Service, do not have complete control over the volume of timber actually harvested from the public lands. They sell timber contracts to forest products firms, estimating the volume that will actually be cut. Sale volume and cut volume may differ because of errors in the presale cruise. In addition, purchasers of timber sale contracts are usually not required to cut the timber purchased immediately; they may harvest a particular sale area when the lumber market is most advantageous. Thus, sale volume is a better measure than timber-cut volume of the agencies' timber decisions.

To some extent, a similar situation exists with respect to grazing leases, discussed below. Ranchers may take "nonuse permits" if they do not wish to run livestock on their federal allotment in a given year but wish to retain rights to their permit or lease.

6. See pages 112–117 and 120–124, for outlines of the agencies' timber, range, minerals-special uses, and Wilderness management processes. See pages 141–145 for a description of the levels of the various outputs in the sample regions. The Wilderness-primitive policy output was a weighted sum, with Wilderness areas weighted by 2 and primitive or similar areas weighted by 1. The distribution of weighted Wilderness-primitive *approvals* was as follows: minimum of zero (twenty-four units at minimum), maximum of 6, mean of .59, standard deviation of 1.14. Distribution of weighted Wilderness-primitive areas *considered* was as follows: minimum of zero (fourteen units), maximum of 8, mean of 1.18, and standard deviation of 2.38.

7. The use of ratio outputs also has a technical advantage. Absolute output levels require a model (which is more complicated than that shown in the public lands group influence model) in which various outputs appear on the right-hand side of the equations. The difficulties with the more complicated model are briefly described in appendix C. The use of ratio outputs avoids the technical problems of the more complicated model; since the absolute outputs equations show higher correlations than the ratio outputs model, the use of the latter is slightly conservative.

8. On the controversy over the FARR plan, see Jack Shepherd, *The Forest Killers* (Weybright and Talley, 1975) pp. 96–104; and page 57. On the nondeclining even-flow issue, see text pages 12–13, 112, and 274–277. On the adjudication of grazing carrying capacity, see text pages 89–92.

9. In other words, the use of ratio output indicators controls for both physiographic potential and prior political influence on allowable cut and carrying capacity. Political factors, of course, can have only a marginal effect on an individual unit's determination, compared with the whole range of carrying capacity and allowable cut found in the sample regions. No amount of pressure, to use an extreme example, could induce a national grasslands ranger district to authorize an allowable cut of 20 million board-feet. (In addition, maximum outputs are used as divisors in constructing ratio indicators; as divisors, small variance errors have slightly less arithmetic effect on the quotient than if the same error had occurred in the dividend.)

10. This use of the term *interests* should not be confused with interests as

value preferences that groups and their members have with respect to policy alternatives. See pages 156–173 and 189–192, especially tables 5-6 and 6-1, for a description of the interest sets and the groups comprising them. In addition to simplifying the presentation of results, a technical reason for reducing the number of groups is that, with thirty-seven ranger district and resource area units of analysis, one cannot have fifty group variables in the model because of the mathematical requirements for solution of the regression equations.

11. ORV groups were included in the "other interests" set in the analyses reported below. Statistically, it makes almost no difference whether ORV groups are included with conservationists or "others"; the multiple correlation of the preservation function is the same, and interests' influence indexes change by a maximum of only .02. Even though the ski industry nationally has been the object of environmentalist criticism, it was not deleted from the conservationist-recreationist set because, on balance, ski area operators in the sample supported environmentalists. Because of the proenvironmentalist operators of the two largest ski areas in the sample, there was a strong correlation between the ski industry group and preservation decisions ($r = .38$ between ski operators' V and the Wilderness-primitive area ratio).

12. See appendix C for details on the scaling and combining of the terms in the model. For the distributions of the various variables, see text pages 173–179, especially table 5-9, on groups contacts' and administrators' attitudes; pages 159–172, especially table 5-7, on group resources; pages 145–149, especially table 5-2, on administrators' resources; pages 190–195, especially tables 6-1 and 6-2, on the number of interactions; pages 235–236, especially table 8-1, on public participation events; and pages 266–268, especially chapter 9, note 2, and table 9-2 on strength of supervision.

13. See note 7, above, and appendix C on this important assumption.

14. On regression analysis, see Ronald Wonnacott and Thomas Wonnacott, *Econometrics* (New York, Wiley, 1970). For readers who are unfamiliar with regression analysis, the basic regression statistics are R, F, and b. The correlation R measures how well the equation fits the data (and thus the total effect of all the predictor variables on the dependent variables); R ranges from 0.0 (no relationship) to 1.0 (perfect relationship with every case lying exactly on the equation's regression line). R^2, the square of R, which can be interpreted as the proportion of variance (in the dependent variable) explained by the predictor variables, is the common measure of how much the predictors affect the dependent variable. The F statistic is a measure of statistical significance (the probability, if the data were from a random sample, that there would not be a zero relationship in the whole population, given the size of the sample). The b statistic is a slope coefficient between a predictor and the dependent variable. The analysis uses "beta," b standardized or transformed as if all the variables were in exactly the same units of measurements. Beta is a better measure of the influence index (i) than b because bs are not directly and intuitively comparable; two variables with the same relative effect (for example, $beta_1 = beta_2 = .40$) can have very different bs (for example, $b_1 = 259.63$ and $b_2 = 0.00718$) if they have very different means and standard deviations.

15. The most rigorous criterion for deleting variables from a regression is the hierarchical F test; see Wonnacott and Wonnacott, *Econometrics*, p. 130. More liberal rules of thumb were used for the purpose of exposition, that is, to see what effects interests—which might be excluded under strict criteria—would have if they were included in the model. Adjusted R^2 controls for the fact that the inclusion of almost any variable in a regression results in at least some R^2 increase (Wonnacott and Wonnacott, *Econometrics*, p. 311). In practice, this criterion is the same as including only variables with F-on-entry of 1.0 or greater. Also see appendix C.

16. The standard procedure for testing interactive effects involves regressing all possible multiplicative terms together. For the group influence model, this test was impossible because of insufficient degrees of freedom (eighty-five combinations of variables, but an N of only 37) and multicollinearity (the combinations of N, R, P, and V for any interest are highly intercorrelated because N, P, and V are partly functions of the number of contacts in the interest set). A less standard method, the logic of which is similar to the standard test of interactive effects, was used to select optimum arguments. Correlation analysis (bivariate r equals bivariate beta), scatterplot inspection, and test regressions were used to examine different arguments, within an interpretation of the arguments as $b_r R b_n N b_p P b_v V$; see appendix C for a demonstration of this interpretation.

17. See text pages 123. In addition, the bivariate scatterplot between EcoPV and the mineral/O&G ratio was very heteroscedastic, with thirty cases along the horizontal axis and the remaining nine cases fanned out within a 60-degree angle. (Mineral/O&G activity was very skewed, since exploration occurred in only a few districts and resource areas.) Because of this unusual data distribution, the mineral/O&G ratio function's results should be regarded as highly suspect.

18. Critical values at the 5 percent significance level for the F test on the regression line as a whole are $F_{4,32} = 2.67$, $F_{3,33} = 2.89$, $F_{2,34} = 3.28$. In addition to tests of statistical significance, it is standard practice to inspect the residuals (the error or e terms in the public lands influence model) for two adverse conditions. The ratio outputs–optimum predictors functions are free from any casewise grouping effects (analogous to autocorrelation of ordered residuals) or heteroscedastic relationships between predictors and residuals. See appendix C for further discussion of these points.

19. Conservationist-recreationist public participation dominance (R in RV_{cr}) had a bivariate correlation of .46 with the preservation ratio, while the correlation of the V term (which, in the logic of the model, reflects solely organization-set characteristics, was only .09.

20. That is, on the basis of probability, one cannot be confident that their indexes were really different from zero. However, the study's purposive sample was not random (and thus one cannot technically generalize from the results of the analysis to the whole population of public lands administrative units). In such a situation, interpreting significance statistics like F is difficult, though

they are useful as benchmarks of how large a statistic should be before one treats a relationship as significant.

21. The purpose of this exercise was to double-check the assumption underlying the use of ratio outputs and thus rule out any effects of potential on ratio level policy outputs. The relationship between allowable cut and the timber sales ratio was almost certainly an artifact of the construction of the timber sales ratio (in which timber sales were divided by allowable cut), which mathematically built in an inverse relationship between the timber sales ratio and allowable cut.

22. See, for example, William Devall, "The Forest Service and Wilderness: A Sociological Interpretation" (Arcata, California State University at Humboldt, 1973), pp. 29 and 42–44, mimeo.

23. Recall that *PV* stands for sum of power-times-values, summed over all contacts in the interest set. Thus, the case-by-case variation in an interest's *PV* scores is a function of the number of contacts in the set, as well as the contacts' power and values scores.

24. That is, since there is no real variation in these interests' variables, they could not be correlated with policy outputs.

25. See, for example, Sally Fairfax, "Public Involvement and the Forest Service," *Journal of Forestry* vol. 73 (October 1975) pp. 657–659.

26. The influence indexes (betas) included in table 10-3 are those that are in the expected direction, based on the scaling of the *V* term. Indexes in the wrong direction are included in parentheses to show what they would be if included in the functions; if these variables were allowed into the functions, some other betas would change slightly (with the largest being the change of forest products *PV* from −.64 to −.60 on the MBF% function). The correlation statistics (*R*s) are for the regressions in which all seven predictors were included. Table 10-3 thus provides some information on the sensitivity of the model to the criteria used to exclude interests from the analysis presented in table 10-1.

27. See note 17 and accompanying text. With all entities included, the mineral/O&G function's adjusted R^2 was only .01, and its *F* was only 0.89 ($F_{7,29}$ greater than 2.35 is significant at the 5 percent level).

28. Tinkering with the administrators' variables is not likely to improve this situation. For example, another plausible treatment of the administrators involved in local decision making would be to include functional staff assistants and treat all relevant administrators as one entity in the model. On the importance of functional staff assistants, see Herbert Kaufman, *The Forest Ranger* (Baltimore, Md., Johns Hopkins University Press, 1960) pp. 103–107. Thus, the officers involved in administrator variables for the timber sales function would be the ranger, the forest supervisor, and the supervisors office timber staff officer. But such a variable would probably not perform any better in the analysis because it would still have minimal real variance (that is, a constant number of people, three, all with essentially similar professional attitudes). See Kaufman, *The Forest Ranger*, especially chap. 6, on the techniques used to produce line officers who think alike on land management issues.

29. National agency policies might account for differences between the Forest Service and the BLM. This topic will be addressed in chapter 11.

30. Kaufman, *The Forest Ranger*.

31. Bentley, *The Process of Government*, especially pp. 214–215; and Truman, *The Governmental Process*, pp. 505–507. Also see chapter 1 of this volume, pages 23–24.

IV
CONCLUSIONS

IV

CONCLUSIONS

11

Conformity, Capture, Multiple Clientelism, and Multiple Use

Public lands policy has traditionally been enmeshed in fundamental political process issues. From Gifford Pinchot and John Muir down to today's environmentalists, the most visible critics of public lands policies have complained that the federal lands are monopolized by consumptive user special interests. A second line of political process criticism has focused on the relative absence of efficiency and expertise in public lands management; as with today's anti-special interests critics, modern efficiency-expertise critics are the philosophical descendents of such early critics of public lands management as Pinchot and John Wesley Powell.

These two lines of political process criticism form the basis of the capture-conformity debate, the most important evaluative issue in public lands administration. The tone and substance of the capture-conformity debate were set largely in 1960, the year in which the major studies of the Forest Service and the Bureau of Land Management (BLM) were published. Public lands politics has changed in several significant ways since 1960, but the tone of the debate has not. Before examining how public lands politics has changed, and the implications of those changes for evaluations of the public lands agencies, it is necessary to review the capture-conformity debate to show its relevance to the agencies' own historic aspirations and administrative evaluative criteria generally. While substantive debates about timber, grazing, preservation, and similar policy issues may be unique to public lands management, the capture-conformity debate in public lands politics is directly linked to fundamental, long-standing issues in American public administration.

The Capture-Conformity Debate

The capture and conformity arguments are largely advanced by the public lands agencies' critics and defenders, respectively. Both sides in the debate agree that some form of conformity is desirable, but they disagree on whether the agencies' behavior is marked by conformity or conformity's supposed opposite, capture.

The capture thesis occupies an important niche in the academic literature on public lands politics. Wesley Calef attributed the problems of early BLM administration primarily to the influence of the livestock industry on western congressmen, who controlled the Interior committees in Congress, which, in turn, controlled the Department of the Interior and the BLM.[1] Phillip Foss argued that western ranchers also used the grazing advisory boards to capture local BLM officers.[2] Charles Reich made a similar charge: the service's and bureau's policymaking was irresponsible because the general public was systematically excluded from agency decision processes, thereby implicitly allowing field officers to be captured by vested user interests.[3] The charge of agency capture was also at the heart of the most widely circulated nonacademic critiques of the Forest Service in the 1970s, those by Jack Shepherd, an environmental journalist, and "Nader Raider" Daniel Barney.[4] The same theme has been developed in environmental groups' periodicals and membership alerts— the Forest Service is being dragged up the mountain, bound and gagged, behind the loggers' skidder, and rape and ruin await the national forests unless the public protests.

The mainline academic view of the Forest Service—the conformity thesis—differs sharply from the capture thesis. The service is generally regarded by academics as one of the elite, uncaptured, professional agencies in the federal bureaucracy. This view has been shaped largely by Herbert Kaufman's *The Forest Ranger,* which detailed the administrative techniques the service used to ensure that field officers conformed to official agency policy.[5] One important consequence of the service's effective use of these techniques was that field officers escaped capture by local interests.

Capture-Conformity and Progressive Conservation

The capture-conformity debate is especially relevant to the Forest Service and BLM because of their origins in the progressive conservation era. As discussed in chapter 1, there were three basic tenets of progressive conservationism. The first was the belief that the public's natural resources should be managed to provide multiple benefits. The second was opposition to the "special interests,"[6] as manifested in rhetoric about the evils of exploitation of the western public lands by the cattle and timber barons. The third was the belief that expert, apolitical management of natural resources by public agencies would rectify the errors of past resource despoilation.[7] These three tenets were intertwined in progressive conservationists' minds. Pinchot argued that the public interest was best served if public natural resources were managed for "the greatest good of the greatest number in the long run." The greatest good was obtained by maximizing resource benefits through multiple-use management. Management for multiple use meant opposition to "single uses" of public resources, that is, opposition to giving away a public resource to a single special interest. Management by expert professionals was required to achieve the greatest good because professional expertise was needed to determine the optimum levels of multiple use that could be sustained over the long run. Progressive conservationists believed that professional resource management should be apolitical, not only because they expected political considerations to frequently conflict with the dictates of professional expertise, but because politics implied special interest influence, which was by definition at variance with the "greatest good of the greatest number."

The service still strongly identifies with the key elements of Pinchot's progressive conservationism.[8] Forest Service officers have continued Pinchot's role as leaders of professional forestry. The progressive conservation movement remained vital into Franklin D. Roosevelt's administration, and the BLM's predecessor, the Grazing Service, was the last progressive conservation agency established in the federal bureaucracy. The early Grazing Service did not have so messianic a self-image as the Forest Service, but under Director Rutledge it borrowed heavily from the Forest Service model of professional range management, and later BLM directors moved the agency along the path to becoming a professional multiple-use agency and fulfilling its progressive conservation heritage.

The two sides of the capture-conformity debate are obviously related to the key tenets of progressive conservation. Concern about capture is simply the modern expression of progressive conservationists' distrust of the special interests. The conformity ideal is a restatement of progressive conservationists' belief in professional resource management and corresponding opposition to special interest influence that could sway administrators from the path of professionalism. Thus, the debate has firm roots in both agencies' institutional histories.

Capture-Conformity and Public Administration Theory

The capture-conformity debate in public lands policy is a variation on an important and long-standing academic disagreement in American public administration. On the one hand, the key principles advocated by the traditionalist theorists of public administration were that civil servants should be politically neutral (reflecting a belief in the so-called politics–administration dichotomy), professionally expert, and thoroughly subordinate to hierarchical superiors. It was no accident that the first two principles paralleled two tenets of progressive conservation, since the traditionalist civil service reformers made up another wing of the progressive movement in American politics.

On the other hand, critics of traditional public administration dogma argued, beginning in the late 1940s, that federal agencies were not really apolitical. In particular, these critics argued that if an agency wished to survive politically and to carry out its mission effectively, it had to co-opt interest groups, that is, enter into a political exchange with them (consulting them on decisions, providing them with policy benefits, and so forth) in the hope they would support the agency and its policies.[9] Co-opting clientele groups is a tricky business. It involves subordinating peripheral (at least from the agency's point of view) federal policies to clientele preferences, but a successful agency co-opts its clientele groups, not vice versa. Capture represents a degenerated clientelist relationship, one in which the agency has been co-opted by its clientele.

According to the clientele theorists, the key to a manageable relationship, one that will not degenerate into capture, is similarity between an agency's mission and its clienteles' inherent interests. The capture thesis has assumed the status of conventional wisdom largely because of studies of one type of policy system, business regulation, in which agency mission and constituency interests are thought to be inherently antithetical. A regulatory agency, so the argument goes, has only its regulated industry as a constituency; strong regulation is not in its industry's interests, so the agency becomes captured as time goes on.[10] The history of the Grazing Service and BLM from 1936 into the 1950s is another case in point. If one assumes that the BLM's mission was to regulate range use in a conservationist fashion and that such regulation would impose hardships on the agency's sole constituency—western stockmen—the BLM's capture was inevitable.

The capture thesis is at the core of the dominant contemporary position on public administrative responsibility. That position is perhaps best expressed by McConnell's attack on "private power." Capture is doubly irresponsible, according to McConnell, because it inevitably transfers public power to private groups, subordinating the public interest to narrow group interests, and, more important, because an agency, in attempting to co-opt a clientele, actively fosters and institutionalizes its own capture. The establishment of the BLM's grazing advisory boards, as described by Foss, was McConnell's prime example of an agency's complicity in its own downfall.[11]

Thus, the capture-conformity debate echoes the core administrative responsibility arguments in American public administration theory. The capture thesis in the public lands politics version of the debate is virtually identical to the capture thesis in public administration theory. Proponents of the capture thesis, who are essentially condemning bureaucratic politics and clientelism, largely advocate a return to many of the traditional principles of public administration. The conformity thesis, which implies the existence of political neutrality (at a minimum, the avoidance of capture) and subordination of field officers' decisions to the policies of their superiors in the Forest Service and BLM hierarchies, is congruent with those traditional administrative principles.[12]

Professionalism and Conformity

The professionalism of BLM and Forest Service administrators is the key to their conformity to agency policy. The basis of any profession is a specialized body of knowledge (usually accompanied by a distinct mode of analysis by which existing knowledge is applied and additional knowledge discovered). In powerful and well-organized professions, the profession's national association controls the educational programs leading to the degree that is the minimum prerequisite for professional employment; the most powerful professional associations also control a certification process, which is an additional hurdle to entry into professional employment. Professional knowledge is not politically neutral. A profession's body of knowledge may represent the best available "truth" about its area of concern, but the very fact that the professionals' mode of analysis and body of knowledge are specialized means that the professionals ignore other truths and ways of looking at problems. The other trappings of professionalism tend to amplify the biases inherent in the profession's body of knowledge. Professional control over education and entry into professional employment produces individuals who thoroughly understand and appreciate the profession's body of knowledge, and thus usually share its biases. On the job, a professional's peers are generally other members of the profession, so his interpersonal social environment reinforces the belief that the profession's biases are correct. To understand Forest Service and BLM policies, one must understand the dictates of the collective knowledge of the agencies' professionals, dictates to which the agencies' officers conform largely because of their professionalism.[13]

Professionalism and Public Lands Management

Forest Service and BLM line officers share almost all the characteristics of professionals described above. Except for small cadres of engineers and business managers who fill staff positions, employees above the GS-7 level are trained in forestry, range management, or the newer hybrid, natural resources management. Most are members of the Society of American Foresters (SAF) or the Society for Range Management (SRM), which play very important roles in education programs in forestry, range management, and natural resources management. Degrees in these fields are practically mandatory for employment, and hiring and promotion decisions are controlled by line officers in the agencies, who are themselves trained in the same fields and members of the same professions.

There are considerable similarities among the forestry, range management, and natural resource management fields. All three are based on the biological sciences, and their mode of operations involves scientific application and planned manipulation of biological processes. Thus, professionals in all three share a dual bias: a predisposition to use their skills to intervene actively in the natural processes of the lands under their jurisdiction, and a thorough understanding of the biological tolerances of those lands.

These professional-disciplinary biases dovetail well with the agencies' progressive conservationist histories and multiple-use missions. The commitment of progressive conservationism and the multiple-use philosophy to active, technically sophisticated, and optimum use of natural resources is facilitated by agency professionals' technical skills. Similarly, the resource protection aspect of multiple-use policy (that is, the sustained yield component) and progressive conservationism is reinforced by agency professionals' ecological science training. Multiple use thus represents a convergence of the dictates of agency policy, the legacy of agency history, and the training of agency professionals.

Multiple use is a widely misunderstood concept. The most common criticism of the multiple-use acts is that they are so vague (giving no indication of the emphasis to be placed on different uses or even guidance as to how such emphasis might be determined) as to be meaningless.[14] Descriptions of the multiple-use principle usually descend to an angels-on-a-pinhead discussion about how much emphasis on how many uses constitutes multiple use, as opposed to single or dominant use.[15]

The multiple-use policy does, in fact, instruct agency professionals to provide as many uses as possible within the large tracts of lands under their jurisdiction, and one of its consequences is that agency professionals have an aversion to dominant use of large tracts (including Wilderness dominant use or nonuse). The multiple-use policy also requires an optimum mix of uses. But contrary to the opinions of most critics of multiple use, the professionals' notion of optimum use is not so ill-defined as to be meaningless as a general principle. Professionals focus not on the number or levels of use, per se, but on their effects on the land. In practical multiple-use management, an optimum use in any given area is the highest level of a use that does not foreclose the possibility of other possible uses by diminishing the capability of the land to provide these other uses in perpetuity.[16] When the notion of an "optimum and high level of many uses" is combined with the land conservation and sustained yield concepts, multiple use becomes a very meaningful and operational principle for people with the education and training of Forest Service and BLM professionals.

It is worth noting that BLM and Forest Service officials are professional public administrators as well as professional resource managers.[17]

At a minimum, this means they have a variety of basic administrative and bureaucratic skills. Several developments in public lands management in the 1970s have placed additional emphasis on this dimension of agency officers' professionalism. In particular, public participation, clearly a political bureaucratic activity, has been perceived by many land managers as being in conflict with their resource management technical skills and professional values. The initial reaction of service and bureau officers to public participation was often that such participation required them to subordinate their professional judgments to the opinions of laymen. The agencies overcame this resistance by convincing their officers that public participation skills were just as much professional skills—and just as critical to the effective administration of the public lands—as the ability to conduct a range survey or mark a timber sale.

Professionalism and the Convergence of BLM and Forest Service Administration

The importance of professionalism in public lands management is perhaps best seen in a comparison of the contemporary BLM and Forest Service. The two agencies are generally regarded as representing opposite poles in the capture-conformity debate. The service has been considered a highly professional, uncaptured, elite agency in the federal bureaucracy, while the BLM has been regarded as unprofessional, a bureaucratic mediocrity, and the prototypical captured agency. The findings of this study, however, suggest that there are almost no significant, systematic differences between the two.

For example, one of the most basic characteristics of an agency is the beliefs of its administrators about the policies under its jurisdiction. The BLM managers, according to the conventional wisdom, should be more development-oriented than the service's because of the BLM's historic sympathies with stockmen. However, the attitude analysis in chapter 5 reveals that Forest Service and BLM officers' attitudes on public lands issues were virtually identical. On the E-U attitude scale, in which scores ranged from $+2.4$ to -1.9, the BLM's mean was $+0.511$ and the service's $+0.513$. (In this same analysis, the supposedly development-oriented service and bureau officers had more conservationist-oriented scores than did state game and fish officers, the active defenders of wildlife interests in league with conservationist groups.)

If the BLM were more captured than the service, there should be significant differences in the two agencies' public participation programs. The study's findings, however, reveal no such differences. The well-developed participation style, which is essentially aimed at conservationist and recreationist clients, was found on the BLM's NRL7 as well as the service's NF1 and NG2, while the service's NF5 and the BLM's NRL8 and NRL9 exhibited the underdeveloped participation style. The agencies' specialized participation arrangements with stockmen are especially interesting because of Foss's allegations about the role of district advisory boards in capturing the BLM.[18] By the 1970s, the BLM's grazing advisory boards had lost their effective veto over significant range management decisions. While the BLM boards still had greater formal authority than the service's grazing boards, the service's national grassland grazing associations had even broader authority. None of the grazing advisory boards or associations exercised real *practical* domination over agency administrators: their primary function was to serve as forums in which agency range managers could persuade ranchers to adopt such professional innovations as rest-rotation range management.

The most important similarity between the two agencies was in the functioning of their policy processes. The interview data indicated there was little systematic difference between the agencies in terms of use administration. Some users felt the service was more restrictive than the BLM, some thought the reverse, and many felt the agencies were equally restrictive. As one mining firm official put it, "The Forest Service is getting tougher, but the BLM is getting tougher faster."

The agencies were also similar in the degree to which they were subject to group influence. In particular, there was no significant difference between the service's ranger districts and the bureau's resource areas as seen in the quantitative analysis of group influence reported in chapter 10.[19] The bureau had a different local constituency mix, across all local administrative units, than did the service. Because it managed primarily desert or semidesert rangeland, the bureau had relatively more Type II (that is, stockmen-oriented) local organization-sets than the service (although many district rangers, such as those on NG2 and NF5, had Type II sets as well). Because it managed more high-country forestland, the service had more Type I constituencies, with balanced forest products and livestock industry clients, than the bureau. But such differences were clearly extrinsic; they related to the agencies' organizational environments, not to differences in the ways the agencies' policymaking was affected by their group environments.

The improved professionalism of the BLM is the main explanation for the similarities between the service and bureau of the 1970s. The image of the BLM as radically less professional than the service is based on studies published in 1960—Kaufman's *The Forest Ranger,* Foss's *Politics and Grass,* and Calef's *Private Grazing and Public Land.* There were considerable differences between the agencies' situations in 1960. The service, with the passage of the Multiple Use–Sustained Yield Act, was at the height of its statutory authority. The bureau, in contrast, had to wait until 1964 for the Classification and Multiple Use Act, and its organic act was not passed until 1976. The bureau's main statutory authority in 1960 was the Taylor Grazing Act, which provided a fairly weak conservation mandate and primarily supported and promoted the BLM's dominant users, stockmen. Furthermore, in 1960 the Forest Service was a fully professional agency, staffed by trained foresters with an organizational history of strong conservation and administrative independence, while the bureau was still dominated by administrators who were former ranchers without professional training.

These disparities have been eliminated. As explained in chapter 3, the bureau's line officers are now trained professionals, with college degrees in range management, resource management, or forestry. They are as active in professional associations as their counterparts in the service. Basically, the trained professionals who were junior staff officers in 1960 have replaced the ex-ranchers as line officers.[20] Today's BLM officers also operate under a set of statutory mandates that are quite similar to the service's. The BLM's core mandate in the Federal Land Policy and Management Act (FLPMA), and its earlier Classification and Multiple Use Act, is identical to the service's in the 1960 Multiple Use Act. Moreover, FLPMA gave the bureau a land use planning mandate very similar to that of the Forest Service's National Forest Management Act and included the bureau, along with the service, the National Park Service, and the Fish and Wildlife Service, under the Wilderness Act mandate. The National Environmental Policy Act (NEPA) applies equally to the service and the bureau (as it does to all federal agencies whose actions affect the environment).

As professionally trained land managers having identical statutory multiple-use missions, Forest Service and BLM line officers are indistinguishable on objective criteria. In 1960 Kaufman remarked on the striking similarities among Forest Service officers. In the 1970s, the similarities among Forest Service *and* BLM professionals were striking, as was the extent to which both groups emphasized, as Kaufman had put it, "multiple use management as the cardinal principle underlying every decision they make about the handling of their districts."[21]

There are, of course, superficial differences between the agencies. Their formal rules, procedures, and jargon differ slightly. The Forest Service still exudes a more professional aura than does the bureau, an *esprit de corps* that many people in and out of the service associate with the uniform greens and Smokey the Bear hat.[22] (Non-service people who comment on the service officers' aura do not, however, necessarily mean the observation as a compliment.) And the large stained wood signs outside the service's and bureau's office buildings display different agency shields.

In summary, there are very few significant differences between the service and bureau. On most counts there is much greater variation within both agencies than there is between them. (Note, for example, the range of public participation styles from "well-developed" to "underdeveloped," and the E–U attitude scores' standard deviations of .588 and .424, compared with the difference of .002 between the agencies' means.) Those differences that exist are not functions of intrinsic agency characteristics relevant to an understanding their policy processes, but either trivial contrasts or consequences of differences in physiographic jurisdictions.[23]

Capture and Clientelism

The key technical management doctrine of BLM and Forest Service professionals—multiple use—is also a political doctrine, a method for managing the agencies' political environments as well as physiographic jurisdictions. One of the scientific and political doctrines of the progressive conservation movement, the multiple-use principle became even more influential in the postwar period, when it was viewed as a means of dealing with increasingly complicated pressures on the agencies. The service sought to have multiple use enshrined in statutory law during the 1950s as a way of fending off conflicting constituency demands, particularly those of the forest products industry, which was placing increasing pressure on the national forests as postwar lumber demand rose and private standing timber inventories declined; the livestock industry, which had made the "Great Land Grab" proposed in the late 1940s to sell off federal rangelands to stockmen for a pittance; and the increasingly militant conservationist groups, which were pressing hard for more emphasis on Wilderness and recreation use. After passage of the service's Multiple Use Act in 1960, the bureau recognized the usefulness of a similar mandate, particularly for dealing with its livestock industry clients. Carved in statutory stone, multiple use was an excellent device for resisting the dominant use demands of client groups.

Viewed from the perspective of the 1955–64 emergence of multiple use as a political as well as technical management doctrine, the public lands agencies' current relations with their constituencies make a great deal of sense. While multiple use was a defense against public lands users in the 1950s, public lands constituents in the 1970s reinforced the multiple-use policy.

Group Influence and Capture

The capture–conformity debate needs to be severely revised—if not discarded altogether—because it implies that the existence of group influence is tantamount to capture and that both are antithetical to professionalism and conformity.[24] In public lands management in the 1970s, group influence has not been synonymous with capture; in fact, group influence has even complemented professional conformity.

There is a systematic pattern of group influence at the lowest levels of Forest Service and BLM management. An obvious precondition for group influence is the existence of interest group constituencies at the local level. These exist in abundance. The sample's 37 local administrators had a combined constituency of over 350 interest groups, representing some 45 different types of groups, and these were just the groups that were significant enough for their leaders to be important contacts of local administrators. Many of these groups were closely allied with regional and national organizations that were also involved in public lands politics; most timber firms belonged to regional and national forest products associations, Sierra Club groups were part of the close-knit national structure, grazing association leaders usually had overlapping memberships with state stockmen's associations and the National Livestock Association. Interest group politics at the Washington office level was just the tip of a

11: CONFORMITY, CAPTURE, MULTIPLE CLIENTELISM, AND MULTIPLE USE 333

political iceberg extending down to the ranger district and resource area level.

Leaders of local groups had access to and regular dealings with their local rangers and area managers (and frequently with higher-level officers in the agencies, as well). Many agency contacts with group leaders occurred during the performance of routine administrative tasks. Not leaving anything to chance, the agencies' public participation programs provided access for group leaders who might not have occasion to deal with administrators on a day-to-day basis. Public participation is not a passive public relations exercise. It is so thoroughly intertwined in the agencies' formal decision-making sequences that it is an integral part of public lands policymaking. Each land use plan requires its own multistage participation program. Wilderness reviews are accompanied by extensive public participation processes. Timber management and grazing allotment management plans and many other types of decisions are subject to the NEPA process, which entails public participation not only through public comments on the environmental impact statement (EIS), but also through the public meetings and informal consultations that accompany the EIS. Underlying all this public participation is the land managers' realization that, if they do not properly anticipate and accommodate public reactions to their decisions, they may find themselves caught squarely in the middle of a public controversy.

Interest groups appear to have significant influence on local public lands policymaking. The statistics in the analysis of the group influence model reported in chapter 10 may not convey the compelling nature of the issues local participants wrestle with, the force of their different philosophies, or the intricacies of their pressure on the agencies. But the numbers confirm that a large local livestock constituency (or one with very well developed access or very strong views) can stave off reductions in range use down to carrying capacity, that a strong timber industry can force rangers to maximize their timber sales, that a well-organized set of local environmentalists can obtain relatively favorable preservation designations, and that influential local government officials can successfully minimize such designations.

Such patterns of influence, however, do not constitute capture, as that term is commonly used. The simplest version of the capture thesis, as applied to public land management, is plainly wrong. That version is predicated on the assumption that, since rangers and area managers work in rural communities whose economies are dominated by the livestock and forest products industries, land managers' local constituencies consist solely of consumptive users. It is true that large proportions of most rangers' and area managers' contacts are direct consumptive users, and that the interests of many of their other local contacts (for example, local businessmen and local government officials) reinforce consumptive users' interests. But most local administrators' constituencies also include some conservationists or recreationists, who give administrators' organization-sets a good degree of balance. Only two of the sample's thirty-seven local organization-sets conformed to the capture thesis' presumption of homogeneous consumptive user constituencies, and these two are offset by two other sets that were dominated by conservationists and recreationists.

Another assumption of the capture thesis is the proposition that a decision maker's policies are primarily determined by his constituency. Groups, as noted above, do influence public lands managers, but because local constituencies are not composed solely of commodity users, as the capture thesis assumes, the resulting pattern of influence is quite different from that posited by thesis adherents. The service and bureau are neither uniformly captured nor uncaptured, but variably captured. Local administrators could be termed captured on timber sales policy when the forest products industry was strong, for example, and uncaptured when it was not. Similarly, when environmentalists were strong, they obtained their Wilderness rewards, and one might call local officers captured in that situation as well. This kind of group influence is not the same as that which triggered the 1960 capture–conformity debate, however, because the agencies are responding in variable and locally appropriate ways to balanced, heterogeneous constituencies. It is especially instructive to examine the livestock industry, the group whose influence over the BLM in 1960 was so construed as to give rise to the capture–conformity debate. The fact that it had one of the lowest total influence scores in the quantitative influence analysis supports the claims of stockmen participants in local public lands politics that far from being masters of the agencies, their influence was on the wane.[25]

Multiple Clientelism

The main reason why the pattern of group influence in public lands politics does not constitute capture is that group influence is not the only important determinant of Forest Service and BLM policy, as the capture critics (and the more extreme of the interest group theorists) assume. The influence of the agencies' balanced constituencies is consistent with national agency policies, the other important determinant of local decision making.

To conform to national agency policy, local administrators must be a little captured. The very existence of local constituencies is required by agency policy. The service, for example, requires its rangers to maintain a "key man list" (which became the starting point in the organization-set analysis reported in chapter 6). Public participation programs are invitations to agencies to be responsive-captured. NF1, with the best public participation program in the sample, was simply following the letter and spirit of *Inform and Involve*. Decision making based on anticipated reactions, a mechanism for responding to group influence while avoiding outright political pressure, is also consistent with the agencies' norms of apolitical administration: land managers are not "captured," but are obtaining "public input," or are "considering all relevant factors," or are being "responsive." Finally, the uniformity with which both BLM and Forest Service officers cited the need for responsiveness to local constituencies as an important factor in their decision making supports the notion that those officers were conforming to informal agency and professional norms of responsiveness (presumably a desirable trait for public officials in a democracy).

Group influence can be consistent with agency policy because contemporary constituency influences reinforce the public lands agencies' core policy, the multiple-use doctrine. Balanced constituencies support different aspects of the multiple-use mission: traditional commodity users support the resource development aspects, recreationists and conservationists support the recreation use aspects, and conservationists support the resource protection and sustained yield aspects.

As noted above, capture is a degenerate form of clientelism. Clientelist theory assumes that an agency's clientele is relatively homogeneous. As explained earlier, however, the constituencies of the Forest Service and the BLM are not now homogeneous. Furthermore, even when they were homogeneous, they were not conducive to a co-optive or clientelist relationship because they did not fully support the agencies' resource protection missions. The emergence of environmentalists and recreationists creates an unusual double-clientele situation. In sample units with a well-developed participation style, the agencies clearly and successfully practiced co-optation, usually with respect to their new environmentalist constituents, but also with traditional users. Even when local administrators did not actively use co-optive tactics, the agencies' balanced constituencies supported the different aspects of the agencies' multiple-use missions.

This support, especially by environmentalists, was not always obvious, but it existed nonetheless. Nationally, environmentalists provide some support for the agencies in the budgetary process, the arena in which clientele support is most critically needed, with their criticisms of inadequate appropriations for such programs as recreation and reforestation.[26] Most important, environmentalists provide the agencies with a public constituency that supports stricter resource-protection conditions on traditional consumptive uses. As described in chapter 7, local service and bureau officers actively used the existence of the environmental movement to pressure industry clients to accept use administration policies, even though those policies originated at least as much in the agencies' progressive conservationist missions as in explicit environmental group demands.

The Forest Service and BLM thus find themselves in a very powerful position. Clientele support is one of the four basic sources of bureaucratic power, along with officers' professional expertise, cohesion and *esprit de corps*, and mastery of the game of bureaucratic politics.[27] Both the service and bureau are fully professionalized agencies, and their officers' dedication to the multiple-use doctrine gives both a high degree of cohesion. Especially in the areas of public participation and use administration, they use rational and sophisticated tactics to manipulate their political environments to further their multiple-use objectives. Most important, the agencies, whose commitment to multiple use demands a balanced course of action, can play their more extreme constituents off against each other to reinforce the agencies' preferred middle course. By using both extreme elements in their constituencies, the bureau and service generate a multiple clientele for their multiple-use mission.

Why Does the Capture Thesis Persist?

It is unclear why the capture thesis gained such credence in public lands policy analysis. Capture means that an agency faced by a hostile and homogeneous constituency has come to identify with its captors and abandoned the pursuit of its proper mission. The behavior of neither the Forest Service nor the BLM fits that description. Very early in its history, the service began to introduce professional range regulations. By the mid-1920s, those regulations were so strict that stockmen supported management of the public domain by the Interior Department to keep more land from falling under the service's jurisdiction. From the 1920s into the 1950s, the service also worked to obtain authority to regulate forestry practices on private as well as public lands. Nor could the BLM ever be characterized as being in league with western stockmen. The Taylor Grazing Act could be viewed as a single-use statute that sought to stabilize the western livestock industry by eliminating overcompetition, but from 1939 on, Grazing Service and BLM directors, especially Rutledge, Clawson, and Stoddard, sought to develop the bureau into a truly conservationist, professional, multiple-use agency. The worst one could say about the first half of the bureau's history is that McCarran and the stockmen thwarted Rutledge's policies in the 1940s and that continuing resistance by stockmen (plus some residual sympathy for the industry on the part of the ex-rancher line officers) made the BLM leadership's task very difficult during the 1950s.[28]

By the 1970s, multiple clientelism and professionalism (especially the BLM's improved professionalism) made it fairly easy for the public lands agencies to avoid capture. In this regard, public lands politics resembles a number of other policy areas to which the capture thesis has been applied to explain supposed policy failure. Water resources development has been portrayed as a classic irresponsible, single-clientele policy system, but constituency balance, generated by public participation programs that institutionalized environmentalist influence in agency policymaking, has made water resources policy in the 1970s a political twin of public lands policy.[29] The capture thesis has also been widely applied to business regulatory policy, yet the EPA has deliberately cultivated environmentalists as a clientele to offset industry opposition to pollution regulation.[30] Consumer groups and other elements of the public interest movement have balanced the constituencies of many other regulatory agencies, as well. For example, when Donald Kennedy, former commissioner of the Food and Drug Administration, was faced with decisions on saccharin, nitrates, and a host of other substances, he knew that industry opposition to bans would be balanced by the prodding of Public Citizen's Sidney Wolfe and other consumer activists.[31]

The capture thesis emerged as an important academic critique of federal bureaucratic politics in the late 1960s.[32] By the mid-1970s, it seemed to have become accepted theory among journalists, political activists, and popular writers, as well. Ironically, this acceptance coincided with mounting evidence that the capture thesis did not reflect the real world.

That the capture thesis remains popular in the face of opposing evidence indicates how thoroughly accepted it was by its adherents. Although some industry and consumptive users in public lands politics attribute their trials to agency capture by preservationists, the thesis is most popular among the agencies' environmentalist critics (although the evidence probably supports the users' charge more than the environmentalists'). Today's public interest groups, of which environmentalists are a part, are heirs of the progressive movement, and the capture thesis is a natural extension of the progressives' belief that the special interests are the root of all evil.

The nature of interest group politics makes it difficult for political activists to recognize the realities of agency politics. Neutral observers can see that the service and bureau are in the middle of a fairly polarized, one-dimensional policy system (as illustrated by figure 5-1). But when environmentalists in that system look to the right, so to speak, they see the service and bureau aligned with the consumptive user industries, and when industry users look to the left, they see the agency aligned with environmentalists. Among participants, only the agencies' officers know they are in the middle. Interest group leaders usually interact with agency decision makers in one-on-one situations, so it is difficult for those leaders to appreciate the tensions between the agencies and the "other side."

In addition, interest groups usually operate on an absolute standard —decision makers should agree with them always. When a decision maker decides in a group's favor, he is viewed by the group as following the only sensible course of action; when he decides against the group, there must be some sinister explanation for his behavior. Since the era of the muckrakers, a favorite explanation of Americans for adversity has been some form of conspiracy theory. Americans facing long lines in a gasoline shortage spread "cargo cult" rumors of oil company tankers lurking offshore awaiting crude oil deregulation. When the service recommends millions of acres of roadless areas for Wilderness designations, consumptive users charge the rangers are in league with the Sierra Club and the Wilderness Society. If the bureau's rangeland is in poor condition, the BLM is viewed by environmentalists as having been captured by the cowboys. As Josh Billings, a nineteenth-century American humorist, put it, "The less we know, the more we suspect."

Committed interest group activists have little reason to disabuse themselves of theories that agencies are captured by malevolent special interests or are themselves malevolent.[33] Such theories allow group leaders to mobilize the faithful to do battle (write their representatives, attend public meetings, make special donations, and so forth) with the miscreants. In short, the myth, which group leaders and followers are predisposed to believe, helps leaders maintain group cohesion in the face of a common enemy.

Multiple Clientelism and the Public Interest

As a substantive policy area, public lands politics is enveloped in the special concerns and rhetoric typical of narrow policy subsystems. Contestants in public lands politics passionately care about the direction of the management of the 661 million acres of federal lands entrusted to the Forest Service and BLM. Their broad concerns are expressed in debates on specific issues, conducted in specialized languages, that are peripheral and somewhat mystifying for the rest of the population: the treatment of productive deferred timber inventory in calculating annual allowable cut, the criteria for allocating class A roadless areas to Wilderness designations, and so forth. A study such as this cannot prove that the specific policies of the Forest Service and BLM are objectively good, bad, or somewhere in between. In our sample regions, grazing leases averaged 112 percent of carrying capacity, timber sales averaged 71 percent of annual allowable cut, and 24 percent of the areas considered were recommended as Wilderness or primitive areas. The forest products industry argues that a 24 percent rate of Wilderness approvals is not in the timber-using public's interest, while the Sierra Club argues that it is too little to preserve a precious wilderness heritage for ourselves and succeeding generations. Sportsmen argue that 12 percent excess of grazing over carrying capacity does not adequately accommodate wildlife, and stockmen reply that grass is going to waste on undergrazed public rangeland. Such arguments are the basic substance of politics.

The standard general answer to such conflicting claims is that an agency's policies should serve the public interest. Unfortunately, the definition of the public interest has been the subject of considerable debate.[34] The problem is not that policies labeled as being in the public interest never appear on the public policy stage, but that all policies are labeled by their proponents as being in the public interest. All sides of public lands issues were so presented by interviewees: decreasing livestock use of the public lands was in the public interest because the use of the federal lands by the national recreational public ought not be diminished for the marginal economic benefit of a few local ranchers; livestock use of the public lands was in the public interest because it "put beef in the store"; and so forth. Wrapping one's group's preferences in the mantle of the public interest would seem to be a sacred right of citizens in a democracy. Moreover, most such arguments possess considerable plausibility.

Because it is so difficult to define the public interest objectively, administrative theorists generally treat agencies' policies as being in the public interest if the agencies' behavior meets some criterion of administrative responsibility. The traditionalist-constitutionalist criteria of responsible administration assume that the elected representatives of the public determine the public interest; thus, bureaus act responsibly if they execute statutory law faithfully and expertly. Since the 1950s, the Congress has consistently proclaimed that multiple use is to be the cornerstone of Forest Service and BLM management. Of course, the multiple-use policy has been advocated most consistently by the agencies themselves and the professions from which agency officers have been drawn, rather than by the general electorate. But Congress has at least satisfied the constitutionalists' assumption by writing multiple use into statutory law. And the agencies, whose officers' professional skills and personal ideologies are built around the multiple-use doctrine, have persisted in managing their lands according to multiple-use principles.

The so-called pluralist criterion of responsible administration is quite different from the traditionalist-constitutionalist criterion. Because of the subjectivity of the public interest, the pluralists argue that the public interest should be defined as the result of a decision process in which all interested groups are afforded access and due process and participate effectively.[35] This definition of the public interest is not much more generally accepted than that of the public interest as any policy that puts beef in the store. The pluralist criterion, however, places a premium on political rationality, which is more compelling for public administrators in a very controversial policy area than the constitutionalists' legal rationality or the subjective rationality of those who argue the merits of maximizing particular social values, such as forest products or recreational services.

In the 1970s, public participation and the NEPA process effectively ensured that any group interested in the management of the federal lands had effective access to BLM and Forest Service decision makers. As a result of that access, a strong argument can be made that public lands politics meets the pluralist criterion of administrative responsibility. Though often complex in a technical–scientific sense, public lands management is simple politically; the lineup of contestants from one public lands controversy to the next parallels the one-dimensional continuum of natural resources philosophies, from utilitarianism to preservationism, that has existed since the turn of the century. Since both ends of this policy spectrum are now well entrenched in service and bureau policy processes, all possible interests are inevitably represented in public lands policymaking since the positions of all potential participant groups must fall between those of the opposing extremes. Given the demonstrable impact on public lands policies of the various opposing groups, the service and bureau seem to be striking a valid political balance, which would satisfy the pluralist notion of public interest policymaking.

The Forest Service and Bureau of Land Management thus find themselves in a fortuitous position in which all criteria of administrative responsibility converge. They have so arranged matters that the political necessity of responding to their multiple clienteles reinforces the dictates of their professional expertise and statutory mandates. Most agencies in the federal bureaucracy are not so fortunate. The service's and bureau's strong positions have been immeasurably aided by the access to agency decision making granted to environmentalists and other new clients by the much-criticized NEPA and public participation programs. Public participation enabled the agencies to pursue a multiple-clientele strategy and thereby buttress their professional commitment to conformity and avoidance of capture. While the benefits accruing to the agencies from public participation and NEPA were only partially anticipated by the environmentalist advocates of public participation, they vindicate those procedural reforms of the 1970s.

NOTES

1. Calef, *Private Grazing and Public Lands* (Chicago, Ill., University of Chicago Press, 1960), especially pp. 259–261.
2. Foss, *Politics and Grass* (Seattle, University of Washington Press, 1960), especially chap. 5 and 6. See ibid., especially p. 262, which also notes that some local BLM officers were overly sympathetic to their rancher clients.

3. Reich, *Bureaucracy and the Forests* (Santa Barbara, Calif., Center for the Study of Democratic Institutions, 1962). As we noted in chapter 6, the capture thesis has two parts: (1) the agencies have a homogeneous constituency of users; therefore (2), their policies are biased in favor of users. Reich addresses only the first point, making no attempt to demonstrate pro-user biases in substantive public lands policies. Interestingly, he subjects the National Park Service to the same criticism as the BLM and Forest Service.

4. Shepherd, *The Forest Killers* (New York, Weybright & Talley, 1975); and Barney, *The Last Stand* (New York, Grossman, 1974). Most books in the Nader series, like Barney's, are premised on the capture thesis.

5. Kaufman, *The Forest Ranger* (Baltimore, Md., Johns Hopkins University Press for Resources for the Future, 1960). More recently, John Hendee and Gordon Bultena (in "Capture–Conformity Orientations of Foresters in the U.S. Forest Service," Paper read at the Meeting of the American Sociological Association, New Orleans, August 1972) argued that the service is still conformist. Hendee, a sociologist, is a second-generation Forest Service employee.

6. See Grant McConnell, "The Conservation Movement—Past and Present," *Western Political Quarterly* vol. 7 (September 1954) pp. 463–478.

7. See Samuel Hays, *Conservation and the Gospel of Efficiency* (Cambridge, Mass., Harvard University Press, 1959). The reliance on professional expertise described by Hays, as well as McConnell's anti-special-interests theme, characterized the entire progressive movement.

8. As noted earlier (see, for example, table 7-1), Forest Service administrators still cite multiple use and Pinchot's "greatest good of the greatest number in the long run" as cornerstones of their decision making. Kaufman (*The Forest Ranger*, p. 207) noted the same phenomenon in 1960.

9. Notably Norton Long, "Power and Administration," *Public Administration Review* vol. 9 (Autumn 1949) pp. 257–264. Also see chapter 1, pages 26–27.

10. This argument is most closely associated with Marver Bernstein, *Regulating Business by Independent Commission* (Princeton, N.J., Princeton University Press, 1955). The capture thesis is not universally subscribed to by academics. See, for example, James Wilson, ed., *The Politics of Regulation* (New York, Basic Books, 1980). The major revisionist interpretation of the regulatory agencies' failures is that the agencies were not really established to regulate in the public interest in the first place, but to manage competition to their industries' advantage; see Gabriel Kolko, *The Triumph of Conservatism* (New York, Free Press, 1963).

11. Grant McConnell, *Private Power and American Democracy* (New York, Knopf, 1966); see especially pp. 200–211 on the role of Foss's *Politics and Grass* in McConnell's argument. The other important contribution to this administrative responsibility position is Theodore Lowi, *The End of Liberalism* (New York, Norton, 1969).

12. The traditionalism of the capture critics is best seen in Lowi's advocacy of "juridical democracy," a formal-legal version of the politics-administration

dichotomy of traditional public administration theory. The comparison between the conformity position and traditional public administration principles leads into an interesting gray area of public administration theory. The conformity position is rightly associated with Kaufman's *The Forest Ranger,* yet that is a case-study application of the organization theory expounded in Herbert Simon's *Administrative Behavior* (New York, Macmillan, 1947); and Simon was the archcritic of traditional public administrative theory and a proponent of the theory of clientelism. However, Kaufman was also a student of Luther Gulick, the leading traditional public administration theorist. (Gulick supervised Kaufman's dissertation, which led to *The Forest Ranger.*) *The Forest Ranger* is actually a subtle demonstration of the ways traditional and modern management practices can coexist and complement each other in a real organization, despite the general supposition that traditional and modern organization theories are antithetical.

13. On the importance of professionalism in contemporary public administration, see Frederick Mosher, *Democracy and the Public Service* (New York, Oxford University Press, 1968), especially chap. 4.

14. See, for example, Reich, *Bureaucracy and the Forests;* Christopher Curtis, "Managing Federal Lands: Replacing the Multiple Use System," *Yale Law Journal* vol. 82 (March 1973) pp. 787–805; and even Kaufman, *The Forest Ranger,* p. 207.

15. See, for example, Shepherd, *The Forest Killers,* especially pp. 35–36. One of the more sensible treatments of this issue can be found in Glen O. Robinson, *The Forest Service* (Baltimore, Md., Johns Hopkins University Press for Resources for the Future, 1975) pp. 55–59.

16. See George Hall, "The Myth and Reality of Multiple Use Forestry," *Natural Resources Journal* vol. 3 (October 1963) pp. 276–290; and Philip Martin, "Conflict Resolution through the Multiple Use Concept in Forest Service Decision Making," *Natural Resources Journal* vol. 9 (April 1969) pp. 228–236.

17. The Forest Service, in particular, has had a long-standing program of mid-career public administration education for its officers, and one of the BLM district managers in the study's sample had been an American Political Science Association Congressional Fellow. As they have dominated professional forestry associations like the Society of American Foresters, Forest Service officers have come to play a significant leadership role in the public administration profession. For example, to date two of the four chairmen of the Section on Natural Resources and Environmental Administration of the American Society for Public Administration (the primary professional association of public administration academics and practitioners) have been the regional forester of the service's Alaska Region and the supervisor of the Chippewa National Forest.

18. Foss, *Politics and Grass,* especially chap. 5 and 6.

19. That is, once the interest group and administrator variables were included in the analysis, there was no residual difference between the service's and bureau's units. For example, the correlations between a dummy or binary

variable, "agency" (in which ranger districts were coded 1 and resource areas zero) and the residuals of the group influence functions were for the MBF% function, −.07, for AUMs%, +.09; and for Wilderness-primitive%, −.04. None of the correlations is statistically significant. In fact, the largest of the three correlations is in the opposite direction from what one would expect: positive correlation makes it appear that the service is more responsive to group influence on grazing policy. But in addition to being insignificant, the correlation is artifactual and misleading. The conventional wisdom is that the BLM's land is, if anything, more overgrazed than Forest Service rangeland. However, the mean of the Forest Service districts' AUMs% CC figures is 117.2 percent, while the BLM mean is 96.5 percent. In other words, the Forest Service is more conservative in computing carrying capacity than is the BLM.

20. See Calef, *Private Grazing and Public Lands*, pp. 261–262, on the BLM's staffing in 1960. One of Calef's recommendations was the professionalization of the BLM's higher ranks. Interestingly, one of the junior-level BLM professionals who participated in Calef's 1960 study was the district manager of NRL7 in 1973.

21. Kaufman, *The Forest Ranger*, pp. 206–207; also see pp. 165–166, 214–215, and 223–224, on the conformist tendencies of professionals in the Service.

22. One BLM district manager, conscious of the symbolic value of the Forest Service uniform, designed a BLM uniform, with the BLM shield as a shoulder patch, and so forth.

23. This argument has a bearing on the perennial issue of reorganizing public lands management by transferring the Forest Service into the Department of the Interior or a new Department of Natural Resources. If the Forest Service and BLM are already so similar, what could be gained by such a reorganization? See Paul Culhane and H. Paul Friesema, "Federal Public Lands Reorganization: Deja Vu, 1979," in Frank Convery, Jack Royer, and Gerald Stairs, eds., *Reorganization: Issues, Implications and Opportunities for U.S. Natural Resources Policy* (Durham, N.C., Duke University School of Forestry, 1979) pp. 44–46.

24. The notion that conformity means an absence of group influence seems to be an example of a proposition's becoming drawn in more absolute terms than was intended by its initial formulator. Kaufman, in a footnote, wrote that rangers often made concessions to local pressures on grazing policy—the policy area around which Foss constructed the capture argument—because it was national Forest Service policy that range decisions be "tied closely to local customs" (*The Forest Ranger*, pp. 218–219).

25. See table 10-3. The stockmen's low score needs to be taken with a few grains of salt. For one thing, the differences among the total influence scores of the "economic users," "others," "conservationists-recreationists," and "livestock industry" interests—especially between the last two—are not statistically significant (extrapolating from the confidence intervals of the regression *b*s on which the influence index betas are based). In addition, some readers may feel the livestock industry's relative score was excessively depressed by some of the criteria used to construct the table (the deletion of indexes that were in the

wrong direction and the inclusion of those from the analysis of the questionable mining policy function). However, even if these criteria were reversed (with wrong direction indexes included and mining function betas excluded), the stockmen's total score of .66 would still not be significantly greater than the conservationist-recreationist score of .57.

26. A key policy recommendation of Barney (*The Last Stand*, p. 135), who was generally very critical of the service, was that Congress should "supply the Forest Service with more generous, balanced funding."

27. Francis Rourke, *Bureaucratic Power in National Politics* (Boston, Little, Brown, 1972) pp. 240–262.

28. Both Foss and Calef described the process of adjudication, the chief means by which the BLM broke the stranglehold of the livestock industry. Calef also noted the beginning of the process of professionalization, arguing in *Private Grazing and Public Lands* (p. 263) that to improve range management, the BLM had to professionalize its staff and offset stockmen's influence with political support from "the East" (a 1950s codeword for conservationists from eastern states). The BLM has, essentially, accomplished both objectives.

29. The best-known critique of the Corps of Engineers' collusion with water development interests is Arthur Maass's *Muddy Waters* (Cambridge, Mass., Harvard University Press, 1951). The reformation of the corps in the face of a balanced constituency in the 1970s is described by Daniel Mazmanian and Jeanne Nienaber in *Can Organizations Change? Environmental Protection, Citizen Participation, and the Corps of Engineers* (Washington, D.C., Brookings Institution, 1979).

30. On regulatory agency capture, see Bernstein's *Regulating Business by Independent Commission*. On EPA's co-optation of environmentalists to counterbalance industry opposition and forestall the decay of regulatory vigor Bernstein described, see Paul Sabatier, "Social Movements and Regulatory Agencies: Toward a More Adequate—and Less Pessimistic—Theory of Clientele Capture," *Policy Sciences* vol. 6 (September 1975) pp. 301–342; and Paul Culhane, *The Lake Michigan Federation* (Evanston, Ill., Northwestern University, Center for Urban Affairs, November 1974) pp. 46–47 and 118–119.

31. Jim Lehrer, "Donald Kennedy Interview," *The MacNeil/Lehrer Report* (New York, WNET/WETA, Library no. 979, Show no. 4259 (transcript), June 28, 1979).

32. For example, McConnell's *Private Power and American Democracy* was published in 1966, and Lowi's *End of Liberalism* in 1969.

33. For an interesting discussion of the caricature of agencies as malevolent, see Sally Fairfax and Barbara Andrews, "Debate Within and Debate Without: NEPA and the Redefinition of the 'Prudent Man' Rule," *Natural Resources Journal* vol. 19 (July 1979) pp. 505–535.

34. A good example of such disputation occurred a few years ago at a political science meeting when a panelist proposed to define a public interest policy as one that benefited 90 percent of the citizens, even though it might harm the other 10 percent (Andrew McFarland, "The Public Interest and

Market Failure," Paper presented at the Meeting of the Midwest Political Science Association, Chicago, January 1974, p. 5). Since this was a gathering of academics, the questions addressed to the panelist were predictable. What if the harm done to the 10 percent was worth nine times the benefit to the 90 percent? What if the policy benefited only 89 percent of the citizens?

35. See Glendon Schubert, " 'The Public Interest' in Administrative Decision Making: Theorem, Theosophy, or Theory?" *American Political Science Review* vol. 51 (June 1957) pp. 360–366. This pluralist definition is the only one that can be realistically examined by a study such as this of agency dealings with interest groups.

APPENDIXES

APPENDIXES

Appendix A
Data-Gathering Methodology

All the Bureau of Land Management (BLM) and Forest Service line officers (area and district managers, district rangers, and forest supervisors) in the three sample regions were interviewed. The interviews consisted of an open-ended conversation on local land management and politics and a list of specific questions. After the specific questions, each district administrator was asked to identify his key contacts in the local area, those people whom he dealt with on agency business and whom he considered important contacts. Those contacts who seemed the most important representatives of local interests, especially those who had contacts with several administrative units in the area, were personally interviewed, but an effort was made to interview a balanced representation of key contacts in each region in terms of interest groups and geographic spread. The remaining key contacts were telephoned (to introduce the researcher and explain the study) and sent return-mail questionnaires.

Interview and Questionnaire Response Rate

The organization-sets of the sample regions' units in the study included 9 supervisory administrators, 37 local administrators, and 393 interest group representatives. In addition to the administrators, 51 interest group representatives were interviewed. Thus, 97 of the 439 individuals (22.1 percent) were interviewed personally.

Of the remaining 342 interest group people, 318 received mail questionnaires. Twenty-four did not receive questionnaires for a variety of reasons. In some cases current addresses could not be determined from administrators' address lists or current telephone books. In other instances, individuals who were excluded from the questionnaire list because members of the same organizations had been interviewed or sent questionnaires were later included as technical nonrespondents for various specific reasons (for example, a conservationist whose group's staff person was interviewed turned out to be an important special use permittee on one ranger district).

Of the 318 questionnaires actually delivered to individuals, 194 (61 percent) were returned with usable information. Table A-1 presents a breakdown of respondents by type of group affiliation and state. Group response rates followed two distinct patterns. Stockmen, the mining or oil and gas industry, recreationists, and local government officials had response rates in the 50 percent range, while the forest products industry, conservationists, and businessmen (other than the categories mentioned above) had rates in the 70 percent range. Questionnaire response rates also varied by state. State B's response rate was particularly low.

Group and regional response rates were somewhat related. First, all the mining and oil and gas contacts were in States B and C, so their low rates affected the states' rates. Second, the lowest rate for any appreciable group was the 44.2 percent rate for State B stockmen.

Because of the importance of maximizing overall response rate, a second wave of questionnaires was sent out to individuals who had not returned the first questionnaire. Responses received from this second mailing amounted to 23 percent of all returned questionnaires. Whereas the questionnaires returned in the second wave improved the State B response rate from 30 percent to 48 percent, the response rate of State B was also the lowest on the second wave, so the second mailing just made the relative State B rate worse.

There are no good explanations for the low State B rate in general or the low State B stockmen's rate in particular. The author had some difficulties with phone calls to questionnaire recipients in State B (with inadequate phone facilities for about one-third of the State B field days), and Postal Service complaint rates are objective evidence of postal delivery problems in that state. These explanations alone, however, cannot ac-

Table A-1. Response Rates by Selected Categories

Category	Total N	Interviewees	Questionnaire respondents	Non-respondents	Questionnaire response rate (%)[a]	Overall response rate (%)[b]
By group type						
Forest products industry	34	8	19	7	73.1	79.4
Livestock industry (+ advisory board)	120	18	52	50	51.0	58.3
Conservationists, environmentalists, and preservationists	33	8	17	8	68.0	75.6
State game and fish administrators	11	1	7	3	70.0	72.7
Recreation operators	17	2	8	7	53.3	58.8
ORV groups	12	2	5	5	50.0	58.3
Other recreationists	20	2	9	9	50.0	55.0
Mineral/O&G firms	32	3	15	14	51.7	56.3
Chambers of commerce, businessmen	25	2	16	7	69.6	72.0
Other economic interests	30	4	18	8	69.2	80.0
State and local government, schools	36	1	18	17	51.4	52.8
Others	23	0	10	13	43.5	43.5
Forest Service, BLM	46	46	N.A.	N.A.	N.A.	100.0
Totals	439	97	194	148	56.7%	66.3%
By sample region						
State A	93	38	37	18	67.3%	80.6%
State B	196	34	79	83	48.8	57.7
State C	150	25	78	47	62.4	68.7

Note: N.A., not applicable.

[a] Questionnaire response rate = $\dfrac{\text{No. Questionnaire Respondents}}{\text{No. Questionnaire Respondents + No. Nonrespondents}}$

[b] Overall response rate = $\dfrac{\text{No. Questionnaire Respondents + No. Interviewees}}{\text{Total N}}$

count for the 15 percent spread between the State B rate and the State A and C rates.

Interview and Questionnaire Formats

All interviews and questionnaires included five parts: (1) a series of broad, open-ended questions intended to stimulate a discourse on local land management processes; (2) a series of forced-choice, attitudinal items; (3) a set of questions on the organizational resources of the interviewees'/respondents' organization; (4) a request for the group affiliations of the respondent or interviewee; and (5) a request for a list of administrators' interest group contacts (or, vice versa, a list of service and bureau officials with whom interest group individuals dealt). The questions' phrasing sometimes varied slightly for the three types of interviewees and respondents. District administrators were asked three additional sets of questions on the number of public participation events during the preceding year, levels of a variety of tangible outputs of the district, and the frequency and style of their interaction with their immediate supervisors.

Open-Ended Question

The initial purpose of the brief, open-ended question was to obtain interviewees' perceptions about the important processes of and forces affecting local land management. The question was phrased, "What factors do you feel are most important in Forest Service and/or BLM decisions in managing the public lands?" The responses were only minimally structured by the interviewer, and ranged widely from anecdotal and analytical observations about local politics, to lectures on professional topics in land management, to personal gripe sessions. This part of the interview was fairly lengthy, ranging from thirty minutes to an hour with interest group people and supervisory administrators and from one and a half to two hours with district administrators. This interview material formed a primary data base for the findings reported in chapters 7 through 9.

Early in the fieldwork it became apparent that the open-ended question was also producing a series of content-analyzable response patterns. The very broad question usually stimulated a brief listing of the interviewees' basic beliefs, followed by supporting, often subjective, observations. Thus, the open-ended question appeared to tap attitudes just as much as did the deliberately attitudinal questions.

Attitudinal Questions

A nine-part question asked of all interviewees and questionnaire recipients was designed to tap individual attitudes about public land management through responses to current public lands issues. The issues were drawn from disputes discussed in the trade and professional journals, as well as from litigation involving public lands policies. Each item was accompanied by a five-point Likert scale ranging from 1 as "always for" through 5 as "always against." The question was phrased:

> What is your personal opinion on the following issues as they relate to Forest Service/BLM lands?
> The general use of even-aged management (sometimes called 'clear-cutting')?
> Mineral exploration, as it is currently practiced?
> Establishing more Wilderness or similar types of areas?
> Permitting off-road vehicles on trails or open lands?
> Using or allowing predator control techniques like 1080 or coyote-getters?
> Increasing grazing fees?
> Increasing fees for recreational use of public lands?
> Increasing the allowable cut or carrying capacity?
> BLM or Forest Service administrators giving preference to local economic considerations in making decisions?

In the initial phase of field interviews in State A, one question was phrased, "Should fees for use of public lands be increased?" The field interviewing experience suggested that the question was too broad. A common reaction was "Which fees?" Grazing fees and recreation fees were the two types interviewees usually had in mind, and several interviewees responded with two answers, one about grazing fees and the other about recreation fees. Before the second field trip, the fees item was divided into two separate items.

Early in the data analysis, the large number of "missing" data on the two fees items caused by the change in the question's wording (48, or 16.5 percent, of the 291 administrator and group interviewees and respondents) seemed unacceptably high. Therefore a number of indicators were chosen on a purely empirical basis to obtain the best fits possible, to substitute estimated values for the missing grazing and recreation fees items. As it turned out, neither of the fees variables significantly affected the main function of the attitude indicators, the construction of an attitude scale. "Recreation fees," because of poor loadings, was dropped from the factor analysis that produced the E–U scale, and "grazing fees" loaded highly on the second factor, which was not used in the analysis of the model in chapter 10. In short, the substitution was inconsequential: the study could easily have gotten along without it, and the indicators involved played no important role in subsequent analyses.

Organizational Resources

All inteviewees and respondents were asked several objective questions about the level of their organization's resources. The questions varied with the type of organization. People from voluntary organizations were asked for their current annual budget, number of members, and number of staff (on a full-time equivalent basis). Business representatives were asked for their gross dollar volume of business and the number of professional and managerial and other employees. Forest Service and BLM line officers were asked about their unit's budget and staffing. For descriptive purposes, administrative staff was broken down into professional (subdivided into functional categories), technical, and other.

Group Affiliations

Each interviewee and respondent was also asked what organizations he belonged to in addition to his primary organization. Based on the interviews and responses, more than 60 percent of the individuals in the sample were known to be officers or members of, or to have some other relationship with, more than one type of organization. The actual percentage of multiple-group memberships was probably much higher, since only one group affiliation was known for certain for most nonrespondents and only 5 percent of interest group interviewees and respondents had only one affiliation. The nature of the interviewee or respondent's affiliation with his organization was also explored (for example, whether the

APPENDIX A: DATA-GATHERING METHODOLOGY   355

individual was an officer, member, or had some other relationship with the organization, and whether the individual's primary organization was related to his or her occupation).

Contact List

A prerequisite for constructing the organization sets of district administrators and identifying group representatives was obtaining a list of the individuals administrators considered key contacts in their districts. The same information was obtained from interest group interviewees and respondents. Administrators were asked to list people not a part of their agency, while interest group individuals were asked only for contacts in the service or bureau. Administrators and interest group individuals were also asked to indicate the number of times they interacted with each contact in person or by phone or mail. Both the identification of contacts and the reporting of interactions were based on individual recollection.

Individuals usually reported the number of interactions in terms of rate, such as "twice a month." Such rates were converted to number per year; for example, "twice a month" became "twenty-four." There were frequently differences between administrators' reported frequencies of interaction with given individuals and the individuals' recollections. In such cases, relatively greater credence was given to the administrator's response.

Such adjustments were made as a part of a FORTRAN aggregating program. The program read in data cases with the following information: individual's name, power and value scale scores, primary and secondary groups, the individual's unique identifier number, and the identifier numbers of and associated reported frequencies of interactions with administrators. This information was read in for four classes of cases: interest group interviewees and respondents; interest group nonrespondents, with substituted or inferred data; district and supervisory administrators, for instances when an administrator reported an administrator in a different agency as a key contact; and a set of inferred power and values scores for "generic" categories. (See appendix C on power, values, and inferred scores.)

The program then read in district administrators' records, processing one set of district administrator contacts at a time. Each reported administrator-group contact was identified by a search of administrator-reported contacts or a secondary search of all interest group contacts' lists for contacts not reported by the administrator.

When a district administrator-interest group contact was established, the routine rectified any disagreement between the reported frequencies of interaction by the algorithm:

$$\text{Rectified } \# = \text{DA}\# \pm \sqrt{|\text{DA}\# - \text{IG}\#|}.$$

Once the number of interactions was set, the program wrote out the organization set map of the district administrator, listing the contacts' identifier numbers, names, numbers of interactions, and power and values scores. These maps were then used in the analysis of organization-sets reported in chapter 6. (The program, as noted in appendix C, also produced the power, values, and interactions scores used to evaluate the group influence model shown in chapter 10.)

Local Administrators' Data

All interviewees were asked the questions described above (open-ended question through contact lists), but rangers and area managers were asked for three additional types of information.

First, district administrators were asked to list the public participation events they held by themselves or with other administrative units. They were asked the type of each event (e.g., public meeting, advisory board meeting), the subject matter of the event, and their perception of the composition of interest groups represented at the event.

Second, in a short series of questions, district administrators were asked about the level of supervisory control over their actions. In particular, they were asked about the number of consultations with supervisors, the number of important reports made to supervisors, the number of instructions received from supervisors, and the style of their relations with their supervisors.

Finally, district administrators were asked to list the relevant output levels of their districts. All this information was available from district or supervisors' office records. The major commodity outputs—timber sales and cut, grazing permit numbers and animal-unit-months, plus allowable cut and carrying capacity—were reported for the fiscal years ending June 1971, 1972, and 1973; designations of special areas (Wilderness, primitive, scenic, and other), special use permits, and mineral or oil and gas claims, leases, or permits were reported for 1973 only.

Appendix B
The Unidimensionality of Public Lands Attitudes

An important assumption in the analysis of the group influence model is that attitudes of participants in public lands politics are unidimensional (see chapter 10 and appendix C). This assumption simplifies the output functions shown in the public lands group influence model (see page 297) by permitting the use of only one term for each interest set, as opposed to N terms per interest set, which would be required if there were N attitudinal dimensions. In addition, as discussed in chapter 2, a unidimensional attitude assumption is consistent with the historic philosophical positions on public lands, as well as in other environmental policy areas.

The assumption of unidimensional attitudes can also be justified by factor analysis. Factor analysis does not automatically tell the user how many dimensions or factors exist in a set of variables. Given N variables, factor analysis initially produces N factors; the user then specifies the number of factors to be used for further analysis (rotation). A common method of selecting the number of factors is to retain those with eigenvalue greater than 1.0, that is, those that explain about as much variance as is contained in one variable. (The whole set of variables has variance equal to the number of variables; for ten variables, for example, the variance would equal 10.0. The eigenvalue of a factor is the proportion of total variance "explained" or summarized by the factor; thus, with total variance of 10.0, an eigenvalue of 1.0 would mean the factor explains 10 percent of the total variance, or as much as a single variable possesses.) The criterion used to select the number of variables for further analysis is a critical aspect of factor analysis. The criterion used to determine the number of basic factors or dimensions is the *discontinuity test*, which identifies the number of useful factors by identifying the point at which there is a clear drop-off in the magnitude of eigenvalue.[1] This test is normally used in conjunction with the eigenvalue-one criterion and the *scree test* (which calls for deleting factors after the point on a plot of eigenvalue at which eigenvalue levels off).

All the forced-choice attitude items plus a series of dummy variables representing open-ended response patterns and various combinations of response patterns were factor-analyzed. After a number of analyses, one of the forced-choice items ("recreation fees") and all the dummy variables except one combined dummy variable (called "perceived group domination") were excluded from further analysis. The distribution of responses to the forced-choice, Likert-scale items is shown in table B-1. (For simplicity of presentation, the responses in table B-1 combine the three favorable positions into one category, the three middle responses into another, and the three-opposition responses into a third.[2]) Table B-2 contains a listing of the response patterns used to construct the "perceived group dominance" dummy variable and the distribution of that variable.

Table B-3 shows the intercorrelations among the eight forced-choice and one open-ended variables remaining in the analysis. The additudinal items are not extremely highly intercorrelated, with some effective zero correlations and most correlations in the .2 to .4 range, and intercorrelations explaining only one-eighth to one-third of the variance of any given variable.

However, the variables do reflect a definite unidimensionality. As table B-4 shows, the first factor has an eigenvalue of 2.88, while the second and third factors have eigenvalue not much greater than the eigenvalue-one criterion cutoff point. The sharpest drop in eigenvalue occurs between the first and second factors, with an initial drop of 1.62 and subsequent drops of .25, .15, .10, .07, .07, and .12. The second and third factors meet the eigenvalue-one and scree test criteria, but the discontinuity criterion clearly indicates a cutoff point after the first. Thus, the first factor can be considered the single significant underlying dimension.

For the purposes of comparison, and as a slight hedge for future stages in the analysis, two factors were extracted in the final solution, the main factor and the second factor (as a residual factor and as the only other

Table B-1. Administrators' and Interest Group Leaders' Attitudes Toward Selected Public Lands Issues

Issue[a]	Strong-weak favor (0-2)(%)	Mixed or neutral (3-5)(%)	Weak-strong oppose (6-8)(%)	No answer (%)	Total[b] (N = 291)(%)	Mean[c]	Standard Deviation
Clear-cutting	26.7	38.2	22.7	12.4	100.0	4.00	2.06
Current mineral exploration practices	37.4	26.4	30.6	5.5	99.9	3.94	2.04
(Less) designated Wilderness	40.5	20.6	36.8	2.1	100.0	3.86	2.51
Unrestricted ORV use	22.7	21.3	54.0	2.1	100.1	4.90	2.23
Predator controls	44.3	19.6	32.3	3.8	100.0	3.70	2.72
(Lowered) grazing fees[d]	26.4	22.0	32.8	28.9	100.1	4.22	2.42
Increasing the allowable cut and carrying capacity	33.7	34.4	22.7	9.3	100.1	3.77	2.13
Administrator preferences for local economic considerations	60.1	19.5	16.8	3.4	99.8	2.59	2.25

[a] For exact wording, see appendix A. High scores (more opposed) are presumed to reflect a more conservationist position. Items in parentheses asked in opposite way from table presentation; for example, the "grazing fees" item asked about support for increased fees.
[b] Some totals do not equal 100 percent because of round-off error.
[c] Mean of the valid responses (deleting cases with "no answer"), with "strong favor" equal to yes; "weak favor," 2; "mixed/neutral," 4; "weak opposed," 6; and "strong opposed," 8. Some respondents answered in the half-spaces between, for example, "neutral" and "weak favor"; to avoid rescoring these responses, the scale was expanded to a nine-point range.
[d] The "grazing fees" item was altered after fieldwork in State A. Thus, most State A participants do not have valid responses to this question. See appendix A.

Table B-2. Local Participants' Perceptions About Interest Group Dominance in Local Public Lands Policymaking

Response pattern mentioned[a]	Code[b]	No.	%	Relative %
"Environmentalist/conservationist/recreationist interest group pressure" "Overcommitment to wildlife/recreation use"	−1	68	23.4	25.1
Neither or both types of response	0	138	47.4	50.9
"Developmentalist philosophical/pressure" "Economic factors/demand/use" "Environmental destruction"	+1	65	22.3	24.0
No answer to open-ended question[c]	N.A.	20	6.9	N.A.
Totals		291	100.0	100.0

Mean = −0.01   Standard deviation = 0.702

[a] For all patterns of response to the open-ended question, see table 7-1. On the context of the question in interviews and questionnaires, see appendix A.

[b] Code used as the "perceived group dominance" attitude measure in subsequent analyses (for example, table B-3).

[c] The "no answer" (N.A.) cases are not included in calculations of mean and standard deviation.

factor with eigenvalue much above the 1.0 cutoff). The factor matrix for this two-factor solution is presented in table B-5. (The factor loadings of the first factor in table B-5 are almost identical to those for a one-factor solution.) As discussed in chapter 5, the first factor can be easily interpreted as a general "environmental-utilitarian" attitude dimension. The second factor, with only two highly loading indicators (the "grazing fees" and "ORV" items), is not so easily interpretable. (In factor analysis, conceptual interpretability is an important supplement to the quantitative criteria for determining the number of factors.) If the "predator control" item had loaded on this factor, it might have been interpreted as a grazing issue factor. As it is, the second factor seems only a residual dimension.

After the indicators and factors shown in table B-5 were determined, the factor scores on the two factors were retained for later use as attitude scales.[3] It seemed that the factor scores from the main E-U scale would be the only scores worth using, but the residual factor's scores were also retained to double-check for the possibility of a slightly better fit of the model with a multidimensional attitude assumption. Since the analysis of the model using the second factor's scores as the attitude or V term pro-

Table B-3. Correlation Matrix of Selected Attitude Items

Variable	Initial estimated communality	Clear.	Min.	Wild.	ORV	Pred.	GFee	AC/CC	Local econ.
Clear-cutting	0.16	1.0							
Mineral exploration	0.26	0.19	1.0						
Wilderness	0.34	0.21	0.23	1.0					
ORV use	0.12	0.004	0.20	0.04	1.0				
Predator control	0.36	0.32	0.34	0.46	−0.004	1.0			
Grazing fees	0.22	0.12	0.18	0.29	−0.21	0.27	1.0		
Allowable cut/carrying capacity	0.23	0.25	0.28	0.32	0.12	0.36	0.16	1.0	
Preference for local economy	0.27	0.06	0.35	0.28	−0.01	0.30	0.35	0.28	1.0
Perceived group dominance	0.22	0.21	0.25	0.39	0.002	0.20	0.18	0.24	0.26

Determinant of correlation matrix = 0.2204.

Table B-4. Eigenvalue of Initial Unrotated Factors

Factor no.	Eigenvalue	Percentage of variance
1	2.88	32.0
2	1.26	14.0
3	1.01	11.2
4	0.85	9.5
5	0.75	8.4
6	0.68	7.6
7	0.61	6.8
8	0.54	6.0
9	0.42	4.7
Total	9.00	100.0%

duced results consistently inferior to those of analyses using the E-U scale scores, and since the second attitude dimension added nothing significant to the model, the second factor was eliminated from the analyses reported in the text (especially in chapters 5 and 10).

Researchers often delete items with loadings of below .40 from factors. However, three items with loadings below .40 were retained in the E-U scale scores. First, two of the items' loadings—"grazing fees" at .396 and "clear-cutting" at .378—are very close to the .4 level (which is only a rough rule of thumb, not a rigid cutoff point based on statistical theory). The two items' attitudes also involve substantively important issues. Sec-

Table B-5. Attitude Factor Matrix

Attitude item	Main factor: Environmental-utilitarian scale	Residual factor
Predator control	0.642	−0.082
Wilderness	0.613	0.107
Allowable cut/carrying capacity	0.556	−0.099
Mineral exploration	0.545	−0.137
Preference for local economy	0.498	0.178
Perceived group dominance	0.463	0.066
Clear-cutting	0.378	−0.016
Grazing fees	0.396	0.501
ORV use	0.124	−0.529
Eigenvalue	2.88	1.26

Total variance = 9.00.   2-Factor percentage of total variance = 46%.

APPENDIX B: THE UNIDIMENSIONALITY OF PUBLIC LANDS ATTITUDES 363

ond, the one very low loading item, "ORV use" at .12, loads highly on the residual factor, and thus should be included in computing the E-U scale scores.[4] In addition to the fact that ORV use is an important issue and its inclusion in the analysis slightly improves the E-U scale (both conceptually and according to statistical theory), it was more efficient to retain the item in the scale than to recompute dozens of analyses for the sake of a marginally more parsimonious attitude scale.

NOTES

1. See R. J. Rummel, *Applied Factor Analysis* (Evanston, Ill., Northwestern University Press, 1970), especially pp. 361–365, on the discontinuity test and related criteria for the number of factors.
2. For the exact distribution of responses, see Paul Culhane, "Politics and the Public Lands," Ph.D dissertation, Evanston, Illinois, Northwestern University, Department of Political Science, June 1977, p. 148.
3. Attitude scales based on scores from factors with eigenvalue greater than 1.0 are generally considered reliable; see Rummel, *Applied Factor Analysis*, p. 356, and references cited therein.
4. It is preferred practice to leave low-loading items in factor scores from a multifactor solution. See, for example, Jae-On Kim, "Factor Analysis," in Norman Nie, C. Hadlai Hull, Jean Jenkins, Karen Steinbrenner, and Dale Brent, eds., *Statistical Package for the Social Sciences* (2nd ed., New York, McGraw-Hill, 1975) pp. 488–489; and Rummel, *Applied Factor Analysis*, pp. 365, 439, and 441.

Appendix C
The Group Influence Model/
Technical Aspects

The discussion of the quantitative analysis of group influence in chapter 10 omits a number of important, but fairly technical topics, including the logic and basic mathematics of the formulation of the group influence model, the scaling procedures used to construct the variables used in the analysis of that model, and the results of analyses of several variations of the model.

Derivation of the Model

The extensive literature on interest group theory contains a wide range of concepts, propositions, critiques, and empirical (although almost always qualitative rather than quantitative) findings. Group theory is much richer than the simple proposition that groups are a major force in governmental decision making, as the very brief review in chapter 1 shows.

Formalization of the Basic Model

The basic proposition of group theory is that group influence causes policy outputs or decisions. That assertion can be represented as

$$\text{Influence}_{kj} \longrightarrow \text{Outcome}_j$$

or, the influence of the kth interest group, with respect to the jth deci-

APPENDIX C: THE GROUP INFLUENCE MODEL

sional event, causes the jth event outcome. Influence is, however, arguably not a property of the kth interest group, but an imputed characteristic that really describes the effect of the kth group's having caused event outcome$_j$.

Therefore, the basic assertion needs to be refined to more precisely specify some property of the kth entity, rather than its effect, as the causal agent. Numerous observers of politics have identified power as the property of political groups that leads to influence. Thus the *effect*, Influence$_{kj}$, would be described by the following control process:

$$\text{Power}_{kj} \longrightarrow \text{Outcome}_j,$$

that is, the power (hereafter, P_{kj}) of the kth group, with respect to j, causes the jth event outcome (hereafter, O_j).

For the concept of influence to be meaningful, in the sense of controlling decision outcomes, the kth group must be trying to achieve a specific outcome within the range of possibilities for O_j. That is, the notion of choice is implicit in the concept of group influence. The group is seen as having an interest in (or preference about) the outcome of the event. In formalizing the theory, we add a term representing preferences and interests, called *values* (V_{kj}). Thus, the reformulation of group theory's main assertion becomes

$$(P_{kj}, V_{kj}) \longrightarrow O_j.$$

That is, the power and value preferences of the kth entity with respect to j cause or control the jth event's outcome.

Interest group theory is usually concerned with competition among groups for policy rewards. It would thus be logical to extend the formulation of influence to accommodate more than one entity's participation in the decisional event. To do this it is helpful to use two new concepts in the decisional control system, a *regulator* and a *decision table*.[1] A decision table specifies the set of possible outcomes, O_j. A regulator is that element in the system that translates entities' attempts to control the outcome of the event into a selection from the decision table. The regulator is, in short, the decision maker who processes the power and value preferences of the group entities in the system. In the case of a political system, the decision table would be the decision procedures and preexisting legal rules that structure or specify possible decision outcomes.

The decision maker can be thought of as a perfect regulator, a homeostat who accurately reflects the result of the various (P_{kj}, V_{kj}) attempts to control the event. A form of imperfect regulation would be variable regulation of, or response to, attempts by the various entities to control the decision outcome. Allowing for imperfect regulation, the decision system could be diagrammed:

$$(P_{1j}, V_{1j}) \longrightarrow \boxed{R_{1j}}$$
$$(P_{2j}, V_{2j}) \longrightarrow \boxed{R_{2j}}$$
$$\vdots \qquad \qquad \vdots \qquad R_j \longrightarrow [T_j] \longrightarrow O_j$$
$$(P_{nj}, V_{nj}) \longrightarrow \boxed{R_{nj}}$$

where R_j is the regulator or decision maker in the system, T_j is the decision table, $R_{1j}, R_{2j}, \ldots, R_{nj}$ are regulations with respect to entities 1, 2, ..., and n, and P_{kj}, V_{kj}, and O_j are as previously defined. The concept of imperfect regulation adds a nongroup element to the system that may or may not be controlled by the group entities. This concept, however, is a familiar one in group literature. Regulation (R_{kj}) is a relative screening that affects the attempts of any kth entity to control the regulator, R_j, the government decision maker—that is, the relative access of the kth entity to the decision maker.

The next step in the formalization of group theory is to express the above diagram in mathematical terms. For any given event, R_j is a homeostatic process and not consequential. However, R_{kj} may vary and *is* consequential. Thus, the previous diagram can be generally expressed:

$$O_j = f(P_{1j}, V_{1j}, P_{2j}, V_{2j}, \ldots, P_{nj}, V_{nj}, R_{1j}, R_{2j}, \ldots, R_{nj})$$

or, the outcome of the jth event is a function of the power and value preferences of the entities in the system and the relative access of those entities to the regulator or decision maker.

V_{kj} represents value preferences that give direction to the entities' power, for example, embodying a choice from the decision table T_j. In other words, the combination of P_{jk} and V_{kj} is a vector. Take a simple case in which T_j is a dichotomy with possible outcomes yes and no, such as a roll-call vote in a legislature. Any kth entity's value preferences with respect to event j would have to be expressed as a dichotomy; mathe-

APPENDIX C: THE GROUP INFLUENCE MODEL

matically, V_{kj} could then be expressed as positive ($+1$) or negative (-1). The term P_{kj} is, then, a magnitude variable, and the combination of P_{kj} and V_{kj} would be multiplicative, $P_{kj} \times V_{kj}$. For simplicity's sake, and since V_{kj} takes only the values $+1$ and -1 so far, we will henceforth write the term as PV_{kj}.

Insofar as R_j is a homeostat, the output function would appear to be additive. For example, the result of the evaluation by R of two entities with equal power but opposite preferences should be cancellation. Thus, the decision-making function would add the various PV terms and "decide" yes if the function were positive and no if negative. A number of common pictorial diagrams of group theory, which are variations on a tug-of-war in which the more powerful group pulls policy in its direction, are good representations of the additivity of group pressure.

The PV term can easily be generalized for attitude preferences more complicated than dichotomies. If attitudes are unidimensional, V_{kj} is a combination of both direction and intensity of preferences. Groups with strong preferences can be presumed to exercise their power more diligently in pursuit of their desired decision outcome than groups with weak preferences; that is, intensity of preference modulates application of power, and is thus also multiplicative. (If attitudes were multidimensional, the function could be expanded using V_{kjd} for each dth dimension of the outcome, O_{jd}. Fortunately, the more cumbersome multidimensional model can be ignored in our case because public lands attitudes can be safely assumed to be unidimensional, as discussed in appendix B.)

The effect of the variable access, R_{kj}, is mathematically similar to the effect of value preferences. Regulation enhances or dampens PV_{kj}, and is thus also multiplicative. The basic outcome function thus becomes:

$$O_j = f(R_{1j}PV_{1j} + R_{2j}PV_{2j} + \ldots + R_{nj}PV_{nj}).$$

The next generalization of the model is to aggregate all decisional events O_j to arrive at a function that summarizes all outcomes in the class of which O_j is a part. Assuming that all O_js are measured in the same units (for example, legislative roll-call votes or board-feet of timber sales), then the class of events O could be defined by the following function:

$$O = \sum_{j=1}^{m} O_j = f\left(\sum_{j=1}^{m} \sum_{k=1}^{n} R_{kj}PV_{kj}\right).$$

If we assume that P_{kj} and V_{kj} remain constant for all events over the class O_j, we can rewrite the previous function:

$$O = f(A_1 PV_1 + A_2 PV_2 + \ldots + A_n PV_n)$$

where A_k is the sum of access over all m events in the class O_j; that is,

$$A_k = \sum_{j=1}^{m} R_{kj}.$$

Most observers of the decisional events in a policy area are likely to be less interested in the influence of an individual group than in the influence of a set of groups that share some common interests, are commonly perceived to be similar, coordinate their activities, and so forth. The arguments in the function can be grouped according to these common interests, perceptions, or activities as follows:

$$O = f(A_1 PV_1 + \ldots + A_b PV_b + A_c PV_c + \ldots + A_e PV_e + \ldots + A_n PV_n).$$

The role of decision makers in the model has not gone beyond regulation, maintaining differential access and tabulating the homeostatic aggregation function. Much of the criticism of group theory has been directed at the notion that decision makers are mere homeostats, so it would be prudent to allow for the possibility of independent decision-maker influence in the outcome function. The model will stipulate that at least one group may be members of the decision-making institution.

Aggregating the various similar groups and reserving one group set for decision makers result in:

$$O = f(APV_{dm}^* + APV_1^* + APV_2^* + \ldots + APV_{n'}^*)$$

where

$$APV_{k'}^* = \sum_{k=1}^{q} A_k PV_k$$

for all q entities in the class k', and APV_{dm}^* is the class of decision makers of O. Note that this summation makes the argument $APV_{k'}^*$ partly a function of the number of groups in the set q, as well as the power, values, and access of the individual groups.

The final part of the formalization of the group influence model is specifying the form of the function f. Group theory simply says that group influence is the effect of group activity on policy. Policy is O, and APV^* is group activity. In the general linear model $Y = a + b_1X_1 + \ldots + b_nX_n + e$, the slope coefficients, b_k, signify the effect of the predictors, X_k, on Y. As the most direct translation of group theory's concept of influence (and since we have already formalized the function as additive), f can be treated as a general linear model,

$$O = a + i_1APV_1 + i_2APV_2 + i_3APV_3 + \ldots + i_nAPV_n + e$$

where the coefficient i_k signifies the effect or influence of the kth set of groups on the policy O.

A model of this form implies that each of the terms that comprise the APV arguments has a significant effect on outputs. That assumption can be restated by saying that all the bs in the following equation are significant:

$$i_kAPV_k = i_k(\Sigma APV_k) = \Sigma(i_kA_kP_kV_k) = \Sigma(b_{ka}A_kb_{kp}P_kb_{kv}V_k)$$

where $i_k = b_{ka} \cdot b_{kp} \cdot b_{kv}$. (These equalities are presented for the purpose of demonstration. In actual least squares regression the equalities, while mathematically correct, do not hold exactly; that is, b_{pv} only approximates $b_p \cdot b_v$.) If b_{ka} is insignificant, it will decrease i_k; while PV_k may influence a policy, A_k is unimportant. Thus, the final form of the model can be expected to contain arguments that, for the various sets of groups, are various combinations of access, power, and values terms, based on the empirical importance of those different properties for specific sets of groups.

Structural Versions of the Model

The basic group influence model can become more complex if it is applied to a policy system in which there are different types of outputs. In the case of public lands policy, there are various reasons why the different policy outputs might be interrelated, and the resulting set of simultaneous equations would thus be structural (that is, the output terms, O, would appear on both the right- and left-hand sides of the equations). If the unit of analysis were a fixed area of typical national forest land, for example, the physiographic potential of the land would affect the rate at which timber production could be substituted for grazing use over time. In a cross-sectional design in which the units of analysis are administrative subdivisions, marginal substitution of outputs is not a compelling explanation of physiography-based interrelationships among outputs. Administrative workload distribution provides one possible explanation of such interrelationships. Assuming that the agencies attempt to maintain roughly comparable workloads for local administrators, units that are major producers of one output will have proportionately lower responsibilities in other areas. This is not a matter of artificially lowering other outputs, but of arranging administrative boundaries to even out workloads. (In the sample, such a workload reorganization took place on NF5 prior to the field research; because of systematically decreased timber management work, the forest was reorganized from seven to five ranger districts.) Some relationships among outputs might also be artifacts of purely legal–administrative factors. For example, BLM resource areas and national grassland ranger districts, with relatively high grazing outputs, were not included in the RARE I Wilderness review for legal reasons; this seems to account completely for the observed negative correlation between grazing and preservation outputs in the sample.

Whatever the reason for the interrelationship among outputs, it affects the form of the model. Using the public lands outputs most affected by intercorrelation (and assuming a fairly simple function appropriate to the workload-based interrelationship), one has $b_1 O_t + b_2 O_g = C + e$, or the weighted sum of timber and grazing outputs is approximately constant. This relationship can be rewritten in separate equations and combined with the basic group influence functions to produce:

$$O_t = a_1 + b_3 O + i_{11} APV_1 + i_{12} APV_2 + \ldots + i_{1n} APV_n + e_1$$

$$O_g = a_2 + b_4 O + i_{21} APV_1 + i_{22} APV_2 + \ldots + i_{2n} APV_n + e_2$$

(and so forth for as many outputs as are included in the system and seem to be plausibly interrelated).

These structural equations are mathematically and methodologically more complicated than the basic group influence functions.[2] Moreover, the structural equation model is somewhat at variance with interest group

APPENDIX C: THE GROUP INFLUENCE MODEL 371

theory, on which the (nonstructural) group influence function was based. Group theory implicitly ignores relationships among different types of policy outputs because groups seem to ignore those relationships in their demands, treating group politics as, for all practical purposes, a positive-sum game. (Such behavior is an often-criticized, if understandable, flaw of group demands. However, the neglect of policy interrelationships is not necessarily a flaw in the group theory description of such behavior.)

The use of absolute public lands outputs levels (for example, thousands of board-feet sold, animal-unit-months grazed) would seem to require the use of structural equation methods. However, there are no obvious reasons to expect, *a priori,* that measures that control for physiographic characteristics—such as the ratio outputs discussed in chapter 10—would be interrelated. The analysis of the public lands group influence model presented in chapter 10 uses such ratio-type outputs because of (1) the conceptual superiority of ratio outputs as "decisional" measures; (2) the congruence of the nonstructural ratio outputs model with the form of the basic group influence model and the simplicity of that model in comparison with the structural absolute outputs model; (3) several critical technical inadequacies, to be noted later in this appendix, in the results of the analysis of the absolute outputs data and structural model; and (4) the absence of such technical inadequacies in the ratio outputs model.

Scale Construction

The data used in the public lands group influence model consist of scales of interest group participants' and administrators' attitudes, organizational resources, and access to local administrators. The goal of the scaling procedure was to develop variables that met three criteria. First, missing data problems should be minimized; in particular, the failure of some individuals in an interest set to respond on a given unit of analysis did not cause that interest set's arguments to be coded as "missing." Second, index units should be in equivalent units of measurement so multiplication of terms would not result in artificial bias of the resulting product. Thus, all component arguments were standardized to unit variance (variance = standard deviation = 1.0). Third, so that the sign of the resulting products would be consistent, only one term was allowed to take negative values. As indicated above, the attitude item is the directionality variable in the model. Therefore, while other terms would have unit variance, they would have positive means, medians, and minimum values.

The attitude, or "values," indicator is the set of scores on the E-U scale, the factor scores on the first factor in the analysis presented in appendix B and table 5-5. Factor scores are automatically computed in standardized form, with a zero mean and unit variance.

Power Scale

There were several noncomparable indicators of organizational resources or power, depending on the individual contact's type of organization; moreover, all but three interest group contacts had missing data (that is, inapplicable, or in some cases no answer was given) on one or more resources indicators.

The first step in the power-scaling procedure for interest groups was to standardize (to zero mean and unit variance) all comparable organizational resources indicators. The four basic indicators were "number of members," "budget," "firm's gross volume of business," and "staff size." As table 5-7 shows, there were sometimes radical and systematic (and misleading) differences in the magnitude of certain groups' resources within a given class of resources. For example, schools and local government units have budgets of hundreds of thousands of dollars, sometimes millions, while voluntary associations' budgets are in the low tens of thousands of dollars. Assuming that an organization with high levels of resources in its resource class was as "powerful" as an organization with high levels in another resource class, resources were also standardized within resource classes. Table C-1 shows the groups in the various categories and the category means and Standard Deviations. Groups were assigned to categories on the basis of group mean levels of resources and conceptual similarity to other groups.

After the comparable resources indicators were standardized, the second step in the scaling procedure was to average each group contact's nonmissing indicators' standard scores and standardize the resulting averages.

The third step was to raise the values of the standardized indicator averages so the median of the resulting power scale was 1.0. (The scale was raised to a median of 1.0, rather than a mean of 1.0, because the indicators were quite skewed.) For example, if a Sierra Club contact had

Table C-1. Group Categories on Which Standardizing of Resources Indicators Was Based, by Resource Category

Resource indicator groups in category	Category N	Mean	Standard Deviation
Membership			
A. Sierra, wildlife, wilderness, general environmental, *ad hoc* environmental, archeologists, sportsmen, ORV, other recreationists, NRA, recreation operator, fraternal, school, non-land-management professional association	36	325.3	646.0
B. Stockmen/grazing association, irrigation, SRM	50	216.6	631.2
C. Mining/O&G, chamber of commerce, boosters	14	92.1	133.5
D. Forest product, BLM advisory board, state and local government, RC&D	9	8.5	2.3
Budget			
A. Stockmen, irrigation association	42	$21,108	55,677
B. Forest products, mining/O&G, chamber of commerce, booster association	14	$23,771	33,327
C. Sierra, wildlife, wilderness, sportsmen, recreation operator, ORV, other recreationists, archeologists, non-land-management professional associations	32	$6,216	14,843
D. State game and fish department, state and local government, schools, soil conservation district, RC&D	13	$304,833	435,582
Firm gross $ volume			
A. Forest products, stockmen, businessmen, recreation operator, media, water/irrigation association, realtors	57	$925,439	2,169,757
B. Mining/O&G, contractors, utilities	17	$69,610,000	2.403×10^8
Professional staff			
A. Sierra, wildlife, sportsmen, ORV, general environmentalists, non-land-management professional association	13	0.77	1.79
B. Forest products, livestock, chamber of commerce, recreation operator, state game and fish department, state and local government, media, irrigation, realtor	76	4.18	7.38
C. Mining/O&G, contractors, utilities, schools	20	63.90	139.99

nonmissing "number of members," "budget," and "staff" indicators, the standard score of each ("members" standardized against a mean of 325.3 and standard deviation of 646, and so forth) would be added together and the sum divided by three; the resultant would then be standardized along with the resultants of all other contacts, and that standard score added to a constant (1.295).

Administrative resources were treated in a more straightforward manner, since all administrators had the same nonmissing indicators. Field interviewing experience and correlation analysis suggested that professional staff resources were more important than other resource categories, so professional staff was weighted by a factor of 2 and its standard score added to standardized budget and total staff, then averaged, standardized, and then increased to a median of 1.0. (Each supervisory administrator's power score was divided by the number of subunits, that is, ranger districts or resource areas, he supervised.)

Access Scales

There were three different "access" variables. The first was the number of interactions between an individual contact and a district administrator; these were standardized and raised to a median of 1.0.

The second access variable also applied to interest groups. Chapter 8 presented data on the public participation events held on ranger districts or resource areas. In addition to data on number and type of events, district administrators were asked which groups, if any, dominated each public participation event. For each district, then, it was possible to determine the number of participation events dominated by each primary interest set. The event domination distribution, before standardization, is shown in table C-2. This set of data for each ranger district and resource area was also standardized and raised to a median of 1.0.

The third set of access indicators applied to supervisory administrators only. The supervisory access is the factor scores of the "strength of supervision" factor. (See chapter 9, table 9-2, and note 2). The factor scores were raised to a median of 1.0. There is no access term for the local administrators' argument in the model since local officials are posited as the decision-making units of analysis. There may be some plausible interpretations of "a ranger's access to himself" (for example, his propensity to allow his own biases to influence his decisions), but those

Table C-2. Public Participation Event Dominance

Group dominating event	Minimum	Maximum	Mean	Standard deviation
Forest products industry	0	1	0.05	0.23
Livestock industry	0	46	7.00	9.36
Economic users (not forest products or livestock)	0	2	0.24	0.49
Conservationists and/or recreationists	0	12	1.65	2.83
Other interests[a]	0	4	0.30	0.88
Total events	3	47	14.95	10.78

[a] Includes only dominance by groups listed in "other" category in chapter 10 and tables 5-1 and 6-1. Events not dominated by one or more groups in a particular interest set, or with balanced participations, are not listed (except in the totals).

interpretations seemed too tenuous and reactive to be included in the model.

Scale Aggregation

The final stage in the scaling process was to produce the case-by-case arguments that would be used in the analysis of the model. In the case of administrators' arguments, this was a simple matter of multiplying the variables discussed above: local administrators' E-U scores times their power index scores; supervisory administrators' E-U scores times their power scores times their "strength of supervision" scores.

The same FORTRAN aggregating program used to produce the organization set results reported in chapter 5 was used to aggregate the interest group power, values, and access variables as follows: (1) when a contact was identified for a particular local administrator, the contact was typed as belonging to one of the five interest sets (see table 6-1); (2) various products of the contact's power, value, and number of interaction scores were calculated; and (3) these products were added to the existing sum of the particular interest set's products of the same type. After the products for each contact in the interest set were added, the sums were multiplied by the appropriate "participation event dominance" score. It was impractical to attempt to obtain contact-by-contact data on public participation event dominance. Thus, it was assumed that the effects of an interest set's event dominance affected each contact equally; that is,

$$\Sigma(R_k \cdot NPV_k) = R_k \cdot (\Sigma NPV_k)$$

where participation dominance, R_k, is a constant for all groups within the interest set (for any given administrator's organization-set).

The aggregating program produced a composite variable for each interest set in each district administrator's organization-set of the following form: Public Participation Dominance times the sum of each of the interest's contacts' Power times Values times Number of Interactions. These composite variables are the APV_k terms in the group influence model. The aggregating program also produced all possible combinations of the N_k, P_k, and V_k terms. Thus, in the "optimum arguments" analysis reported in chapter 10, the arguments are the sum of products—for example, $\Sigma(P_k \cdot V_k)$—not the products of sums (for example, $\Sigma P_k \cdot \Sigma V_k$) or some other argument.

The scaling and aggregating procedures discussed above entail a tradeoff that is necessary in light of the model formalized at the beginning of this appendix. The resulting arguments are composed of equivalent variables and are signed consistently, but they are short on intuitive meaning. For example, a forest products interest interactions–power–values product sum score of -11.999 does not have the same conspicuous reality as the following rough interpretation of the number: a set of six timber mill operators, each with about \$1 to \$1.5 million gross, once-a-week interactions with the ranger, and attitudes typical of the forest products industry as a whole. Because the arguments do not have a clear intuitive meaning, the regression analyses presented in chapter 10 do not report the unstandardized regression coefficient (b) or the regression line intercept (a).

Missing Data

There are no missing data on administrators' variables in the model. As noted in appendix A, the effective response rate for all interest group contacts was 62.3 percent. In the tables in chapters 5 and 6, the missing 37.7 percent is no more of a problem than the normal problem of the questionnaire response rate bias. However, at the interest-aggregating stage of the scaling process, nonresponses present a potentially fatal prob-

APPENDIX C: THE GROUP INFLUENCE MODEL 377

lem. One way to handle nonrespondents was to code any interest set that had one or more nonrespondents as missing data. Since this would eliminate most observations in the model analysis, especially for those interest sets with many contacts per set (that is, the most important sets) and would also eliminate good data along with nonrespondents, the procedure was unacceptable. A second way to deal with nonrespondents was to simply exclude them from organization-set sums. A third way was to make assumptions about nonrespondents, based on their group affiliations, and infer substitute scores for their missing power and values scale scores. (Nonrespondents' numbers of interactions with most administrators were also known.)

The third alternative was chosen. After the attitude (E-U) and power scales were generated for respondents, the scales were broken down by primary and secondary group affiliations, obtaining group and subgroup means, medians, and standard deviations. The primary group median power scale was substituted for missing data. The average of the individual's primary and secondary group mean E-U scores was substituted as an estimate of his attitudes.

Table C-3 presents the scores that were substituted by type of group. For the most part, the inferred scores appear to be good approximations, although for some groups (with few total contacts) some of the inferred values seem somewhat out of line. Note, for example, the large differences between the primary and secondary group E-U scale values for schools (several environmental group leaders were schoolteachers) and general environmental groups.

The so-called generic contacts' "missing" scores were inferred in the same way as other nonrespondents'. For generic groups for which there were valid respondents in the type, the respondents' mean/median was used, as per normal procedure. However, for the federal agency contacts, no valid data were available. By convention, the substituted scores were the mean power score (1.295) and the values index of a similar interest group; for example, for the National Park Service, a preservation- and recreation-oriented agency, a low conservationist E-U score of 1.25 was used.

A procedure of substituting estimates for missing data involves possible bias, but less than treating interest sets with nonrespondents as missing or deleting missing individuals from the interest set sums. Table C-4 gives a heuristic example of the three types of bias. Two of four ranchers in a hypothetical ranger's livestock industry interest set are nonrespondents

Table C-3. Parameters Used as Substitutes for Nonrespondents and Other Missing Data Cases

Group type	Power score	E-U score primary group	E-U score secondary group
Forest products industry	1.127	−0.758	−0.700
Stockmen, grazing associations,	0.950	−0.575	−0.462
BLM advisory board members	0.948	−0.816	−0.884
Mineral or oil and gas firms or associations	1.297	−0.629	−0.587
Chambers of commerce, businessmen	0.969	−0.354	0.006
Water/irrigation corporations or associations	1.011	−0.142	−0.229
RC&D, other conservation districts	1.613	−0.151	−0.355
Realtors	1.008	0.266	0.266
Utilities	4.213	−0.725	1.536
Contractors	1.948	−0.832	−0.504
Sierra Club	1.216	1.496	1.215
Wildlife federations	0.977	1.255	0.877
Wilderness societies/committees	1.179	1.397	0.901
Sportsmen	0.923	0.401	0.085
ORV clubs	0.937	−0.146	−0.477
Other recreational users	0.967	1.536	1.536
Recreation-related businesses	1.285	0.362	0.601
State game and fish departments	1.051	0.439	0.272
Archeologists	1.055	1.133	1.133
General environmental groups	0.936	2.139	0.113
Booster or tourism associations	1.028	0.497	1.106
Fraternal	0.980	0.124	−0.017
State and local government	1.618	−0.241	−0.524
Schools	0.625	−0.096	1.159
Media	0.957	−0.607	2.440
Others	1.000	various	various
National Park Service	1.295	1.250	N.A.
Soil Conservation Service	1.295	0.060	N.A.
U.S. Geological Survey	1.295	−0.629	N.A.
Bureau of Indian Affairs	1.295	−0.920	N.A.

(rancher 3 and rancher 4). Assume that nonresponse has caused a major bias: both ranchers, though unknown to the coder, are quite powerful and hold extreme views. The hypothetical ranger's livestock industry organization-set would have a real sum-PV score of −4.05. Substituting mean and median livestock industry value and power estimates results in a 46 percent bias [(4.05 − 2.19)/4.05]; clearly in this case the implicit assumption of intragroup homogeneity has produced a significant bias. However, the other methods are even more biased. Deletion of nonre-

APPENDIX C: THE GROUP INFLUENCE MODEL 379

Table C-4. Heuristic Ranger's Livestock Industry Interest Set

Individuals	The "real" scale scores		Substitution of inferred scores		Deletion of nonrespondents		Exclude set with missing data	
	P	V	P	V	P	V	P	V
Rancher 1	1.1	−0.6	1.1	−0.6	1.1	−0.6	deleted	
Rancher 2	0.9	−0.5	0.9	−0.5	0.9	−0.5	deleted	
Rancher 3[a]	(1.47	−1.0)	(0.95	−0.57)	deleted		deleted	
Rancher 4[a]	(1.47	−1.0)	(0.95	−0.57)	deleted		deleted	
$\Sigma PV_{live.}$ =	−4.05		−2.19		−1.11		0	

Note: P is power score; V is value (E-U) score.
[a] Nonrespondents.

spondents leads to a 73 percent bias [(4.05 − 1.11)/4.05], and exclusion of the interest set causes, effectively, a 100 percent bias. Thus, though possibly biased, substitution of estimates for missing variables seems the best possible method of processing nonrespondents.

Model Results—Additional Details

Based on two distinctions, there are four logical version of the public lands group influence model. The first distinction is between absolute level outputs (for example, "MBF sold") and ratio level outputs (for example, "MBF sold as a proportion of allowable cut"). The second distinction is between "full argument" predictors (for example, "stockmen's RNPV") and "optimum argument" predictors (for example, "stockmen's RV"). Thus, the four versions of the model are (1) "absolute outputs, full arguments," (2) "absolute outputs, optimum arguments," (3) "ratio outputs, full arguments," and (4) "ratio outputs, optimum arguments." The first and second versions were statistically analyzed using two-stage least squares regression because the model was a structure set system; the third and fourth were analyzed using ordinary least squares regression because those versions were nonstructural. For several reasons the fourth version, the "absolute outputs, optimum arguments" model, was the best, and its results have been reported in chapter 10. In addition to the conceptual reasons noted in the text and earlier in this appendix, there were several technical-statistical reasons for the selection of the fourth version.

Alternative Versions of the Model

The primary problem with the absolute outputs versions of the model was that the set of functions of the form

$$\text{MBF} = b_1 \text{AUMs} + \ldots + i_1 \text{ForRNPV} + i_2 \text{StockRNPV} + \ldots + e_1$$

was grossly unidentified.[3] The theory and substantive considerations about public lands policy used to construct the model provided minimal information on how to exclude output or predictor variables, or both, so as to identify the model's functions. The timber and grazing outputs were more likely to be structural (that is, endogenous predictors) than the preservation or mining outputs; it also seemed likely that some groups would be less influential on certain functions than other groups (for example, that "other interests" would be less important than the forest products industry on the timber sales function). The analysis employed an *ad hoc*, empirical strategy to identify the structural absolute outputs systems. While not recommended or standard practice, the empirical identification strategy did not violate the basic theory (group theory) under examination and is not definitionally unreasonable.[4] Excluding interest group variables empirically does not involve model misspecification, but merely a recognition that certain interests do not significantly influence a given policy output. The key points, however, are that the nonstructural ratio outputs version was better than the absolute outputs versions on a number of conceptual grounds and that the absolute outputs model had a number of technical problems that more extensive specification or more complex methods were not likely to overcome.

The preliminary step in the data analysis was a visual inspection of bivariate scatterplots and correlations; if a correlation was based on one or two extreme outlying cases, it was included in the analysis only in unusual circumstances. (An example of such an unusual circumstance was the $r = -.65$ relationship, generated largely by one very extreme outlying case, between EconRNPV and mineral/O&G approvals. The relationship was included in the analysis because the economic user set included the mining industry, the primary clientele of mining approvals.) Outlyer-based correlations were treated with special skepticism if the relationship was anomalous (that is, in the wrong direction or suspiciously large) based on *a priori* qualitative understandings of the roles of different groups in public lands politics.

APPENDIX C: THE GROUP INFLUENCE MODEL

The primary criterion for excluding variables was a combination of the significance of individual regression coefficients and the overall significance of the resulting function. The standard statistical criterion for inclusion of additional variables in a regression model is the hierarchical F test. The hierarchical F test, however, would have excluded more variables than preferred; because of a judgment that it was beneficial to include as many variables as possible in the model (so the relative influence of as many entities as possible would be reported), more liberal inclusion criteria were used. Variables were not added to functions if their addition would result in the F for the function as a whole dropping below the 5 percent significance level or a decrease in adjusted R^2. (Adjusted R^2 decreases when the F significance statistic of the entered variable's b is less than 1.0 at entry; since the critical value for F-of-b is about 4.1, such a variable is statistically very insignificant.) Even the liberal adjusted R^2 (and F-of-b greater than 1.0) criterion was relaxed occasionally to allow entry of a variable (for example, an administrators' argument for the purposes of exposition. For any given function, a fairly large number of regression analyses were performed to determine the entry order that would maximize adjusted R^2 and the number of variables included in the function while maintaining a regression line F significant at the 5 percent level. Even using these liberal inclusion criteria, it was possible to include only four to six variables (out of ten possible) on the grazing, timber, and preservation absolute outputs structural functions. Thus, it was easy to overidentify the functions using these liberal, reverse-order procedures. (Using the same liberal criteria, it was possible to include a maximum of only four variables, out of seven possible, in the ratio outputs functions.)

Table C-5 presents a summary of the results of the two-stage least squares (2SLS) analysis of the absolute outputs, optimum arguments version of the model (omitting some statistics such as the Fs of predictors' bs and adjusted R^2s at entry). In one respect, this version of the model obtained good results; the multiple correlations were all high (higher than the corresponding version of the ratio outputs model). However, there were problems with the results. Because of the 2SLS procedures and intercorrelations among forest products PV, AUMs, and MBF, there were some confounding effects in the second stage of 2SLS. The forest products PV coefficient is very unstable on the MBF function, with its beta and F-of-b dropping radically when predicted $\overline{\text{AUMs}}$ is entered into the function; its beta was $-.55$ before $\overline{\text{AUMs}}$ entry. The forest products PV was also excluded from the AUM's function, though it met the inclusion

Table C-5. Summary of Results for Alternative Model Versions

Interest set, other parameters	Absolute outputs, optimum arguments				Ratio outputs, full RNPV arguments			
	AUMs	MBF	W–P	Min/O&G	AUMs%	MBF%	W–P%	Min/O&G
Stockmen (RV)[a]	−0.41[d]	c	c	c	−0.09	0.38[d]	c	c
Forest products (PV)[a]	c	−0.27	0.28	c	−0.30	−0.41[d]	0.17	c
Economic users (RNPV)[a]	−0.26	c	c	−0.61[d]	0.24	c	c	−0.26
Conservationists and recreationists (RV)[a]	c	−0.31[d]	0.57[d]	c	c	−0.21	0.42[d]	c
Others (NPV)[a]	c	c	0.30	−0.15	c	−0.08	0.53[d]	c
Supervisory administrators (RPV)[a]	0.19	c	c	c	−0.25	c	0.11	c
District administrators (PV)[a]	c	0.17	0.08	c	c	c	c	c
MBF[b]	−0.28	N.A.	c	c	N.A.	N.A.	N.A.	N.A.
AUMs[b]	N.A.	−0.35	−0.17	c	N.A.	N.A.	N.A.	N.A.
Multiple R	0.67	0.69	0.59	0.66	0.50	0.49	0.53	0.26
F, whole function	6.36[d]	7.37[d]	3.23	13.30[d]	2.73[d]	2.59	3.12	2.56
Residuals[e]	2H/Y	4H/Y	3H/Y	1H/?	4H/N	4H/Y	4H/Y	1H/?

Note: N.A., not applicable.
Source: Paul Culhane, "Politics and the Public Lands," Ph.D dissertation, June 1977, Northwestern University (University Microfilms #77-32292). For "Absolute outputs, optimum arguments" columns, see pages 200–208 and 216–220; for "Ratio outputs, Full RNPV arguments" columns, see pages 209–212 and 216–220.

[a] Betas of the variables in 2SLS and OLS regressions, respectively. (Absolute output version's optimum argument shown in parentheses.)
[b] Beta of endogenous outputs predictor (predicted from first stage of 2SLS).
[c] Variable excluded from analysis (because of failure on one or more inclusion criteria).
[d] F-of-b or F of whole function statistically significant at the 5 percent level.
[e] Two sets of codes summarizing visual analyses of residuals. First code (before slash): "xH," where x is the number of predictors in the function with heteroscedastic plot of the predictor with the residual. Second code (after slash): presence of (autocorrelation-like) casewise grouping of residuals, yes (Y), no (N), and indeterminant (?).

APPENDIX C: THE GROUP INFLUENCE MODEL   383

criteria, because of its confounding multicollinear effect on predicted $\overline{\text{MBF}}$. (If the forest product PV is entered into the AUM's function, the forest products set's beta is .35 with an F-of-b of 2.28; $\overline{\text{MBF}}$ shows a multicollinear effect, with its beta dropping to .01 and F-of-b dropping to 0.001. The other variables' parameters remain stable. The forest products PV was excluded because of a judgment that the "real" relationship was between grazing and timber outputs, with the forest products industry relationship being arguably spurious.) While the instability of the parameters of the AUM's and MBF absolute outputs, optimum arguments functions was quite serious, the same multicollinearity problem was disastrous in the absolute outputs, full (RNPV) arguments version (the results of which are not shown). For example, after $\overline{\text{AUMs}}$ are added to the MBF function, the forest products RNPV's beta drops from $-.32$ to $.02$ (and F-of-b drops from 4.17 to 0.01). Because of this multicollinearity in two functions, some key parameters in the absolute outputs versions of the model must be considered unreliable.

The "absolute-optimum" version of the model had another, less critical flaw. The betas of administrators on the two primary commodity functions were in the wrong direction. In terms of the model's assumptions, an interpretation of these betas is counterintuitive: the more conservation-oriented the administrator, the more he influences decisions in favor of increased timber or grazing use. (A better explanation, which field experience suggested might be the case, is that the more protection-oriented officers were assigned to some high potential units to hold down overexploitation, while more utilitarian administrators were used to get an underproductive unit going again.) The only strong point of the "absolute-optimum" version (apart from high overall multiple correlations) was the strong .57 beta of conservationists-recreationists on the Wilderness function.

Table C-5 also provides a summary of the ratio outputs, full arguments version of the model. These results are primarily useful for comparison with the results shown in chapter 10 of the ratio outputs, optimum arguments version, indicating the sensitivity of the model to the "optimum aguments" specification. The multiple correlations of the "ratio-full" version were lower than those in the "ratio-optimum" model (just as the optimum arguments version of the absolute outputs functions had higher correlations than its full arguments counterpart). The main weakness of the ratio-full version is the beta of stockmen's RNPV in the AUM's percentage function; stockmen's effect when alone in the AUM's percentage function (beta = −.24) is overriden when forest products RNPV enters the function.

Analysis of Residuals

Inspection of the residuals (the *e* terms in the model's functions) shows further problems with the absolute outputs and ratio-full versions of the model. Two standard potential problems in regression analyses are autocorrelation of error terms and residual-predictor heteroscedasticity. Normal autocorrelation analysis is inappropriate for our data because the casewise ordering of the data represents only one grouping; district rangers on the same national forest were grouped together and area managers were grouped together by BLM district; cases were not ordered in any meaningful way within supervisory units or from one supervisory unit to the next. However, there were some clear patterns of casewise grouping of error terms within supervisory units on most of the absolute-full, absolute-optimum, and ratio-full versions' functions. (See the last row, table C-5.) For example, in the absolute-level AUM's optimum argument functions, NF1's residuals were slightly to the minus side, NG2's to the plus side, NF5's to the minus side, NRL7's and NRL8's to the plus side, NRL9's to the minus side, and so on. The groupings of residuals suggested some effect at the supervisory administrative level was not being adequately measured by the supervisory variables in the model. No pattern of systematic error by Forest Service region or BLM state was evident.

The second standard type of residuals analysis involves a visual inspection of plots of residuals against the standardized pedicted dependent variable and the various predictor variables. The only problem that emerged from such inspections was heteroscedasticity, but that problem was drastic enough. Most of the predictors in the absolute-level outputs functions and all of the ratio-full functions' predictors were affected by heteroscedasticity. Some of the residual-predictor plots in the absolute-level outputs functions are textbook examples of heteroscedasticity (that is, a perfectly horizontal, funnel-shaped pattern); the heteroscedastic ratio-full functions' plots were somewhat less well defined.

The skewed nature of the data led to heteroscedasticity. Sometimes the bivariate scatterplots of predictors on outputs suggested that the relationship was nonlinear (neither straight-line nor curvilinear). In some other scatterplots, there was a tight cluster of data cases at the origin, where there were few contacts in a particular interest set and few outputs of a certain type, but as the cases moved away from the origin, there was a normal deviation of the data points around the regression line. This latter pattern applied, in particular, to preservation and mineral/O&G outputs. In the case of some full argument predictors, heteroscedasticity was also compounded by the scaling procedures; that is, the multiplication of extreme values in the RNPV argument produced greater skewness in the full arguments than in the optimum arguments versions of the model.

The predictors affected by heteroscedasticity were not altered to correct the problem because (1) the problem could not be effectively resolved by standard methods such as weighted least squares or data transformations; (2) such methods, especially data tinkering like log transformations, complicate the interpretation of the model; (3) the problems seemed to be rooted in the basically skewed distribution of the real-world variables being measured; and (4) heteroscedasticity was only one of a series of problems that led to the rejection of the affected versions of the model.

It is important to note that the ratio outputs–optimum arguments version of the model discussed in chapter 10 was *not* affected by either heteroscedasticity or casewise residuals grouping problems. Only the ratio mineral/O&G–optimum arguments function had even a faint casewise grouping, and only four of the "ratio-optimum" functions' predictor-residual plots had even slightly heteroscedastic plots (and those were for predictors with small betas, such as supervisors RPV on the AUM's % function). The absence of heteroscedasticity was caused, at least in part, by the transformationlike effect of the radio outputs and optimum predictor variables' specifications (that is, the distributions of both ratio outputs and optimum predictors were much less skewed than those of their absolute outputs and full argument predictor counterparts).

The Ratio Outputs–Optimum Arguments Model—Technical Details

The ratio outputs versions of the model assumed that the set of ratio-level outputs functions was nonstructural because there was no apparent, valid, and plausible explanation for interrelationships among ratio (as opposed to absolute-level) outputs. The only apparent rationale for interrelationships among the ratio outputs is that some propensity for utilitarianism or conservationism pervades a local unit's policies. However, such a propensity would presumably result from administrators' predilections or constituency influences, both of which are included in the model, so the effects of such a propensity would be spurious. Moreover, the largest correlation among ratio outputs is a *positive* (and fairly low) .16 betwen the timber sales and Wilderness ratios; based on an inspection of the raw data, this correlation is clearly an artifact of the legal differences between the BLM (no Wilderness mandate, no trees) and the Forest Service (Wilderness mandate, trees).

Nonetheless, the nonstructural assumption was double-checked by running a test 2SLS regression on the ratio outputs, optimum arguments data. The salient results of that analysis were as follows. On the AUM's % function, with six predictors included, predicted $\overline{\text{Wilderness-primitive}}$ % (entered third) had beta $= -.06$, F-of-$b = 0.08$, and R^2-added $= .003$, and predicted $\overline{\text{MBF}\%}$ (entered fourth) had beta $= -.29$, F-of-$b = 0.36$, and R^2-added $= .009$; predicted $\overline{\text{MBF}\%}$ was multicollinear with forest products PV (that is, on $\overline{\text{MBF}\%}$ entry, forest products PV's beta balloons from $-.41$ to $-.63$, while its F-of-b drops precipitously). On the MBF% function, with five predictors included, predicted $\overline{\text{AUM's}\%}$ (entered second) had beta $= .15$, F-of-$b = 0.83$, and R^2-added $= .02$. (There were some suspicious partial correlation and 2SLS flip-flop effects in the MBF% and AUM's% relationships: the correlation between MBF% and AUM's% was $-.11$; the correlation between predicted $\overline{\text{MBF}\%}$ and $\overline{\text{AUM's}\%}$ was $+.16$; and their betas in the second stage of 2SLS were negative, $-.29$ and $-.15$.) On the Wilderness-primitive ratio function, with six predictors included, predicted $\overline{\text{AUM's}\%}$ (entered third) had beta $= .10$, F-of-$b = 0.26$, and R^2-added $= .005$. Except for the ballooning b, beta, and Standard Error of b of the multicollinear forest products PV on the AUM's% function, all exogenous predictors' parameters remained fairly stable in spite of the inclusion of endogenous predictors. On the basis of these results—especially the endogenous predictors' very insignificant F-of-b statistics—the null hypothesis, that the ratio outputs system was nonstructural, was accepted.

The criteria for including variables in the ratio-optimum model were the same, described above, used for other versions of the model. The only unusual exclusion was stockmen's RV, with $r = +.34$, on the MBF% function. (The correlation matrix among ratio outputs and optimum argument predictors is shown in table C-6.) It was excluded because the anomalous correlation (there is no good substantive interpretation of stockman's opposition to timber sales) was based on two outlying cases

Table C-6. Correlation Matrix, Ratio Outputs, and Optimum Arguments

	AUMs%	MBF%	W-P%	Min%	S.A.	D.A.	For.	Stoc.	Econ.	Oth.	CnRc
AUMs%	1.00										
MBF%	−0.11	1.00									
Wild/Prim%	0.16	−0.09	1.00								
Min/O&G%	0.13	0.14	0.0006	1.00							
SAdmRPV	−0.29	−0.07	0.14	−0.03	1.00						
DAdmPV	−0.11	−0.04	0.22	−0.02	0.10	1.00					
ForPrPV	−0.23	−0.56	−0.0005	−0.15	0.22	−0.08	1.00				
StockRV	−0.34	0.34	0.12	0.08	0.17	0.10	−0.39	1.00			
EcoPV	0.19	−0.03	0.17	−0.30	0.04	0.21	−0.33	−0.06	1.00		
OthNPV	−0.06	0.17	0.35	−0.11	0.09	0.30	−0.32	0.24	0.41	1.00	
CnRcRV	−0.05	−0.10	0.22	0.02	−0.08	−0.06	0.03	0.22	−0.06	−0.37	1.00

Note: Table entries are bivariate *r*.

in an otherwise very weakly correlated bivariate scatterplot. The results of the full analysis of the ratio-optimum version of the model are presented in chapter 10. For information on the sensitivity of the model to the exclusion criteria used in the study, compare the parameters in table 10-3 with those in table 10-1.

In summary, the ratio outputs, optimum predictors version of the model was superior to the alternate versions for the following reasons. First, its multiple correlations were adequate and its functions statistically significant; its lower R statistics, compared with the absolute-outputs, optimum-arguments version, seemed caused by the otherwise beneficial effects of lowered skewness in the ratio outputs measures. Second, its regression coefficients (bs, and thus betas) were stable, especially in comparison with the severe multicollinearity in several of the other versions' functions. Third, its error terms were free from any discernible problems, such as residual-predictor heteroscedasticity or autocorrelationlike casewise groupings. Fourth, a structural ratio outputs model was not plausible conceptually and was insignificant statistically. Since it is nonstructural, the ratio outputs–optimum predictors model is simple, parsimonious, and a direct translation of interest group theory, unencumbered by endogenous predictors that are not specified by group theory.

NOTES

1. These concepts are adapted from the discussion of regulation and control in W. R. Ashby, "Self-Regulation and Requisite Variety," in F. E. Emry, ed., *Systems Thinking* (Harmondsworth, England, Penguin Books, 1969) pp. 105–124. *Regulation*, in Ashby's use of the term, has two functions, maintaining the system within acceptable parameters and registering exogenous control influences and random disturbances. (Ashby's random disturbances have been omitted from the diagram for simplicity.) The use of the concept of regulation in the development of the model relies primarily on the second function. Arthur Bentley, in *The Process of Government* (Chicago, University of Chicago Press, 1908, p. 163), refers to decision makers as "registration clerks." As has been noted throughout this book, public lands decision makers also perform the first function, keeping decisional responses within bounds acceptable to agency policy (for example, the multiple-use policy).

2. Structural set models are evaluated using so-called econometric methods, such as two-stage least squares regression. See Ronald Wonnacott and Thomas Wonnacott, *Econometrics* (New York, Wiley, 1970) chap. 6 to 9 and 16 to 20; and Otis Dudley Duncan, *Introduction to Structural Equation Models* (New York, Academic Press, 1975) chap. 6.

3. On the mathematical problem of identification, see Wonnacott and Wonnacott, *Econometrics*, chapter 8, and Duncan, *Introduction to Structural Equation Models*, chapter 6.

4. Wonnacott and Wonnacott (*Econometrics*, p. 312) note that empirical identification is a reasonable, last-ditch method in the case of a model that is unmanageable and a theory that does not exclude variables *a priori*.

Index

Abbey, Edward, 6
Access. *See also* Interest groups.
  indicator, 374–375
Adjudication. *See* Range administrator.
  attitudes of, 359
  budgets, 146–147
  decision-making role, 135
  discretion of, 18–19
  influence of, 308
Alaska Native Claims Settlement Act (1971), 96–97
Alaska Purchase (1867), 43
Alaska Statehood Act (1959), 96
Allowable cut, 11, 72n, 112, 266, 273, 293, 303, 339
Allowable sale quantity. *See* Allowable cut.
American Association for the Advancement of Science, 5, 45
American Forestry Association, 45
American Horse Protection Association, 168
American National Livestock Association, 88
American Society for Public Administration, 343n
AMPs. *See* Grazing allotment.
Anderson, James, 207n
Animal protectionist groups, 168
Anticipated reactions, 279–283, 284, 290, 311
Antiquities Act (1906), 97
Archeologist, 172
Area manager, 109n, 146–147, 296. *See also* Bureau of Land Management; District manager; Rangers.
  assignments, 309
  background, 147–154
  contacts, 334
  and decision-making, 263–264, 283
  economic responsiveness, 215
  employment history, 150
  independence of, 268
  and management plans, 266
  organization-set of, 150–154, 300
  politics of, 271
  and public participation, 235–236
  and staff assistants, 269
  supervison of, 267

Army Corps of Engineers, 232, 259n, 260n, 344n
Aspen blading, 216, 231n, 271
Aspinall, Wayne, 93, 219
Attitudes, 365. *See also* Interest groups.
  indicator, 372
  about public land management, 353
  unidimensional, 357–363
AUMs. *See* Grazing fees.

Ballinger–Pinchot affair, 46–47, 70n, 80, 86
Bankhead–Jones Act (1937), 48, 253, 261n
Barney, Daniel, 17–18, 57, 322
Bentley, Arthur, 22, 290, 311
Benton, Thomas, 78
Bernstein, Marver, 342n
Berry, Jerry, 25–26
Biocentrism, 7
Bitterroot National Forest (Montana), 57
BLM. *See* Bureau of Land Management
Board-foot, 74n
Bolle Report, 32n, 57
Brower, David, 51
Brownlow Commission, 50
Budgetary process, and clientele support, 336
Bureaucracy, reorganization of, 70n, 86, 88, 256, 344n
Bureaucratic politics. *See* Group theory.
Bureau of Indian Affairs, 189–191
Bureau of Land Management. *See also* Area manager; District manager; Grazing allotments; Professionalism.
  activity of, 30
  administration, 103–104, 327–328
  Alaska lands, 96
  constituencies, 215, 248, 283, 292, 336
  district office, 103
  environmental impact statements, 102
  E-U attitude scale, 328
  formal organization, 97–105
  formation, 88
  geographic decentralization, 100
  grazing advisory boards, 18, 85, 88–92, 157, 160, 197, 232, 236, 247–251, 257, 325, 329
  history of, 75–97
  ideologies, 20–21

continued

390

INDEX   391

Bureau of Land Management (cont'd.)
  intraagency influences, 209
  management framework plan, 233, 275
  managerial *esprit de corps*, 105
  mandate, 330
  mission, 325
  multiple-use advisory boards, 257
  multiple-use management, 98
  organic act, 94. See also Federal Land Policy and Management Act.
  personnel, 103, 104, 110
  planning process, 276
  policymaking factors, 210–211
  politics of, 16–20, 181
  professionalism of, 92, 248, 328–331
  and public participation, 244–245
  and range conditions, 13
  receipts, 100
  resource area, 136
  state office, 102–103
  timber management, 114
  wilderness review, 293
Business regulation, 337
Butz, Earl, 57

Cabin owners, 217, 224
Calef, Wesley, 330
California Desert Conservation Area, 96, 98
Callaway, Howard (Bo), 64–65
Campgrounds, 119, 221
Capture–conformity debate, 1–2, 27–29, 226–229, 259, 322–325. See also Capture thesis; Conformity thesis.
  basis of, 321
  origins, 2
  problems with, 332
Capture thesis, xiv, 19, 28, 186, 322, 331–339. See also Capture-conformity debate; Clientelism; Conformity thesis.
  administrators' perceptions of, 215–218
  as degenerate clientelism, 335
  environmentalist perceptions of, 212–215
  persistence of, 336–339
  simplest version of, 333
Carhart, Arthur, 54
Carpenter, Farrington, 84, 104
Carter, Jimmy, 97, 256
Carrying capacity, range, 90, 115, 247, 293, 294, 339
Carson, Rachel, 55
Chaining, 272
Chambers of Commerce, 157, 165
Church, Frank, 57
Civilian Conservation Corps, 48, 83, 111
Clark–McNary Act (1924), 47, 48, 70*n*
Classification and Multiple Use Act (1964), 32*n*, 93–94, 110, 216, 275, 330

Clawson, Marion, 12, 36*n*, 89, 91, 337
Clear-cutting, 11–12, 57, 113, 115
  attitudes toward, 174
  Bitterroot controversy, 216
  critique, 32*n*
Clientelism, 27, 324, 331–339. See also Capture thesis.
  balance, 227
  multiple, 227, 334–336, 339–341
CODINVOLVE, 262
Colson, Charles, 18
Commoner, Barry, 5, 7, 9
Conformity thesis, 65, 216, 274, 309–310, 325–331, 343*n*, 344*n*. See also Capture-conformity debate; Capture thesis; Professionalism.
  and Forest Service, 322
Congressional committee subsystem, 18, 37*n*, 63, 100–102, 322
Congressional inquiry, 67, 271
Conservationists. See Environmentalists.
Conspiracy theory, 338
Constituency. See also Clientelism.
  balance, 255, 334–336
  management, 218–226, 228–229
Contacts. See Interest groups.
Contractor, 164
Council on Environmental Quality, 56. See also Environmental impact statements; National Environmental Policy Act.
Crested Butte ski area, 64–65
Cruise, 113
Cutler, M. Rupert, 34*n*, 60, 73*n*

Decision making
  back end, 222–226
  front end, 220–222, 271, 289–290
  local latitude, 265–269
  locus of, 264–269
  mechanisms, 274–283
  merged group, 309–310
Desert Land Act (1877), 78
Devall, William, 33*n*, 74*n*
DeVoto, Bernard, 51, 89
Disney Industries, 58
District manager, 91, 146, 266, 296. See also Area manager; Rangers.
Douglas, William O., 6
Dust Bowl, 79

EAR. See Environmental analysis report.
Earth Day, *xiii*, 55, 166, 216
Echo Park Dam, 51, 71*n*
Efficiency, progressive movement theorem, 5, 17

Eisenhower administration, natural resources management, 51
Endangered Species Act (1973), 118
Environmental Action, 167
Environmental analysis report, 113, 117, 225–226
Environmental impact statement, 225, 232, 333. *See also* Council on Environmental Quality; National Environmental Policy Act.
   as public participation process, 279
Environmentalism, 7–10, 212
   administrators' reactions to, 218–219
   agency awareness of, 216
   ideology, 21, 55
   as social movement, 20
Environmentalists, 94–95, 157, 166–169, 209–218, 242, 255, 295, 309
   access, 195
   adversaries of, 8
   as agency critics, 338
   as counterbalance, 289
   and extremism, 240, 246
   and Forest Service, 213
   function of, 154, 280
   and influence index, 300–302, 307
   as moderates, 244
   as multiple-use tool, 228
   organizational resources, 168
   and public lands politics, 180
   and public participation, 203–205, 238–246, 306
   in public meetings, 238
   as recreationists, 217
   rise of, 222
   types of, 166–169
   urban influence, 202–203
   and wilderness, 15–16, 54–55, 59–60, 167, 212–214, 300–302, 334
Environmental Protection Agency, 337
Environmental–Utilitarian Scale, 177–179, 292, 308, 331, 360, 372. *See also* Interest groups.
Esprit de corps, 331, 336
E–U Scale. *See* Environmental–Utilitarian Scale.
Even-aged management, 11–12, 113

Factor analysis, 176, 285*n*, 357
   discontinuity test, 358
Farm Bureau, 158
FARR. *See* Forest and Related Resources plan.
Federal Advisory Committee Act (1973), 256–258
Federal Land Policy and Management Act (1976), 32*n*, 45, 97, 110, 121, 123, 227, 257, 274, 330
   as answer to organic act, 95–96
Federal Range Code, 90
Federal Timber Purchasers Association, 158, 161
Fernow, Bernard, 46
Fish and Wildlife Service, 10, 189
   authority of, 118
Fishing, state control of, 119
Flooding, increase in, 4
FLPMA. *See* Federal Land Policy and Management Act.
Food and Drug Administration, 337
Forest and Related Resources plan, 57, 294
Forest products industry, 161–163, 214, 220–221, 222, 244, 270, 273, 295, 339
   demands of, 331
   and extremism, 240
   influence of, 300, 303, 307
Forest Products Laboratory, 60
Forest Reserve Act (1891), 6, 46
Forest reserves, 46, 80
Forest roads, 271
   building standards, 224
   in multiple-use management, 127
Forestry practices, on private lands, 337
Forestry research, 60
Forest Service. *See also* Professionalism; Rangers.
   activity of, 30
   administration, 60–69, 327–328
   advisory boards, 236, 250–256
   campgrounds, 119
   centrifugal forces, 65–66
   conflict with Park Service, 191
   congressional committees, 63
   consolidation period, 47–50
   constituencies, 215, 283, 292, 336
   cooperative forestry, 61
   and decision-making, 64
   development control, 125
   division of labor, 60
   and environmental decade, 55–60
   established, 41
   grazing management, 82–83, 116, 250–256
   group influence on, 329
   harvesting policy, 11
   ideology, 20
   interpretive programs, 120
   intraagency influences, 66–69, 209
   leaders, 323
   manual, 66, 264
   mounting pressure period, 50–55
   multiple-use concept, 93

continued

Forest Service (cont'd.)
  officer transfer, 67, 226–227
  organization of, 60–69
  origins, 45–47
  personnel responsibilities, 110
  planning processes, 66–67, 275, 276
  politics of, 16–20, 181, 311
  policymaking factors, 210–211
  professionalism of, 29, 68, 328–331
  public participation, 56, 244
  recreationist pressure, 52
  recreation visitation, 217
  reorganization issue, 17, 50
  timber sales decisions, 64
  U regulations, 55
  Washington office, 63
  and wilderness, 14, 59–60, 293
Forest supervisors, 61–63, 266, 296
Forsling, Clarence, 88
Foss, Phillip, 18, 28, 216, 226, 247, 259n, 322, 330
Free-rider problem, 24
Friedrich, Carl, 280, 287n
Friends of Animals, 168
Friends of the Earth, 51, 167
Friesema, H. Paul, 34n, 72n, 286n

Gadsden Purchase (1853), 43
Garden clubs, 168
General Land Office, 43, 46, 98
  commissioners, 79
  corruption of, 80
  organized, 75
GLO. See General Land Office.
Graves, Henry, 47
Grazing. See also Range; Rest-rotation.
  animal-unit months, 84, 106n–107n
  management, 115–117
  on national forest land, 82
  predator controls, 174–175
  privileges allocation, 116–117
Grazing advisory boards, 18, 85, 88–89, 157, 160, 197, 232, 236, 247–250, 257, 325, 329
Grazing allotments, 160, 251. See also Bureau of Land Management.
  management plans, 117, 249, 275, 277, 278–279, 284, 333
Grazing associations, 160, 295
  resources, 161
Grazing fees, 14, 82, 87–88, 96
  increases, 91, 94, 95, 219
  rancher attitudes, 175
Grazing permits, 164, 292, 309, 339
  capitalized value, 91–92, 116–117
  group influence on, 300

Grazing Service, 28, 84–88, 323, 337
  advisory boards, 159
  dependence on range users, 88
  expenditures, 88
  personnel, 104, 248
  reorganization, 86
Great land grab, 51, 88, 332
Greeley, William, 47
Group theory. See Interest groups.
Guide services, 169
Gulick, Luther, 36n, 73n
Gypo, 161, 183n, 221

Hall, George, 343n
Hardin, Garrett, 9, 89
Hayes, Samuel, 5
Hendee, John, 262n
Homesteading, 76–84
Hoover Commission, 50
Hormay, August, 14, 117, 252
Hough, Franklin, 45–46
Humphrey, Hubert H., 52, 57, 63
Hunting
  as management tool, 118
  state control of, 119

Ickes, Harold, 50, 83, 107n
  confrontation with Forest Service, 86
I & E. See Information and education.
I & I. See Inform and Involve.
Inform and Involve, 232, 241, 246, 259, 282, 335
Information and education, 205, 235, 238, 241
Influence. See Interest groups.
In-lieu payments. See Payments in lieu of taxes.
Interaction frequency. See Interest groups.
Interest groups, xiii, 23. See also Attitudes; Environmental–Utilitarian Scale; Organization-set; Organization theory; Public participation; names of specific groups
  access, 23–24, 195, 311, 366, 374
  affiliations, 155–159, 180, 354
  attitudes of, 173–180, 359
  balance, 200–201, 205, 217–218, 227–229, 334–336
  contacts, 187–195, 312, 332, 355, 377
  dominance, 175, 185n, 360
  explanations for existence, 25
  industry, 159–166
  influence of, 208, 263, 284, 290–312, 332–334, 364, 379–388
  influence model, 297–301, 310–313

continued

Interest groups (cont'd.)
  interactions of, 192, 193, 374
  lobbying, 25–26, 285
  local policy, 219
  major blocs, 136
  nonindustry, 166–173
  open systems theory, 27
  organizational resources, 162, 354, 372
  perceptions of, 265–269
  power, 23, 312, 365, 372
  properties of, 291, 296
  reification, 24, 311–312
  reputational study, 310–311
  theory, 22–27, 311
  use administration policies, 289
Interview
  format, 352–357
  response rate, 349–352
Irrigation, 164
Izaak Walton League, 52, 88, 89, 93, 169, 243
  and clear-cutting lawsuit, 57

Jeffersonian agrarian democracy, 76–78
Job Corps, 111, 138
Journal of Forestry, 60
Judeo-Christian tradition, relation to nature, 3
Kaufman, Herbert, xi, xiv, 65, 128, 216, 226, 268, 322, 330, 343n, 344n
  conformity thesis, 28–29, 68–69, 332
Kincaid Act (1904), 79
Knutson–Vandenburg Act (1930), 114
Kolko, Gabriel, 108n, 342n
Krutilla, John V., xi

Laissez-faire capitalism, 17
Laissez-faire conservatism, 3
Land, physiographic potential of, 370
Land grants, 76
Land patent, 78
Land sales, 75
Land use planning, 58, 95, 212, 233, 268, 274–279, 284, 333
  public meetings, 236, 245
Leases, oil and gas, 95, 98, 122
Leopold, Aldo, 6
Litigation, 273–274. *See also specific cases.*
Livestock grazing. *See* Grazing; Range.
Livestock industry. *See* Ranchers.
Lobbying, 285, 288n
  function of, 25–26
Local business, contacts, 189
Local constituencies, 205–206
Local government, 157, 171, 295
  contacts, 189

Local land manager. *See* Area manager; Rangers.
Long, Norton, 27, 342n
Louisiana Purchase (1803), 43
Lowi, Theodore, 27, 342n–343n, 345n

Maass, Arthur, 345n
McArdle, Richard, 52
McCarran, Patrick, 247, 337
  investigation of Grazing Service, 87–88
McConnell, Grant, 5, 325
  and clientelism, 27
Marsh, George Perkins, 4
Marshall, Robert, 48, 54
Mazmanian, Daniel, 259n, 345n
Mexican cession, 43
MFPs. *See* Bureau of Land Management, management framework plans.
Mineral King, 58, 124–125, 169
Mineral Leasing Act (1920), 122
Mining industry, 157, 163, 295
  and agency delays, 225
  claims, 122
  contacts, 189, 202
  exploration practices, 174
  influence of, 300
  minerals management, 122–123
  patents, 122
  permits, 292
  postlease monitoring, 123
  restrictions on, 222
  and use rights decisions, 221
Mining Laws (1872), 52, 122, 174
Minority organizations, 172
Mizpah–Pumpkin Creek association, 83
Monongahela National Forest (West Virginia), 57
Muckrakers, 338
Muir, John, 6, 21, 25, 166, 321
Multiple use, 6, 69, 95, 110, 227, 250, 252, 283, 323, 340
  advisory boards, 248
  agency responsiveness to, 282
  as cardinal principle, 69, 105, 331
  concept of, 52, 327
  legal definition, 53
  management, 125–128, 215, 223
  philosophy, 6, 9, 10, 15
  plans, 275
  as political doctrine, 331
  and range land, 91–97
  restrictions of, 223
Multiple Use Mining Act (1955), 52
Multiple Use–Sustained Yield Act (1960), 15, 32n, 50–54, 110, 275, 330, 332

INDEX

Nash, Roderick, 3
National Environmental Policy Act (1970), 56, 102, 109n, 216, 232, 270, 330, 340. *See also* Council on Environmental Quality; environmental impact statement.
National forests, 49
　administrative structure, 61
　ranger districts, 61
　recreational use, 51
　transportation systems, 126
National Forest Management Act (1976), 57, 274, 330
National Forest Products Association, 161
National grasslands, 253
　acquisition, 48
　environmental constituency, 255
　grazing associations, 253–254, 329
National Livestock Association, 332
National Park Service, 10, 120, 138, 189, 217, 244, 295
　Mission '66 proposal, 52
　public meetings, 242
National Rifle Association, 169
National Timber Supply Act, 18
National Wildlife Federation, 167, 238
Natural resources
　apolitical management of, 323
　and interagency competition, 188
　management fields, 326
　philosophy continuum, 2–10, 176, 341
Natural Resources Defense Council v. *Morton*, 95, 108n, 117
NEPA. *See* National Environmental Policy Act.
New Deal, and Forest Service role, 48
NFMA. *See* National Forest Management Act.
Nicholson Plan, 91
Nienaber, Jeanne, 34n, 72n–73n, 259n, 345n
Nixon, Richard M., 18, 57
Nondeclining even-flow, 12, 33n, 112, 286n, 294
NRA. *See* National Rifle Association.

O&C lands, 86, 98, 114–115, 182n
　timber production, 98
OCS. *See* Outer continental shelf.
Off-road vehicles, 130n, 138, 184n, 243
　groups, 157, 170, 171, 223, 315n
　opposition to, 174
　restrictions on, 120, 223
Oil and gas firms. *See* Mining industry.
Olson, Mancur, 24
Open systems theory. *See* Interest groups.
Oregon Compromise, 43
Organic Act (1897), 6, 32n, 46, 52, 58

Organization-set, 27, 186, 329. *See also* Interest groups.
　balance, 196
　and capture thesis, 205
　and commodity user groups, 198–199
　contacts, 190–191
　imbalance of, 199–200
　mining industry dominance, 198
　rancher dominance, 197
　typology, 195–205
　urban influence, 202–203, 204
Organization theory, 26–27, 264. *See also* Interest groups; Public administration.
　modern, 343n
　open systems, 186, 209
ORV. *See* Off-road vehicles.
Outer continental shelf, leases, 95, 100, 123
Overstory removal, 261n

Parker v. *United States*, 73n, 171, 184n–185n
Pasturage districts, 81, 83
Payments in lieu of taxes, 16, 111, 172, 302
Pestigo (Wisconsin) fire, 4, 45
Pinchot, Gifford, 4–5, 46, 48, 69, 80, 86, 321
　conservation values, 212
　and public interest, 323
Pioneer mentality, 212
PLLRC. *See* Public Land Law Review Commission.
Pluralism, 22
Powell, John Wesley, 81, 321
Power. *See* Interest groups.
Prescribed burning, 74n
Pressure politics, 269–274
Private forest regulation, 50
Professionalism, 323, 325–331, 341. *See also* Bureau of Land Management; Conformity thesis; Forest Service.
Progressive conservation, 3–6, 8, 21, 323–334
Progressive movement, 338
Property taxes. *See* Payments in lieu of taxes.
Public administration. *See* also Organization theory.
　apolitical thesis, 324
　pluralist criterion, 340
　traditional theory, 28, 186–187, 324–325, 340, 343n
Public domain. *See* Public lands.
Public goods, 24, 35n
Public interest, 323, 339–341
　pluralist notion of, 341
Public Land Law Review Commission, 93–94

Public lands
  access to, 252
  acquisition, 41–43
  agencies, 44–45
  disposal, 43, 75–81, 116
  efficiency in, 321
  end of disposal era, 84, 94, 96
  management eras, 41
  management issues, 10–21, 216–217
  origins, 42
  policy outputs, 293–294
  politics of, 155, 220, 339
  and recreation, 214, 217, 223
  secondary benefits, 111
  withdrawal, 43–44
Public participation, 233, 237, 296, 328, 333, 374. *See also* Interest groups.
  and access, 306
  cases of, 246–258
  educational value of, 280
  efficacy, 246, 258, 302
  events, 235
  function, 310
  informal, 242–243, 255
  interactions during, 306
  in planning process, 278
  professionalism, 242
  as responsive-capture, 335
  scope of, 233–236
  styles of, 236–246
Public Rangelands Improvement Act (1978), 96

Questionnaire format, 352–357

Ranchers, 79, 87, 155, 159–161, 197, 212, 221, 223, 295
  and Bureau of Land Management officers, 104–105, 322
  commensurability, 116
  contacts, 189
  cooptation, 254–255
  and Forest Service, 82–83, 87
  grazing associations, 157, 250–256
  influence of, 299, 333
  organization-sets, 197
  and public lands politics blocs, 180
  and public participation, 235–236, 237, 246–258, 306
  and recreation, 214
  relationship with hunters, 119
Range. *See also* Grazing; Rest-rotation.
  carrying capacity, 90, 115, 247, 293, 294, 339
  inventory, 115
  management, 13–14, 104, 250–256, 270

overgrazing, 81
regulations, 337
rights adjudication, 85, 89–92, 247, 249
wars, 86–91
Rangelands Improvement Act (1978), 257
Rangers, 68, 69, 268, 296. *See also* Area manager; District manager; Forest Service.
  apolitical nature of, 271
  assignments, 226–227, 308
  background, 147–154
  contacts, 189–192, 334
  decision-making, 263–264, 283
  districts, 61, 141–145
  district staff assistants, 145–147, 269
  district work plan, 266
  employment history, 150
  image of, 135, 266
  local constituencies, 201–202
  managerial style, 242
  organization-set, 196–205, 243, 334
  and public participation, 235–236
  supervision of, 65, 267
  and timber management, 64
  urban districts, 243
RARE. *See* Roadless Area Review and Evaluation.
Rational decision model, 277–279, 287n
RC & D. *See* Rural Conservation and Development Districts.
Reagan, Ronald, 97
Realtors, 164–165
Reclamation Act (1902), 79
Recreation, 51
  industry, 169
  management, 119–120
  private development, 124
  restrictions on, 223
Recreationists, 157, 169–171, 242, 281, 295
  and influence index, 300
  participation measures of, 306
Redford, Emmette, 29
Reforestation, 11, 48, 114
Regression analysis, 298, 315n
Reich, Charles, 19, 322
Reorganization. *See* Bureaucracy.
Resource areas. *See* Area managers.
Rest-rotation, 14, 117, 209–212, 223, 310, 329. *See also* Grazing; Range.
  attitudes toward, 252–253, 255
Rights-of-way, 123, 144
Roadless Area Review and Evaluation, 15, 59–60, 144, 237, 284, 287n, 293, 302. *See also* Wilderness.
  criteria, 121, 305
  public meetings, 236, 239, 272, 279

Romantic preservation, 6–7
Roosevelt, Theodore, 4, 43
Rural Conservation and Development districts, 165
Rutledge, Richard, 86, 337

Sabatier, Paul, 345n
Sagebrush Rebellion, xiii
Salisbury, Robert, 25
Scaling, 114
Scenic Hudson Preservation Conference, 168
Schubert, Glendon, 32n
Search and rescue groups, 170
Seed tree cutting, 113
Selective cutting, 113
Selznick, Phillip, 27
Sequoia National Forest, 58
Sheep, 86
Shelterwood cutting, 113
Shepherd, Jack, 17–18, 57, 322
Sierra Club, 7, 25, 51, 54, 89, 154, 184n, 203, 216, 243, 255, 332, 338, 339
  contacts, 189
  resources, 166
Silent Spring (Carson), 55
Simon, Herbert, 26, 343n
Ski areas, 169
  operators influence, 315n
  permits, 124–125, 131n
Slash, 114
Snowmobiles. *See* Off-road vehicles.
Social Darwinism, 3
Society for Range Management, 92, 105, 150, 172, 295, 326
Society of American Foresters, 46, 150, 172, 326
Soil Conservation Service, 165, 191
Soldier Creek controversy, 89–92
Special use permit, 123, 144
Sportmen's groups, 169
Standard operating procedures, 110
Standing to sue, 58, 73n
State government, fish and game departments, 118, 172, 238, 295
State wildlife federations, 167
Stockmen. *See* Ranchers.
Stockraising Homestead Act (1916), 79, 82
Stoddard, Charles, 93, 337
Study sample, 136–145
Stumpage value, 113
Supervision, 374
Sustained yield, 6, 327
  nondeclining even-flow, 12, 33n, 112, 286n
  result of multiple-use management, 126

Taylor, Edward, 83
Taylor Grazing Act (1934), 43, 81–86, 93, 257, 337
  as conservation mandate, 330
  grazing districts, 98, 103
  land management provisions, 84
Technology, linear nature of, 9
Tennessee Valley Authority, 8, 27, 51
Thoreau, Henry David, 6
Timber and Stone Act (1878), 78
Timber Culture Act (1873), 78
Timber harvest scheduling. *See* Nondeclining even-flow.
Timber management, 112–115, 147, 333
  controversy, 10–13
  plans, 273, 279
Timber Resources Allocation Method, 112
Timber sales, 114, 141, 157, 220, 266, 270, 272, 292, 293, 334, 339
  alternative model, 304
  controversy over, 271
  group influence on, 300, 302
  limitations, 202
  market explanation, 304–305
  planning, 112, 113
  ranger sale, 221
  restrictions on, 222
Tourism association, 170
"Tragedy of the commons," 89
Transmission lines, 144
Treaty of Guadalupe Hidalgo, 43
Truman, David, 23, 233, 290, 311
Tucker, William, 34n
TVA. *See* Tennessee Valley Authority

Udall, Morris, 97
Udall, Stewart, 93
United Mine Workers, 158
U.S. Geological Survey, 98, 123, 191
U.S. House of Representatives, Interior and Insular Affairs Committee, 63, 102
U.S. Senate
  Agriculture and Forestry Committee, 63
  Energy and Natural Resources Committee, 63, 102
Use administration, 126–127, 144–145, 222–226, 309
Users, complaints of, 224–225
Usufruct, 4
Utilitarianism, 2–3
Utilities, 163

Water resources, 337
Watershed management, 127–128, 131n–132n
Weber, Max, 36n

Weeks Act (1911), 47
Western Forest Industries Association, 158
Western frontier, 3
Western Wood Products Association, 161
Wilderness, 14–16, 54–55, 59–60, 71n, 109n, 119, 174, 236, 239, 244, 272, 279, 306, 309, 333. *See also* Roadless Area Review and Evaluation.
  administrative concept of, 54
  designations, 292–293, 338
  group influence on, 299
  guides, 144
  litigation, 58–59, 171
  local effects of, 16
  management, 120–122
  and mining, 122
  permits, 122, 240
Wilderness Act (1964), 54–55, 96, 293, 330
Wilderness Society, 54, 154, 167, 338
Wild and Free-Roaming Horses and Burros Act (1971), 118, 270
Wildlife management, 117–118
Wilson, James, *xiv*, 207n, 342n
Wolfe, Sidney, 337

Yellowstone National Park, 43
Yellowstone Timber Reserve, 46
Youth Conservation Corps, 111